Inside Investigative Criminal Procedure

What Matters and Why

Inside Investigative Criminal Procedure

What Matters and Why

Julian A. Cook, III
J. Alton Hosch Professor of Law
University of Georgia School of Law

Wolters Kluwer
Law & Business

Copyright © 2012 CCH Incorporated.

Published by Wolters Kluwer Law & Business in New York.

Wolters Kluwer Law & Business serves customers worldwide with CCH, Aspen Publishers, and Kluwer Law International products. (www.wolterskluwerlb.com)

No part of this publication may be reproduced or transmitted in any form or by any means, electronic or mechanical, including photocopy, recording, or utilized by any information storage or retrieval system, without written permission from the publisher. For information about permissions or to request permissions online, visit us at www.wolterskluwerlb.com, or a written request may be faxed to our permissions department at 212-771-0803.

To contact Customer Service, e-mail customer.service@wolterskluwer.com, call 1-800-234-1660, fax 1-800-901-9075, or mail correspondence to:

Wolters Kluwer Law & Business
Attn: Order Department
PO Box 990
Frederick, MD 21705

Printed in the United States of America.

1 2 3 4 5 6 7 8 9 0

ISBN 978-0-7355-8425-9

Library of Congress Cataloging-in-Publication Data

Cook, Julian A.
Inside investigative criminal procedure : what matters and why / Julian A. Cook III.
    p. cm.
Includes bibliographical references and index.
ISBN 978-0-7355-8425-9
1. Criminal procedure—United States. 2. Criminal investigation—United States. 3. Searches and seizures—United States. 4. Arrest—United States. 5. Due process of law— United States. 6. Civil rights—United States. I. Title.

KF9619.C66 2012
345.73'052—dc23

2012013026

About Wolters Kluwer Law & Business

Wolters Kluwer Law & Business is a leading global provider of intelligent information and digital solutions for legal and business professionals in key specialty areas, and respected educational resources for professors and law students. Wolters Kluwer Law & Business connects legal and business professionals as well as those in the education market with timely, specialized authoritative content and information-enabled solutions to support success through productivity, accuracy and mobility.

Serving customers worldwide, Wolters Kluwer Law & Business products include those under the Aspen Publishers, CCH, Kluwer Law International, Loislaw, Best Case, ftwilliam.com and MediRegs family of products.

CCH products have been a trusted resource since 1913, and are highly regarded resources for legal, securities, antitrust and trade regulation, government contracting, banking, pension, payroll, employment and labor, and healthcare reimbursement and compliance professionals.

Aspen Publishers products provide essential information to attorneys, business professionals and law students. Written by preeminent authorities, the product line offers analytical and practical information in a range of specialty practice areas from securities law and intellectual property to mergers and acquisitions and pension/benefits. Aspen's trusted legal education resources provide professors and students with high-quality, up-to-date and effective resources for successful instruction and study in all areas of the law.

Kluwer Law International products provide the global business community with reliable international legal information in English. Legal practitioners, corporate counsel and business executives around the world rely on Kluwer Law journals, looseleafs, books, and electronic products for comprehensive information in many areas of international legal practice.

Loislaw is a comprehensive online legal research product providing legal content to law firm practitioners of various specializations. Loislaw provides attorneys with the ability to quickly and efficiently find the necessary legal information they need, when and where they need it, by facilitating access to primary law as well as state-specific law, records, forms and treatises.

Best Case Solutions is the leading bankruptcy software product to the bankruptcy industry. It provides software and workflow tools to flawlessly streamline petition preparation and the electronic filing process, while timely incorporating ever-changing court requirements.

ftwilliam.com offers employee benefits professionals the highest quality plan documents (retirement, welfare and non-qualified) and government forms (5500/PBGC, 1099 and IRS) software at highly competitive prices.

MediRegs products provide integrated health care compliance content and software solutions for professionals in healthcare, higher education and life sciences, including professionals in accounting, law and consulting.

Wolters Kluwer Law & Business, a division of Wolters Kluwer, is headquartered in New York. Wolters Kluwer is a market-leading global information services company focused on professionals.

To my lovely, wonderful wife and children — for their constant love and support during the preparation of this book

Summary of Contents

Contents

Chapter 15. Fourth Amendment Violations and Their Associated Remedies 183

Chapter 16. The Privilege Against Self-Incrimination — General Principles 211

Preface

I routinely tell my criminal procedure students that irrespective of their intention to ultimately pursue a career in criminal litigation, criminal procedure is likely to be one of their most enjoyable courses. Television and cinema are filled with programs and movies that depict the criminal process. Whether it is law enforcement in the performance of its investigative, arrest and search functions, or criminal attorneys litigating in a courtroom setting, the seemingly endless depictions are undoubtedly a by-product of the public's fascination with cops, robbers, and the criminal litigation process.

While some criminal courses, such as criminal law, are very statutory intensive, criminal procedures is, in essence, a course in constitutional law. Throughout your criminal procedure course, it is likely that you will study a plethora of Supreme Court cases in which the Court has had to engage in a constitutional balancing act of sorts. Indeed, this balance is often a delicate one, with compelling arguments and interests on each side. In case after case, the Supreme Court has had to address questions pertaining to the latitude that the government should be afforded to investigate and prosecute and the degree that individual liberties should be safeguarded against such governmental interference. Invariably, these questions arise under the Fourth, Fifth, Sixth, and Fourteenth Amendments. As you will discover, often the answers to these quandaries are less than clear.

Throughout, the book will cite, discuss, and review the most salient Supreme Court opinions addressing certain topics. However, the book is much more than a mere regurgitation of facts, holdings, and rationales. Instead, this work is designed to present and review the most central topics that you will commonly encounter in your studies and break down the complexities of each subject area in a manner that is easy to comprehend. This study guide is designed for students of criminal procedure. To accomplish these objectives, the book has adopted a format design and employed various graphic features that will assist in your understanding and retention of the material.

In the end, this book will provide you with explanations that are clear and easy to understand. Naturally, I welcome any and all comments on the book as I continuously strive to make it, and thus the comprehension of criminal procedure, as fluid and beneficial as possible.

Julian A. Cook, III
April 2012

Acknowledgments

I am indebted to the University of Georgia School of Law, its students, Wolters Kluwer Law & Business, and an array of anonymous reviewers for their tremendous assistance during all phases of the preparation of this book. The contributions of so many have not only made this book possible but greatly enhanced its overall quality. I am and will remain extremely grateful to each and every individual who gave their time to assist in the making of this book.

Inside Investigative Criminal Procedure

What Matters and Why

Incorporation

Though not as riveting and sensational as the myriad of issues that will typically characterize your criminal procedure studies, the incorporation

O V E R V I E W

question is arguably the most critical criminal procedure question ever to confront the Supreme Court. To comprehend the issue's significance one must appreciate not so much the factual nuances of the particular cases presented before the Court (though such comprehension is not without relevance), but rather the broader implications underlying their resolution. Indeed, had the Court not interpreted the Fourteenth Amendment due process clause so expansively, the American criminal justice process (and perhaps societal perceptions of its fairness) would, in all likelihood, differ noticeably from the system (and societal perceptions) that exist today.

A. THE BILL OF RIGHTS

B. THEORIES OF INCORPORATION

1. Total Incorporation
2. Fundamental Rights
3. Selective Incorporation

A. The Bill of Rights

Yale law professor Akhil Reed Amar commented in his book *The Bill of Rights: Creation and Reconstruction* that "[t]he Bill of Rights stands as the high temple of our constitutional order—America's Parthenon—yet we lack a clear view of it."[1] This statement is quite apt, for, among other things, it is descriptive of this nation's ongoing struggle to appropriately comprehend the Bill's origin, to interpret its provisions, and to properly apply the initial ten amendments of this country's constitution to its populace. One aspect of this struggle is reflected in the issue of incorporation. Adopted as a restraint upon actions undertaken by the federal government, the Supreme Court ultimately had to decide which of the Bill's safeguards, if any, also served as a restraint upon state government conduct. At the center of the incorporation controversy was the Fourteenth Amendment. Enacted in 1868, that Amendment provides, in pertinent part:

> No State shall make or enforce any law which shall abridge the privileges or immunities of citizens of the United States; nor shall any State deprive any person of life, liberty, or property, without due process of law; nor deny to any person within its jurisdiction the equal protection of the laws. . . .

In the incorporation context, this single sentence has been parsed, interpreted, and fiercely debated by academics, legal observers, and even among the Supreme Court justices themselves over the course of several decades. In *Adamson v. California*,[2] which in 1947 rejected the contention that the Fourteenth Amendment incorporated the Fifth Amendment's privilege against self-incrimination, Justices Hugo Black and Felix Frankfurter rather pointedly expressed their contrasting viewpoints on the incorporation issue. In his concurrence, Justice Frankfurter wrote:

> Between the incorporation of the Fourteenth Amendment into the Constitution and the beginning of the present membership of the Court—a period of 70 years—the scope of that Amendment was passed upon by 43 judges. Of all these judges, only one, who may respectfully be called an eccentric exception, ever indicated the belief that the Fourteenth Amendment was a shorthand summary of the first eight Amendments theretofore limiting only the Federal Government, and that due process incorporated those eight Amendments as restrictions upon the powers of the States.

The "eccentric exception" was Justice John Marshall Harlan, who advocated that the Fourteenth Amendment did, in fact, absorb the Bill of Rights. Justice Black, who subsequently championed Justice Harlan's position, wrote the following pointed retort in his *Adamson* dissent:

> I cannot consider the Bill of Rights to be an outworn 18th Century "strait jacket" as the *Twining* opinion did. Its provisions may be thought outdated abstractions by some. And it is true that they were designed to meet ancient evils. But they are the same kind of human

---

[1]Akhil Reed Amar, *The Bill of Rights: Creation and Reconstruction*, xi (R.R. Donnelley & Sons Company 1998).
[2]332 U.S. 46 (1947).

evils that have emerged from century to century wherever excessive power is sought by the few at the expense of the many. In my judgment the people of no nation can lose their liberty so long as a Bill of Rights like ours survives and its basic purposes are conscientiously interpreted, enforced and respected so as to afford continuous protection against old, as well as new, devices and practices which might thwart those purposes.

Did you notice the tinge of rancor? What is it about the issue of incorporation that stirs up such emotion? At least some explanation can be gleaned from the previous quotations. To incorporate the Bill of Rights to the states constitutes, in the view of some, an unjust intrusion upon state sovereignty. It is argued that states should be free to establish their own rules and processes — unencumbered by the Bill of Rights — by which criminal cases should be adjudicated. Others, however, believe that the Bill of Rights is a necessary hedge against the dangers of undue governmental infringements that have emerged in various societies.

Aside from the question of federalism there is another, more practical, concern that emerges from this debate. Every day, federal and state prosecutors decide what cases to pursue and what cases to forgo. Invariably many of these decisions are predicated upon any number of factors, including qualitative evidence assessments, associated penalties, and a defendant's criminal history, to name but a few. But what if such decisions were also based upon meaningful jurisdictional procedural variances? Does the federal constitution envision a criminal justice structure where such profound systemic differences can exist? If so, then prosecutorial decisions can — and arguably should — be influenced by procedural distinctions that may exist between federal and state jurisdictions.

An example may be helpful. Assume in a particular fictitious state, an individual, in desperate need of money, decides to steal money from a federally insured financial institution. After entering the bank, the individual approaches a teller and successfully takes, by force and intimidation, several thousand dollars. Unfortunately for the robber in our hypothetical, he is apprehended by federal authorities within hours of the robbery.

Assume further that bank robbery is punishable under both federal and state law. Federal prosecutors contemplate whether to pursue prosecution of the case or defer prosecution to the state authorities. In evaluating the merits of the case, the prosecutors come to the conclusion that the evidence linking the suspect to the case is weak. In the end, the federal prosecutors decide to decline prosecution, believing that a conviction can be attained more easily in the state system. They reason that while the Bill of Rights grants a defendant in federal court a jury trial as well as a right to counsel, they note that such similar rights are not afforded criminal defendants in our fictitious state court system. The prosecutors believe that a defendant, without the benefit of counsel, would be less likely to persuade a judge (as opposed to a jury) of his innocence. Moreover, they note that while the suspect made an incriminating statement to law enforcement after his arrest, that statement was made without the provision of *Miranda* warnings, which are mandated by the Fifth Amendment. Given their fear that this confession will be suppressed in federal court, the prosecutors reason that the statement could be used locally given that such Fifth Amendment protections are inapplicable at the state level. In light of these procedural and substantive distinctions, the federal prosecutors conclude that the case should be submitted to the local authorities.

As you can see, the issue of incorporation is of considerable significance. If the Bill of Rights is not incorporated, either fully or meaningfully, to the states, then state sovereignty is largely respected and federal and state prosecutors can — and perhaps should — make prosecutorial decisions based upon procedural and substantive differences between the respective systems. On the other hand, if there is, at a minimum, substantial incorporation, then greater procedural and substantive uniformity is produced, thereby depriving prosecutors of considering such procedural and substantive dissimilarities when deciding whether to litigate a particular case.

Your Criminal Procedure course will not focus upon the entire Bill of Rights. Rather, the primary focus of your course will, in all probability, be upon three of these amendments — the Fourth, Fifth, and Sixth. In the context of the incorporation debate, the question therefore becomes whether the rights contained in the Fourth, Fifth, and Sixth Amendments are made applicable to the states via the Fourteenth Amendment.

It is important to understand that, with limited exceptions, the Fourteenth Amendment has fully incorporated the Bill of Rights. Accordingly, when this book (and your professor) makes reference to rights and privileges embodied within the Fourth, Fifth, and Sixth Amendments, you should understand that those protections are equally applicable to state court jurisdictions. The next section will briefly discuss the evolution of the incorporation debate followed by a review of the predominant theories of incorporation.

B. Theories of Incorporation

Since the ratification of the Fourteenth Amendment in 1868, the Supreme Court's conception of the Amendment's incorporative breadth has undergone an interesting evolution. As evidenced in cases such as *Hurtado v. California*[3] (presentment of a case before a grand jury is not required by the due process clause of the Fourteenth Amendment), *Twining v. New Jersey*[4] (the Fourteenth Amendment due process clause does not incorporate the Fifth Amendment privilege against self-incrimination), and *Palko v. Connecticut*[5] (the Fifth Amendment protection against double jeopardy does not apply to the states), the Supreme Court initially interpreted the Amendment narrowly. However, at or around 1932 when the landmark decision in *Powell v. Alabama*[6] (the Fourteenth Amendment due

[3]110 U.S. 516 (1884).
[4]211 U.S. 78 (1908).
[5]302 U.S. 319 (1937).
[6]287 U.S. 45 (1932).

process clause guarantees the assistance of counsel in capital cases) was rendered, and accelerating through the 1960s, the Court began to incorporate more of the Bill of Rights guarantees to the states.

(1) Total Incorporation

Out of this debate emerged three predominant views regarding incorporation. A view that has never garnered a majority of justices but managed to attract a meaningful minority of the Court is the total incorporation theory. These theorists advocated that the Fourteenth Amendment encompassed the Bill of Rights in its entirety. In their view, *every* clause of *every* amendment was fully applicable to the states by virtue primarily of the due process clause of the Fourteenth Amendment. Indeed, in their view, anything short of complete incorporation would not only risk the curtailment by governmental entities of individual freedoms but would also grant the Court a windfall of subjective interpretive authority. As noted, Justice Black, a chief proponent of this view, insisted that anything short of complete incorporation would "hold that this Court can determine what, if any, provisions of the Bill of Rights will be enforced, and if so to what degree," which would "frustrate the great design of a written constitution."

Sidebar

JUSTICE HUGO BLACK

Justice Hugo Black was appointed by President Franklin D. Roosevelt to the U.S. Supreme Court and served from 1937 to 1971. At the time of his ascendancy to the High Court, Justice Black served as a U.S. Senator from Alabama.

Justice Hugo Black
Library of Congress,
LC-USZ62-95031

(2) Fundamental Rights

The theory that prevailed from the 1930s until the 1960s, however, was the fundamental rights approach. Under this approach, only those rights that were considered fundamental were made applicable to the states. The determination of whether a right was fundamental was not determined by reference to the Bill of Rights. Rather, the source was the Fourteenth Amendment due process clause. With a determinative source outside the Bill of Rights, fundamental rights were therefore not limited to the Bill. In other words, due process protections could exceed those delineated within the Bill of Rights. So, theoretically at least, the fundamental rights approach could afford greater overall protections to individuals than the total incorporation model. As stated by Justice Frankfurter, due process protections are rights that are neither fixed nor predetermined.

> The faculties of the Due Process Clause may be indefinite and vague, but the mode of their ascertainment is not self-willed. In each case "due process of law" requires an evaluation based on a disinterested inquiry pursued in the spirit of science, on a balanced order of facts exactly and fairly stated, on the detached consideration of conflicting claims. . . .

Due process of law, as a historic and generative principle, precludes defining, and thereby confining, these standards of conduct more precisely than to say that convictions cannot be brought about by methods that offend "a sense of justice."

Sidebar

JUSTICE FELIX FRANKFURTER

Justice Felix Frankfurter was appointed to the Supreme Court by President Franklin D. Roosevelt and served from 1939 to 1962. Prior to assuming this position, Justice Frankfurter was a law professor at Harvard University. Justice Frankfurter is widely viewed as the leading proponent of the fundamental rights theory of incorporation.

Justice Felix Frankfurter
Library of Congress,
LC-USZ62-36966

As an illustration of this process, consider *Powell v. Alabama*. In that case, where the defendants were charged with rape and sentenced to death, the Court held that the Fourteenth Amendment due process clause mandated the appointment of counsel. But it did not conclude that the Fourteenth Amendment incorporated the right to counsel found in the Sixth Amendment. Rather, the Court found that the right was independently provided for in the due process clause of the Fourteenth Amendment. And it further found that the right existed in light of the particular facts in that case. As you review the following quotation from the Court's opinion, notice the Court's employment of the due process clause and the absence of any language of incorporation, as well as the factual appendages to its holding.

All that it is necessary now to decide, as we do decide, is that in a capital case, where the defendant is unable to employ counsel, and is incapable adequately of making his own defense because of ignorance, feeble-mindedness, illiteracy, or the like, it is the duty of the court, whether requested or not, to assign counsel for him as a necessary requisite of due process of law; and that duty is not discharged by an assignment at such a time or under such circumstances as to preclude the giving of effective aid in the preparation and trial of the case. To hold otherwise would be to ignore the fundamental postulate, already adverted to, "that there are certain immutable principles of justice which inhere in the very idea of free government which no member of the Union may disregard."

What is also interesting about this passage is the reference to "certain immutable principles of justice which inhere in the very idea of free government." Pursuant to this theory of interpretation, the Court must ascertain what rights are fundamental. To make this determination a Court must develop a standard by which to adjudge claims that a particular right is encompassed within the due process clause. So then, what was the governing standard for determining whether a right was fundamental or was an "immutable principle of justice"? The standard has been alternately stated and is, arguably, subjective and indeterminate. Justice Frankfurter, as referenced earlier in this section, described the standard as whether the practice at issue offends "a sense of justice." And in *Palko v. Connecticut*, Justice Cardozo stated that a fundamental right is one that is part of "the very essence of a scheme of ordered liberty."

(3) Selective Incorporation

The fundamental rights doctrine gave way in the 1960s to another methodology that, ultimately, became the predominant approach to resolving questions of incorporation.

Known as the selective incorporation doctrine, this approach, as its name suggests, maintains that certain (selective) provisions within the Bill of Rights are so fundamental that they should be incorporated to the states via the Fourteenth Amendment due process clause. It looks in the abstract at the entirety of the right (as opposed to a singular case application) and inquires whether the entirety of that right is fundamental. If so, then it should be incorporated to the states and should be every bit as binding upon the states as it is upon the federal government.

The selective incorporation doctrine is a hybrid approach to the incorporation issue. Within its definition, one can see aspects of both the fundamental and total incorporation theories. Before a Bill of Rights safeguard can be selectively incorporated, that right must be deemed to be fundamental. In other words, a finding that a particular right is fundamental is a prerequisite to its selective incorporation. Once this threshold is satisfied, then that right is totally incorporated to the states.

To see this at work, consider the 1968 case of *Duncan v. Louisiana.*[7] At issue was whether the right to a trial by jury guaranteed by the Sixth Amendment was applicable to the states via the Fourteenth Amendment. Answering in the affirmative, the Supreme Court held that since "trial by jury in criminal cases is fundamental to the American scheme of justice, we hold that the Fourteenth Amendment guarantees a right of jury trial in all criminal cases which—were they to be tried in federal court—would come within the Sixth Amendment's guarantee." In contrasting the selective incorporation approach—employed in *Duncan*—with the fundamental rights approach, the Court drew the following distinctions between the two approaches:

> Earlier the Court can be seen as having asked, when inquiring into whether some particular procedural safeguard was required of a State, if a civilized system could be imagined that would not accord the particular protection. . . . The recent cases, on the other hand, have proceeded upon the valid assumption that state criminal processes are not imaginary and theoretical schemes but actual systems bearing virtually every characteristic of the common-law system that has been developing contemporaneously in England and in this country. The question thus is whether given this kind of system a particular procedure is fundamental—whether, that is, a procedure is necessary to an Anglo-American regime of ordered liberty.

Notice the Court's emphasis on the "American scheme of justice" and the "Anglo-American regime of ordered liberty." Whereas the fundamental rights approach focuses upon whether a particular aspect of a Bill of Rights guarantee is fundamental to "a civilized system" or "a scheme of ordered liberty," the selective incorporation approach examines the right in light of the scheme of justice as it has developed in this country. Rather than focusing upon "imaginary and theoretical" justice systems and inquiring whether a particular right is fundamental in such scenarios, the selective incorporation model examines the safeguard in the context of the common-law justice system as it has developed in the United States.

---

[7]391 U.S. 145 (1968).

To date, the adoption of the selective incorporation approach has resulted in the incorporation of virtually all of the Bill of Rights. As stated by Yale Law School Professor Akhil Reed Amar, "[I]n the cases they decided, Justice [William J.] Brennan and his brethren never met a right in the Bill they didn't like or deem fundamental enough to warrant incorporation."[8] In the criminal context, only the Fifth Amendment grand jury requirement and, arguably, the Eighth Amendment prohibition against excessive bail have yet to be incorporated.

Today the incorporation debate, at least within the criminal procedure context, is essentially settled. Rather than debating whether a particular Fourth, Fifth, or Sixth Amendment right is applicable to the states, the Supreme Court now concerns itself with how each of these rights should be interpreted. The Court's interpretation of these amendments is what the remainder of this book will address.

Sidebar

JUSTICE WILLIAM J. BRENNAN

Justice William J. Brennan was appointed by President Dwight Eisenhower to the U.S. Supreme Court and served from 1956 to 1990. At the time of his appointment, Justice Brennan was a judge on the New Jersey Supreme Court. Justice Brennan is considered to have been the leading voice behind the theory of selective incorporation.

Justice William J. Brennan
Library of Congress,
LC-USZ62-60138

SUMMARY

- The Bill of Rights has been almost completely incorporated to the states via the Fourteenth Amendment.

- Historically there have been three competing theories regarding incorporation that members of the Supreme Court have advocated.

  1. Total Incorporation: Principally advocated by Justice Black, supporters of this theory argued that the Fourteenth Amendment encompassed the Bill of Rights in its entirety.

  2. Fundamental Rights: Vigorously advocated by Justice Frankfurter, supporters of this theory argued that a right should be made applicable to the states via the Fourteenth Amendment due process clause if the particular right at issue (irrespective of whether it is part of the Bill of Rights) was fundamental.

  3. Selective Incorporation: This became the predominant approach to incorporation. Advocates of this theory examine the entirety of a particular right delineated in the Bill of Rights and inquire whether that right is fundamental and, therefore, applicable to the states via the due process clause of the Fourteenth Amendment.

---

[8]Akhil Reed Amar, *supra* note 1, at 220.

CONNECTIONS

Relationship to Fourth Amendment: Essential Concepts (Chapter 2)

This chapter provides an overview of many essential Fourth Amendment foundational concepts. Each of these concepts has been fully incorporated to the states.

Relationship to Searches and Seizures: Exceptions to the Warrant Requirement and Residential Arrests (Chapter 6)

This chapter commences this book's discussion of the many exceptions to the warrant requirement. Each of the exceptions discussed (e.g., exigent circumstances) are applicable to the states.

Relationship to Searches Incident to Arrest (Chapter 7), the Automobile Exception (Chapter 8), the Plain View Doctrine (Chapter 9), and Consent Searches (Chapter 10)

Each of these chapters discusses additional exceptions to the warrant requirement, all of which are applicable to the states.

Relationship to Searches and Seizures on Less than Probable Cause — *Terry v. Ohio* (Chapter 11)

This chapter provides an introductory discussion regarding Fourth Amendment seizures on less than probable cause. The law regarding this type of seizure is also applicable to the states.

Relationship to Fourth Amendment Violations and Their Associated Remedies (Chapter 15)

This chapter discusses the exclusionary rule and the standing concept. This common remedy for constitutional violations and the prerequisite standing requirement are applicable to the states.

Relationship to the Involuntary Confessions and the Due Process Clause Cases (Chapter 17) and the *Miranda* Rule (Chapter 18)

These chapters discuss the law regarding confessions, including the Fifth Amendment right to counsel, which apply to the states and federal governments equally.

Relationship to The Sixth Amendment Right to Counsel — General Principles (Chapter 19)

This chapter discusses the right to counsel that attaches upon the commencement of adversary proceedings. These constitutional principles apply with equal force to federal and state courts.

Fourth Amendment: Essential Concepts

2

Though the incorporation debate is, arguably, the most significant criminal procedure issue to have confronted the High Court, the most entertaining

discussions and lively debates among my students unquestionably have arisen in the context of Fourth, Fifth, and Sixth Amendment interpretation. It seems that almost everyone has an opinion regarding the thematic debate that invariably characterizes such discussions — the appropriate balance that should be struck between allowing the police to pursue their investigative function and the safeguarding of individual liberties. This chapter begins this discussion by providing an overview of the essential components of the Fourth Amendment.

A. ESSENTIAL FOURTH AMENDMENT TERMS

1. People
2. Persons, Houses, Papers, and Effects
3. Reasonableness
4. Seizures
5. Searches
6. Warrants

B. CRITICAL THRESHOLD ISSUES

1. Government Action Requirement
2. Standing

C. REMEDIES: THE EXCLUSIONARY RULE

A. Essential Fourth Amendment Terms

A significant portion (if not a majority) of your time in your Criminal Procedure course will be spent analyzing the Fourth Amendment. Again, the text of the Fourth Amendment reads:

> The right of the people to be secure in their persons, houses, papers, and effects, against unreasonable searches and seizures, shall not be violated, and no Warrants shall issue, but upon probable cause, supported by Oath or affirmation, and particularly describing the place to be searched, and the persons or things to be seized.

Sidebar

HISTORY UNDERLYING THE ADOPTION OF THE FOURTH AMENDMENT

The following historical account is excerpted from the 1965 Supreme Court opinion in *Stanford v. Texas*.[1]

[The words of the Fourth Amendment] reflect the determination of those who wrote the Bill of Rights that the people of this new Nation should forever "be secure in their persons, houses, papers, and effects" from intrusion and seizure by officers acting under the unbridled authority of a general warrant. Vivid in the memory of the newly independent Americans were those general warrants known as writs of assistance under which officers of the Crown had so bedeviled the colonists. The hated writs of assistance had given customs officials blanket authority to search where they pleased for goods imported in violation of the British tax laws. They were denounced by James Otis as "the worst instrument of arbitrary power, the most destructive of English liberty, and the fundamental principles of law, that ever was found in an English law book," because they placed "the liberty of every man in the hands of every petty officer." The historic occasion of that denunciation, in 1761 at Boston, has been characterized as "perhaps the most prominent event which inaugurated the resistance of the colonies to the oppressions of the mother country." . . .

James Otis was a Massachusetts lawyer and legislator in the mid-1700s.
Library of Congress, LC-USZ62-45327

    But while the Fourth Amendment was most immediately the product of contemporary revulsion against a regime of writs of assistance, its roots go far deeper. Its adoption in the Constitution of this new Nation reflected the culmination in England a few years earlier of a struggle against oppression which had endured for centuries. . . .

    What is significant to note is that this history is largely a history of conflict between the Crown and the press. It was in enforcing the laws licensing the publication of literature and, later, in prosecutions for seditious libel that general warrants were systematically used in the sixteenth, seventeenth, and eighteenth centuries. In Tudor England officers of the Crown were given roving commissions to search where they pleased in order to suppress and destroy the literature of dissent, both Catholic and Puritan. In later years warrants were sometimes more specific in content, but they typically authorized of all persons connected of the premises of all persons connected with the publication of a particular libel, or the arrest and seizure of all the papers of a named person thought to be connected with a libel.

---

[1] 379 U.S. 476 (1965).

This single passage has been the subject of seemingly endless litigation before the Supreme Court. To understand the basis for this litigation, however, it is initially necessary to analyze the essential components of the Fourth Amendment.

(1) People

To date, the term "the people" has been somewhat loosely defined by the Supreme Court. However, some guidance can perhaps be gleaned from *United States v. Verdugo-Urquidez*,[2] where the majority observed that, in contrast to the Fifth and Sixth Amendments, the Fourth Amendment:

> extends its reach only to "the people." . . . "[T]he people" seems to have been a term of art employed in select parts of the Constitution. The Preamble declares that the Constitution is ordained and established by "the People of the United States." The Second Amendment protects "the right of the people to keep and bear Arms," and the Ninth and Tenth Amendments provide that certain rights and powers are retained by and reserved to "the people" (citations omitted). While this textual exegesis is by no means conclusive, it suggests that "the people" protected by the Fourth Amendment, and by the First and Second Amendments, and to whom rights and powers are reserved in the Ninth and Tenth Amendments, refers to a class of persons who are part of a national community or who have otherwise developed sufficient connection with this country to be considered part of that community.

Thus, to be entitled to Fourth Amendment protections an individual would seemingly have to possess a "connection with this country" that is, at a minimum, more substantial than simply a fleeting or temporary presence. Certainly U.S. citizens are included in this term. Permanent resident aliens would also appear to be encompassed within the definition. However, the Court in *Verdugo-Urquidez* found that Fourth Amendment safeguards did not extend to a Mexican citizen on trial in the United States whose residence in Mexico was searched by U.S. and Mexican government officials. As stated by the Court, "[a]t the time of the search, he was a citizen and resident of Mexico with no voluntary attachment to the United States, and the place searched was located in Mexico. Under these circumstances, the Fourth Amendment has no application." Nevertheless, there are some issues that remain unresolved, including the applicability, if any, of the Fourth Amendment's protections to non-citizen residents who are lawfully within the country but are here on a temporary (nonpermanent) basis.

(2) Persons, Houses, Papers, and Effects

The Amendment further provides that "the people" are protected or "secure[d]" in their "persons, houses, papers, and effects." The term "persons" has been interpreted to include not only an individual's physical body, but also his clothing and conversations. When, for example, an individual is arrested his freedom of movement is significantly curtailed. This conduct constitutes a seizure of a "person" within the meaning of the Fourth Amendment. Similarly, if bodily fluids are extracted in order to detect the presence of alcohol or narcotics, or if an officer performs a search of an individual's outer garments, such activity also constitutes a search of a

---

[2] 494 U.S. 259 (1990).

"person." In addition, electronic eavesdropping upon telephonic conversations can also constitute a search and seizure of an individual's person.

The term "houses"[3] includes not only permanent and nonpermanent residences (e.g., houses, apartments, hotels) but also structures attached to a home (e.g., garages), as well as detached areas provided they fall within a home's curtilage.[4] This term will be discussed at greater length in Chapters 3 and 6. The term "papers" is comparatively more straightforward in definition. Written and electronic correspondence, whether personal or business-related, are encompassed within the term, as are papers such as tax returns and billing statements. In contrast to the definitions attendant to "houses" and "papers," the term "effects" is considerably broader in scope. It includes items that are frequently the subject of government searches, such as computers, automobiles, luggage, briefcases, purses, wallets, and backpacks. It also includes countless other possessory items, including currency, household products, pictures, identification cards, and credit cards, to name just a few.

(3) Reasonableness

So now we know that "the people" are secured by the Fourth Amendment in their "persons, houses, papers, and effects." But from what are "the people" protected? Are the people protected against all governmental searches and seizures affecting their "persons, houses, papers, and effects"? As I'm sure you suspect, the answer to that is no. To see why, let's examine the language of the Amendment a bit further. The text provides that the Amendment affords protection against searches and seizures that are unreasonable. In other words, individuals who are subject to government searches and seizures that are reasonable are not protected by the Fourth Amendment. Thus, a critical issue is whether a particular search or seizure is, in fact, reasonable. This book will soon examine the plethora of contexts in which this issue has been debated.

(4) Seizures

The text of the Fourth Amendment plainly protects the "people" from unreasonable governmental seizures of their "persons" and of their property. But when there is some sort of governmental interference with these interests a critical question must be asked: What constitutes a "seizure" within the meaning of the Fourth Amendment?

With respect to the seizure of individuals, certainly an individual is considered to be seized when he is under arrest. Well, then, what constitutes an arrest? Is it necessary for an officer to utter the words "You're under arrest"? Does an arrest occur if the officer verbally or physically attempts—albeit unsuccessfully—to exercise her authority to restrain an individual?

The answer to the latter two questions is "no." Though the answer to the arrest question varies depending upon context, a commonly held understanding of the term, as enunciated by the Fifth Circuit, is that a person is under arrest "if a reasonable person in the suspect's position would understand the situation to be a restraint

---

[3]The term "houses" is discussed at greater length in Chapter 6.
[4]The term "curtilage" is discussed at greater length in Chapter 3.

on freedom of the kind that the law typically associates with a formal arrest."[5] Certainly an individual who has been officially placed under arrest by a law enforcement agency in anticipation that charges will be sought is, in all likelihood, seized for Fourth Amendment purposes. However, a person who has not been formally arrested by the police for a particular crime may yet be under arrest for constitutional analysis purposes if the circumstances of his detention would cause a reasonable person to believe that the restraint on his liberty is tantamount to a formal arrest.

Even in the absence of an effective arrest, a person may yet be seized for Fourth Amendment purposes. As explained in greater depth in Chapter 11, there is a distinction in the law between an individual who is arrested and one who is merely detained. Individuals who are merely detained by law enforcement may also present cognizable challenges to their seizure under the Fourth Amendment.

A different definition of seizure applies with respect to property. In essence, a seizure of property "occurs when there is some meaningful interference with an individual's possessory interests in that property."[6] Thus when an officer, in the midst of a search of an individual's home, merely touches an object it is highly unlikely that such slight handling constitutes "meaningful interference" within the meaning of the Constitution. On the other hand, if this same officer destroys a piece of property or permanently displaces the property from the search scene, then it is certainly more likely that a "meaningful interference" has occurred.

(5) Searches

As the text of the Fourth Amendment makes clear, a governmental search of an individual and her property potentially infringes the constitutional rights of that individual. I use the term "potentially" because not every government search is prohibited. Only those that are unreasonable are proscribed. As will be made clear in the next chapter, the determinative test for whether or not a search is reasonable has gone through an interesting transition. Suffice it to say, today the predominant test for reasonableness is whether an individual has a reasonable expectation of privacy in the location of the search and whether that right was properly respected by the government. If the individual does not have a reasonable expectation of privacy, then usually there is no search within the meaning of the Fourth Amendment. If, on the other hand, a reasonable expectation of privacy is present, then the government must comply with the demands of the Fourth Amendment prior to engaging in a search.

So as you study the material in Chapter 3 ask yourself in each instance whether the individual has a reasonable expectation of privacy in the person, the home, the paper, or the effect that was searched. If not, then in most instances there is no Fourth Amendment violation. If so, then a further examination must take place to determine whether the search in question complied with Fourth Amendment standards.

You will also discover through your study that the rules regarding the propriety of government searches are not uniform but are contextually influenced. Factors such as "who" is being searched (e.g., prisoners versus non-prisoners), "why" the search is taking place (criminal purposes versus noncriminal objectives), and "where" the search occurs (e.g., a home versus a car) can also influence the ultimate outcome.

---

[5]*Freeman v. Gore*, 483 F.3d 404 (5th Cir. 2007).
[6]*United States v. Jacobson*, 466 U.S. 109 (1984).

Do I hear some of you saying, "Now wait a minute. Where are all these distinctions in the Fourth Amendment text?" Well, stay tuned folks! The Supreme Court has developed an interesting jurisprudence that will be sure to test your own personal sense of justice and fairness. Remember, in all these cases the Supreme Court is tackling the ever-present and difficult dilemma of how to properly balance the government's law enforcement objectives against the individual's liberty interests. These variances will be explored in much greater depth later in this book.

(6) Warrants

As noted, the second half of the Fourth Amendment text provides, "[A]nd no Warrants shall issue, but upon probable cause, supported by Oath or affirmation, and particularly describing the place to be searched, and the persons or things to be seized." Though this passage will be dissected in much greater depth in later chapters, a few general, preliminary observations are warranted at this juncture.

The latter part of the Amendment primarily addresses the various prerequisites that must be satisfied before a judicial warrant to search or seize will issue. For example, the Amendment plainly requires that before a search warrant can be authorized, the place to be searched as well as the items to be seized must be described with sufficient particularity. This same level of particularity is expected prior to the issuance of an individual arrest warrant. The passage further provides that a warrant shall not issue unless probable cause is established. Thus, unless this minimum threshold of evidentiary support is satisfied, neither a search warrant nor an arrest warrant will be issued by a court. Ordinarily, one might believe that the term "probable cause" would equate to a "more likely than not" standard. Not true. Though a set percentage has not been affixed to the term, a warrant can be validly issued with less than a 50 percent belief in the "cause" underlying the warrant request.

B. Critical Threshold Issues

(1) Government Action Requirement

Defense attorneys routinely submit motions to the court alleging governmental violations of their client's constitutional rights. Prosecutors, in turn, file responses to these motions justifying the challenged conduct. When I was a federal prosecutor I filed innumerable such responses. Prior to assessing the merits of the defendant's contention, however, I would always review certain threshold issues. In fact, I routinely tell my students that, when taking their Criminal Procedure final examination, they should always ensure that certain threshold requirements have been satisfied prior to analyzing the merits of a defendant's constitutional claim. If these threshold matters have been satisfied, then a court may proceed to address the merits of the defendant's arguments. If, on the other hand, these preconditions have not been satisfied, then a court should dismiss the defendant's motion without reaching the constitutional issues.

One such threshold issue that I rather routinely addressed concerned the identity of the individual or entity that performed the challenged search or seizure. It is essential to remember that the Bill of Rights regulates *only government* conduct.

Therefore, only searches and seizures performed by government actors implicate a review under the Fourth Amendment. If this essential element is not satisfied then a court's work is done. A court can dismiss a defendant's motion without further review of the facts underlying the challenged search.

Think of the court as a gatekeeper. The court performs an array of functions, one of which is to assess the validity of purported constitutional violations. A defendant might claim, for example, that he was illegally arrested, that his automobile was illegally searched, or that items found in his briefcase were illegally seized. The court may, in fact, consider the facts underlying the search and seizure in question particularly offensive. However, no matter how offensive or egregious the underlying conduct, a court is devoid of authority to consider the constitutionality of such conduct unless the challenged actions were performed by a government actor.

F   A   Q

Q: Can a search or seizure performed by a private citizen ever constitute a constitutional violation? How about a search or seizure performed by a foreign government official on an American while traveling abroad?

A: *Private Conduct.* Ordinarily private conduct falls outside the ambit of the Fourth Amendment. However, if a sufficient government link to the private conduct can be established, then a constitutional challenge can be heard. The establishment of this linkage would effectively render the private search a governmental endeavor. So if a police officer arrests a private citizen who was transporting illegal narcotics and then asks that individual to search for and seize evidence relevant to narcotics trafficking from the residence of his source of supply, a subsequent search conducted by this individual could very well constitute state action.

B: *Foreign Officials.* Generally, Americans who are present in another country and are subject to a search or seizure by foreign government officials may not later challenge the constitutionality of that conduct in a subsequent criminal prosecution in the United States. The Fourth Amendment is concerned primarily with searches and seizures performed by government actors in this country. However, searches performed by foreign officials are subject to constitutional challenge if a sufficient nexus can be established between the American government and the foreign actor.

(2) Standing

Another critical threshold issue that will be discussed in much greater depth in Chapter 15 involves the issue of standing. Broadly speaking, only those individuals who have sustained an injury as a result of the government's conduct are eligible to have their claims heard. However, this statement is over-inclusive as to the issue of standing, for not every individual so affected actually has standing. Rather, and more particularly, only those defendants who have a constitutionally protected interest in the person, house, paper, or effect that was searched or seized can present such claims.

In the context of a Fourth Amendment search claim, for example, this requirement may be satisfied if a defendant can demonstrate that he has a reasonable expectation of privacy in the area that was searched. If such a showing is made then a defendant has standing to challenge the government's conduct. Thus, a defendant who asserts that the police unconstitutionally searched and seized items from within a home will likely have standing if he can demonstrate that he was residing at the residence at the time of the search. Similarly, a defendant who is challenging the search of an automobile will likely have standing if he can show that he owned and operated the vehicle at the time of the search. Standing issues can also arise, albeit far less frequently, in the Fifth and Sixth Amendment contexts.

C. Remedies: The Exclusionary Rule

When a defendant presents a claim alleging a violation of his Fourth, Fifth, or Sixth Amendment rights, he is seeking more than simply a judicial declaration of inappropriate governmental conduct. A doctrine called the exclusionary rule will often require that the prosecution be precluded from using at trial evidence obtained as a result of the government's unconstitutional conduct. Thus, if the defendant submits that his automobile was illegally searched, then he is seeking via the exclusionary rule the suppression of some, if not all, of the evidentiary material discovered by law enforcement as a result of that Fourth Amendment violation. Similarly, if a defendant asserts that statements he uttered were the product of police coercion in violation of the Fifth Amendment due process clause, he is seeking to preclude the government from introducing those statements at his trial.

SUMMARY

- The first half of the Fourth Amendment protects the people in their persons, houses, papers, and effects against unreasonable government searches and seizures.

- The "people" are individuals "who are part of a national community or who have otherwise developed sufficient connection with this country to be considered a part of that community." This includes citizens and permanent resident aliens. The people are protected in their persons (which includes their physical body and outer clothing), houses (e.g., actual houses, apartments, some temporary living quarters), papers, and effects (e.g., automobiles, luggage, purses, etc.).

- A person is seized when he has either been arrested or otherwise detained by the government.

- The predominant test employed by the courts to determine whether a government search was reasonable is whether the individual who is asserting the claim has a reasonable expectation of privacy in the searched location and whether the government properly respected that right.

- The latter half of the Fourth Amendment provides that judicial warrants will only issue if probable cause is established that is supported by an oath and a particularized description of "the place to be searched, and the persons or things to be seized."

- The Fourth Amendment's proscriptions are applicable only against governmental conduct.

- An individual must have standing to assert a claim that a governmental search or seizure was unconstitutional. A person has standing if he can show that he has a constitutionally protected interest in the person, house, paper, or effect that was searched or seized.

- Absent a demonstration that a claimant possesses a reasonable expectation of privacy in the subject of the search or seizure, a court usually will not consider the merits of his constitutional claim.

- The exclusionary rule often requires that evidence seized (physical and/or testimonial) in violation of the Constitution be suppressed at trial.

CONNECTIONS

Relationship to Searches and the Reasonableness Inquiry (Chapter 3)

Whether an individual has a reasonable expectation of privacy in his telephone conversations, residence, trash, and financial records are among the many issues addressed in Chapter 3. The concept of reasonableness is explored in greater depth in this chapter.

Relationship to Searches, Seizures, and the Warrant Clause (Chapter 4)

This chapter provided an introduction to the warrant clause of the Fourth Amendment. As detailed in Chapter 4, a warrant must describe with particularity the place to be searched and specifically describe the items to be seized. In addition, the government must satisfy a magistrate that probable cause exists to believe that evidence of crime will be found at the stated location.

Relationship to Searches and Seizures on Less than Probable Cause — *Terry v. Ohio* (Chapter 11)

This chapter provided an introduction to the concept of a seizure within the Fourth Amendment. Chapter 11 discusses the different types of Fourth Amendment seizures (arrests, which require probable cause, and so-called *Terry* stops, which require reasonable suspicion) as well as the concept of encounters that do not implicate Fourth Amendment interests.

Relationship to Searches and Seizures: Exceptions to the Warrant Requirement and Residential Arrests (Chapter 6), Searches Incident to Arrest (Chapter 7), the Automobile Exception (Chapter 8), the Plain View Doctrine (Chapter 9), and Consent Searches (Chapter 10)

This chapter provided an introductory discussion about the reasonableness concept. Chapters 6-10 explore how the Supreme Court has interpreted the term "reasonable" in several different contexts and how the Court's interpretations have resulted in several exceptions to the general requirement that the state secure a warrant prior to a search. At times, the Court has granted the government the right to conduct searches without any suspicion whatsoever.

Relationship to Fourth Amendment Violations and Their Associated Remedies (Chapter 15)

The concepts of standing and the exclusionary rule—introduced in this chapter—are the focus of Chapter 15. In most instances, unless an individual can establish a personal expectation of privacy that is deemed reasonable by society, that individual cannot successfully exclude evidence pursuant to the exclusionary rule.

Searches and the Reasonableness Inquiry

3

OVERVIEW

Invariably, I tell my students that when I was an assistant U.S. attorney, among the first issues that I would explore when confronted with a motion challenging the legitimacy of a government search was whether the "search" term as defined by the Fourth Amendment was even implicated by the purported police violation. If the answer to that question was "no" then there was no Fourth Amendment issue for the court to consider and the challenge could be readily denied. This chapter will discuss the issue of what constitutes a "search" within the meaning of the Fourth Amendment and examine several Supreme Court precedents that address situations where this question has arisen.

A. *KATZ* AND THE REASONABLE EXPECTATION OF PRIVACY TEST

1. Consensual Exposure of Telephonic Conversations
2. Houses, Curtilage, and Unprotected Areas
3. Trash
4. Bags on Public/Commercial Modes of Transportation
5. Financial, Utility, Telephonic, and Other Business Institutions; Pen Registers
6. Technology
7. Use of Dogs as a Sensory Enhancement Tool

A. *Katz* and the Reasonable Expectation of Privacy Test

In your Criminal Procedure course — often toward the beginning of the discussion of the Fourth Amendment — you will, in all probability, discuss the case of *Katz v. United States*.[1] That case provides some basic guideposts that help courts determine whether a search or a seizure falls within the ambit of the Fourth Amendment.

The case centered on the electronic surveillance by FBI agents of Katz's telephone conversations while he was in a public telephone booth. The agents were able to listen to Katz's conversations by virtue of having attached electronic surveillance equipment to the outside of the booth. In holding that the government's conduct breached Katz's Fourth Amendment rights, the Court found that, despite Katz's presence in a public phone booth, he nevertheless had a legitimate expectation of privacy in his conversations. The Court reasoned that "[w]hat a person knowingly exposes to the public, even in his own home or office, is not a subject of Fourth Amendment protection. But what he seeks to preserve as private, even in an area accessible to the public, may be constitutionally protected."

Thus, the Court focused its attention not upon the public status of the telephone booth where the call was placed, but upon Katz's subjective expectation that his conversation was private. This was significant because it changed the course of how such search questions had traditionally been analyzed. Prior to *Katz*, the Court focused upon a trespass doctrine. In essence, the doctrine provides that an unconstitutional search occurs when the government penetrates a "constitutionally protected area." In fact, the litigants before the Court — the government and Katz — debated whether the phone booth was, in fact, an area that was constitutionally protected. The government further argued that there was no physical penetration of the phone booth given that the surveillance devices were attached to the booth's exterior. In rejecting this property-based approach, the Court observed that the protection of the Fourth Amendment concerns "people, not places." Since Katz had a legitimate expectation of privacy in his phone booth conversations, the Court found that the FBI surveillance violated his Fourth Amendment interests.

There remained the question of how to determine whether a government search was permissible under the Amendment. The answer was ultimately found in Justice John Harlan II's concurring opinion that set forth a two-part test that has since become the predominant test governing this determination. The test is as follows: 1) whether an individual has exhibited a subjective expectation of privacy; and 2) whether that subjective expectation is one that society deems to be reasonable. Notice that the test requires both a subjective as well as an objective

---

[1]389 U.S. 347 (1967).

inquiry. When both prongs are answered affirmatively, an individual is deemed to have a reasonable expectation of privacy and is entitled to the protections extended by the Fourth Amendment.

While the test is easy to state, it is unquestionably more difficult to apply. As you might expect, the subjective prong is rarely a point of contest. Defendants routinely assert that they subjectively believed that the area searched would remain private. Indeed, as a practical matter, it would be difficult for a prosecutor to successfully wage a battle on this front. The central inquiry invariably concerns the objective prong. What activities society reasonably considers private is obviously more difficult to gauge. Certainly any resolution of this question inevitably requires a degree of subjective speculation. And this subjective disagreement is evident in many of the Court's decisions. As you review the upcoming cases, remember the Court's admonition that what an individual knowingly exposes to the public is not protected by the Fourth Amendment. Virtually all (if not all) of the considered cases are characterized by at least some public exposure. But whether society, despite such public disclosure, is prepared to accept as reasonable a defendant's subjective expectation of privacy under such circumstances is the critical issue.

As noted, the Court indicated that people and not places are protected by the Fourth Amendment. While this is true, I would suggest that you not unduly emphasize this proclamation. True, the Fourth Amendment plainly provides that the "people" are protected from various government intrusions. However, when ascertaining whether a particular government intrusion is justified, the Court frequently considers the place where the search is conducted. As you will see in your studies, time and again great significance is placed by the Court upon the location of the search. Searches justified in one particular locale are plainly unconstitutional in another. Indeed, the Court's continued emphasis upon location can plausibly be cited as a reason why *Katz* has yet to live up to its perceived promise as being a harbinger for expansive individual liberties under the Amendment. Many believed that *Katz*, with its emphasis upon people and de-emphasis upon place, would lead to judicial findings of protected privacy interests in a multitude of public fora. However, as is evident in much of the remaining material in this chapter, such has not been the case.

What follows next is a discussion of the *Katz* principles in various contexts. As you study these applications, ask yourself whether you believe that the individual's subjective expectation of privacy is one that should be considered reasonable by societal standards. Also ask yourself whether the Court, in addressing the various factual scenarios, has been consistent in its application of these factors.

(1) Consensual Exposure of Telephonic Conversations

As noted, the Court found that Katz could successfully challenge the electronic surveillance of his conversations within a public phone booth given that he possessed a reasonable expectation of privacy in his conversations. But let's change the facts slightly. What if the individual on the other end of the conversation with Katz consented to have the government tape or listen in on the conversations? Or what if the individual, upon completing his call with Katz, elected either to testify regarding his communications or to convey the substance of his conversation to a government agent? Would someone in Katz's position retain his Fourth Amendment protections? Would the revelation of the substance of Katz's conversations violate his expectation of privacy?

The Supreme Court has said that the reach of the Amendment does not extend to such situations. Remember *Katz*'s admonition that when a person knowingly exposes something to the public he cannot retain a reasonable expectation of privacy. As in *Katz*, it is certainly plausible to believe that a majority, perhaps even a vast majority, of telephone conversationalists subjectively expect that their conversations will be private. They do not normally expect that, say, an unknown third party, whether or not the party is a government official, will be listening in on their conversations. Nevertheless, when one conveys words to another individual the expresser of those words is making a public exposure of his words and thoughts.

Through such exposure, he naturally runs the risk that the person listening to those words may not elect to keep those words private. But should this mere risk render a subjective expectation of privacy unreasonable? The Supreme Court thinks so. Thus, whether the person on the other end consents to governmental eavesdropping or simply elects to subsequently relate the nature of the conversation, there is nothing in the Fourth Amendment prohibiting such disclosure.

Sidebar

UNDERCOVER POLICE WORK AND THE USE OF INFORMANTS

The line of authority governing the conveyance of telephonic conversations is commonly referred to as "false friends" cases. It should be noted that the "false friend" rules apply not only to telephonic conversations but also to conversations that occur while in the physical presence of another individual. Law enforcement officials routinely engage in undercover work and similarly employ citizens as police informants. In such roles, it is hardly unusual for informants and undercover officers to meet with investigative targets, misrepresent their true identity and intentions, wear a wire capable of transmitting conversations, and record any conversations. The Fourth Amendment does not prohibit the subsequent use of such statements at trial since an individual who publicly expresses his thoughts to others cannot, in turn, insist that he reasonably expected those conversations to remain confidential.

(2) Houses, Curtilage, and Unprotected Areas

The reach of the Fourth Amendment extends to "houses" as well as those areas beyond the confines of a home where a reasonable expectation of privacy is shown to exist. Well, then, what is the reach of the Fourth Amendment beyond the physical confines of a "house"? What areas or structures might be encompassed within the term? There is no definitive answer to either question. However, there are some guiding principles for the courts to follow when making these assessments.

On the one hand, the safeguards of the Fourth Amendment do not necessarily extend to all activities that occur on property associated with a "house" (e.g., lawn, driveway, shed, etc.). This is true even in situations where the incriminating evidence was discovered by a government trespasser. Even if a homeowner litters his lawn with signs that say "No Trespassing," "Beware of Dog," "No Solicitation," and the like, such actions standing alone will not afford the homeowner Fourth Amendment protections against the prying eyes of the government for activities conducted in an open field or that are otherwise publicly exposed.

On the other hand, if these activities are conducted within the curtilage of the home then the Fourth Amendment might provide the homeowner with some protection. Obviously, then, the critical question is, what constitutes the curtilage of a home? A home's curtilage is considered to be those areas that immediately surround a home where intimate activities associated with a household occur. The courts examine four factors when making this determination: 1) the immediacy of the area in question to the residence; 2) the area's primary use; 3) whether the area is enclosed; and 4) efforts by the homeowner to shield the area from public view.

Land located within the curtilage of a home is protected by the Fourth Amendment. However, land that is beyond the curtilage is not so protected. Such "open fields" do not receive Fourth Amendment protection because, according to the Supreme Court, it is not a person, house, paper, or effect and individuals who conduct activities in the open cannot legitimately expect privacy under such circumstances. Even structures commonly found on residential property, such as unattached garages and sheds, are not presumed to be within a home's curtilage. However, it is important to remember that even if an area or unit falls within a home's curtilage, a government search thereof is not subject to Fourth Amendment scrutiny if that area or unit was otherwise readily observable from a public vantage point. Thus, an officer who observes, while walking along a public sidewalk, the presence of marijuana plants on land within the curtilage of a home did not conduct a "search" within the meaning of the Fourth Amendment.

(3) Trash

Does a Fourth Amendment search occur when the police search an individual's trash? No bright-line rule has been established in regards to this question. However, the location of the trash at the time of the government search may very well be a critical, if not determinative, factor.

In *California v. Greenwood*,[2] the Supreme Court held that when an individual leaves his trash outside the curtilage of his home, that individual has knowingly exposed his trash to the outside world. Such public exposure, the Court concluded, renders any subjective expectation of privacy an individual has in his trash an expectation that society would not consider reasonable. As the Court noted, "plastic garbage bags left on or at the side of a public street are readily accessible to animals, children, scavengers, snoops, and other members of the public." The Court concluded, "having deposited their garbage 'in an area particularly suited for public inspection and, in a manner of speaking, public consumption, for the express purpose of having strangers take it,' *United States v. Reicherter*, 647 F.2d 397, 399 (CA3 1981), [defendants] could have had no reasonable expectation of privacy in the inculpatory items that they discarded."

(4) Bags on Public/Commercial Modes of Transportation

Many people today travel by airplane, train, and bus in order to get from one destination to another. It is also not unusual for these travelers to carry on board luggage or some other form of travel bag and store the items in overhead bins.

In *Bond v. United States*,[3] the Supreme Court addressed an issue pertinent to this situation; namely, "whether a law enforcement officer's physical manipulation of a bus passenger's carry-on luggage violated the Fourth Amendment's proscription against unreasonable searches." The Court held that the manipulation in that case violated the Fourth Amendment.

---

[2]486 U.S. 35 (1988).
[3]529 U.S. 334 (2000).

The case involved a Border Patrol agent who boarded a bus at a permanent checkpoint and, after checking the immigration status of those on board, "squeezed the soft luggage" belonging to one of the passengers that had been placed in an overhead storage bin. As he was squeezing the luggage, the officer noticed that within the bag was a "'brick-like' object." After obtaining consent from the owner of the bag, the officer conducted a search and discovered methamphetamine. The government argued that passengers who travel by bus necessarily expose their traveling bags to the public and, thus, should reasonably expect that those items will be manipulated.

Rejecting this contention and finding that the agent's physical manipulation of the bag's exterior constituted a search, the Court held that while a bus traveler "expects that other passengers or bus employees may move [his luggage] for one reason or another," he does not expect that his baggage will be handled "in an exploratory manner." Again, remember the public exposure rationale. The Court did not declare unconstitutional any law enforcement touching of luggage, only that which was exploratory.

(5) Financial, Utility, Telephonic, and Other Business Institutions; Pen Registers

A *subpoena duces tecum* is a court order requiring the individual or entity identified in the subpoena to produce certain tangible forms of evidence for use at trial or before a grand jury. When I was a federal prosecutor, I would routinely issue subpoenas of this type to private business entities, such as banks, requesting records with respect to certain individuals under investigation. In a fraud prosecution, for example, I might seek to obtain checking and savings account records to learn whether suspicious deposits were made by a suspect on certain specified dates. Or, if information reflected in telephone accounts were essential, I might subpoena those records as well. Or, if I needed to establish that an individual resides at a particular address, I might subpoena cable, water, or electric records that might be in his name at that locale.

Sidebar

SUBPOENAS DUCES TECUM

Subpoenas of this type are, in essence, a type of search. By requesting that a company produce certain records, it is requesting that the company search its records and produce that information that corresponds with what is sought in the subpoena. Like any search that implicates the Fourth Amendment, such a subpoena can be challenged when a reasonable expectation of privacy is infringed.

The use of a pen register device is another commonly employed investigative technique. A pen register is "a device or process which records or decodes dialing, routing, addressing, or signaling information transmitted by an instrument or facility from which a wire or electronic communication is transmitted."[4] In other words, pen registers are used when the government is interested in learning the numbers dialed from a certain telephone line. Judicial approval is required before such devices can be installed. Pen registers are often employed as a prelude to the submission of a wiretap application. Whereas records obtained from telephone service providers reflect information regarding dialed numbers that is somewhat dated, pen registers provide more current information. Indeed, currency of information is vital when seeking a wiretap, given that a court must be satisfied, before an application for electronic surveillance can be

---

[4] 18 U.S.C. § 3127 (3) (2006).

approved, that there is probable cause to believe that a crime has been, is being, or is about to be committed. Thus, information that is dated increases the risk that an application might be denied on account of staleness.

As you may be able to infer, prosecutors enjoy an investigative authority that is quite broad. In fact, this broad authority often enables prosecutors to build an airtight case even before an indictment is returned. By what rationale, then, can the government obtain such wide-ranging information about individuals? The Supreme Court has held that the provision of records, such as banking, electric, telephone, cable, and water bills, by private companies and the employment of pen registers are not searches within the meaning of the Fourth Amendment. Once again, the public exposure rationale governs this result. When individuals make deposits, make withdrawals, and conduct other financial transactions with their bank they necessarily impart information to a third-party financial institution. Not only are they sharing with the bank information regarding their own personal business associations, but they are also requesting that the bank — a third-party institution — assist with the particular financial transaction.

This same rationale applies when an individual secures services with a cable, electric, or water company. A person who seeks such services necessarily must impart certain personal information in order to obtain the desired service. Moreover, during the period that the service is provided the individual continues to impart information to that third-party institution (e.g., monthly electric and water usage, Internet addresses visited, etc.). When an individual orders cable service, for example, the cable company is necessarily provided with information reflective of the type of television programming that is being subscribed to by the customer. The cable company is also aware if any movie or special programming has been ordered. This information, in turn, is reflected in the monthly bill that is submitted to the subscriber at the provided mailing address. Given the nonexclusive nature of these business arrangements, any privacy in the subpoenaed information that an individual might subjectively expect is, in the view of the Supreme Court, one that society is unprepared to accept as reasonable.

(6) Technology

It is not uncommon for my students to readily grasp the public exposure concept and to concur in the results reached by the Supreme Court in the foregoing examples. However, student opinion becomes somewhat more divided when the concept is applied to information gathered pursuant to technology that plainly enhances the ability of law enforcement to learn information about an individual. After all, according to some, it is one thing to gather evidence by virtue of one's natural senses but quite another to use technology to enhance evidence gathering. As we will see, whether a technology-enhanced search is subject to Fourth Amendment review is often dependent upon whether the sought-for information has been exposed to the public. However, sometimes another influence helps to dictate the eventual outcome — the general prevalence of the technology in question. So pay attention to these rationales as you consider the following scenarios.

(a) Flashlights, Binoculars, Beepers, and Global Positioning Systems

The Supreme Court has held that the use of flashlights to assist in the observance of objects in darkened areas is not a search within the meaning of the Fourth

Amendment. Similarly, the use of binoculars, at least when used to illuminate the existence of publicly exposed objects or individuals, seems to be constitutional as well. Quoting *United States v. Lee*,[5] the Court in *Texas v. Brown*[6] stated, "'[The] use of a searchlight is comparable to the use of a marine glass or a field glass. It is not prohibited by the Constitution.' Numerous other courts have agreed that the use of artificial means to illuminate a darkened area simply does not constitute a search, and thus triggers no Fourth Amendment protection."

What about the use of beepers to track the movement of an individual or items in his possession? The Supreme Court has held that the government may employ such tracking devices as long as the beeper is furnishing information that is otherwise publicly observable. Thus, if the police install a beeper to monitor the movements of a vehicle along the public streets or traveling up a comparatively inaccessible rugged mountain, the Fourth Amendment is not violated given that such movements can readily be observed with the naked eye. However, if the beeper is placed within, say, a package and is then used to follow the movements of that package within a suspect's home, then the suspect can assert a Fourth Amendment challenge to such activity. In such circumstances, the beeper is no longer providing publicly exposed information, but rather information about private activities occurring within an individual residence.

This issue was among those presented to the Court in *United States v. Karo*.[7] There, the defendant and two others were suspected of using ether to extract cocaine from imported clothing items. The defendant, who had ordered 50 gallons of ether from an undercover government cooperative, was given several cans of ether. Unbeknownst to the defendant, the government installed a beeper in one of the cans. The beeper enabled the government to monitor the movements of that particular container.

After the defendant had picked up the ether containers, the government's surveillance efforts of the can's movements commenced. In short, the beeper technology enabled the government on different occasions to determine that the beeper was located within the defendant's home, that it had been removed to another associate's residence, that it had been removed once again to that associate's father's home, and then later moved to two different commercial storage facilities, before finally coming to rest at yet another residence rented by some of the defendant's associates. The defendant was eventually arrested and charged with narcotics crimes.

The Court found that the government's conduct violated the Fourth Amendment. In reaching this conclusion, the Court distinguished *Karo* from another beeper case, *United States v. Knotts*.[8] As in *Karo*, the government in *Knotts* installed a beeper in a container containing chloroform (which the Court described as "one of the so-called 'precursor' chemicals used to manufacture illicit drugs") that was delivered to an associate of the defendant. After the delivery, the officers by means of visual surveillance and the beeper technology followed the movements of two vehicles that, at different times, possessed the container. The container eventually came to rest in a cabin that the defendant had occupied. Based, in part, upon the information obtained from this technology, a search warrant for the cabin was obtained.

---

[5]274 U.S. 559 (1927).
[6]460 U.S. 730 (1983).
[7]468 U.S. 705 (1984).
[8]460 U.S. 276 (1983).

An ensuing search uncovered evidence that resulted in the defendant's indictment on narcotics charges.

In *Knotts*, the Supreme Court found that there was no Fourth Amendment violation. The *Knotts* Court acknowledged that the defendant had a privacy interest in his cabin. However, the Court reasoned that an expectation of privacy did not extend to the officers' visual surveillance of the vehicles while traversing the public highways. Even though the officers relied only in part upon their visual capacities when conducting their surveillance, the Court found that the additional reliance upon the beeper technology "does not alter the situation. Nothing in the Fourth Amendment prohibited the police from augmenting the sensory faculties bestowed upon them at birth with such enhancement as science and technology afforded them in this case." The Court concluded that the information provided by the beeper neither revealed information within the cabin nor uncovered information that was not otherwise "visible to the naked eye from outside the cabin."

This was the very fact that distinguished *Karo* from *Knotts*. In *Karo*, the beeper revealed information that was located within a private residence. As noted by the Court, the beeper monitoring

> reveal[ed] a critical fact about the interior of the premises that the Government [was] extremely interested in knowing and that it could not have otherwise obtained without a warrant. The case is thus not like *Knotts*, for there the beeper told the authorities nothing about the interior of Knotts' cabin. The information obtained in *Knotts* was "voluntarily conveyed to anyone who wanted to look . . . " (citation omitted); here, as we have said, the monitoring indicated that the beeper was inside the house, a fact that could not have been visually verified.

As the years progressed, how the rationale of *Karo* and *Knotts* would fare in the context of more sophisticated tracking technology, such as Global Positioning System (GPS) devices, was of great interest to many Court observers. The case of *United States v. Jones*[9] presented the Supreme Court with an opportunity to address this possible application. At issue was "whether the attachment of a GPS tracking device to an individual's vehicle, and subsequent use of that device to monitor the vehicle's movements on public streets, constitutes a search or seizure within the meaning of the Fourth Amendment." The Court answered in the affirmative, and in the process reintroduced and relied upon the long-dormant (pre-*Katz*) property-based perspective to its Fourth Amendment analysis.

At issue was the warrantless placement by the government of a GPS device on the undercarriage of a vehicle being used by the defendant and the subsequent monitoring of the vehicle's movements over the course of 28 days. The device enabled law enforcement to ascertain, via a computer, the "vehicle's location within 50 to 100 feet" and provided them with in excess of "2,000 pages of data over the 4-week period." The defendant was subsequently arrested and indicted for various narcotics offenses.

The Court held "that the Government's installation of a GPS device on a target's vehicle, and its use of that device to monitor the vehicle's movements, constitutes a 'search.'" Though the Court was unanimous in its conclusion that the government's use of a GPS device in this instance was unconstitutional, the Justices disagreed as to

---

[9]565 U.S. ___ (2012).

why. A majority of five, however, reasoned that a search occurred in this instance given the government's trespass upon the defendant's "private property for the purpose of obtaining information." Indeed, to find a search under this trespass approach, it appears that a trespass coupled with an underlying intent to gather information is a necessary precondition. Accordingly, a mere trespass standing alone is an insufficient basis to establish that the government engaged in a Fourth Amendment search. As noted in footnote 5 of the majority opinion, "Trespass alone does not qualify, but there must be conjoined with that what was present here; an attempt to find something or to obtain information."

Notably, the majority in *Jones* sidestepped the government's contention, based upon *Katz* and its progeny (including *Knotts* and *Karo*), that a Fourth Amendment search did not occur given the absence of a reasonable expectation of privacy (in the area of the vehicle where the GPS had been placed and on the public roads where the vehicle had been driven) on the part of the defendant. The Court stated, in part, that the *Katz* test was never intended to replace the common-law trespass test, but merely provided an additional basis upon which to decide such Fourth Amendment issues.

(b) Surveillance from Aircraft

The employment of aircraft to conduct surveillance also presents interesting issues. In *California v. Ciraolo*,[10] the Supreme Court held that aerial observance of an individual's backyard (where marijuana was grown) was permissible when the government used a private plane to fly over the yard. The government was unable to observe the cultivation on land given the existence of fences standing several feet high. As a result, an airplane was obtained and the observation was made at the publicly navigable airspace of approximately 1,000 feet. Though steps had clearly been taken to shield the cultivation activities from public view, the Court held, in part, that the second prong of the *Katz* test was not satisfied. The Court reasoned that an individual who exposes the activities in his yard to public viewing—even if only from publicly navigable airspace—cannot reasonably expect his activities to remain private. The fact that the surveillance was performed in a "physically nonintrusive manner" and that the public *could* view such activities from a public vantage was enough to defeat the defendant's reasonable expectation of privacy claim.

Three years later, the Court reached a similar result in *Florida v. Riley*.[11] There, an officer, who was unable from ground level to observe the activities within a greenhouse on residential property, employed the use of a helicopter in order to hover over the greenhouse. From a vantage point of approximately 400 feet above the greenhouse, and given the absence of two panels from the roof, he was able to see with his naked eye evidence of narcotics cultivation within the greenhouse. The Court found that the government flyover and observation did not constitute a search within the meaning of the Fourth Amendment. It reasoned that the officer's conduct was lawful due to the common employment of helicopters in society, the fact that the law permitted a helicopter to fly within 400 feet of the greenhouse, and the absence of any evidence that helicopter flyovers were uncommon in the area. Given such circumstances, the Court found that the defendant could not reasonably expect that his greenhouse activities would remain private. Finally, the Court found that the helicopter flight did not disrupt the expected uses of the greenhouse and its curtilage,

---

[10]476 U.S. 207 (1986).
[11]488 U.S. 445 (1989).

did not reveal "intimate details" associated with the property, and did not cause any unnecessary external disturbances or hazards.

In both cases, the activities observed by the police were within the curtilage of the home. Yet in neither case was there a search within the meaning of the Fourth Amendment. This is an important point to remember. Just because a "house" is among the enumerated Fourth Amendment protections does not necessarily mandate that a Fourth Amendment analysis attends to every government observation of that house. In *Ciraolo* and *Riley*, the police observation was from a vantage point that was, *in theory at least*, accessible by anyone. The entire populace, including the police, had a right to be where the officers were at the time of the respective observations. This begs the question whether such theoretical possibilities fairly address the contention that the expectation of privacy in such instances was reasonable. For those of you who think that the answer is "no," well, you've got friends on the Court who expressed this point and dissented in both cases!

F   A   Q

Q: *Ciraolo* and *Riley* involved visual surveillance from an aircraft. Is the Fourth Amendment violated if the government employs camera technology during an air flight in navigable airspace to enhance their visualization?

A: The Supreme Court has answered this question at least in part. In *Dow Chemical Co. v. United States*,[12] the Court addressed whether the Fourth Amendment was violated when the government took aerial photographs of the Dow Chemical plant. Though the Court held that the government's conduct did not constitute a Fourth Amendment search, the Court noted that a different outcome may have been reached had the premises photographed been a dwelling area, had more intimate details of the plant been observed (here, only outlines of buildings and equipment on Dow's property were gathered), and had highly sophisticated technology been employed. "We find it important that this is *not* an area immediately adjacent to a private home, where privacy expectations are most heightened. Nor is this an area where Dow has made any effort to protect against aerial surveillance."

(c) Heat Measurement Instruments

The Court in *Dow Chemical* stated, "The mere fact that human vision is enhanced somewhat, at least to the degree here, does not give rise to constitutional problems." How much technological enhancement of the human senses is too much? In *Kyllo v. United States*[13] the Supreme Court tackled such an issue. There, the Court addressed whether the government's employment of a thermal imaging device — an instrument capable of creating images reflecting comparative levels of heat that emanate from various objects — to detect levels of heat emanating from a house qualified as a search within the meaning of the Fourth Amendment.

In *Kyllo*, federal agents suspected that the defendant was growing marijuana within his home. In order to grow marijuana indoors, "typically . . . high-intensity

---

[12]476 U.S. 227 (1986).
[13]533 U.S. 27 (2001).

lamps" must be used. To ascertain whether, in fact, the defendant was emanating high heat levels within his home, federal agents "used an Agema Thermovision 210 thermal imager to scan the complex." The Court explained that a thermal imager detects and, in turn, displays on a video screen infrared radiation that is not observable to the unaided human eye. More specifically, the device depicts relative differences in temperature much like a "video camera showing heat images."

While seated in a vehicle situated in different locations on a public street near Kyllo's residence, the agents used the imaging device to detect heat levels within the home. According to the Court, the imager "showed that the roof over the garage and a side wall . . . were relatively hot compared to the rest of the home and substantially warmer than neighboring homes in the triplex." A search warrant was subsequently obtained and a search found marijuana and other evidence indicative of a manufacturing operation.

The Court found that the government's use of the device in this instance constituted a search. The majority reasoned that the heat instrument revealed information about the interior of the home that was not otherwise discernible absent a physical intrusion. It therefore rejected the dissent's claim that the device merely detected heat that emanated from the home's exterior. The Court cited *Katz* in support. It noted "just as a thermal imager captures only heat emanating from a house, so also a powerful directional microphone picks up only sound emanating from a house. . . . We rejected such a mechanical interpretation of the Fourth Amendment in *Katz*, where the eavesdropping device picked up only sound waves that reached the exterior of the phone booth." Whether a Fourth Amendment violation occurs, according to the Court, is not dependent upon the quality of the evidence obtained. The Court noted that in *Silverman v. United States*,[14] "we made clear that any physical invasion of the structure of the home 'by even a fraction of an inch,' was too much (citation omitted) and there is certainly no exception to the warrant requirement for the officer who barely cracks open the front door and sees nothing but the nonintimate rug on the vestibule floor."[15]

The Court also relied upon the fact that such devices were not commonly used by members of the public. The Court declared that when law enforcement employs such instruments "to explore details of the home that would previously have been unknowable without physical intrusion," the government's conduct constitutes a search within the meaning of the Fourth Amendment. The majority's partial reliance upon this fact raises the prospect that as the use of this technology became more prevalent, the public's expectation of privacy from such technological intrusions would, in the Court's view at least, become increasingly less reasonable.

Justice Stevens spoke for four members of the Court in his dissent. As noted, he argued that the technology at issue simply revealed information — heat — that emanated from the home's exterior. Thus, there was no search of a "house" given that the measurement was of heat emissions from the home's exterior. He analogized such emissions to "aromas that are generated in a kitchen, or in a laboratory or opium den." Do you agree? The Court approved the search in *Dow Chemical* due, in part, to the fact that the camera technology was employed against a commercial establishment. Whether the same result would accrue in *Kyllo* if the imaging device was directed against a commercial establishment is, arguably, an open question.

---

[14]365 U.S. 505 (1961).
[15]*Kyllo v. United States*, 533 U.S. at 37.

(7) Use of Dogs as a Sensory Enhancement Tool

Usually within the first two or three weeks of class a student will come across a statement in the class readings that will, in essence, state that an individual does not have a legitimate expectation of privacy in contraband. This is a true statement. In my experience, this statement has proven to be a bit confusing to some students. So let's discuss this concept. Does it mean that an individual who is harboring cocaine in the bedroom of his home cannot claim a violation of the Fourth Amendment when the police conduct an illegal search? Does it mean that this same individual cannot successfully assert that he has a reasonable expectation of privacy in his home when the police performed their illegal search? The answer to both of these questions is "no." An individual can, indeed, raise a Fourth Amendment claim and often do so successfully!

The second prong of the privacy test is that society must be prepared to accept as reasonable the subjective interest asserted by the individual. The Supreme Court has held, however, that if the subjective interest that is asserted is *solely* an interest in illegal activity then such an interest is not reasonable. In other words, society is not prepared to accept as reasonable an interest of an individual that protects nothing more than illegal contraband. Society is, on the other hand, prepared to accept as reasonable a privacy interest that encompasses legal activities. This makes sense, doesn't it? After all, in our homes are objects and papers, among other effects, that are perfectly legitimate. They were obtained legally. They are possessed legally. It is, therefore, reasonable for society to accept the notion that the people of this country have a subjective expectation that our homes should remain private.

The Fourth Amendment serves as a buffer to guard against unreasonable governmental searches and seizures. Thus, unless certain prerequisites are satisfied, the police cannot simply rush into your home and start searching. However, if there were a type of search that could *only* uncover evidence of illegality, then such a search would not infringe an interest that society would consider reasonable. Are there any searches that can exclusively target illegal contraband? The answer is "yes." Canine sniffs.

Properly trained canines, by virtue of their enhanced ability to smell, are frequently employed by law enforcement agencies to assist them in their criminal investigations. Notably, the evidence that such canines can provide is limited to the detection of illegal contraband. This limitation, as stated by the Supreme Court in *United States v. Place*,[16] is central to the Court's conclusion that such activity is outside the realm of the Fourth Amendment.

> A "canine sniff" by a well-trained narcotics detection dog . . . does not expose noncontraband items that otherwise would remain hidden from public view, as does, for example, an officer's rummaging through the contents of the luggage. . . . Moreover, the sniff discloses only the presence or absence of narcotics, a contraband item. Thus, despite the fact that the sniff tells the authorities something about the contents of the luggage, the information obtained is limited.

Place involved a canine sniff of luggage that was in a public location. Though the Court has also upheld canine searches in regards to other "effects," the Supreme

---

[16]462 U.S. 696 (1983).

Court has yet to decide whether dog sniffs of humans are similarly beyond the reach of the Fourth Amendment.

SUMMARY

■ *United States v. Katz* established a two-pronged test to determine whether government conduct amounted to a search within the meaning of the Fourth Amendment. *Katz* found that an expectation of privacy existed when the government electronically eavesdropped upon conversations the defendant had while on the telephone within a phone booth.

■ The two-pronged *Katz* test consists of: 1) whether an individual has exhibited a subjective expectation of privacy; and 2) whether that expectation of privacy is one that society recognizes as reasonable.

■ The Supreme Court has applied *Katz* to the following contexts and has reached the following conclusions:

    ■ Consensually Monitored Telephone Conversations: The Fourth Amendment is not violated when a person with whom he is speaking on the telephone either elects to share the contents of such conversations with the government or allows the government to eavesdrop upon such conversations. A person who elects to speak assumes the risk that the person with whom he is speaking may decide to reveal the substance of the conversation.

    ■ Homes, Curtilage, and Open Fields: While an individual enjoys Fourth Amendment protection for activities within the home (and its curtilage), that protection is lost when the activity is in an open field and/or is publicly exposed.

    ■ Trash: It is not a search within the meaning of the Fourth Amendment when the trashed items have been placed and searched outside the curtilage of a home.

    ■ Bags on Public/Commercial Transportation: Government manipulation of such bags/luggage may constitute a search within the meaning of the Constitution if the handling of the items is exploratory.

    ■ Pen Registers, Financial/Utility Information: It is not a search within the meaning of the Fourth Amendment since a person who makes telephone calls and engages in business transactions cannot reasonably claim an expectation of privacy in information already conveyed to third parties.

    ■ Binoculars, Flashlights, and Beepers: Law enforcement may properly aid their visual senses with binoculars and flashlights. The use of beepers is permissible as well, provided that the information furnished does not reveal information not otherwise publicly exposed.

    ■ Global Positioning Systems: The Supreme Court has concluded that the installation of a GPS device upon a vehicle when accompanied by a purpose to gather or obtain information constitutes a search within the meaning of the Fourth Amendment.

    ■ Areas Observable from Airspace: It is not a Fourth Amendment search if the government can visually observe with the naked eye publicly exposed areas of a home/property from navigable airspace. A person who exposes property to the public, even if viewed only from the air, cannot claim a reasonable expectation of privacy in those items. The use of technological equipment to enhance such human visualization of a dwelling (as opposed to a business) remains an open question.

■ Thermal Imaging Devices: Use of thermal imaging devices is a search within the meaning of the Fourth Amendment when directed at a residence given, among other things, that the imager reveals intimate details within a home.

■ Dog Sniffs: Dog sniffs (from properly trained canines) do not constitute a search if performed on effects, such as luggage. Such sniffs can only reveal the presence of illegal activity, for which individuals do not possess a reasonable expectation of privacy. It is an open question whether it is a search if performed on humans.

CONNECTIONS

Relationship to Searches, Seizures, and the Warrant Clause (Chapter 4) and Executing the Warrant (Chapter 5)

This chapter examined the reasonableness concept enunciated in the *Katz* case, including the determinative two-pronged test. If each prong is satisfied then the protections of the Fourth Amendment are implicated. Presumptively, a warrant must be obtained prior to performing a search or seizure. The particulars of the warrant clause are explored in greater depth in Chapters 4 and 5.

Relationship to Searches Incident to Arrest (Chapter 7) and the Automobile Exception (Chapter 8)

The Supreme Court has held that though individuals have a reasonable expectation of privacy in their houses and effects, individuals enjoy lesser expectations of privacy in their automobiles than they enjoy in their homes. Sometimes effects (e.g., containers) that enjoy full Fourth Amendment protection if found within a home lose this status when found within a vehicle.

Relationship to Fourth Amendment Violations and Their Associated Remedies (Chapter 15)

The concepts of standing and the exclusionary rule are the focus of Chapter 15. Usually, unless an individual can establish a personal expectation of privacy that is deemed reasonable by society, that individual cannot successfully exclude evidence pursuant to the exclusionary rule.

Searches, Seizures, and the Warrant Clause

4

Chapter 3 discussed what constitutes a search within the meaning of the Fourth Amendment. More particularly, the chapter examined

instances when a search occurred and, more often than not, instances when it did not. This chapter will discuss the prerequisites to conducting a lawful search and seizure, which are found in what is commonly referred to as the "warrant clause" portion of the Fourth Amendment. That clause provides:

> and no Warrants shall issue, but upon probable cause, supported by Oath or affirmation, and particularly describing the place to be searched, and the persons or things to be seized.

The warrant clause and the reasonableness clause are often read together. That is, whether a particular search or seizure is reasonable is often determined by examining whether the particulars of the warrant clause have been satisfied. If a warrant has been properly obtained, then, as detailed at greater length later in this chapter, the search or seizure is presumptively reasonable. In this chapter, the essential elements of the warrant clause — probable cause, oath, and particularity — will be examined in some depth. Each of these elements must be satisfied before either an arrest or search warrant may issue.

A.   WARRANT REQUIREMENTS

1. Sample Search Warrant Application
2. Oath Requirement
3. Particularity and Specificity Requirements
4. Probable Cause to Search and Seize

A. Warrant Requirements

The Supreme Court has declared that ordinarily a search or seizure performed in the absence of a judicially approved warrant is presumptively unreasonable. Alternatively stated, if the government performs a search or seizure prior to securing a warrant from a judicial officer, the government's conduct is presumptively — though not conclusively — unconstitutional. The presumption exists because an opposite rule — one that grants authority to the government to assess the constitutionality of its own conduct — would, for obvious reasons, constitute an inadequate check upon its own exercise of power. Consider the following comment in 1948 by the Supreme Court in *McDonald v. United States*:[1]

> Absent some grave emergency, the Fourth Amendment has interposed a magistrate between the citizen and the police. This was done not to shield criminals nor to make the home a safe haven for illegal activities. It was done so that an objective mind might weigh the need to invade that privacy in order to enforce the law. The right of privacy was deemed too precious to entrust to the discretion of those whose job is the detection of crime and the arrest of criminals. Power is a heady thing; and history shows that the police acting on their own cannot be trusted. And so the Constitution requires a magistrate to pass on the desires of the police before they violate the privacy of the home.

This passage makes reference to a judicial magistrate. It is this judicial officer — an individual who, in the federal system, is a licensed attorney and is both neutral and detached from the government's investigation — from whom a warrant must be obtained. In contrast to federal district court judges, who are lifetime appointees, federal magistrates are appointed to their positions by these same federal judges but only for a term of eight years. Their terms, however, can be renewed. Aside from issuing warrants, magistrates are authorized to adjudicate certain civil and criminal cases as well as to conduct arraignments and bail hearings, among various other duties.

With respect to the stated presumption, it must be strenuously emphasized that this presumption is littered with exceptions. You will discover later in this book that while the presumption of unreasonableness exists and while government actors often do obtain warrants prior to performing searches and seizures, law enforcement is granted substantial leeway to engage in such conduct in lieu of a warrant. But before we discuss the myriad of exceptions to the warrant requirement, it is necessary to review the essential requirements to obtaining a warrant.

---

[1] 335 U.S. 451 (1948).

(1) Sample Search Warrant Application

United States District Court

_____ DISTRICT OF _____

In the Matter of the Search of
(Name, address or Brief description of person, property or premises to be searched)

**APPLICATION AND AFFIDAVIT
FOR SEARCH WARRANT**

CASE NUMBER:

I,_____being duly sworn depose and say:

I am a(n)_____ and have reason to believe that ___ on the person of or ___ on the property or premises known as (name, description and/or location)

in the _____ District of _____
there is now concealed a certain person or property, namely (describe the person or property to be seized)

which is (state one or more bases for search and seizure set forth under Rule 41(b) of the Federal Rules of Criminal Procedure)

concerning a violation of Title____United States code, Section(s)
The facts to support a finding of Probable Cause are as follows:

Continued on the attached sheet and made a part hereof. ___ **Yes** __ **No**

_____
Signature of Affiant

Sworn to before me, and subscribed in my presence

_____   _____
Date   at
                                                                                            City and State

_____, U.S. Magistrate Judge
Name and Title of Judicial Officer

_____
Signature of Judicial Officer

A sample application and affidavit for a search warrant

(2) Oath Requirement

As noted, when the government applies for a search warrant they must present the request to a magistrate who makes an assessment as to whether the requested warrant shall issue. However, before making this determination, the government must satisfy the strictures of the Fourth Amendment. First, an individual must take an oath that the information that is presented to the magistrate is true to the best of his knowledge. You will notice that on the top two lines of the sample search warrant application the government official, typically a law enforcement officer or agent, puts her name on the document and indicates her job title. This person is the affiant and it is this person who declares an oath before the magistrate. At the bottom of the document you will notice several lines. On the bottom right side are lines where the affiant as well as the magistrate affix their signatures. On the bottom left side are lines for the magistrate's name and the date of the application.

(3) Particularity and Specificity Requirements

Remember *Katz*'s admonition that the Fourth Amendment protects people not places? Though the statement is an inapt descriptor of the Amendment's jurisprudence, what the statement does accurately convey is the Amendment's overarching concern with the protection of individual liberties. It is the individual's person, house, paper, and effects that are protected. The protections against unreasonable searches and seizures are liberties that are, therefore, personally possessed. Each qualifying individual is entitled to assert these rights against the government whenever his or her constitutional rights are impacted.

Given this concern with the individual, the Fourth Amendment contains a particularity requirement. This requirement is there in part to help ensure that warrants issued are sufficiently descriptive so as to prevent an officer from either mistakenly or purposefully searching the premises of another for which probable cause to search and seize does not exist. Whether such a description passes constitutional muster is assessed pursuant to a reasonableness standard. If an officer can reasonably ascertain the location of property to be searched then the particularity requirement is satisfied. As stated by the Supreme Court in *Maryland v. Garrison*, satisfaction of the particularity clause as to location "depends on whether the officers' failure to realize the overbreadth of the warrant was objectively understandable and reasonable."[2] This particularity requirement applies with equal force to the issuance of arrest warrants. An arrest warrant must describe the person to be arrested with sufficient particularity so as to avoid reasonable confusion as to the subject's identity.

In the upper left-hand corner of the sample search warrant application (beneath the heading "In the Matter of the Search of") there is a space for a brief description of the property to be searched. That space will typically contain the address of the property to be searched. However, it is not unusual for a more detailed description of the property (e.g., external features of the residence, characteristics of the surrounding area, etc.) to also be included in that space or on an attached sheet. A description might include references to the placement and types of shrubbery that fronts a home, the location of the front door, the color of roof, the presence of brick, tile, or stone on the home's exterior, among numerous other characteristics. This same level of precision is required for other properties, including apartments, storage units, and the like.

As noted, the reason for such exacting detail is to guard against unwarranted government intrusions. Many of your fellow students, for example, may live in apartment complexes. As you are certainly aware, individual apartment units often

[2]480 U.S. 79, 88 (1987).

possess a high degree of external resemblance. There may be several doors adjacent to one another, all with the same color paint and external features. Perhaps the principal feature distinguishing one residence from another is the presence of a single letter or number. By requiring that the premises be described with particularity, the particularity clause helps guard against the searches of units where probable cause does not exist.

This brings us to another aspect of particularity, often referred to as the specificity requirement. The Fourth Amendment also mandates that the items to be seized be specifically described. Notice in the middle of the sample search warrant application the words "there is now concealed a certain person or property, namely. . . ." This is the location where the government is required to list all the items of evidence it submits that there is probable cause to believe are located at the particularly described premises and are evidence of criminal activity. As with the premises description, the government will often make reference in this space to an attachment that will then detail an extensive laundry list of items that it is seeking authorization to search for and seize.

The principal rationale underlying the specificity requirement is to protect against general searches. In other words, simply because a search warrant has been issued does not authorize a general rummaging by the government of the premises. Rather, the specificity requirement serves primarily as a constraint upon the government's authority to search and seize. This is why a warrant must be exacting in its detail. As stated by the Supreme Court in *Maryland v. Garrison*:

> Thus, the scope of a lawful search is "defined by the object of the search and the places in which there is probable cause to believe that it may be found. Just as probable cause to believe that a stolen lawnmower may be found in a garage will not support a warrant to search an upstairs bedroom, probable cause to believe that undocumented aliens are being transported in a van will not justify a warrantless search of a suitcase."[4]

Aside from this limitation rationale, the particularity clause also provides an important notice function: In *Groh v. Ramirez*,[5] the Court declared that "[a] particular warrant also 'assures the individual whose property is searched or

Sidebar

MERE EVIDENCE RULE

As noted, the government will typically include in a search warrant application a detailed listing of the items it seeks to seize. The right of the government to seek such broad authority is greatly influenced by the case of *Warden v. Hayden*,[3] decided by the Supreme Court in 1967. Prior to that case, the spectrum of evidentiary items subject to government seizure was more restricted. Though "instrumentalities, fruits of crime, or contraband" could be properly seized, the government was prohibited from seizing items that were merely evidentiary in nature. In a murder investigation, for example, the government would certainly be permitted to seize the body of the victim as well as any weapons used during the homicide. However, more tangential items such as letters or a diary (depending on their content), or records reflective of the suspect's depressed mental state could potentially prove to be more problematic. In abandoning this rule, the *Hayden* Court reasoned that the Fourth Amendment does not distinguish between evidentiary types. "Nothing in the language of the Fourth Amendment supports the distinction between 'mere evidence' and instrumentalities, fruits of crime, or contraband. On its face, the provision assures the 'right of the people to be secure in their persons, houses, papers, and effects. . . . This 'right of the people' is certainly unrelated to the 'mere evidence' limitation. Privacy is disturbed no more by a search directed to a purely evidentiary object than it is by a search directed to an instrumentality, fruit, or contraband."

[3]387 U.S. 294 (1967).

[4]*Id.* at 84-85.
[5]540 U.S. 551 (2004).

seized of the lawful authority of the executing officer, his need to search, and the limits of his power to search' (citations omitted)."[6]

| F | A | Q |

Q: If the Fourth Amendment requires a specific listing in the warrant of the items to be searched for and seized, how can the government possibly anticipate and list every evidentiary item that they may encounter?

A: While compliance with the specificity requirement is a constitutional mandate, the Supreme Court has upheld the use of broad "catch-all" phrases so as to allow for the search and seizure of items that were not listed. In *Andresen v. Maryland,*[7] the Supreme Court rejected an argument that certain "catch-all" verbiage appearing at the conclusion of the government's detailed listing rendered the search warrant at issue too general. The Court held that the subject language ("together with other fruits, instrumentalities, and evidence of crime at this (time) unknown"), when read in context, "did not authorize the executing officers to conduct a search for evidence of other crimes but only to search for and seize evidence relevant to the crime of false pretenses and Lot 13T." Nevertheless, even if evidence is seized pursuant to an overly broad descriptive term, the entire warrant is not necessarily tainted. Instead, the court will admit at trial those evidentiary items seized pursuant to the warrant's properly descriptive phrases, and excise those items obtained by virtue of the overly broad terminology.

(4) Probable Cause to Search and Seize

(a) Foundational Concepts

Though we will later learn that some Fourth Amendment seizures can be based upon evidence short of the probable cause standard, the arrest, which requires a finding of probable cause, is, according to the Supreme Court in *California v. Hodari D,*[8] "the quintessential 'seizure of the person' under Fourth Amendment jurisprudence." Though difficult to define with meaningful exactitude, the Supreme Court in *Maryland v. Pringle*[9] provided the following useful guideposts for making probable cause determinations:

> The substance of all the definitions of probable cause is a reasonable ground for belief of guilt (citation omitted), and that the belief of guilt must be particularized with respect to the person to be searched or seized (citation omitted). In *Illinois v. Gates*, we noted:
>
>> As early as *Locke v. United States*, 7 Cranch 339, 348, 3 L. Ed. 364 (1813), Chief Justice Marshall observed, in a closely related context: "[T]he term 'probable cause,' according to its usual acceptation, means less than evidence which would justify condemnation. . . . It imports a seizure made under circumstances which warrant suspicion." More recently, we said that "the *quanta* . . . of proof" appropriate in ordinary judicial proceedings are inapplicable to the decision to issue a warrant (citation omitted).

---

[6]*Id.* at 561.
[7]427 U.S. 463 (1976).
[8]499 U.S. 621 (1991).
[9]540 U.S. 366 (2003).

Finely tuned standards such as proof beyond a reasonable doubt or by a preponder-ance of the evidence, useful in formal trials, have no place in the [probable cause] decision (citation omitted).

To determine whether an officer had probable cause to arrest an individual, we examine the events leading up to the arrest, and then decide "whether these historical facts, viewed from the standpoint of an objectively reasonable police officer, amount to" probable cause (citation omitted).

A more succinct and oft-cited definition was set forth by the Supreme Court in *Brinegar v. United States*:[10]

Probable cause exists where "the facts and circumstances within their [the officers'] knowledge and of which they had reasonably trustworthy information [are] sufficient in themselves to warrant a man of reasonable caution in the belief that" an offense has been or is being committed [by the person to be arrested].

The *Brinegar* passage provided a definition of probable cause in the arrest con-text. In regards to searches, the Supreme Court in *United States v. Grubbs*[11] declared that "probable cause exists when 'there is a fair probability that contraband or evidence of a crime will be found in a particular place.'" Despite the vagaries asso-ciated with the term, what is seemingly settled is that a finding of probable cause to arrest or search does not require a judicial "belief" of at least 50 percent.

In making a probable cause assessment, the court will examine the evidence presented in the warrant application and make what amounts to an anticipatory determination. As stated in *Grubbs*, "In the typical case where the police seek per-mission to search a house for an item they believe is already located there, the magistrate's determination that there is probable cause for the search amounts to a prediction that the item will still be there when the warrant is executed."

In making this prediction, the court will examine the facts from the perspective of a reasonable officer. This certainly suggests that the standard is objective. However, an assessment of reasonableness does not preclude the consideration of certain subjective factors. An officer's subjective beliefs based upon his previous work-related experiences are often considered by a reviewing court. Factors such as the term of years of an officer's service as well as his investigative experience in relation to a particular crime can be relevant to this assessment. None of these factors are neces-sarily determinative nor are they necessarily worthy of significant weight. However, their relevance to a determination of probable cause is certainly not precluded.

(b) The *Spinelli/Aguilar* Two-Pronged Test

At the top of the sample search warrant application, you will notice the phrase "Application and Affidavit for Search Warrant." With each warrant application, the government will typically submit a written affidavit that details the facts that it believes establish probable cause to either search or seize. The court will, in turn, review the substance of that affidavit in light of the general principles described in the preceding subsection.

Given that each case presents its own unique facts, each warrant application will necessarily vary in the type and quality of evidentiary support. However, the type of

---

[10]338 U.S. 160 (1949).
[11]547 U.S. 90 (2006).

evidentiary support will often contain a description of the affiant's (typically a law enforcement officer's) personal observations, the statements and observations of a third party (someone who is neither the affiant nor the suspect), or both. Generally, when the affidavit includes the personal observations of the affiant, the courts will lend greater credence to such accounts. This makes sense. Under such circumstances, the officer/affiant has taken an oath to declare the truth, and the information conveyed to the court consists of events that the affiant — as opposed to, for example, an informant who is not swearing to the truth of submitted facts — personally observed. Of course, such declarations do not mandate a finding of probable cause. For whatever reason, the court may find the affiant to be untrustworthy or the quantum of evidence to be lacking. So a court is free to assign little, or no, weight to the affiant's submissions. Nevertheless, as a general rule, firsthand observations will be afforded greater weight than evidence received from second- and thirdhand sources.

Well, what happens when the affidavit relies upon the statements and observations of third parties? How should a court assess evidence presented in this manner? When presented in this form, the affidavit will include statements and observations of persons who are neither under oath nor available for questioning. This presents an obvious assessment problem. Think about the myriad of ways this situation can present itself. An affidavit may, for example, include an assertion that a named third party informed the affiant that he observed his roommate commit a bank robbery and hide the proceeds inside their apartment. Or the affidavit may include statements purportedly made by the bank robbery suspect to his roommate regarding the former's involvement in the bank heist. Or assume the same scenarios except now the source of the eyewitness identification and verbal admissions is an unnamed third party. Thus, a court is not uncommonly faced with the difficult task of assessing the appropriate weight to assign to such third-party information.

Traditionally, a two-pronged test — enunciated by the Supreme Court in *Aguilar v. Texas*[12] and *Spinelli v. United States*[13] — had been employed by the courts. Before either an arrest or search warrant could issue, the following two prongs had to be satisfied:

1. the court must be apprised of information that provides the basis for the outside source's knowledge (commonly referred to as the "basis of knowledge" prong); and
2. the court must be satisfied that the outside source is credible (commonly referred to as the "veracity" or "reliability" prong).

---

[12]378 U.S. 108 (1964).
[13]393 U.S. 410 (1969).

To satisfy the "basis of knowledge" requirement, the government had to present evidence to the court that demonstrated how this outside source was aware of the information being conveyed. There were at least three ways — all identified in Justice Byron White's concurrence in *Spinelli* — that this prong could be satisfied. One is if the affidavit reflected that the source learned of this information through firsthand observation. Referring to the bank robbery example, if the source of information personally observed the suspect's bank robbery activity or personally heard the suspect's admissions, then this prong would likely be satisfied. If, on the other hand, the information source learned of the information from another individual, then such information could properly be considered if the outside statements were otherwise reliable. For example, if the statement made by the suspect was significantly against his penal interest at the time it was made (commonly referred to as a "declaration against interest") or, perhaps, satisfied some other exception to the hearsay rule, then the first prong could be met.

Finally, Justice White indicated that in certain circumstances an informant third party who provides "sufficiently detailed" information might satisfy this requirement. In essence, he argued that a strong correlation often exists between the breadth of information provided and the likelihood that the information presented to the court is reliable. Consider the following explanation by Justice White.

> I am inclined to agree with the majority that there are limited special circumstances in which an "honest" informant's report, if sufficiently detailed, will in effect verify itself — that is, the magistrate when confronted with such detail could reasonably infer that the informant had gained his information in a reliable way (citation omitted). Detailed information may sometimes imply that the informant himself has observed the facts. Suppose an informant with whom an officer has had satisfactory experience states that there is gambling equipment in the living room of a specified apartment and describes in detail not only the equipment itself but also the appointments and furnishings in the apartment. Detail like this, if true at all, must rest on personal observation either of the informant or of someone else. If the latter, we know nothing of the third person's honesty or sources; he may be making a wholly false report. But it is arguable that on these facts it was the informant himself who has perceived the facts, for the information reported is not usually the subject of casual day-to-day conversation. Because the informant is honest and it is probable that he has viewed the facts, there is probable cause for the issuance of a warrant.

Sidebar

PRESUMPTIONS REGARDING INFORMANTS

Courts sometimes elect to assign certain presumptions to outside sources. Law enforcement routinely employs private citizens to assist them in their investigations. Often these citizens are paid or receive some tangible benefit by virtue of their cooperation (e.g., sentencing concessions, reduced charges, etc.). The courts, at a minimum, do not attach a presumption of reliability to the statements proffered by these individuals. The information they provide is more suspect given the other considerations that might taint their objectivity. This same practice and accompanying rationale applies to citizens who provide information but elect to remain anonymous. As the Supreme Court acknowledged in dicta in *Illinois v. Gates*,[14] "the veracity of persons supplying anonymous tips is by hypothesis largely unknown and unknowable." In contrast to citizens who reveal their identities (for whom a presumption of reliability attaches), persons who shield their names are not entitled to a favorable presumption given the ill motives that might accompany their decision to remain anonymous.

[14]462 U.S. 213 (1983).

As part of its attempt to determine whether the information provided amounts to probable cause, a court, especially when confronted with an affidavit containing information from an unsworn source, must make an assessment of that source's credibility. This naturally brings us to the second requirement—the veracity or reliability prong. So how does the government present evidence of an informant's reliability?

Perhaps the most commonly employed method is to provide the court with information relating to the informant's past performance. When I was a prosecutor, I would routinely inform the court in the attached affidavit of prior instances when the cited third party has provided reliable information. In other words, the government will inform the court that the informant has a track record of reliability. The following section will discuss *Illinois v. Gates* and how that case altered the aforementioned two-pronged test for determining probable cause. The inclusion of information relative to an informant's past reliability takes on added significance under the new test. So remember this practice as you consider the following materials.

F   A   Q

Q: Sometimes an outside source does not have a track record. How does a court assess credibility in the absence of a proven record?

A: The Court has identified certain ways that the government can satisfy this requirement. One such way is by verifying the information that the informant has provided. By corroborating many, if not most, of the details provided by the informant, a court can be satisfied that the outside source's information is trustworthy. Even if the information corroborated is activity that can be classified as innocent in character, this type of verification could satisfy the second prong. For example, if the police receive a tip that an individual is planning to rob a bank next week and the police, in turn, corroborate some of the seemingly innocent details provided — such as the type of car he drives, his financial debts, the proximity of his home to the bank, etc. — these innocent details, among others, could theoretically satisfy the reliability prong.

(c) Replacement Test: *Gates* and "Totality of the Circumstances"

The *Aguilar/Spinelli* two-pronged test was a rigid requirement, requiring that both prongs be satisfied before either a search or arrest warrant could issue. Failure of either prong would defeat the application. All this changed in 1983 when the Supreme Court enunciated a new test in *Illinois v. Gates*. The replacement test, still in effect today, reviews warrant applications on the basis of the "totality of the circumstances." Though the two prongs in the former *Aguilar/Spinelli* test remain "highly relevant" in a probable cause determination, no longer must the government satisfy both prongs in order to secure a warrant. The "totality of the circumstances" test reflects the Court's view that a probable cause determination is a "common-sense, practical question" and that the courts should have the flexibility that necessarily accompanies such a test when evaluating applications.

In contrast to the former test, insufficient evidence in support of one factor can be compensated by stronger evidence in the other. If, say, the affidavit largely fails to establish an informant's reliability, the insufficiency of this prong can be overcome by the strength of the basis of knowledge prong. Thus, an affidavit rich in descriptive detail might be sufficiently strong to compensate for the weaker veracity prong. If, on the other hand, an informant has a long track record of reliability, such strength can now compensate for comparatively weak evidence in support of the basis of knowledge prong. In each situation, the "totality of the circumstances" test grants the courts the flexibility to consider "all the circumstances set forth in the affidavit before [them], including the 'veracity' and 'basis of knowledge' of persons supplying hearsay information," and decide whether "there is a fair probability that contraband or evidence of a crime will be found in a particular place."

The *Gates* Court offered various rationales in support of its decision. In particular, the Court asserted that the factual assessments invariably associated with probable cause determinations require flexible, as opposed to rigid, analytical standards. According to the Court, a flexible approach is better suited to address the fluidity in factual patterns that are inevitably presented. It added that the new test better enables the government "to provide for the security of the individual and of his property." The Court noted that, in the context of information provided by anonymous sources, the former test would typically preclude the securing of a warrant based upon such information. However, the new standard would allow the government to pursue such leads, particularly when the tips are verified through independent police investigation.

In dissent, Justice Brennan acknowledged the fluidity of the probable cause determinative process, but insisted that abandonment of the *Aguilar/Spinelli* test was not needed to accommodate this reality. He believed that the "totality of the circumstances" test would be a significant and unnecessary boon to law enforcement at the expense of individual liberties. He wrote, "Words such as 'practical,' 'nontechnical,' and 'commonsense,' as used in the Court's opinion, are but code words for an overly permissive attitude towards police practices in derogation of the rights secured by the Fourth Amendment." He further argued that the *Aguilar/Spinelli* test had several benefits. He argued that *Aguilar/Spinelli* "require[d] the police to provide magistrates with certain crucial information," that it "provide[d] structure for magistrates' probable cause inquiries," and that it

> preserve[d] the role of magistrates as independent arbiters of probable cause, insure[d] greater accuracy in probable cause determinations, and advance[d] the substantive value of precluding findings of probable cause, and attendant intrusions, based on anything less than information from an honest or credible person who has acquired his information in a reliable way. Neither the standards nor their effects are inconsistent with a "practical, nontechnical" conception of probable cause. Once a magistrate has determined that he has information before him that he can reasonably say has been obtained in a reliable way by a credible person, he has ample room to use his common sense and to apply a practical, nontechnical conception of probable cause.

Who do you think is right?

Sidebar

CONCLUSORY STATEMENTS

Despite the newfound flexibility inherent in the new standard, the *Gates* Court was clear that mere bare, unsubstantiated allegations in an affidavit will not satisfy this new test. Thus, unsubstantiated statements such as "The informant has indicated to the affiant that there are narcotics in the suspect's residence" will not meet this new standard. As the Court stated, such allegations are "mere conclusory statement[s] that give[ ] the magistrate virtually no basis at all for making a judgment regarding probable cause." Instead the affidavit "must provide the magistrate with a substantial basis for determining the existence of probable cause."

(d) Stale Information

When submitting an affidavit to the magistrate, it is critical that the information provided be relatively current. In other words, if the information contained in the affidavit is outdated, then the warrant application will likely fail. This makes sense. A search warrant application is suggesting to the court that the government believes that probable cause exists to believe that currently on the identified premises is evidence of criminal activity. If the information included in the affidavit is too remote, then there is hardly a substantial basis for a court to believe that a warrant should issue.

Sidebar

PRESENTMENT OF THE WARRANT APPLICATION

Often the prosecutor and/or a law enforcement officer personally presents the warrant application to the reviewing magistrate. The magistrate is empowered, however, to require that the affiant himself appear before the magistrate in order to answer any questions or concerns on the part of the court. Such questioning would take place under oath. In addition, the magistrate is empowered to grant a warrant "by telephone or other reliable electronic means." In doing so, the affiant must be placed under oath and "a verbatim record of the conversation" must be made "with a suitable recording device, if available, or by a court reporter, or in writing."

(e) Challenging the Sufficiency of a Warrant

As noted earlier, a search or seizure performed in the absence of a warrant is presumptively unreasonable. This principle obviously implies that searches and seizures can be performed either with or without a warrant. It is important to remember that when a search and seizure is performed in the absence of a warrant, that does not mean that the probable cause requirement has been dispensed with. Subject to certain exceptions, the Fourth Amendment mandates that the government have probable cause before a search or seizure can take place. Thus, if an individual is arrested or his property searched in the absence of a warrant, he may subsequently challenge the legitimacy of the government's conduct by filing a pretrial motion alleging that his arrest or the search of his property was not based upon probable cause. In such instances, the government, not the defendant, bears the burden of demonstrating that probable cause existed to justify the search or seizure. If the government does not fulfill its burden, then the defendant can seek an order suppressing the evidence found as a result of the government's impropriety. This is known as the exclusionary rule, which you can read about in Chapter 15.

However, if a warrant has been obtained prior to the search or seizure, then challenging the legitimacy of the government conduct is much more difficult. In most instances, the defendant is challenging the sufficiency of the warrant affidavit. He is arguing that the warrant application, though previously approved by a magistrate, did not establish probable cause. In other words, he is arguing that the magistrate committed an error; that the court incorrectly found the existence of probable cause. When probable cause has already been found and the government acts in response to this judicial finding, the defendant, not the government, bears the burden of persuasion. This makes sense given that the government, having secured a warrant, has already satisfied its burden of demonstrating probable cause. There has already been a judicial determination of the issue and it is this judicial determination that the defendant is now challenging.

Franks v. Delaware,[15] decided by the Supreme Court in 1978, enunciated the principles that guide this type of hearing. When a defendant seeks to challenge a warrant, a hearing on the matter is not automatic but is dependent upon whether the defendant submits to the court substantial proof that a false statement was intentionally or recklessly included within the affidavit by the person swearing to the truth of the document.

In addition, a defendant must preliminarily show that the judicial finding of probable cause was dependent upon the purportedly false information. If these requirements are satisfied, then a hearing can be scheduled. If at the hearing the defendant is able to establish, by a preponderance of the evidence, each of the aforementioned elements, then the defendant must finally show that the "affidavit's remaining content is insufficient to establish probable cause." If this can be shown, "the search warrant must be voided and the fruits of the search excluded to the same extent as if probable cause was lacking on the face of the affidavit."

As you can no doubt tell, the defendant bears a heavy burden under such circumstances. Such high hurdles certainly provide the government with an incentive to seek warrants prior to conducting searches and seizures that implicate Fourth Amendment interests. When the government performs a warrantless search or seizure, such actions may be challenged in court, with the government bearing the burden of persuasion. If a hearing is scheduled, the defendant is present and is permitted to cross-examine the government's witnesses and present his own case. If the government, on the other hand, obtains a warrant, the review of the probable cause evidence is performed in an ex parte hearing. Only one party — the government — is present before the magistrate and, thus, the defendant has no opportunity to challenge the sufficiency of the claims detailed in the affidavit at that time. His first opportunity to challenge the sufficiency is during a so-called *Franks* hearing. And you can see the difficult burden he bears in such instances.

Sidebar

PRELIMINARY SHOWING UNDER *FRANKS*

There are a couple of aspects concerning the preliminary showing that require some elaboration. First, it is not enough that the defendant simply demonstrate that the affidavit contained a falsehood. In addition to this showing, the defendant must demonstrate that the falsehood was either knowingly or recklessly included in the affidavit. Thus, a showing that the false statement was inadvertently or negligently included will not suffice. Second, the knowing and reckless standard is focused upon the mind-set of the affiant. The defendant must show that the affiant (typically a law enforcement officer) either knowingly or recklessly included the cited information. If, say, an outside source (an informant) purposefully lied to the officer with respect to certain information and the officer, in turn, included this information in the affidavit, the defendant must still demonstrate that the officer knowingly or recklessly included the material. It is, therefore, not enough to show that the informant purposefully misrepresented the information. However, this principle does not apply if the informant in such circumstances is another law enforcement officer. A rule of collective knowledge applies to law enforcement personnel, thereby preventing less scrupulous officers from insulating themselves by recruiting an unsuspecting officer to secure a warrant.

---

[15]438 U.S. 154 (1978).

SUMMARY

- There is a presumption that a search or seizure performed in the absence of a warrant is unreasonable.

- The Fourth Amendment requires that before a warrant authorizing a government search or seizure is issued, certain prerequisites must be satisfied.

  1. First, the government must establish the existence of probable cause. Probable cause has been succinctly defined as existing when "'the facts and circumstances within [the officers'] knowledge and of which they had reasonably trustworthy information [are] sufficient in themselves to warrant a man of reasonable caution in the belief that' an offense has been or is being committed [by the person to be arrested]."
  2. Second, the government must particularly describe the place to be searched (or the person to be seized) as well as the evidentiary items that are believed to be on the cited premises.
  3. Third, this information must be presented under oath to a neutral and detached magistrate.

- The magistrate previously assessed warrant applications pursuant to a strict two-pronged test (basis of knowledge and informant veracity). However, that test has since been abandoned in favor of a totality of the circumstances analytical framework.

- If there has been a prior judicial determination of probable cause, a defendant may still challenge this finding. However, the defendant must show not only that the affiant either knowingly or recklessly included such information in the warrant affidavit, but that the remaining affidavit content did not amount to probable cause if the challenged material is excluded.

CONNECTIONS

Relationship to Executing the Warrant (Chapter 5)

Whereas this chapter discussed the warrant requirements, Chapter 5 discusses issues relevant to the execution of the warrant.

Relationship to Searches and Seizures: Exceptions to the Warrant Requirement and Residential Arrests (Chapter 6), Searches Incident to Arrest (Chapter 7), the Automobile Exception (Chapter 8), the Plain View Doctrine (Chapter 9), and Consent Searches (Chapter 10)

Chapters 6-10 explore how the Supreme Court has interpreted the reasonableness concept in several different contexts and how the Court's interpretations have resulted in several exceptions to the general requirement that the state secure a warrant prior to a search. At times, the Court has granted the government the right to perform searches without prior demonstration of any suspicion whatsoever.

Relationship to Searches and Seizures on Less than Probable Cause — *Terry v. Ohio* (Chapter 11)

Chapter 11 discusses seizures and searches that the government can perform during a criminal investigation that require neither a warrant nor the establishment of probable cause. Rather, the government may perform so-called *Terry* searches and seizures upon a showing of reasonable suspicion.

Relationship to Administrative and Special Needs Searches and Seizures (Chapter 14)

Chapter 14 discusses government searches that serve noncriminal objectives. Virtually every administrative and special needs search can be performed in the absence of a warrant. Nevertheless, the warrant requirements still influence government searches that fall within this category.

Relationship to Fourth Amendment Violations and Their Associated Remedies (Chapter 15)

Searches performed in the absence of a warrant are presumptively unreasonable. Though there are a myriad of exceptions to this rule, the standard remedy for Fourth Amendment violations is to exclude the evidence obtained pursuant to the exclusionary rule.

Executing the Warrant

5

When the government obtains judicial approval of an arrest or search warrant request, the reasonableness clause of the Fourth Amendment

OVERVIEW

governs the conduct of the officers during the warrant's subsequent execution. It goes without saying that there are a myriad of factual contexts where questions regarding the propriety or reasonableness of government performance in this area can arise. In the search context, for example, issues involving the mode of entry, the performance of the actual search, the membership of the search participants, and the duration of the search are among the critical questions that the Supreme Court has addressed in this area. These issues, among other matters relevant to the execution of a judicially approved warrant, are the subject of this chapter.

A. WHEN A WARRANT MUST BE EXECUTED

1. Sample Search Warrant

B. KNOCK AND ANNOUNCE REQUIREMENT

1. Length of Time Prior to Entry
2. The Search and Detention of Individuals on the Premises When Executing the Warrant

A. When a Warrant Must Be Executed

After a warrant application has been approved, the magistrate will complete a warrant form reflecting the court's authorization. A sample search warrant form is reproduced here.

(1) Sample Search Warrant

As you begin reading the sample warrant, you will notice that the form states that an affidavit in support of a warrant has been submitted to the court, that the application identified a particular individual or location where the affiant had reason to believe

United States District Court

_____ DISTRICT OF _____

In the Matter of the Search of

(Name, address or Brief description of person, property or premises to be searched)

SEARCH WARRANT

CASE NUMBER:

TO:_____ and any Authorized Officer of the United States

Affidavit(s) having been made before me by_____ who has reason to
Affiant
believe that _____ on person_____ on the premises known as (name, description and/or location)

in the _____ District of_____

there is now concealed a certain person or property, namely (describe the person or property to be seized)

I am satisfied that the affidavit(s) and any recorded testimony establish probable cause to believe that the person or property so described is now concealed on the person or premises above-described and establish grounds for the issuance of this warrant.

YOU ARE HEREBY COMMANDED to search on or before _____ Date

(not to exceed 10 days) the person or place named above for the person or property specified, serving this warrant and making the search (in the daytime - 6:00 A.M. to 10:00 P.M.) (at any time in the day or night as I find reasonable cause has been established) and if the person or property be found there to seize same, leaving copy of this warrant and receipt for the person or property taken, and prepare a written inventory of the person or property seized and promptly return this warrant to _____ as required by law.

U.S. Judge or Magistrate Judge

_____   at   _____

Date and Time Issued   City and State

Honorable _____, US Magistrate Judge
Name and Title of Judicial Officer

Signature of Judicial Officer

AO 93 (Rev. 5/85) Search Warrant

A sample search warrant

that a certain individual or evidence of crime could be located, that the request had been approved by the court (with language in the bottom middle indicating the court's probable cause finding as well as a magistrate's signature line at the bottom of the warrant), and that law enforcement personnel were authorized to search the person or the described location.

In addition, the form delineates certain parameters regarding when the warrant can be executed. Rule 41 of the Federal Rules of Criminal Procedure requires that a search warrant be performed within ten days of a court's order approving the warrant. Remember the staleness rationale described in Chapter 4. To allow a warrant to be executed at a more distant date would, obviously, present issues regarding the currency of the information justifying the court's finding of probable cause. The rule also requires that the search be performed during the "daytime." The search warrant displayed requires that the search be performed between 6 A.M. and 10 P.M. This certainly does not require that the entire search be performed within that time but the search should at least be commenced within the time frame specified by the court. Finally, the warrant indicates that a copy of the warrant, as well as a receipt for the items seized, must be given to or left for the person from whom the property was taken.

F A Q

Q: Can law enforcement ever detain individuals located on a premise or secure the premises themselves *prior to* the actual execution of a search warrant?

A: In *Illinois v. McArthur*,[1] the Supreme Court answered this question in the affirmative. Officers who had probable cause to believe that marijuana would be found inside a residence belonging to the defendant were in the process of securing a search warrant for the premises. While awaiting the warrant, the defendant was prevented from reentering his residence unless accompanied by law enforcement. After approximately two hours, a search warrant was obtained and illegal narcotics were discovered. The Court found that this detention pending the warrant was reasonable within the meaning of the Fourth Amendment. The Court reasoned that exigent circumstances (e.g., the risk that evidence could be destroyed pending the attainment of a warrant) justified the detention. The Court also noted that the detention at issue was temporary, that probable cause existed that illegal narcotics would be found on the property, and that the police reasonably reconciled their law enforcement interests with the defendant's Fourth Amendment privacy interests (e.g., neither was the trailer searched nor was the defendant arrested pending the attainment of a search warrant).

B. Knock and Announce Requirement

The Fourth Amendment reasonableness requirement underlies the enactment of laws at the federal level and across many states requiring that officers knock and announce their authority and purpose prior to conducting a search of a dwelling. In *Wilson v. Arkansas*,[2] the Supreme Court held that "the method of an officer's entry

[1]531 U.S. 326 (2001).
[2]514 U.S. 927 (1995).

into a dwelling was among the factors" that a court should consider in ascertaining whether a search or seizure satisfied the Fourth Amendment's reasonableness clause. Compliance with the knock and announce rule generally requires that an officer, prior to entering a dwelling, identify himself and announce his intent to search.

Three policy rationales underlie this requirement. As identified in *Hudson v. Michigan*[3] (see discussion of this case in the FAQ that follows) these are: 1) protection of "human life and limb," given that residents surprised by an unanticipated entry into their home may respond with violence; 2) protection against the destruction of property that may accompany an unnecessarily forceful entry; and 3) safeguarding of personal privacy and dignity by giving residents "the 'opportunity to prepare themselves for' the entry of the police."

Nevertheless, the *Wilson* Court did not find that the Fourth Amendment mandated a knock and announcement in all circumstances. Thus, the knock and announce requirement is merely part of an overall reasonableness inquiry required by the Fourth Amendment. The adoption of a "rigid" mandate, according to the Court in *Wilson*, might unduly restrict other legitimate interests in law enforcement. Indeed, the Court in *United States v. Banks*[4] (see discussion of the *Banks* case later in this chapter) commented that a reasonableness inquiry in such matters must be flexible since the facts in any given case are "so various that no template is likely to produce sounder results than examining the totality of circumstances in a given case; it is too hard to invent categories without giving short shrift to details that turn out to be important in a given instance, and without inflating marginal ones." For example, the *Wilson* Court noted that the rule might not apply when there is "a threat of physical violence," when "a prisoner escapes from [the officer] and retreats to his dwelling," and "where police officers have reason to believe that evidence would likely be destroyed if advance notice were given."

F   A   Q

Q: What happens if a court finds that the knock and announce rule was violated? Must the evidence found during the search be suppressed at trial?

A: The Supreme Court in *Hudson v. Michigan* held that the exclusionary rule is inapplicable to knock and announce rule violations. It reasoned, in part, that the interests served by the knock and announce requirement (outlined earlier) "have nothing to do" with the actual search for and seizure of the evidence. Given this disconnect, exclusion is an inappropriate remedy. The Court also referenced the existence of other exceptions to the exclusionary rule, the considerable social costs associated with exclusion, and the current incentives to comply with the rule (e.g., civil rights actions, internal training, reforms and disciplines within police departments) as additional support for its holding.

---

[3]547 U.S. 586 (2006).
[4]540 U.S. 31 (2003).

(1) Length of Time Prior to Entry

When the executing officers knock and announce their authority to search, sometimes an occupant will promptly open the door and not pose an impediment to the search mission. But life isn't always so ideal! In situations that are, perhaps, less ideal, can the knock and announce requirement ever be dispensed with by law enforcement? What if an occupant is slow or even refuses to respond to an officer's announcement? What principles govern an officer's conduct in such situations?

The Supreme Court addressed the first of these questions in *Richards v. Wisconsin*.[5] There, the Court reversed the holding of the Wisconsin Supreme Court, which held that the knock and announce principle was per se inapplicable to searches pertaining to felony drug investigations. The Wisconsin Court reasoned, in part, that such cases presented "an extremely high risk of serious if not deadly injury to the police as well as the potential for the disposal of drugs by the occupants prior to entry by the police." Though the Supreme Court rejected such a categorical exclusion, the Court held that a "no-knock" entry may sometimes be reasonable. It found that a no-knock entry is justified in instances where an officer reasonably suspects that compliance with the rule would be dangerous, futile, or would frustrate or impede their criminal investigation (e.g., evidence destruction).

This book will discuss the concept of "reasonable suspicion" in Chapters 11-13. Suffice it to say, however, that the level of police certainty required by this concept is less than the probable cause standard. Accordingly, if law enforcement reasonably suspects that compliance with the knock and announce rule might result in the destruction of evidence or pose a danger to the officers or others, then a no-knock entry may be permitted. Sometimes officers may reasonably suspect such dangers prior to the submission of a warrant application. In such instances, a magistrate may grant, upon request, a warrant authorizing a no-knock entry.

Some guidance regarding the length of time officers must actually wait prior to effectuating an entry after knocking and announcing their presence can be gleaned from the Supreme Court's opinion in *United States v. Banks*. There, the Supreme Court addressed whether the government violated the Fourth Amendment when officers, after having knocked and announced their presence, waited less than half a minute prior to entering the defendant's residence. Specifically, in *Banks* officers had obtained a warrant to search an apartment for evidence of narcotics distribution. Upon arrival, the officers knocked and announced their presence. After waiting approximately 15 to 20 seconds without obtaining a response, the officers "broke open the front door with a battering ram." Banks, who claimed that he was in the shower at the time of the announcement and was unaware of the officers' presence until after they gained entry, argued that the short duration between the knock and announcement and the officers' entry rendered the execution of the warrant unreasonable.

The Court defined the issue presented as "whether it was reasonable to suspect imminent loss of evidence after the 15 to 20 seconds the officers waited prior to forcing their way." The Court concluded that the entry was reasonable, though it acknowledged that the ultimate outcome was less than clear cut. In reaching this conclusion, the Court applied the same reasonable suspicion test applicable in the no-knock scenarios described previously. Finding that the forced entry was justified,

---

[5]520 U.S. 385 (1997).

the Court stressed that the disposable nature of the narcotics at issue, the daytime execution of the warrant (suggesting that people would likely be awake), and the 15 to 20 seconds of wait time provided the officers with the reasonable suspicion to believe that the narcotics could be destroyed. The fact that the officers were looking for narcotics — an item easily disposable — was central to its conclusion that the 15- to 20-second wait time was reasonable.

Sidebar

THE PARTICIPATION OF THIRD-PARTY PERSONNEL IN SEARCH WARRANT EXECUTION

Sometimes individuals who are not employed in a law enforcement capacity may accompany, or seek to accompany, the police in the execution of a search warrant. The Supreme Court has held that such accompaniment is permissible only when the outsider participation is related to the objectives underlying the search. Thus, for example, a citizen whose property was stolen might be permitted to accompany officers during the execution of a search warrant in order to help identify stolen items. The Supreme Court did not find such a nexus in *Wilson v. Layne*,[6] when the Court held that the presence of a photographer and a reporter with the *Washington Post* did not directly aid in the search.

---

[6]526 U.S. 603 (1999).

(2) The Search and Detention of Individuals on the Premises When Executing the Warrant

Once inside, it is hardly unusual for officers, armed with a search warrant, to encounter individuals within the residence. Naturally, this begs at least a couple of questions. For example, may the police detain the individuals found inside? May these individuals be searched? Imagine the conflicts presented by this dilemma. On the one hand, it is not difficult to envision that individuals present at a search scene — particularly those who are involved in criminal activity — might seek to hamper the police search effort. Physical dangers and the destruction of evidence are certainly plausible outcomes. Obviously law enforcement would prefer rules limiting individual freedom during such encounters. On the other hand, to allow the search and detention of individuals merely because they happened to be present at the time of a search would, in the eyes of many, unjustly compromise basic Fourth Amendment protections. After all, it could be argued, why should a search warrant for physical evidence justify the search and seizure of an individual? Should not an individual be allowed to freely move within and outside his own home, particularly in the absence of any evidence linking him to criminal activity?

In regards to searches, the Supreme Court has held that an individual found on the premises during the execution of a search warrant cannot be searched merely because he happened to be present at the time of execution. Instead, the Fourth Amendment generally requires that either probable cause or reasonable suspicion be established before this additional intrusion will be justified. It is important to remember that, upon a finding of probable cause, a search warrant can authorize not only the search of a place (e.g., a residence) but the search of an individual as well. Therefore, if the search warrant has authorized the search of premises as well as a particular individual, then a search of that individual, if found on the property, would be justified.

The issue of detention is a little less straightforward. Normally, an individual may not be detained absent the establishment of either probable cause or reasonable suspicion to believe that the individual has been engaged in criminal activity. Thus, an individual is free from governmental seizures unless the government can establish at least some level of connection between that individual and criminal activity. However, these general principles of protection are compromised in the context of a search warrant execution. The Supreme Court in *Michigan v. Summers*[7] held that an individual "occupant" or "resident" found on the premises during the execution of a search warrant may be detained, even in the absence of any individualized suspicion.

> If the evidence that a citizen's residence is harboring contraband is sufficient to persuade a judicial officer that an invasion of the citizen's privacy is justified, it is constitutionally reasonable to require that citizen to remain while officers of the law execute a valid warrant to search his home. Thus, for Fourth Amendment purposes, we hold that a warrant to search for contraband founded on probable cause implicitly carries with it the limited authority to detain the occupants of the premises while a proper search is conducted.

The reasonableness of such searches, according to the Court in *Summers*, is premised upon a number of normative characteristics. The Court noted where a magistrate has found probable cause to believe that a particular residence contains contraband,

> [t]he detention of one of the residents while the premises were searched, although admittedly a significant restraint on his liberty, [is] surely less intrusive than the search itself. Indeed, we may safely assume that most citizens — unless they intend flight to avoid arrest — would elect to remain in order to observe the search of their possessions. Furthermore, the type of detention imposed here is not likely to be exploited by the officer or unduly prolonged in order to gain more information, because the information the officers seek normally will be obtained through the search and not through the detention. Moreover, because the detention in this case was in respondent's own residence, it could add only minimally to the public stigma associated with the search itself and would involve neither the inconvenience nor the indignity associated with a compelled visit to the police station.

This holding arguably suggests that an individual who is neither an "occupant" nor a "resident" of a premise identified in a search warrant would not be subject to the aforementioned rule. Thus, for example, if a pizza delivery carrier happens to be present at a location during the execution of a warrant, he or she would seemingly be beyond the reach of the rule enunciated in *Summers*. It bears reemphasis, however, that this apparent rule with respect to nonresidents would not constitute a per se exclusion from detention during a search. The police retain the authority to detain such individuals if either probable cause or reasonable suspicion of criminal wrongdoing can be established.

SUMMARY

■ The government's execution of a warrant is governed by the Fourth Amendment's reasonableness clause.

---

[7]452 U.S. 692 (1981).

- Rule 41 of the Federal Rules of Criminal Procedure details various nonconstitutional requirements that officers must follow when executing a warrant (e.g., calendar execution limitations, permissible hours of execution, etc.).

- The knock and announce rule is not a constitutional mandate but is part of the Fourth Amendment's reasonableness inquiry.

- The knock and announce rule generally requires that officers announce their intention to search prior to entering the subject premises and commencing their search activities, but there are exceptions to this rule. If the officers reasonably suspect that compliance with the rule would jeopardize their safety or the seizure of evidence within the dwelling, then officers may enter the dwelling without satisfying this requirement. The elapsed time span between the officers' announcement and the government entry is also adjudged pursuant to the reasonableness standard.

- The government may detain "residents" or "occupants" of a dwelling during the execution of a search warrant at that location. Authority also exists justifying the detention of individuals prior to the attainment of a warrant to search.

- However, the government does not have an automatic right to search individuals found on the premises absent some other justification.

CONNECTIONS

Relationship to Searches, Seizures, and the Warrant Clause (Chapter 4)
The requirements necessary to securing a warrant are discussed in Chapter 4.

Relationship to Searches and Seizures: Exceptions to the Warrant Requirement and Residential Arrests (Chapter 6)
In order to obtain a warrant to search or seize, the government must establish the existence of probable cause. Chapter 6 introduces the reader to some of the exceptions to the warrant requirement. However, the exceptions to this requirement do not dispense with the government's need to satisfy the probable cause standard. Included in Chapter 6 is a discussion regarding the timing of the probable cause hearing when an arrest is made in the absence of a warrant.

Relationship to Searches and Seizures on Less than Probable Cause — *Terry v. Ohio* (Chapter 11)
This chapter explained that the government's execution of a warrant is governed by the reasonableness standard within the Fourth Amendment. Chapter 11 discusses so-called *Terry* seizures and searches that do not require a warrant. However, *Terry* stops and frisks are assessed pursuant to the Fourth Amendment's reasonableness clause.

Relationship to Fourth Amendment Violations and Their Associated Remedies (Chapter 15)

This chapter provided an introductory discussion of some of the exceptions to the warrant requirement. In addition, the chapter discussed the knock and announce rule. Chapter 15 discusses the general principle that evidence obtained in contravention of the Fourth Amendment is subject to exclusion pursuant to the exclusionary rule. However, a knock and announce violation does not implicate this remedy.

Searches and Seizures: Exceptions to the Warrant Requirement and Residential Arrests

6

As noted previously, the law does not forbid an officer from performing a search or seizure in the absence of a warrant. However, the law does pro-

vide that such conduct, without prior judicial authorization, is presumptively unreasonable. What this means, at least in part, is that the government always retains the burden of demonstrating that a particular search or seizure is justified. Thus, whenever a warrantless arrest or search is performed the government may be required to subsequently demonstrate to a court why the challenged conduct is constitutionally permissible.

This chapter will discuss some of the exceptions that serve to justify government searches and seizures in the absence of a warrant. More particularly, this chapter will review, among other topics, those exceptions that apply when the attainment of a warrant prior to an arrest or search is impractical. In addition, the rules that govern the effectuation of arrests in public spaces and within a "house" will be examined.

A. EXCEPTIONS TO THE WARRANT REQUIREMENT

1. Exigent Circumstances
2. Arrests in Public Places

B. ARRESTS IN THE HOME

1. Definition of "House"

C. WARRANTLESS ARRESTS: HOW SOON MUST A PROBABLE CAUSE DETERMINATION BE MADE?

A. Exceptions to the Warrant Requirement

(1) Exigent Circumstances

As noted, there is a presumption that searches and seizures performed in the absence of a warrant are unreasonable. However, this presumption is just that—a mere presumption. In fact, you will discover that this presumption is largely toothless. Each of these exceptions will be examined in this and the next several chapters. However, before some of the more particularized exceptions are examined, this chapter will commence with a review of a comparatively broader exception, namely, the exigent circumstances doctrine. The exigent circumstances rationale, you will discover, will invariably arise again and again throughout your study of the exceptions to the warrant clause. Whether exclusively, or in conjunction with other rationales, the exigent circumstances concept often serves as a direct or underlying justification for warrantless government search and seizure activities.

The rationale underlying the exception is not difficult to digest. The law recognizes that, on occasion, the attainment of a warrant prior to an arrest or a search may be impractical. Sometimes an emergency circumstance is presented that mandates a swift governmental response. In fact, it is not unusual for an initial exigency to give rise to additional exigencies. When such exigencies, either individually or collectively, are found, the government may perform a search or seizure without prior attainment of a warrant.

An officer need not correctly gauge the existence of an exigency in order to take advantage of the doctrine. Instead, an officer's conduct is assessed in accordance with the reasonableness clause of the Fourth Amendment. That clause requires that government officers act reasonably when performing a search or seizure. We saw this clause at work earlier in the "Knock and Announce Requirement" section in Chapter 5. Just as officers must act reasonably when they search and seize in connection with a search warrant, officers must also act reasonably when they search and seize in the absence of a warrant. Therefore, whether officers accurately assessed the purported exigency that confronted them is not the determinative inquiry. Rather, the test is whether the officers had a reasonable basis for believing the existence of the exigency. If so, then that reasonable basis will justify the officers' conduct in the absence of a warrant.

(a) Destruction of Evidence and Hot Pursuit Rationales

What situations has the Supreme Court recognized as sufficiently exigent so as to overcome the presumption of a warrant? One such circumstance is when officers are required to act swiftly to prevent the destruction of evidence. When evaluating such claims, a court will consider several factors, including the immediacy of the possible destruction, the feasibility of securing a warrant, and the materiality of the evidence, as well as the gravity of the criminal offense. Accordingly, a government showing that the evidence seized was readily disposable or destructible (e.g., illegal narcotics), that the criminal offense under investigation was comparatively serious (e.g., a felony as opposed to a misdemeanor or petty offense), and that the evidence was central or material to an investigation (e.g., the murder weapon used in a homicide) would tend to strengthen a government claim of an exigent circumstance.

Another recognized exigency excusing the prior attainment of a warrant is the hot pursuit doctrine. As its name suggests, an arrest or search warrant may be excused when law enforcement are in hot pursuit of a fleeing suspect and reasonably believe that the suspect may escape prior to the attainment of a warrant. Often, the suspect who is hotly pursued is aware that the police are seeking his apprehension. Certainly individuals engaged in any criminal endeavor possess some degree of motivation to shed incriminating evidence. But a suspect who is cognizant that he is being pursued by the police has a heightened motivation to swiftly conceal or destroy evidence or evade police apprehension. However, such awareness is not a prerequisite for the doctrine to be invoked.

(b) Police/Public Safety Rationales

Finally, a warrant will be excused when the prior attainment of a warrant would pose a reasonable risk of death or serious bodily injury to the public or the police. The actions of the officers under such circumstances are subject to an objective reasonableness review.

In *Brigham City v. Stuart*,[2] officers responded to a residence upon receiving a call regarding "a loud party." Upon arrival, the officers, while located outside the residence, observed and heard indicia of a physical fracas and human injury, as well as evidence suggesting a possible escalation of violence within the home. Finding that the officers' warrantless entry "was plainly reasonable under the circumstances," the Court made the following observations:

RISK OF EVIDENCE DESTRUCTION — CASE STUDY

Consider *Ker v. California*,[1] in which California police officers had probable cause to believe that at least one of the defendants (Diane and George Ker) had recently purchased illegal narcotics from a known drug supplier and that evidence associated therewith could be found within their residence. After obtaining a passkey to the Kers' apartment from the apartment manager, the officers entered the apartment without a warrant and found George Ker sitting in the living room. Shortly thereafter, Diane Ker entered the living room from the kitchen. After one of the officers approached the kitchen area (without entering) and observed marijuana and a scale, the Kers were placed under arrest. Subsequent to the arrest, the officers, again without a warrant, searched the kitchen and seized the marijuana as well as evidence found elsewhere in the residence. The Kers sought to suppress the evidence, contending that their arrests were illegal given the officers' unconstitutional entry to their residence. In rejecting this claim, the Supreme Court relied upon the fact that the narcotics in question could be easily discarded. As stated by the Court, "In addition to the officers' belief that Ker was in possession of narcotics, which could be quickly and easily destroyed, Ker's furtive conduct in eluding them shortly before the arrest was ground for the belief that he might well have been expecting the police."

---

[1]374 U.S. 23 (1963).

As they approached the house [at approximately 3:00 A.M.], they could hear from within "an altercation occurring, some kind of a fight" (reference omitted). "It was loud and it was tumultuous" (citation omitted). The officers heard "thumping and crashing" and people yelling "stop, stop" and "get off me." . . . The noise seemed to be coming from the back of the house; after looking in the front window and seeing nothing, the officers proceeded around back to investigate further. . . . From here, they could see that a fracas was taking place inside the kitchen. A juvenile, fists clenched, was being held back by several adults. As the officers watch, he breaks free and strikes one of the adults in the face, sending the adult to the sink spitting blood.

In these circumstances, the officers had an objectively reasonable basis for believing both that the injured adult might need help and that the violence in the kitchen was just beginning. Nothing in the Fourth Amendment required them to wait until another blow rendered someone "unconscious" or "semi-conscious" or worse before entering. The role

---

[2]547 U.S. 398 (2006).

S i d e b a r

HOT PURSUIT — CASE STUDY

Let's review another case — *Warden v. Hayden*[3] — that you will likely encounter in your class studies. Officers received a report that an individual (later identified as Hayden) had just robbed a cab company and had entered a residential home. "Within minutes" the police arrived at the house and obtained entry after talking briefly with a Mrs. Hayden. After searching throughout much of the home, defendant Hayden was discovered in an upstairs bedroom. A search uncovered various pieces of evidence that were subsequently introduced into evidence at his trial. In upholding both the warrantless entry and search, the Supreme Court held that exigent circumstances justified the officers' actions. The Court found that the police, who arrived no more than five minutes after the arrival of defendant Hayden, "acted reasonably when they entered the house and began to search for a man of the description they had been given and for weapons which he had used in the robbery or might use against them. The Fourth Amendment does not require police officers to delay in the course of an investigation if to do so would gravely endanger their lives or the lives of others. Speed here was essential, and only a thorough search of the house for persons and weapons could have insured that Hayden was the only man present and that the police had control of all weapons which could be used against them or to effect an escape."

---

[3]387 U.S. 294 (1967).

of a peace officer includes preventing violence and restoring order, not simply rendering first aid to casualties; an officer is not like a boxing (or hockey) referee, poised to stop a bout only if it becomes too one-sided.

In this regard, the Court made another notable finding. It flatly rejected as "irrelevant" the claim that the police entry was unreasonable, and therefore unconstitutional, given that the officers' subjective intentions in entering were to effectuate arrests, not to protect the public. The Court stated that the subjective intentions of the officers had no bearing whatsoever upon whether the government acted reasonably under the circumstances.[4]

(c) Manufactured Exigencies

One final note regarding the exigent circumstances doctrine: the government cannot avail themselves of this justification if the exigency was improperly manufactured. Elaborating upon the meaning of this concept, the Supreme Court in *Kentucky v. King*[5] declared that an exigency is improperly manufactured only in circumstances where the government agents either violated the Fourth Amendment or threatened to do so. In the words of the Court:

> [W]arrantless searches are allowed when the circumstances make it reasonable, within the meaning of the Fourth Amendment, to dispense with the warrant requirement. Therefore, the answer to the question before us is that the exigent circumstances rule justifies a warrantless search when the conduct of the police preceding the exigency is reasonable in the same sense. Where, as here, the police did not create the exigency by engaging or threatening to engage in conduct that violates the Fourth Amendment, warrantless entry to prevent the destruction of evidence is reasonable and thus allowed.

---

[4]*Brigham* was followed by the Supreme Court in *Michigan v. Fisher*, 130 S. Ct. 546 (2009). There, the Court found that a warrantless police entry into a residence was justified given that the officers had an objectively reasonable basis for believing that an "emergency aid" safety situation presented itself. The Court deemed *Fisher* to be a "straightforward application" of *Brigham*, declaring that both cases involved reported disturbances that prompted a law enforcement response, that "a tumultuous situation" within each home was encountered by the respective officers upon their arrival (including indicators outside the homes that personal injuries had been sustained), and the officers in each instance observed violent behavior within the residence.
[5]131 S. Ct. 1849 (2011).

Consider the facts in *King*. After a controlled purchase of narcotics from an individual outside of an apartment building and the suspect's rather swift departure from the scene of the purchase, law enforcement officers decided to pursue their target. Though the officers were aware that the suspect had entered a residence within a particular apartment building, they were unsure which of two apartment units the suspect had actually entered. Having smelled an odor of marijuana emanating "from the apartment on the left" the officers then "banged on the left apartment door 'as loud as [they] could' and announced" their presence. At that moment, the officers heard sounds associated with the movement of people and objects within the residence. The officers then kicked in the door and found therein three individuals, as well as various narcotics, drug paraphernalia, and cash.[6]

It was argued that the government's warrantless entry could not be justified on exigent circumstances grounds given that the exigency at issue — here, the likely destruction of evidence — was impermissibly manufactured. Assuming the existence of a true exigency, the Supreme Court of Kentucky declared that the police could not prevail on an exigent circumstances rationale whenever it creates an exigent circumstance in bad faith or it can reasonably foresee that its actions would create the relied-upon exigency. Based upon this test, the Kentucky court found that the search was not justified given that the exigency at issue was reasonably foreseeable. It reasoned that when the officers knocked on the door it was reasonably foreseeable that people within the residence would destroy evidence.

The Supreme Court, however, reversed. The Court rejected both the bad faith and reasonably foreseeable tests, instead declaring "that the exigent circumstances rule applies when the police do not gain entry to premises by means of an actual or threatened violation of the Fourth Amendment." Thus, the subjective motivations underlying the officers' actions as well as the likely foreseeable consequences of their conduct are of no consequence to whether the exigent circumstances exception applies in a given situation.

(2) Arrests in Public Places

In *United States v. Watson*,[7] the Supreme Court held that law enforcement had the right to arrest individuals in public places in the absence of a warrant. In *Watson*, the defendant was arrested without a warrant at a public establishment for possessing stolen credit cards. The officers were acting in accordance with a federal statute that authorized such warrantless apprehensions.

For many students this result seems rather unremarkable. After all, long before any of us enrolled in law school most individuals who spent any meaningful time in the United States were fully cognizant of this police practice. Television, the movies, and, for some, personal experiences have taught us that the police rather routinely arrest individuals without seeking prior judicial authorization. Moreover, the arrest in *Watson*, like so many other arrests, occurred not in a private setting but, rather, in the public sphere. What's the big deal, you may ask, about a declaration that an officer may conduct a warrantless arrest in a public space? When one delves a bit

---

[6]As it turned out, the initial target of their investigation (the individual who made the controlled purchase) had entered the apartment unit on the right side. The officers searched that unit as well.
[7]423 U.S. 411 (1976).

deeper into the facts of Watson, certain interesting considerations are presented by this issue.

The Court noted "the ancient common law rule" — which remains the governing rule to this day — "that a peace officer was permitted to arrest without a warrant for a misdemeanor or felony committed in his presence as well as for a felony not committed in his presence if there was reasonable ground for making the arrest." In *Watson*, the facts are devoid of any suggestion that law enforcement did not have ample time to obtain an arrest warrant. Moreover, the criminal offense at issue was nonviolent in nature. In the absence of an exigency requiring swift government action, coupled with the nonviolent character of the offense, was *Watson* correctly decided? Consider the dissent's contention that "[j]ust as it is virtually impossible for probable cause for an arrest to grow stale between the time of formation and the time a warrant is procured, it is virtually impossible for probable cause to become stale between procurement and arrest."

At the outset of this book, I indicated that this course largely addressed the tug of war between two competing interests — the safeguarding of individual liberties and the provision of power to law enforcement. The *Watson* case is a classic example of this struggle. Should law enforcement be empowered with the authority to decide on its own when and where to invade an individual's Fourth Amendment protection against unreasonable seizures? Should any such authority be restricted to only those instances when an emergency situation is presented? Or did the majority correctly reason that a contrary ruling would invite "endless litigation" regarding, inter alia, exigencies, the feasibility of obtaining a warrant, and suspect flight concerns? These are interesting questions for sure!

(a) "Reasonableness" of Government Arrests and Seizures

Though the police are permitted to seize individuals in the absence of a warrant, the Fourth Amendment requires that officers act reasonably in the process. As stated by the Supreme Court in *Graham v. Connor*,[8] "the 'reasonableness' of a particular seizure depends not only on *when* it is made, but also on *how* it is carried out." Irrespective of whether the seizure involved the use of deadly or non-deadly force, the Court employs a balancing test that weighs "the nature and quality of the intrusion" upon an individual's Fourth Amendment rights against the competing government interests. The Court observed that this review requires that "careful attention" be paid to the peculiar facts and circumstances presented in a given case. In this regard, the Court cited certain factors as germane to this inquiry, including "the severity of the crime at issue, whether the suspect poses an immediate threat to the safety of the officers or others, and whether he is actively resisting arrest or attempting to evade arrest by flight." Whether a particular seizure is reasonable is assessed objectively in light of the circumstances confronting the officer.

Consider *Tennessee v. Garner*,[9] which addressed the reasonableness of a government seizure in the deadly force context. The Court found that the Fourth Amendment restricts the use of deadly force to circumstances where such force is necessary to apprehend the suspect, and probable cause exists that the suspect poses a serious physical safety threat to the public or the police (e.g., threats to an officer involving a

---

[8]490 U.S. 386 (1989).
[9]471 U.S. 1 (1985).

weapon; instances where the suspect has committed a crime involving "the infliction or threatened infliction of serious physical harm"). As explained by the Court:

> Where the suspect poses no immediate threat to the officer and no threat to others, the harm resulting from failing to apprehend him does not justify the use of deadly force to do so. It is no doubt unfortunate when a suspect who is in sight escapes, but the fact that the police arrive a little late or are a little slower afoot does not always justify killing the suspect. A police officer may not seize an unarmed, nondangerous suspect by shooting him dead.

This reasonableness inquiry was also addressed by the Court in the context of an arrest for a comparatively minor traffic offense. In *Atwater v. City of Lago Vista*,[10] the Court examined the constitutionality of a Texas statute that authorized, but did not mandate, the warrantless arrest of either a front-seat passenger of a vehicle who was not wearing a safety belt or a driver who failed to secure a small child riding in the front seat with a safety belt. Punishable as a misdemeanor (including a fine), the statute provided officers with the discretionary authority to either issue a citation or make a custodial arrest.

After engaging in a lengthy historical review of English statutory and common law as well as American history, the Court upheld the statute and Atwater's arrest. The Court acknowledged the very troublesome facts presented in *Atwater*. However, the Court reasoned, in part, that Atwater's arrest was justified given two important facts. First, probable cause existed that Atwater violated the seatbelt statute. Second, the manner of her arrest was otherwise reasonable. In making this latter point, the Court distinguished *Atwater* from other cases, including *Garner*, where the Court found that the seizure, though supported by probable cause, was nevertheless executed in an "extraordinary" manner:

> Nor was the arrest made in an "extraordinary manner, unusually harmful to [her] privacy or . . . physical interests" (citation omitted). . . . . [T]he question whether a search or seizure is "extraordinary" turns, above all else, on the manner in which the search or seizure is executed (citations omitted). Atwater's arrest was surely "humiliating," . . . but it was no more "harmful to . . . privacy or . . . physical interests" than the normal custodial arrest. She was handcuffed, placed in a squad car, and taken to the local police station, where officers asked her to remove her shoes, jewelry, and glasses, and to empty her pockets. They then took her photograph and placed her in a cell, alone, for about an hour, after which she was taken before a magistrate, and released on $310 bond. The arrest and booking were inconvenient and embarrassing to Atwater, but not so extraordinary as to violate the Fourth Amendment.

F   A   Q

Q: Are there situations where the police may properly arrest an individual even though he is not suspected of any criminal activity?

A: Yes. Section 3144 of Title 18 of the U.S. Code authorizes the detention of material witnesses to criminal activity. Before "a judicial officer may order the arrest of the person,"

---

[10]532 U.S. 318 (2001).

the affidavit presented to the court must satisfy two conditions: 1) "the testimony of a person is material in a criminal proceeding," and 2) it is "impracticable to secure the presence of the person by subpoena." Whenever an individual is arrested, that person is entitled to a judicial determination regarding his continued detention. A court may order his detention to continue or may order his release. In the material witness context, the statute contains safeguards that, at least arguably, assure that the length of any imposed detention be *reasonable*. The statute requires that the duration of an individual's detention be no longer than is necessary to secure his testimony by means of a deposition provided that "further detention is not necessary to prevent a failure of justice."

B. Arrests in the Home

We have learned that officers are permitted under the Constitution to effectuate warrantless *public* arrests, and that sometimes the requirement of an arrest or search warrant can be excused if exigent circumstances are present. Assuming, however, the absence of an exigency or a consensual entry, may an officer arrest an individual in his *home* in the absence of an arrest warrant?

The Supreme Court addressed this issue in *Payton v. New York*.[11] There, officers had probable cause to believe that the defendant had murdered a gas station manager. Several officers went to the defendant's apartment with the intent to effectuate a warrantless arrest. After receiving no response after knocking upon the door, the officers, approximately 30 minutes thereafter, used a crowbar to break down the door and enter the apartment. Though no one was present at the time of the entry, a .30-caliber shell casing was gathered at the scene that was subsequently introduced into evidence against Payton in his murder trial.

In a companion case, defendant Obie Riddick had been arrested for two armed robberies while he was at home sitting in a bed. The officers, who did not have an arrest warrant, entered after the defendant's son had opened the door. Subsequent to the arrest, the officers searched a chest of drawers located near a bed and discovered illegal narcotics and related material.

The Supreme Court reversed the judgments in each case, holding that, absent exigent circumstances, an officer must obtain an arrest warrant before an individual may be arrested within his home. The Court emphasized the special sanctity afforded a home and noted that this sanctity exists irrespective of whether the intrusion at issue involves a search for property or a seizure of an individual. As observed by the Court, "neither history nor this Nation's experience requires us to disregard the overriding respect for the sanctity of the home that has been embedded in our traditions since the origins of the Republic."

Lastly, the Court rejected the government's contention that a warrantless entry was justified since "only a search warrant," as opposed to an arrest warrant, can protect individual privacy in this instance and the attainment of a search warrant under such circumstances "is manifestly impractical." Despite the added protections attendant to a search warrant, the Court found that a magistrate's independent determination of probable cause to arrest was sufficient to protect the privacy interests of an individual within his own home. The Court reasoned that if a court found

---

[11]445 U.S. 573 (1980).

probable cause to arrest, it is not asking too much of the suspect "to require him to open his doors to the officers of the law" when the officers arrive at his home.

(1) Definition of "House"

Given the requirement of an arrest warrant prior to effectuating an arrest within a suspect's house, it is essential to understand what constitutes a house for Fourth Amendment purposes. As you will see, the term "house" takes on various meanings.

Some things are not in dispute. For example, courts agree that residential homes, including apartments, certainly qualify as "houses." In addition, hotel and motel rooms occupied by paying customers during the agreed-upon rental period qualify as "houses." The term also encompasses certain nonresidential structures such as office spaces and storage units. On the other hand, the courts agree that public establishments and other locations, such as restaurants, casinos, and hotel lobbies, to name just a few, do not fall within the meaning of the term. Thus, these public locales are not subject to the *Payton* warrant requirement, but are subsumed within the *Watson* doctrine that authorizes warrantless seizures in public places.

Yet there are some gray areas where the division between a "house" and a public area is less than clear. For the moment we will consider this division in the context of the traditional residence (either the standard residential house or an apartment). Obviously, when an individual is situated outside his home, the person is subject to a warrantless arrest. But when that individual approaches his home, at what point does he become entitled to the protections enunciated in *Payton*? Stated another way, when an individual departs from his residence, at what point does he lose his *Payton* protections? The answer might not be what you suspect.

The Supreme Court has held that, in a limited circumstance, an individual might be subject to a warrantless arrest even when situated within his own home. In *United States v. Santana*,[12] the Court held that an individual who is standing in the doorway of his home, but not in the vestibule, is subject to warrantless arrest. The Court reasoned that such an individual is situated in a position no different than an individual situated "completely outside her house." The Court declared that, in either circumstance, the individual is capable of being publicly viewed, heard, or touched.

As noted, the preceding discussion focused upon what I referred to as "the traditional residence." However, others live in less conventional housing, such as homeless shelters or in outdoor public spaces. To date, the Supreme Court has not addressed the applicability of the Fourth Amendment in these contexts. However, among the lower courts there is judicial precedent for extending Fourth Amendment protections to those who reside in homeless shelters as well as outdoors on public property. Other courts have been reluctant to find privacy expectations for individuals who reside outside on public spaces.

Let's now turn our attention to another common scenario. Whether for business or pleasure, people are often situated in the homes of other individuals. Friends visit friends or other family members. They may, for example, stop by for a few minutes to simply chat, or come for a few hours to watch a program on television or to have dinner, or even spend the night. People in business may enter a home to clean a carpet or repair a television. Others might come by to sell a product or a service. What

---

[12]427 U.S. 38 (1976).

Fourth Amendment protections, if any, are extended to individuals who are located in a residence other than their own?

As a general rule, the Supreme Court has held that, absent exigent circumstances or a consensual entry, the government must secure both an arrest and a search warrant prior to arresting an individual located within the home of a third party.[13] Why a search warrant? Remember, the Fourth Amendment protects an individual's privacy interest from unreasonable government interference. The third-party home-owner or lessee has a privacy interest in his residence. Generally, this interest may be pierced only through the securement of a warrant. In the situation presented, the government, in effect, is conducting a search of a third party's premises for a suspect. Thus, the government must demonstrate that there is probable cause to believe that the suspect is located within the third party's residence.

While this constitutes the general rule, this scenario raises another significant issue — the issue of standing — that will be addressed in greater detail in Chapter 15. Imagine that the police conduct a warrantless search of a third party's residence and find evidence therein that incriminates five individuals found within the home. If the five individuals seek to suppress the evidence on the ground that the search was unconstitutional, whether they ultimately succeed may not depend upon whether or not the government should have obtained a search warrant. Rather, the result may depend, at least initially, upon whether the complainants had standing to contest the search.

C. Warrantless Arrests: How Soon Must a Probable Cause Determination Be Made?

When an arrest occurs in the absence of a warrant several important questions and concerns are presented. Among the more critical questions concerns the time frame within which the government must satisfy its evidentiary burden. Imagine the following. An individual robs a bank late in the morning on a Tuesday. Though the police are cognizant of his whereabouts they intentionally wait until early Friday evening before arresting the suspect without a warrant and placing him in a jail cell. Moreover, all government offices, including the courthouses, will be closed the following Monday on account of a national holiday. As a result, the suspect faces the prospect of remaining in confinement for at least three full days without a judicial determination regarding the propriety of his arrest. What, if any, protections are afforded individuals in such circumstances?

In 1975 the Supreme Court held in *Gerstein v. Pugh*[14] that our hypothetical individual may not simply languish in jail for the period of time described therein without a judicial determination of probable cause. Specifically, the Court held that the Fourth Amendment requires that a judicial officer make a "fair and reliable" probable cause determination "either before or promptly after arrest." The detention of an individual following a warrantless arrest can be for only a "brief period" in order "to take the administrative steps incident to arrest." Several years later, in *County of Riverside v. McLaughlin*, the Court elaborated upon the meaning of the "prompt"

---

[13]*Steagald v. United States*, 451 U.S. 204 (1981).
[14]420 U.S. 103 (1975).

standard. The Court declared that "a jurisdiction that provides judicial determinations of probable cause within 48 hours of arrest will, as a general matter, comply with the promptness requirement of *Gerstein*."

Sometimes this probable cause proceeding, often referred to as a "*Gerstein* hearing,*" will occur in open court, in the presence of the defendant and his counsel. More often, however, a magistrate makes this probable cause determination on an ex parte basis. Whether in the privacy of the judge's chambers, at the magistrate's residence, or at some other locale, a magistrate will typically meet with the government attorney and the affiant and review the sufficiency of the complaint detailing the alleged offense. Neither the defendant nor his counsel is present during this deliberative process. Indeed, this evaluative step is analogous to the pre-arrest warrant application process. When seeking an arrest warrant, the magistrate meets only with government representatives and not with the defendant or his counsel.

SUMMARY

- There are several exceptions to the requirement that the government secure a warrant prior to effectuating a warrantless arrest or search.

- The following exigent circumstances can justify a warrantless arrest or search in the absence of a warrant:
  - Public Safety: A warrant may be excused if the officer has a reasonable fear for his or the community's safety.
  - Hot Pursuit: A warrant may be excused if the officer is hotly pursuing a suspect.
  - Destruction of Evidence: A warrant may be excused if the officer reasonably believes that material evidence may be destroyed before a warrant can be obtained.

- An officer may effectuate a warrantless arrest at a public location. However, the arrest must be performed in a reasonable manner.
  - An officer may not employ deadly force when seizing a suspect unless that suspect reasonably posed a danger to the officer or the community.
  - The Fourth Amendment does not prohibit an officer from effectuating an arrest, pursuant to a statute, authorizing the arrest for a comparatively minor offense (e.g., a traffic offense).

- Typically, an officer must secure an arrest warrant in order to arrest a suspect within his own residence. A search warrant and an arrest warrant are required if the officer seeks to arrest a suspect in the home of a third party.

- For Fourth Amendment purposes, a person's house includes not only an actual house, but also apartments, hotel and motel rooms, and, in some jurisdictions, homeless shelters.

- If the government makes a warrantless arrest, a probable cause determination must be made by a judicial officer "promptly after arrest." The Supreme Court has declared that a probable cause determination made within 48 hours of arrest is presumptively reasonable.

CONNECTIONS

Relationship to Searches, Seizures, and the Warrant Clause (Chapter 4) and Executing the Warrant (Chapter 5)

Whereas this chapter provided an introductory discussion of some of the exceptions to the warrant requirement, Chapters 4 and 5 examine the essential prerequisites to obtaining a warrant as well as issues related to its execution.

Relationship to Searches Incident to Arrest (Chapter 7), the Automobile Exception (Chapter 8), the Plain View Doctrine (Chapter 9), and Consent Searches (Chapter 10)

This chapter is the first of several chapters that discuss government searches in the absence of a warrant. Chapters 7-10 continue this discussion and explore several additional exceptions to the general requirement that the state secure a warrant prior to performing a search or seizure.

Relationship to Searches and Seizures on Less than Probable Cause — *Terry v. Ohio* (Chapter 11)

Chapter 11 discusses the different types of Fourth Amendment seizures (arrests, which require probable cause, and so-called *Terry* stops, which require a finding of reasonable suspicion) as well as the concept of encounters that do not implicate Fourth Amendment interests. The chapter also discusses *Terry*-level searches or frisks. *Terry* stops and frisks can be performed in the absence of a warrant.

Relationship to Fourth Amendment Violations and Their Associated Remedies (Chapter 15)

If the government performs a warrantless search or seizure, it must still prove that its actions were justified. Thus, depending upon the circumstance, either probable cause or reasonable suspicion must be established. The failure to satisfy the applicable evidentiary standard may result in the exclusion of evidence at trial.

Searches Incident to Arrest

7

As noted earlier in this book, the government enjoys wide latitude to perform warrantless searches and arrests in a public setting. Within

a home, however, warrantless searches and arrests are permissible only if entry is obtained by virtue of an exigency or consent. This chapter will address a matter that invariably presents itself in these search and arrest scenarios. Once an arrest has occurred, what are the rules regarding any subsequent searches that can take place? Supreme Court pronouncements in this area fall under three general rubrics — searches of a person, searches of a home, and searches of an automobile. This chapter will explore in depth the search incident to arrest doctrine and examine how it has been applied in each of these contexts. But first, this chapter will begin with an overview of the pertinent rules and a discussion of the underlying Supreme Court authorities. A more elaborate and collective examination of these rules will follow that will underscore the breadth of the search incident to arrest doctrine, its consequences for law enforcement and individuals, and some inconsistencies that are, arguably, associated with its application.

A. **SEARCHES OF A PERSON INCIDENT TO ARREST**

B. **SEARCHES OF A HOME INCIDENT TO ARREST**

C. **SEARCHES OF AN AUTOMOBILE INCIDENT TO ARREST**

    1. Passenger Compartment — Contemporaneous Requirement

D. **CRITIQUE OF THE SEARCH INCIDENT TO ARREST RULE**

E. **PRETEXTUAL SEIZURES OF INDIVIDUALS**

A. Searches of a Person Incident to Arrest

Let's begin with the rules regarding the search of the individual upon arrest. In *United States v. Robinson*,[1] the Supreme Court held that an officer may search the person of the individual incident to his arrest. In *Robinson*, an officer validly stopped an individual who was driving an automobile. Based upon adequate probable cause, the officer arrested the driver and proceeded to perform a search of the driver's person. During a patdown of the driver, the officer "felt an object in the left breast pocket of the heavy coat [the driver] was wearing." Unable to ascertain the identity of the object, the officer retrieved the object (which turned out to be a somewhat disfigured package of cigarettes). The officer then proceeded to open the package, whereupon he discovered illegal narcotics.

In upholding the search, the Court found that such searches incident to arrest are always reasonable within the meaning of the Fourth Amendment. No warrant is needed. No suspicion that evidence of crime will be found is required. No exigency must be demonstrated. The Court determined that "the fact of the lawful arrest" in and of itself is sufficient justification for these type of searches. The Court added that such searches are further rationalized by the need on the part of law enforcement to preserve evidence and to disarm the arrested individual.

Perhaps many of you believe that such a rule, at least at first blush, makes sense. One can easily envision situations where an individual might seek to discard evidence or endanger officer safety when confronted with the possibility of arrest. But this rule allows officers to perform a search even when the officer has no reason whatsoever to believe that the arrested individual poses a danger or possesses evidence of crime.

Whether or not you agree that *Robinson* was correctly decided, remember the *Katz* presumption about the unreasonableness of government searches in the absence of a warrant. The search incident to arrest rule — for good or bad — creates a giant crater in this presumption. Now, irrespective of whether any evidence exists to suggest that contraband might be found on an arrested individual, the government may constitutionally proceed with a search of that person.

B. Searches of a Home Incident to Arrest

What about searches that extend beyond the individual's person? Should officers, incident to an arrest, be permitted to search nearby locations as well? After all, just as

---

[1]414 U.S. 218 (1973).

searches of individuals implicate privacy interests, searches of nearby areas can implicate such interests as well.

In *Chimel v. California*,[2] the Supreme Court addressed this issue in the context of an arrest that occurred within a residence. There, officers arrived at the defendant's residence armed with an arrest warrant for burglary. After entering the residence, apparently with the consent of the defendant's wife, the officers waited for the defendant to return home from work. Upon his arrival, the officers informed the defendant that he was under arrest. After being denied permission by the defendant to search his home, the officers stated that they were going to conduct a search of the home anyway in light of his arrest. The officers, who did not have a search warrant, proceeded to search "the entire three-bedroom house, including the attic, the garage, and a small workshop." As part of their search, the officers, while "[i]n the master bedroom and sewing room, . . . directed the [defendant's] wife to open drawers and 'to physically move contents of the drawers from side to side so that [the officers] might view any items that would have come from [the] burglary.'"

The issue addressed by the Court was whether this particular search, which was performed without a warrant but incident to the defendant's arrest, was permissible under the Fourth Amendment. The Court answered this narrow question in the negative. In so holding, the Court recognized that searches of an individual incident to an arrest were justified in order to preserve evidence and ensure officer safety. Significantly, however, the Court added that these dual rationales also justified a search of the area in the arrestee's immediate vicinity. As stated by the Court:

> And the area into which an arrestee might reach in order to grab a weapon or evidentiary items must, of course, be governed by a like rule. A gun on a table or in a drawer in front of one who is arrested can be as dangerous to the arresting officer as one concealed in the clothing of the person arrested. There is ample justification, therefore, for a search of the arrestee's person and the area "within his immediate control" — construing that phrase to mean the area from within which he might gain possession of a weapon or destructible evidence.

While the Court held that the particular search performed in *Chimel* was excessive — in part, given that it extended throughout the entire house — the Court upheld, as a general matter, searches incident to an arrest of those areas within the immediate control of an arrested individual. Though the Court did not provide definitive contours of an "immediate control" area, it did place some limitations upon the scope of such searches. Specifically, the Court stated that the mere fact that an arrest occurred within a particular room did not entitle the officers to search "through all the desk drawers of other closed or concealed areas in that room itself." It added that, unless another exception to the warrant clause applies, searches of the type exemplified in *Chimel* require the authority of a search warrant. Thus, a *Chimel* "immediate control" area analysis necessitates a case-by-case factual review, and will require consideration of a host of personal and situational factors. The mobility of the suspect (e.g., age, health condition, etc.), the location of the arrest, the proximity of the areas and effects searched, as well as the number of individuals (including police officers) present at the scene of the search are among the factors that a court will consider when undertaking this review.

---

[2]395 U.S. 752 (1969).

C. Searches of an Automobile Incident to Arrest

Finally, let's examine the search incident issue in the context of an arrest of an individual riding in an automobile. Recently, the Supreme Court enunciated a new rule set that substantially transformed the traditional rules that have long governed this particular subset of the search incident to an arrest rule. However, before reviewing the new rules it is important to recount the old.

For many years, the search incident to arrest rule in the context of automobiles was governed by the case of *New York v. Belton*.[3] There, an officer traveling in a police vehicle stopped a car occupied by four individuals (one of whom was the defendant Roger Belton) that was traveling at an excessive speed. After an inquiry with the passengers revealed that none of the occupants owned the vehicle, and after having smelled marijuana and having observed within the vehicle an envelope with markings that, based upon the officer's experience, he associated with the drug, the four men were ordered by the officer to exit the car. The men were then placed under arrest for possession of narcotics. A subsequent search by the officer of the vehicle uncovered additional narcotics within the envelope as well as within a black leather jacket pocket in the area of the backseat. The jacket belonged to Belton.

The Court upheld the automobile search in this case. Noting the "recurring" nature of the factual scenario presented in *Belton* as well as the absence of a "workable definition" of the *Chimel* doctrine in the automotive search context, the Court made the following bright-line pronouncement:

> [W]e hold that when a policeman has made a lawful custodial arrest of the occupant of an automobile, he may, as a contemporaneous incident of that arrest, search the passenger compartment of that automobile.
>
> It follows from this conclusion that the police may also examine the contents of any containers found within the passenger compartment, for if the passenger compartment is within reach of the arrestee, so also will containers in it be within his reach. Such a container may, of course, be searched whether it is open or closed, since the justification for the search is not that the arrestee has no privacy interest in the container, but that the lawful custodial arrest justifies the infringement of any privacy interest the arrestee may have.

In sum, the Court held that when the police arrest an occupant of a motor vehicle the entire passenger compartment may be searched, including any open or closed containers. In other words, *Belton* deemed the passenger compartment of a car, including all of its containers, to be within the "immediate control" or grabbing area of the arrested passenger and therefore subject to an automatic search.

Remember, the officer in *Belton* initially encountered the passengers while they were within the car and the subsequent arrest occurred only after an order to exit had been commanded. But sometimes an officer's initial encounter with an individual comes after the occupant has departed the vehicle. If an arrest subsequently ensues in this situation, does the search incident to arrest rule justify a subsequent contemporaneous search of the vehicle?

In 2004, the Supreme Court in *Thornton v. United States*[4] answered this question in the affirmative. According to the majority, the ability of a recent occupant of a

---

[3]453 U.S. 454 (1981).
[4]541 U.S. 615 (2004).

motor vehicle to access evidence or weaponry within that vehicle is equally present irrespective of the passenger's location at the time of initial law enforcement contact. Each situation, according to the Court, presents "a highly volatile situation" that "presents identical concerns regarding officer safety and the destruction of evidence."

Nevertheless, the Court acknowledged that evidence within a vehicle will often be inaccessible to recent occupants. In fact, the Court declared that in the case before the justices it was "unlikely" that the defendant could have readily accessed the contraband that was recovered from within his vehicle. In *Thornton*, the defendant had already been handcuffed and placed in the police vehicle prior to the commencement of the search. However, the Court reasoned that the necessity for a bright-line rule justified the application of the *Belton* principle to this context.

Thus, pursuant to *Belton* and *Thornton*, officers were entitled to search the entire passenger compartment, including any containers found therein, incident to an arrest of an occupant (or recent occupant) of a vehicle. And this rule applied even in instances where it was "unlikely" that an arrested individual could access any of the items within the subject vehicle. Needless to say, there was an incongruity between the rule in *Chimel* and that in *Belton*. In *Chimel*, the Court held that an officer could search only the area in the immediate vicinity of the arrestee and that this area did not extend throughout an entire house. In fact, the Court found that it did not even entitle the officers, as a matter of right, to search the entire room where the arrest occurred. The reason for this limitation was because such areas of the home were not necessarily within an arrestee's grab area. It was a rule that, at least arguably, placed a meaningful limitation upon the government's search right. It was a limitation that recognized that, even in a home arrest situation, the Fourth Amendment limited how far the government could venture within such a sacred space. Yet, in *Belton*-type situations the government's search right had no comparable limitation. Officers possessed the right to search the entire passenger compartment of a vehicle, even in the absence of any realistic threat of evidence destruction or access to weaponry.

In 2009, the Supreme Court decided the case of *Arizona v. Gant*,[5] which discarded that aspect of *Belton* that authorized automatic passenger compartment searches incident to arrest. In *Gant*, the officers searched the defendant's vehicle (recovering cocaine in a jacket pocket on the backseat) after the defendant had been arrested, "handcuffed and locked in the back of a patrol car." The Court held that the Fourth Amendment prohibited an officer from searching the passenger compartment incident to arrest when the arrested occupant "has been secured and cannot access the interior of the vehicle." Instead, the Court held that a search of a passenger compartment incident to arrest was constitutionally permissible in only two instances: 1) when an unsecured arrestee is "within reaching distance of the passenger compartment at the time of the search"; and 2) when an officer reasonably concludes that "evidence relevant to the crime of arrest might be found in the vehicle."

In reaching this result, the Court declared that *Belton*'s bright-line pronouncement runs counter to the underlying rationale of *Chimel*. The Court noted that "in most cases" the vehicle's passenger compartment is not within the reach area of the arrested individual. The majority added in a footnote that "it will be the rare case in which an officer is unable to fully effectuate an arrest so that a real possibility of

[5]556 U.S. 332 (2009).

access to the arrestee's vehicle remains." In *Gant*, for example, the Court observed that there were five officers present compared to three arrestees, who, prior to the commencement of the search, had already been secured within patrol vehicles. In this instance, the Court found that the defendant "clearly was not within reaching distance of his car at the time of the search." Moreover, given that the defendant had been arrested for driving with a suspended license, the Court reasoned that an officer could not reasonably expect to find evidence related to that crime within the defendant's vehicle. For these reasons, the Court found that the performed search was unreasonable.

The Court also emphasized, among other things, that motorist privacy interest, though diminished, is nevertheless "important" and is deserving of greater protection than that traditionally afforded under *Belton*. The majority observed that "*Belton* searches authorize police officers to search not just the passenger compartment but every purse, briefcase, or other container within that space. A rule that gives police the power to conduct such a search whenever an individual is caught committing a traffic offense, when there is no basis for believing evidence of the offense might be found in the vehicle, creates a serious and recurring threat to the privacy of countless individuals."

F   A   Q

Q: Does the search incident to arrest rule apply when the occupant of the car is not arrested but is only issued a citation?

A: No. The Supreme Court addressed this issue in *Knowles v. Iowa*[6] where an officer conducted a search of a vehicle incident to an issuance of a citation. An Iowa statute authorized such searches incident to either an arrest or a citation for violations of traffic or motor vehicle equipment laws. According to the Supreme Court, the dual concerns that justified such searches incident to an arrest — evidence preservation and officer safety — are not sufficiently present in the context of a routine traffic citation. As stated by the Court, "In [*United States v.*] *Robinson,* we held that the authority to conduct a full field search as incident to an arrest was a 'bright-line rule,' which was based on the concern for officer safety and destruction or loss of evidence, but which did not depend in every case upon the existence of either concern. Here we are asked to extend that 'bright-line rule' to a situation where the concern for officer safety is *not present to the same extent* and the concern for destruction or loss of evidence is *not present at all*. We decline to do so" (emphasis added).

(1) Passenger Compartment — Contemporaneous Requirement

The search of the passenger compartment, however, must be performed contemporaneously with the arrest. While there is no time restriction affixed to this mandate, the ensuing search need not be performed immediately. In *Belton*, after the subjects were placed under arrest, the officer patted down the four passengers, split up the men into "separate areas of the Thruway," picked up the envelope within the vehicle, returned to the men to administer *Miranda* warnings, and then searched each

---

[6]525 U.S. 113 (1998).

individual prior to conducting a search of the passenger compartment. Despite the delay exhibited in *Belton*, as a general matter the longer the time interval between arrest and search the greater the risk a court will find the search to be insufficiently incident to the arrest to satisfy the exception.

F   A   Q

Q: Since the "passenger compartment" and any "container" found therein may be searched incident to an arrest, how then are the terms "passenger compartment" and "container" defined?

A: In regards to the passenger compartment, the *Belton* Court declared that this area "encompasses only the interior of the passenger compartment of an automobile and does not encompass the trunk." With the advent of hatchbacks and sport utility vehicles, where the integration of the trunk with the passenger area is relatively commonplace, many courts have found that the trunk along with the passenger area may properly be searched pursuant to *Belton*. With respect to containers, the Court stated that it is "any object capable of holding another object. It thus includes closed or open glove compartments, consoles, or other receptacles located anywhere within the passenger compartment, as well as luggage, boxes, bags, clothing, and the like."

D. Critique of the Search Incident to Arrest Rule

Given the various contexts in which the search incident to arrest rule is applicable, a comparative analysis of the doctrine is in order.

Let's begin this review with a hypothetical. Let's assume that an officer has probable cause to arrest an individual walking along a street but has no reason to believe that the suspect is either armed or has incriminating evidence on his person. In fact, let's assume that the officer believes with 100 percent certainty that the suspect possesses neither weapons nor evidence of crime. May the officer who performs an arrest conduct a warrantless search of the person anyway? Well, the answer to this question is yes. The Court in *Robinson* held that the authority to perform a search of a person incident to arrest is in no way dependent upon the likelihood that weapons or other contraband will be recovered pursuant to a search of that individual. In other words, such warrantless searches of a person incident to an arrest are *automatic* and are deemed to be reasonable within the meaning of the Fourth Amendment.

So if there is one word you should remember in relation to this rule in this context it is the word "automatic." The search incident rule allows officers to perform a free search of an individual. Whether an individual is arrested in a public space, within a house, or in an automobile, a free search of the individual may ensue. No warrant is required. No probable cause need be established. No suspicion of any kind is needed. It is a free automatic search. And this automatic right extends not only to a search of the person, but also to the grab area of the individual. However, if an automobile is involved, the automatic search rule regarding the grab area does not apply. Before a search of the passenger compartment can ensue, the arrested individual must be unsecured and within reaching distance of the passenger compartment or the officer must reasonably believe that evidence of the crime of arrest will be found within the vehicle.

Given that the search incident to arrest doctrine extends to places beyond an individual's physical body, this presents other related queries. First, how far (in terms of distance and areas and items searched) can such a search extend? As discussed previously, the search incident rule within a home does not allow officers to freely search the entire house or necessarily the entire room where the arrest occurred. It does not even entitle the officers to open all the drawers in a room. A case-by-case factual analysis is required. In the vehicle context, only the passenger compartment and containers found therein can be searched, assuming the requirements in *Gant* are satisfied.

One could certainly characterize the search incident rule as an end run around the plain text of the Fourth Amendment. After all, some might argue, the Supreme Court could have been more faithful to the letter of the Amendment—and preserved its evidence-gathering and safety rationales—by allowing officers to conduct searches incident to arrest only when a true exigency could be demonstrated. Thus, in the absence of an exigency there could be no search absent probable cause and the attainment of a warrant.

Think about this in the context of a container. Assume the police, during a valid search incident to arrest within a home or car, come across a closed container. The officers have no reason to believe that it poses a danger to the officer or that it contains evidence of crime. Rather than allowing officers to freely examine the contents of the container—which they are permitted to do under the current doctrine—the Supreme Court could have announced a rule requiring officers to secure a search warrant under such circumstances. Advocates of such a rule would argue that the current search incident rule goes too far. It is one thing, they might contend, to allow a free search of an area to protect against danger and evidence destruction. But it is another thing altogether to allow officers to search a closed container in the absence of any suspicion whatsoever that it either poses a danger or possesses incriminating material. They would argue that Fourth Amendment principles would be better respected if the warrant requirement were to apply under these circumstances.

As you consider the propriety of this rule, let's consider another hypothetical (with admittedly exaggerated facts). Assume an officer, armed with an arrest warrant for the theft of a loaf of bread, is walking a mere ten yards behind Suspect on a public street. After following Suspect at that distance for a mile, the officer purposefully waits until Suspect enters his home before attempting an arrest. After Suspect enters his home but before he closes the door, the officer enters the home and arrests Suspect. The officer, who had no suspicion whatsoever that evidence of crime or weapons would be located within the residence, then searches suspect's grab area within the home, opens several containers located within the area, and finds large quantities of illegal narcotics. Suspect is later charged with a more serious felony, possession with intent to distribute narcotics. Is this a valid search incident to arrest? May an officer purposefully wait until a suspect is inside his home before attempting an arrest?

The answer to this question is, once again, yes. There is no rule that requires an officer to effect an arrest when it is most convenient to the arrested person. The government enjoys wide latitude in regards to how it conducts an investigation, including when it decides to arrest and indict. And with respect to arrests, officers are permitted to take advantage of the edicts pronounced by the Supreme Court. The search incident to arrest rule allows officers to conduct searches of the vicinity immediately surrounding the arrested individual. If an officer can effectuate an arrest so as to conduct a free search in an otherwise constitutionally protected area, then the officer can strategically manipulate an arrest to achieve this objective.

The location and timing of an arrest are, therefore, subject to strategic manipulation. Are there any checks in place for this subjective exercise? The next section further explores this issue.

E. Pretextual Seizures of Individuals

Imagine a scenario where an officer, while driving in an unmarked patrol car, observes a vehicle with temporary license plates occupied by two young individuals. The officer also notices that while the vehicle is stopped at a traffic light (for an extended period of time) the driver is looking in the direction of the passenger's lap. Based upon the foregoing, the officer decides to survey the movements of the vehicle. After observing the vehicle turn right without signaling and travel at an excessive speed the officer decides to make a traffic stop. After effectuating the stop and approaching the driver the officer observes a substance that appears to be crack cocaine in the possession of the driver. The officer then places the occupants under arrest. They are later charged with various drug offenses.

This was the factual scenario that the Supreme Court encountered in *Whren v. United States*.[7] In *Whren*, the Court addressed "whether the temporary detention of a motorist who the police have probable cause to believe has committed a civil traffic violation is inconsistent with the Fourth Amendment's prohibition against unreasonable seizures unless a reasonable officer would have been motivated to stop the car by a desire to enforce the traffic laws."

The Court found that the legitimacy of an individual's seizure is not dependent upon the subjective intentions of the officer. Instead, the Court held that so long as the officer has an objectively reasonable basis to effectuate a stop then the seizure is lawful. In other words, as long as the law authorized the officer to effectuate a traffic stop the officer is within his right to make such a stop, irrespective of the officer's subjective intentions at the time of the seizure.

It is, therefore, of no consequence that an officer, suspicious of the intentions of a motorist, awaits the commission of a traffic offense in order to effectuate a stop and conduct an investigation for a wholly unrelated offense. The issue in *Whren* presented a number of interesting considerations. For example, should it make a difference that there are a plethora of traffic regulations? After all, the sheer volume of traffic laws would, arguably at least, allow officers to effectuate a traffic stop on virtually any driver. Given this reality, what about the problem of selective enforcement of traffic laws on the basis of race or ethnicity? Would officers, if allowed to effectuate stops for any technical violation of the traffic laws, be tacitly encouraged to selectively enforce those laws?

These considerations did not persuade the Court. In essence, the Court reasoned that a violation of the law is just that — a violation of the law that officers are authorized to enforce. The Court noted that it was "aware of no principle that would allow us to decide at what point a code of law becomes so expansive and so commonly violated that infraction itself can no longer be the ordinary measure of the lawfulness of enforcement." Regarding the selective enforcement concern, the Court acknowledged that selective enforcement of the nation's laws on the basis of race is constitutionally prohibited. However, the Court indicated that the basis for a selective

---

[7]517 U.S. 806 (1996).

S i d e b a r

EQUAL PROTECTION CLAIMS

You should not be surprised if your Criminal Procedure class devotes little, if any, time to the equal protection issue that underlies a claim of selective enforcement. This topic is typically addressed in your Criminal Procedure Adjudication (Criminal Procedure II) course. In short, however, it is exceedingly difficult for claimants to prove an equal protection violation on account of the procedural hurdles a claimant must clear. A claim of selective enforcement requires two showings: 1) proof that the claimant was disparately treated; and 2) proof that his prosecution was motivated by an improper reason. To satisfy these prongs, a claimant typically needs discovery from the prosecution, who typically possess the identification information relevant to these queries. To obtain this information from the prosecution, however, the claimant must make a "credible" showing of the first prong. This is quite difficult for claimants to do given that the information they need to make a "credible" showing is the very information that is possessed by the government.

enforcement objection does not lie in the Fourth Amendment, but rather the Equal Protection Clause.

One final consideration for you to ponder. In *Atwater v. City of Lago Vista* (discussed in Chapter 6), the Supreme Court upheld the arrest of an individual for a misdemeanor seatbelt violation. Given an officer's right to enforce any infraction of the traffic laws, no matter how trivial or infrequently enforced, do *Whren* and *Atwater* encourage legislatures to enact laws that authorize arrests for comparatively minor traffic offenses?

SUMMARY

■ An officer may search a person incident to a valid arrest.

■ An officer may also search the immediate area surrounding an individual incident to an arrest. If an arrest occurs within a home, the determination of the suspect's grab area generally involves a factual review of several factors.

■ An officer also has the right to open any containers that are found either on the arrested individual's person or in the adjacent areas that are searched.

■ In the automobile arrest context, an officer may search the passenger compartment (and any containers found therein) only if the arrestee is unsecured and the passenger compartment is within his reach or if the officer reasonably believes that evidence related to the crime of arrest will be found within the vehicle.

■ Officers may effectuate a traffic stop so long as there is an objectively reasonable basis for the stop. Therefore, an officer's subjective intentions have no bearing on whether a traffic stop was reasonable under the Fourth Amendment.

CONNECTIONS

Relationship to the Automobile Exception (Chapter 8)

Pursuant to *Arizona v. Gant*, the government may be authorized to search the passenger compartment of a vehicle incident to an arrest of an automobile's occupant. However, this right does not extend to the trunk of a vehicle. The automobile exception discussed in Chapter 8 allows an officer to search any areas of the vehicle, including the trunk, provided that probable cause exists to believe that evidence of crime might be found in that location.

Relationship to the Plain View Doctrine (Chapter 9)

An officer who from a lawful vantage point observes evidence of criminal activity in plain view may seize that evidence provided the officer has lawful access to the item and the item's incriminating nature is immediately apparent. Thus, the plain view doctrine might work in conjunction with the search incident to arrest doctrine (as well as other search justifications) to justify seizure of evidence found by an officer when conducting a search incident to arrest.

Relationship to Fourth Amendment Violations and Their Associated Remedies (Chapter 15)

If the government performs a search incident to arrest but obtains evidence in a manner not authorized pursuant to the rule, the government risks the suppression of the evidence pursuant to the exclusionary rule.

Automobile Exception

8

Chapter 7 addressed the search incident to arrest exception to the warrant requirement. On the one hand, this exception is somewhat restrictive. For

example, the exception allows for a search only of the arrestee's immediate grab area. A search that strays beyond this limited area can be constitutionally justified only pursuant to some alternative search theory. Moreover, there are certain temporal restrictions.

On the other hand, it can be forcibly argued that the search incident to arrest exception is an expansive doctrine. After all, a search performed incident to arrest (excluding vehicular searches) is a free search that can be performed irrespective of any suspicion whatsoever that incriminating evidence or weaponry will be uncovered.

When it comes to the automobile exception you will be hard pressed to find anyone who can persuasively suggest that this exception to the warrant requirement is restrictive in any meaningful way. Pursuant to this exception officers possess broad authority to perform warrantless searches of automobiles, including open and closed containers found therein, even when ample time exists to obtain a warrant. In addition, this exception, unlike the search incident to arrest doctrine, can potentially justify the search of an entire automobile. The following section will detail the general rules attendant to this exception and describe the rule's underlying rationales. Thereafter, this chapter will explore the historical development of this jurisprudence. It will then conclude with a discussion of the law relevant to the inventory searches of motor vehicles and individuals.

A. Essential Elements and Application

It is worth reiterating the admonition found in *Katz* that searches performed in the absence of a warrant are presumptively unreasonable. When it comes to the searches of automobiles, however, I suspect that the Supreme Court might one day proclaim, "Searches of an automobile performed with a warrant are presumptively bizarre!" For good or bad, officers enjoy wide latitude to perform warrantless vehicular searches and much of that authority stems from the automobile exception.

This exception authorizes a warrantless search of an automobile in situations where there is probable cause to believe that evidence of a crime will be found therein. There are some minor limitations upon this authority, but this is the general rule. The rationale for the rule is twofold. First, given the mobility of cars it is frequently impractical for officers to secure a warrant prior to performing a search of a vehicle. This rationale seems fairly plausible. By the time an officer has obtained a warrant to search a vehicle for contraband, often the car will have relocated.

Second, the Court has reasoned that individuals have a lesser expectation of privacy in their vehicles than they do in their homes. The Court has observed that automobiles are subject to substantial government regulation, are driven in public view, and, in the Court's view at least, are seldom the repository for effects intended to be kept private. The same is not true for homes, which have been afforded heightened privacy protections. A search of a home generally requires a search or arrest warrant prior to entry.

Finally, during the course of an automobile search, it is not uncommon for officers to come across effects such as luggage, purses, and other containers. Do officers need a warrant prior to searching these effects? The answer is generally no. The Supreme Court has held that officers may conduct a warrantless search of containers found within a vehicle during the course of an automobile exception search.

These are the general rules and they may be easy to remember in the abstract. However, to truly comprehend the scope of the rule it is essential to understand not only the rule's historical evolution but also the various contexts in which the rule applies. The next section will address these subjects.

B. Historical and Contextual Application

Rather than engage in a mechanistic recitation of the rule's jurisprudential evolution, this chapter will present this historical background through five hypothetical situations. These factual presentments — which build upon one another — not only will teach the rule's historical development but will also provide important contextual applications and demonstrate the interrelationships between this rule and other concepts previously discussed. Note that the first two hypotheticals do not involve vehicular searches. However, they provide a contextual framework for truly comprehending and appreciating the automobile exception doctrine.

(1) First Hypothetical

Suppose Suspect recently departed a hardware store and proceeds to walk along a public street carrying a closed container. Suspect then approaches his residence, opens the front door, and walks inside.

If the police have probable cause to believe that within the closed container are various tools stolen from the aforementioned hardware store, may the police enter Suspect's home and perform a warrantless search of the container? Absent consent or a demonstrable exigency, the police will not be permitted to enter Suspect's residence without either an arrest or a search warrant. Suspect has a reasonable expectation of privacy not only in his house but also in the effects within his home and the government may not infringe upon these rights, in the circumstances presented, unless a judicially approved warrant is obtained. Of course, if the police are validly within the home then a seizure and search of the container might be constitutionally permissible. If, for example, the police had an arrest warrant and the container was on Suspect's person or within his grab area, then the search incident to arrest doctrine would justify a search of the container. However, absent a qualifying justification, the officers in the presented hypothetical are without authority to perform a warrantless search.

Now consider the next hypothetical, which builds upon this first factual scenario.

(2) Second Hypothetical

Now let's assume Suspect departs from his residence with the closed container in hand. Assume further that the police do not want to arrest Suspect at this time. If the police approach Suspect as he walks along a public street, may the police, having probable cause to believe the container contains stolen tools, seize and search the container?

Given the Fourth Amendment's protection against unreasonable searches and seizures of our effects, perhaps the police would need to obtain a warrant. In this instance, however, that statement is only partially true. Yes, the container is an effect within the definition of the Fourth Amendment. However, the mobility of the container in this second hypothetical would certainly create an exigency authorizing a warrantless seizure. This makes sense. By the time the officers obtained a search warrant the container would likely have been transported to a different location. Though a warrantless seizure would certainly be justified, an actual search of the container would probably require a search warrant. In most instances — including the facts presented in this tool theft hypothetical — the exigent circumstances dissipated with the container's seizure. Absent demonstration of another exigency (e.g., suspicion of explosives within the container), the Fourth Amendment would require that the police secure a search warrant prior to searching the container.

The next hypothetical involves our same Suspect but now with an automobile.

(3) Third Hypothetical

For this hypothetical assume that rather than approaching Suspect while he is walking along the street, the police observe Suspect approach his vehicle and place the closed container in the car's trunk. Again, assume that the police wish to refrain from arresting Suspect at this time.

May the police seize and search the container under this scenario? Well, the answer is yes regarding the seizure and probably so regarding the search. You may be saying to yourself, "Ok. I understand why the police may seize the container. After all, it is just as mobile as in the second hypothetical. But why is it likely that the police may perform a warrantless search? Is not a container still an effect? By seizing the container has not the exigency ended, thus obviating the need to perform a warrantless search?"

The mobility of the container in the third hypothetical would certainly entitle the police to perform a warrantless seizure. It is easy to see how impractical it would be to require the police to obtain a warrant for a container that is in transit.

Let's now engage in a preliminary discussion of the search question. It is true that a closed container, even after its placement in a vehicle, is still an effect. And a very compelling argument can be made that any exigency that may have attached to the container typically terminates upon its seizure. Nevertheless, the Supreme Court has held that in most instances the police may perform a warrantless search of such containers found in a car simply due to the fact of its placement therein. Remember this general rule, for it is the principle that unquestionably governs the overwhelming majority of vehicle search cases.

However, before exploring further the niceties of the principle introduced by this third hypothetical it is important to pause for a moment and review some background material relevant to the evolution of this doctrine. The next two sections will do just that and review several cases decided by the Supreme Court that are pertinent to this discussion and that will likely be discussed in your Criminal Procedure class. It is certainly important that you become familiar with these cases for they provide the central rationales underlying the automobile exception and help provide context to the doctrine's current application. Thereafter, the promised exploration of the doctrine's subtleties introduced in the third hypothetical will be examined, answered, and reviewed in this chapter's presentation of the fourth and fifth hypothetical scenarios.

(a) Vehicular Mobility as a Primary Rationale

The mobility of an automobile is what the Supreme Court originally relied upon when, in 1925, it first announced the automobile exception to the warrant requirement. In *Carroll v. United States*,[1] the Court held that officers who had probable cause to stop a vehicle that had been transporting illegal liquor were permitted to perform a warrantless seizure and search of that vehicle for contraband. In *Carroll*, the probable cause that existed extended only with respect to a search of the automobile. It did not exist (prior to the search) to arrest of its occupants. As noted by the Court, "[T]he facts and circumstances within [the officers'] knowledge and of which they had reasonably trustworthy information were sufficient in themselves to

---

[1] 267 U.S. 132 (1925).

warrant a man of reasonable caution in the belief that intoxicating liquor was being transported in the automobile which they stopped and searched."

Although, prior to the search, the officers did not have probable cause to perform an arrest, the Court nevertheless justified not only the warrantless seizure of the effect in this case — the automobile — but also the ensuing search of that effect. In so holding, the Court relied upon the vehicle's mobility as an underlying justification. The Court noted that in contrast to houses, automobiles are capable of swift relocation. At first glance the sufficiency of the mobility rationale might appear to be rather clear. After all, automobiles are mobile and one can easily imagine the difficulty of imposing a warrant requirement to seize and search moving targets. However, this rationale ultimately proved to be an inadequate and incomplete explanation. Many issues remained inadequately addressed.

For example, sometimes government searches are performed upon vehicles that are not readily mobile. Imagine an officer who first encounters an automobile that has been parked at a particular location. Or perhaps an officer stops a traveling vehicle, but prior to the search the automobile has been rendered immobile or has been otherwise secured by the police. Should the automobile exception be applicable in such instances?

(b) The Transition to a Reduced Expectation of Privacy Rationale: *Chambers v. Maroney* and *Coolidge v. New Hampshire*

In 1970 and 1971, the Court decided two cases — *Chambers v. Maroney*[2] and *Coolidge v. New Hampshire*,[3] respectively — that presented such fact patterns. In *Chambers*, the Court upheld a warrantless search of a vehicle despite the fact that prior to the search its occupants had been arrested and placed in police custody and the search of the vehicle took place at the police station. Clinging to the mobility rationale, the Court reasoned that there was little difference between conducting a warrantless search at the scene of the arrest and performing it at the police station. As the Court declared, "[T]he blue station wagon could have been searched on the spot when it was stopped since there was probable cause to search and it was a fleeting target for a search. The probable cause factor still obtained at the station house and so did the mobility of the car. . . ."

The following year the Court decided *Coolidge*, which involved a police search of a vehicle after it had been seized pursuant to a search warrant from the defendant's driveway and towed to a police station. Specifically, a warrant authorizing the vehicle's seizure was signed on February 19, 1964, and the car was subsequently searched on February 21 and twice the following year. Finding the automobile exception to the warrant requirement inapplicable to the facts presented in *Coolidge*, four members of the Court's plurality — Justices Stewart, Brennan, Marshall, and Douglas — focused much of their attention upon the issue of mobility. They expressed an utter disbelief that the automobile at issue in *Coolidge* could be deemed mobile within the meaning of the Fourth Amendment.

> When the police arrived at the Coolidge house to arrest him, two officers were sent to guard the back door while the main party approached from the front. Coolidge was arrested inside the house, without resistance of any kind on his part, after he had

[2]399 U.S. 42 (1970).
[3]403 U.S. 443 (1971).

voluntarily admitted the officers at both front and back doors. There was no way in which he could conceivably have gained access to the automobile after the police arrived on his property. When Coolidge had been taken away, the police informed Mrs. Coolidge, the only other adult occupant of the house, that she and her baby had to spend the night elsewhere and that she could not use either of the Coolidge cars. Two police officers then drove her in a police car to the house of a relative in another town, and they stayed with her there until around midnight, long after the police had had the Pontiac towed to the station house. The Coolidge premises were guarded throughout the night by two policemen. . . .

In short, by no possible stretch of the legal imagination can this be made into a case where "it is not practicable to secure a warrant" (citation omitted), and the "automobile exception," despite its label, is simply irrelevant.

Chambers and *Coolidge* involved searches of vehicles at a police station. There was no plausible argument in either instance that the vehicle was readily movable. Yet the Court reached divergent results. Given the difficulty of reconciling *Chambers* and *Coolidge*, the Court inevitably had to decide upon an interpretive approach to resolving cases involving searches of arguably immobile vehicles. It could follow a more narrow constructive philosophy, such as that followed in *Coolidge*, and limit application of the automobile exception to instances involving true exigencies. Or it could adopt a more flexible standard, such as that exhibited in *Chambers*.

Ultimately, the more flexible interpretive model prevailed. Accordingly, a healthy body of Supreme Court precedent exists affirming the government's right to conduct warrantless searches of seemingly immobile vehicles. But along with this approach came the reliance by the Court upon another entirely separate justification for warrantless automobile searches — the reduced expectation of privacy that individuals have in their automobiles. The Supreme Court in *South Dakota v. Opperman*[4] explained it this way:

> Automobiles, unlike homes, are subjected to pervasive and continuing governmental regulation and controls, including periodic inspection and licensing requirements. As an everyday occurrence, police stop and examine vehicles when license plates or inspection stickers have expired, or if other violations, such as exhaust fumes or excessive noise, are noted, or if headlights or other safety equipment are not in proper working order.
>
> The expectation of privacy as to automobiles is further diminished by the obviously public nature of automobile travel.

F   A   Q

Q: How are motor homes viewed under the Fourth Amendment?

A: The Court in *California v. Carney*[5] addressed this question. There, federal agents observed the defendant accompany a youth to a motor home parked in a lot in downtown San Diego. After the youth left the motor home, the agents approached him. They were told that the defendant had provided him with marijuana in exchange for "sexual contact." The agents and the youth then returned to the motor home. Shortly thereafter, the agents conducted a

---

[4]428 U.S. 364 (1976).
[5]471 U.S. 386 (1985).

warrantless search of the motor home where they found marijuana among other incriminating evidentiary materials.

The Court found that the search was justified pursuant to the automobile exception. *Carney* set forth two factors that a court should consider when assessing whether a motor home should be viewed as an automobile or a home for Fourth Amendment purposes. First, whether the vehicle was observed being driven on a highway. If so, then the motor home resembles an automobile more than it resembles a home. Second, whether the motor home "is readily capable of such use and is found stationary in a place not regularly used for residential purposes — temporary or otherwise. . . ." Thus, a motor home parked in a shopping center parking lot would likely be treated differently under the Constitution than a motor home sitting on blocks in an established motor home residential park.

The significance of the reduced expectation of privacy rationale for automobiles should not be understated. This additional rationale facilitated the expansion of the automobile exception doctrine to encompass not only searches of arguably immobile automobiles but also of containers found therein. With this in mind, consider the fourth and fifth hypotheticals presented next.

(4) Fourth Hypothetical

Let's return to the fact pattern presented in the third hypothetical. As you may recall, Suspect was observed by the police walking along a street before placing a closed container in the trunk of a vehicle. Among the questions presented was whether a warrantless search of the container could be performed. The answer was "probably so." At this point I want to append ever so slightly the following facts to the third hypothetical. I would like you to assume that the search of the container occurs just moments after Suspect places the container in the trunk and before the engine is started.

(a) *United States v. Chadwick*

The facts in this fourth hypothetical are analogous to those presented in *United States v. Chadwick.*[6] *Chadwick* involved a search of a footlocker that officers had probable cause to believe contained narcotics prior to its placement by three individuals into the trunk of a parked vehicle at a railroad station. Prior to the initiation of the vehicle's engine, the footlocker was seized by the officers and all relevant suspects were arrested. A warrantless search of the footlocker conducted approximately 90 minutes later uncovered marijuana. The Court struck down the warrantless search, finding that the diminished expectation of privacy rationale that attached to vehicle searches did not similarly attach to closed containers, such as the footlocker. In contrast to automobiles, the Court noted that luggage contents are shielded from public view, that luggage is not subject to recurrent inspections, and that luggage ordinarily contains an individual's personal items. Accordingly, the Court concluded that the expectation of privacy that attaches to personal luggage is "substantially greater than in an automobile."

---

[6]433 U.S. 1 (1977).

The *Chadwick* Court further found that the warrantless opening of the luggage could not be justified by an exigency. Once the footlocker had been seized and safely secured by the investigating agents,[7] the Court found that the officers had ample opportunity to secure a search warrant given the absence of any possibility of removal or tampering with "the footlocker or its contents."

Thus, pursuant to *Chadwick*, a closed container is not necessarily subject to a warrantless search simply because the effect is, or recently has been, mobile. Therefore, an individual in possession of a closed container within an automobile does not necessarily have a reduced expectation of privacy in that effect. You may have noticed the use of the term "necessarily" in the last two sentences. What the *Chadwick* Court did not address was the applicability of the automobile exception to the facts presented in that case. The government did not present this as a justifying theory. While *Chadwick* is still good law, it is hardly inconceivable that the Court might ultimately reach a different result should this question be revisited.

In the second hypothetical, Suspect emerged from his home and walked along a public street with a closed container that the officers had probable cause to believe contained contraband. *Chadwick* tells us that though the container was mobile and was subject to a warrantless seizure, it could not be searched in the absence of a warrant. In the fourth hypothetical, Suspect walked with the closed container along a public street and placed it in the trunk of a car where it was seized prior to the initiation of the engine. *Chadwick* teaches that in such situations the heightened protections afforded by the Fourth Amendment to effects, such as closed containers, still attach. Despite the fact that the container had been placed within an automobile — where a reduced privacy expectation typically attaches — the effect found within that vehicle did not suffer the same fate.

Consider now the fifth hypothetical.

(5) Fifth Hypothetical

Assume now that after Suspect places the closed container in the trunk Suspect drives the vehicle a quarter mile. Suspect is then stopped by the police and a warrantless search of the container ensues moments thereafter. Does this minor alteration of the facts — the movement of the motor vehicle — alter the outcome of the fourth hypothetical? According to the Supreme Court it does.

(a) *California v. Acevedo*

California v. Acevedo[8] involved the warrantless search of a paper bag recovered from the trunk of an automobile. Prior to its placement in the trunk and its subsequent recovery, officers had probable cause to believe that the bag contained contraband. The bag was seized from the trunk by the police after the vehicle had been stopped. In upholding the search, the Court stated:

> We . . . interpret *Carroll* as providing one rule to govern all automobile searches. The police may search an automobile *and the containers within it* where they have probable cause to believe contraband or evidence is contained (emphasis added).

---

[7]The Court noted that after the agents had seized the footlocker at the station, it was transported to a federal building under the government's "exclusive control."
[8]500 U.S. 565 (1991).

Notice the italicized language. The heightened expectation of privacy that attaches to a container when it is within a home (first hypothetical), outside a home in public space (second hypothetical), or even within an automobile with the ignition off (fourth hypothetical) suddenly yields to the reduced expectation of privacy that attaches to moving vehicles. There is another important fact here that underscores the expanse of the automobile exception doctrine. In *Acevedo* and *Chadwick* the effects at the time of their seizure were in the actual possession of the police. They were under complete police control. No demonstrable exigency — mobility or otherwise — existed that necessitated a warrantless intrusion of those effects.

Notice the expanse of this exception. Not only may officers search those places in a vehicle — mobile or immobile — where probable cause exists to believe evidence of crime might be found, but officers may also seize and search any containers — open or closed — located within the vehicle. Remember *Chadwick*'s declaration that the privacy interest "in personal luggage [is] substantially greater than in an automobile"? Well, that no longer applies once those items are placed within an automobile in transit. Whether in a locked glove compartment, in the passenger compartment, or in the trunk, the police may now seize and search these items in the absence of a warrant. And the police may search these items irrespective of whether probable cause existed to search the containers prior to their placement in the vehicle.

Sidebar

HISTORICAL FOOTNOTE: SUPREME COURT DOCTRINE PRIOR TO *ACEVEDO*

Prior to *Acevedo* (decided in 1991), Supreme Court jurisprudence distinguished two sets of cases: 1) where probable cause to search a container existed prior to its placement in a vehicle; and 2) where probable cause existed to search a vehicle but not a particular container found therein. Again, *Acevedo* dispenses with this distinction.

An example of number 1 is exemplified in *Arkansas v. Sanders*.[9] There, the Supreme Court held that a warrantless government search of luggage found within a vehicle was unconstitutional. The police seized luggage from the trunk of a taxicab after the cab had been stopped and its passengers had been arrested. The Court reasoned that the expectation of privacy attendant to a container, such as the luggage in *Sanders*, was not diminished simply due to the fact that the luggage was discovered within a moving automobile. In his concurrence, Chief Justice Burger wrote, "Here, as in *Chadwick*, it was the *luggage* being transported by respondent at the time of the arrest, not the automobile in which it was being carried, that was the suspected locus of the contraband. The relationship between the automobile and the contraband was purely coincidental, as in *Chadwick*."

United States v. Ross[10] is an example of number 2. *Ross* involved a warrantless search of an automobile in which probable cause existed to believe it contained contraband. After the vehicle had been stopped and the driver arrested, a warrantless search ensued during which the officers opened a paper bag found in the trunk that contained heroin.

In upholding the warrantless search, the Court distinguished this case from *Chadwick* and *Sanders* because "in this case police officers had probable cause to search respondent's entire vehicle." The Court explained that "nice distinctions between closets, drawers, and containers, in the case of a home, or between glove compartments, upholstered seats, trunks, and wrapped packages, in the case of a vehicle, must give way to the interest in the prompt and efficient completion of the task at hand."

---

[9]442 U.S. 753 (1979).
[10]456 U.S. 798 (1982).

C. Searches of Passenger's Effects

The Fourth Amendment protects the people against unreasonable searches and seizures. With this in mind, imagine the following situation. Driver and Passengers A, B, and C are traveling in a vehicle. After a lawful stop of the vehicle by the police, only Driver is arrested (Passengers A, B, and C are not suspected of criminal activity and are, therefore, not arrested). Subsequent to Driver's arrest, the police conduct a search (assume the search is justified pursuant to either the automobile or the search incident to arrest exceptions to the warrant requirement). However, during the search the officers encounter suitcases belonging to Passengers A, B, and C. May the officers search the suitcases in the absence of a warrant?

The Supreme Court addressed this issue in *Wyoming v. Houghton*.[11] There, during a traffic stop an officer observed a hypodermic syringe on the driver's person. After this observation and the driver's admission to using illegal narcotics, the officer conducted a warrantless search of the passenger compartment. During the search, the officer discovered a purse that purportedly belonged to a passenger within the vehicle. A search of the purse uncovered drug paraphernalia. The passenger was charged with possession of a controlled substance.

Notice that probable cause to search the vehicle for contraband existed given the officer's observations and the driver's verbal statements. Hence, the automobile exception plainly comes into play. In fact, this point was conceded before the U.S. Supreme Court. However, the Wyoming Supreme Court deemed the search to be unconstitutional. In reaching this conclusion, the court reasoned that the officer was aware or should have been aware of the lack of any possessory or ownership interest in the purse on the part of the driver, and that probable cause did not exist to believe that evidence of criminal activity would be found therein.

The U.S. Supreme Court, however, disagreed with this analysis. The Court cited *Ross* and *Acevedo* for the principle that where probable cause exists to search a vehicle, it authorizes the search not only of the vehicle but its contents as well. This includes *"all* containers within a car, without qualification as to ownership." The Court added that a warrantless search of the passenger's belongings is permissible since her items were "'in' the car, and the officer has probable cause to search for contraband *in* the car."

The Court added that the privacy interests of drivers and passengers alike are reduced in regards to their property within a vehicle. The Court also noted that a contrary rule — "[a] 'passenger property' rule" — would impair effective law enforcement. The majority stated that such a rule "would dramatically reduce the ability to find and seize contraband and evidence of crime," given the mobility of vehicles as well as the interests of passengers to conceal evidence of crime.

D. Inventory Searches of Automobiles and Individuals

Though administrative in nature, the inventory search rationale has a meaningful place in criminal investigations. Unlike most, if not all, other types of "special needs"

---

[11]526 U.S. 295 (1999).

and administrative searches (see Chapter 14), the inventory search is far more encompassing. It is not directed solely at students, or those who cross the border, or those who apply for certain jobs, or those who are stopped at checkpoints. Rather, its application sweeps broadly, with the *potential* to impact virtually every criminal investigation and prosecution.

It is not uncommon for the inventory search doctrine to find application in the context of automobile searches. For example, assume that an officer effectuates a traffic stop, arrests the driver, and subsequently searches the car pursuant to either the search incident to arrest or automobile exceptions to the warrant requirement. If it is subsequently determined that the subject search is problematic, the admissibility of the evidence found could conceivably rest upon whether the evidence would have been inevitably retrieved pursuant to an inventory search. Or perhaps the officer simply encounters a disabled vehicle on the side of a road. In such circumstances, it may be necessary for the automobile to be towed to the police station or some other alternate location. When this occurs, the Supreme Court has held that as part of its "caretaking" duties, the government may—without a warrant or any level of suspicion—inventory the contents of the entire vehicle. Provided the police department has established departmental regulations authorizing such a broad sweep, the government will be permitted to search and seize virtually all the contents contained within the towed vehicle.

This caretaking function was first established by the Court in *Cady v. Dombrowski.*[12] There, the police encountered a disabled vehicle that had been involved in an accident. The vehicle was later towed to a private garage where a warrantless search by the police uncovered evidence linking the defendant to a murder. Declaring that the government's conduct was reasonable under the Fourth Amendment, the Court found that the search at issue was a "type of caretaking 'search.'" The Court explained that the officers "reasonably believed" that a revolver was in the vehicle[13] and that "concern for the safety of the general public . . . might be endangered if an intruder removed a revolver from the trunk of the vehicle." The Court also observed that the search was conducted pursuant to standard procedures of the police department.

As you may have noticed, the Court cited the officers' reasonable belief that a weapon was within the vehicle prior to the search. However, suspicion that evidence of a crime will be found is not a prerequisite to a valid inventory search. Consider *South Dakota v. Opperman.* There, the police towed a vehicle on account of overtime parking tickets. Following established police procedure, an inventory search of the vehicle was performed, which revealed the presence of marijuana found within the glove compartment.

In upholding the search, the Court referred to the three "caretaking" rationales that underlie the performance of inventory searches: securing of the owner's personal belongings, safeguarding the police from claims of lost or stolen property, and protecting the police from potential danger. The Court also observed that the search was prompted by the officer's plain view observation of personal items within the vehicle, that there was no indication that the inventory search was a pretext for a

---

[12]413 U.S. 433 (1973).
[13]This reasonable belief was not based upon officer suspicion that the driver had committed a murder but due to the driver's assertion that he was a Chicago police officer and the investigating officer's understanding that such officers were required to possess a service revolver.

criminal search, and that the owner of the vehicle "was not present to make other arrangements for the safekeeping of his belongings."

The observation in *Opperman* regarding the inability of the vehicle owner to make alternative arrangements for his possessions was discounted in *Colorado v. Bertine*.[14] There, the Court upheld the inventory search of a vehicle that produced evidence associated with illegal narcotics possession and distribution. In discarding the Colorado Supreme Court's finding that the search was unconstitutional given that the defendant "could have been offered the opportunity to make other arrangements for the safekeeping of his property," the Court declared that the reasonableness of a challenged search is not dependent upon a finding that the pathway chosen by the government was the least intrusive. Thus, the availability of "equally reasonable" procedural alternatives will not defeat governmental inventory regulations that are otherwise reasonable.

The Court also noted that the police performed the inventory search pursuant to standardized criteria. Such criteria, according to the Court, appropriately limited the discretion that police could exercise during such searches. This statement reflects a principle in the context of inventory searches that remains critically important to this day. Before an inventory search can be upheld, it must be found that it was performed in compliance with the policies established by the police department. If an inventory search exceeds these boundaries then the evidence discovered is subject to suppression.

F A Q

Q: Does the inventory search doctrine extend to the search of an individual?

A: Yes. In *Illinois v. Lafayette*,[16] the Supreme Court addressed whether the Fourth Amendment permits a warrantless search of the personal effects of an arrested individual who is taken to the police station for booking. Answering in the affirmative, the Court found that police searches of "container[s] or article[s]" found on a person are reasonable when performed as part of a "routine procedure incident to incarcerating an arrested person" and "in accordance with established inventory procedures."

[14]479 U.S. 367 (1987).
[16]462 U.S. 640 (1983).

SUMMARY

■ The automobile exception authorizes the warrantless search of those areas within an automobile where probable cause exists to believe that evidence of crime might be found.

■ The mobility of an automobile and the reduced expectation of privacy attendant to such vehicles (as opposed to homes) are rationales that underlie the rule.

■ The automobile exception also authorizes the warrantless search of open and closed containers found within the vehicle. However, if the container was seized from a stationary vehicle prior to any actual movement, the automobile exception will likely not justify the warrantless search of that item.

■ An officer may search all containers found within the vehicle irrespective of whether the searched item is the property of an occupant who is not under suspicion of any wrongdoing.

■ The Fourth Amendment sometimes affords motor homes the heightened protections afforded houses, and at other times equates such homes with automobiles. A court will consider the vehicle's location and its ready capability for use on the highways as factors when making this assessment.

■ Though the automobile exception is quite expansive, it is arguably limited in that officers may not search those areas where probable cause does not justify an intrusion. However, Chapter 10, which addresses consensual searches, can grant officers authority to engage in searches that extend beyond the limits otherwise afforded by probable cause.

■ The police may perform an inventory search of a vehicle and of an arrested individual at the police station in order to satisfy its caretaking responsibilities. Examination of the law enforcement agency's policies regarding the permissible scope of the inventory search is a central inquiry when assessing the propriety of such searches.

CONNECTIONS

Relationship to Searches and the Reasonableness Inquiry (Chapter 3)

The *Katz* case established the reasonable expectation of privacy test. In the automobile context, the Supreme Court has declared that individuals have a reduced expectation of privacy.

Relationship to Searches, Seizures, and the Warrant Clause (Chapter 4) and Executing the Warrant (Chapter 5)

A warrant is excused in the automobile context due not only to an automobile's mobility but also to the lesser expectation of privacy that individuals have in their vehicles.

Relationship to Searches Incident to Arrest (Chapter 7)

The automobile exception potentially authorizes a warrantless search of the entire vehicle. By contrast, the search incident to arrest doctrine authorizes a search of only the passenger compartment.

Relationship to *Terry* Stops and Frisks — Contextual Applications and Derivative Lessons (Chapter 12)

In contrast to the more expansive search that is authorized pursuant to the automobile exception, a *Terry* frisk of a vehicle is much more limited. The Supreme Court has declared that an officer may search the passenger compartment of a vehicle pursuant to *Terry* if the officer has a reasonable belief that a suspect is dangerous and that he may gain immediate access to weapons. The officer may only search those areas of the passenger compartment where a weapon might be stored.

Relationship to Fourth Amendment Violations and Their Associated Remedies (Chapter 15)

Like any other government search performed during a criminal investigation, the seizure of evidence that exceeds the boundaries of the automobile exception justification is subject to suppression pursuant to the exclusionary rule.

Plain View Doctrine

9

This chapter introduces you to the plain view doctrine. When studying the various doctrines that you will encounter in your Criminal Procedure studies, it is important to appreciate the potential interrelationships that exist between many of the principles. It is hardly atypical for searches and seizures performed at a particular location to be justified by more than one rationale. However, unlike the other search and seizure doctrines thus far considered, the plain view doctrine cannot serve as an independent justifier of government conduct. Rather, as explained in greater detail in this chapter, the plain view doctrine can only coexist with other search justification rationales.

O V E R V I E W

A. Essential Elements and Application

Have you heard the phrase, "Looks can be deceiving"? Well, that's certainly the case with certain doctrines that you learn during your studies in law school. For example, in my Evidence class I teach a doctrine called the "Best Evidence Rule." I often have to dispel the notion that this principle represents that a litigant must produce at trial the best evidence with respect to a particular evidentiary item. This is not at all what the doctrine represents. The doctrine is much more complex.

I have also had to dispel some preconceived notions regarding the meaning of the plain view doctrine. Though not as complicated as the Best Evidence rule (thank goodness!), the seeming simplicity of a doctrine entitled "plain view" can lull the less attentive into a false sense of security regarding the doctrine's full meaning. This doctrine allows an officer to seize evidentiary items of an incriminating nature that are discovered in plain view. However, the doctrine is not as broad as it may initially appear. When you think about it, any time an officer retrieves incriminating material the evidence is almost invariably discovered in the plain view of the officer.

What the plain view doctrine permits is the seizure of evidence discovered in plain view provided that the officer observed the item (whose incriminating nature is immediately apparent) from a lawfully authorized position and had a right of access to that item. Thus, the plain view doctrine has three essential elements — immediate recognition of the evidentiary item's incriminating nature, observance of the item from a position where the officer was lawfully permitted to be located, and a right to access the seized item. Each of these elements will be reviewed in greater detail next.

As noted earlier, a plain view justification must coexist with some other search rationale. Thus, the plain view doctrine comes into play when, for example, an officer is armed with a search warrant and during the course of the search comes across evidentiary items of an incriminating nature that were not contemplated by the warrant. It can also apply during the performance of warrantless searches. The doctrine may permit an officer who has entered a home on account of an exigency to seize evidentiary items that are subsequently observed in plain view, even if the items seized are wholly unconnected to the exigency.

(1) Immediacy Requirement

Before a seizure can be justified on plain view grounds, the government must establish that the incriminating nature of the item was immediately apparent. In other words, the searching officer must be able to immediately determine that the item observed is evidence of crime. This immediacy requirement is exactly that; an officer, upon noticing the object, must immediately recognize the incriminating nature of that item. Therefore an officer who, upon observing an item, is merely suspicious of its incriminating nature will likely be unable to justify the seizure of the item pursuant to this doctrine.

Consider the following hypothetical, which will help exemplify this requirement.

Assume a scenario where an officer has a search warrant to search a residence for various new (unused) laptop computers believed to have been stolen from a local business that manufactures and sells this type of product. During the course of the search the officer notices in one of the bedrooms ten laptop computers with the logo of the subject company affixed to the front of the laptop. One of the computers happens to be turned on. On the screen is a listing of the files stored on that computer. One such file is entitled "Children.photographs." The officer clicks on the file and several pornographic depictions of children are displayed. If evidence of these images is to be admissible at a subsequent criminal trial, the officer will likely have to find a basis other than the plain view doctrine. Though the officer was lawfully on the premises (by virtue of the search warrant) and had a right to access the object (since the search warrant allowed the officer to seize laptops located within the home), the

Sidebar

PLAIN TOUCH DOCTRINE

Sometimes a situation arises when the seizure of an object is based not upon the officer's visual observation but upon the officer's "sense of touch." In *Minnesota v. Dickerson*,[1] the Supreme Court analogized the seizure of evidence after a plain view observation to the seizure of evidence after a lawful touching. As stated by the Court, whenever a law enforcement officer during a lawful patdown of an individual's outer clothing encounters "an object whose contour or mass makes its identity immediately apparent, there has been no invasion of the suspect's privacy beyond that already authorized by the officer's search for weapons; if the object is contraband, its warrantless seizure would be justified by the same practical considerations that inhere in the plain-view context." Thus, if an officer is lawfully justified to touch or pat down an individual and during such touching immediately determines that the object felt is contraband, then that object may be seized. Plain touch issues frequently arise in the context of searches and seizures of individuals during so-called *Terry* stops.

One additional note: the seizure of contraband pursuant to the plain touch doctrine does not entail an additional search that requires either a warrant or a separate search justification. The rationale is this: if the officer is lawfully patting down an individual, then he has a right to touch and feel the individual in that manner. Thus, any physical sensation attendant to that lawful touching reveals no additional intrusive information. On the other hand, if the officer's touching exceeds the bounds of what he is lawfully entitled to perform, then the information gathered pursuant to this additional intrusion requires a separate rationale.

[1]508 U.S. 366 (1993).

government was not authorized to conduct a search of the computers and will likely have a difficult time persuading a court that the file name ("Children.photographs") was immediately incriminating. The officer was unable to make a determination regarding the incriminating nature of the material until after the subject file had been opened.

(2) Observation of Evidence from a Lawful Position

Secondly, the government must establish that the incriminating evidence was observed by an officer from a lawful location. In other words, the officer must be physically located in a place where the law permits him to be at the time the evidence is observed. Thus, an officer who observes an evidentiary item whose incriminating nature is obvious but from a location where he was not lawfully permitted to be may not seize the evidence pursuant to this doctrine. Consider the following hypothetical.

Assume that Officer receives a report that Suspect has stolen several magazines from a local store. Officer proceeds to Suspect's home and arrests Suspect inside Suspect's residence. Incident to Suspect's arrest, Officer proceeds to search the immediate area within Suspect's home. During this search, Officer observes in plain view within the immediate area an open-faced bowl filled with marijuana leaves (Officer is a trained narcotics detective and is intimately familiar with the appearance and smell of marijuana). Though the incriminating nature of the evidence seized was immediately apparent, Officer's attempt to justify the seizure based upon the plain view doctrine will depend upon whether Officer can establish his lawful presence within the residence. Absent a warrant authorizing his presence, a consensual entry, or a demonstrable exigency, the seizure of the marijuana cannot be justified on plain view grounds given Officer's inability to justify that he viewed the contraband from a lawful vantage point.

(3) Right of Access

Finally, an officer who immediately recognizes incriminating evidence from a lawful position cannot avail himself of the plain view doctrine unless it can also be demonstrated that he had a right to access the subject evidence. Sometimes an officer's observation of an incriminating object may be proper, yet the officer may not lawfully be permitted to effectuate a seizure. Let's consider one last hypothetical that involves a slight twist upon the factual scenario presented in the previous subsection.

This time assume that Officer has entered Suspect's home with a warrant for Suspect's arrest. Upon entering, Suspect is arrested in the foyer of his home. In the previous hypothetical, the existence of a warrant would have provided Officer with lawful access to the home. Given his lawful presence and his right to search the immediately surrounding area, Officer would have likely been able to rely, in part, upon the plain view doctrine to justify the seizure of marijuana found near Suspect.

But in the current scenario, assume that Officer — from his lawful position in the foyer of the home — observed in plain view the marijuana in an open-faced bowl in another room well beyond Suspect's grabbing area. Could Officer justify the plain view seizure of the marijuana located in the other room? Probably so.

As noted, the arrest warrant grants Officer lawful authority to enter the home and arrest Suspect. The search incident to arrest rule further authorizes a search of Suspect's immediate reach area. However, a search beyond this area cannot be justified pursuant to this doctrine. Therefore, to justify his access to the marijuana Officer will have to rely upon another search principle that grants him lawful access to that area of the house. There are other principles that could conceivably provide a justification. For example, Officer could present an exigent circumstances argument, claiming that he reasonably feared that the marijuana might be imminently destroyed. Particularly if other individuals are present within the home, the exigency argument might very well succeed. On the other hand, if the government is unsuccessful in proving an exigency or some separate justification, the marijuana seizure will not be upheld on plain view grounds given that the government did not have a right to access the narcotics.

Sidebar

OFFICER'S PREEXISTING MINDSET IRRELEVANT TO VALIDITY OF A PLAIN VIEW SEIZURE

Assume that during the course of a lawful search for bank robbery proceeds an officer purposefully looks for evidence of crimes separate and apart from the bank robbery. Such subjective motivations on the part of the officer will not defeat any subsequent seizure of evidence found in plain view. As long as the officer can establish her lawful observation position, her right to access the item in question, and the immediacy of the article's incriminating nature, the officer's preexisting mind-set regarding what she might find during the search is irrelevant to the rule's application. You will find throughout your Criminal Procedure studies that a government actor's preexisting mind-set is often — though not always — irrelevant when evaluating the legitimacy of a government search.

SUMMARY

■ The plain view doctrine has three elements: 1) an officer must immediately recognize the incriminating nature of the evidence, 2) the officer must view the evidence from a lawful vantage point, and 3) the officer must have a lawful right to access the item.

■ The plain view doctrine is not a theory that can, by itself, justify the seizure of evidence. Rather, it is a theory that can only be used in conjunction with another search rationale.

CONNECTIONS

Relationship to Executing the Warrant (Chapter 5), Searches Incident to Arrest (Chapter 7), and the Automobile Exception (Chapter 8)

The plain view doctrine cannot in and of itself justify the seizure of an item of evidence. Instead, it must be combined with another search and seizure justification. Thus, if an officer possesses an arrest warrant and searches the arrestee within his home, that officer might be able to employ the plain view doctrine to seize additional evidence discovered therein. Similarly, an officer who has probable cause to search the trunk of an automobile for, say, a stolen large-screen television might develop probable cause to search other smaller areas of the vehicle if that officer discovers evidence of illegal narcotics in plain view within the trunk.

Relationship to Searches and Seizures on Less than Probable Cause — *Terry v. Ohio* (Chapter 11)

An officer who performs a search pursuant to *Terry v. Ohio* might observe additional evidence that provides the officer with probable cause to conduct a more extensive search. Thus, an officer who performs a limited protective sweep of a house might observe in plain sight additional evidence of crime that would then justify a more extensive search of the home.

Relationship to Fourth Amendment Violations and Their Associated Remedies (Chapter 15)

Like any other government search performed during a criminal investigation, the seizure of evidence that exceeds the boundaries of the plain view justification is subject to suppression pursuant to the exclusionary rule.

Consent Searches

10

I routinely tell my students that most of the time prosecutors, especially federal prosecutors, benefit from a number of advantages throughout the criminal litigative process. For example, defendants will often confess to the crimes of which they are accused. When these confessions are uttered, such statements are typically admissible at trial. It certainly makes a prosecutor's work much easier when the defendant has confessed to the very crime you're trying to prove.

Of course, this is not a chapter on confessions. Confessions will be dealt with at much greater length in Chapters 16-19. Nevertheless, there are commonalities between consent searches and confessions that bear mentioning. One such commonality is that, like confessions, it is hardly atypical that an individual being investigated by the police will consent to a search that will culminate in the discovery of incriminating evidence. So this begs a question: Why do so many individuals confess to crimes and consent to searches? No doubt there are many explanations. I suspect that one of the many reasons that underlie this phenomenon is the belief that cooperation with law enforcement may culminate in beneficial treatment. It is believed that through cooperation perhaps punishment can be avoided altogether or, at the very least, lessened.

Cognizant of this reality, it should surprise few that officers will frequently attempt to obtain consent during the course of an investigation. What are the standards that are generally applicable to consent searches? Under what factual scenarios has the Supreme Court upheld government efforts to obtain consent? Under what factual constructs has it not? These are the predominant questions that this chapter will begin to address in the following section.

A. Essential Elements and Application

As noted earlier, the Fourth Amendment protects the people against unreasonable searches and seizures, and searches performed in the absence of a warrant are presumptively unreasonable. However, the Supreme Court has recognized numerous circumstances under which a warrantless search can be performed. Consent searches constitute one of those circumstances.

In *Schneckloth v. Bustamonte*,[1] the Supreme Court stated, "It is . . . well settled that one of the specifically established exceptions to the requirements of both a warrant and probable cause is a search that is conducted pursuant to consent." Therefore, when an individual consents to a search, not only does such consent authorize a warrantless search, but it may also authorize a search under circumstances where probable cause is lacking. In fact, the provision of consent can validate a search in situations devoid of any evidence suggestive of criminal activity. So long as the consent was voluntarily provided (and complied with during the ensuing government search) the search will be upheld.

(1) Burden of Proof

Whenever the government seeks to admit evidence obtained pursuant to a warrantless search, it bears the burden of proving that an exception to the warrant requirement justified the police action. The rule is no different in the context of consent searches. As stated by the Court in *Bumper v. North Carolina*,[2] "When a prosecutor seeks to rely upon consent to justify the lawfulness of a search, he has the burden of proving that the consent was, in fact, freely and voluntarily given." The government's burden, the Court added, is not satisfied if the government shows nothing other than individual compliance to a government demand or request.

(2) Voluntariness Standard and Relevant Factors

As noted, valid consent can be found only if a court determines that it was given freely and voluntarily. In undertaking this review, a court will consider two rather broad categories of evidence: the actions on the part of the government to obtain the consent, and the personal traits of the individual who allegedly provided the consent. As stated by the Supreme Court in *Schneckloth*, "both the characteristics of the accused and the details of the interrogation" should be considered when assessing whether the consent provided was a product of an individual's free will. Such consent questions are fact-specific inquiries necessitating a review of the entirety of the surrounding circumstances. Indeed, it is difficult to imagine how it could be any

---

[1] 412 U.S. 218 (1973).
[2] 391 U.S. 543 (1968).

different given the myriad of factors that invariably impact this review. After all, personal traits vary from human to human as do the circumstances surrounding the government's gathering of consent. Some individuals, for example, may not be proficient in English, or may have mental, physical, or educational handicaps. On the other hand, perhaps the consent was obtained by virtue of coercive governmental activity or other unfair investigative techniques.

Though a laundry list of relevant criteria exists, four such factors will be highlighted next, each of which has been addressed by the Supreme Court: the defendant's awareness of his right to refuse consent, the defendant's custodial status, police misrepresentations, and coercive police activity.

(a) Awareness of Right to Refuse Consent

In *Schneckloth*, the Supreme Court addressed, on habeas review, whether voluntary consent requires that the government demonstrate that the consent provided was given with the understanding that it could be withheld. The Ninth Circuit, in the underlying litigation, had concluded "that a consent was a waiver of a person's Fourth and Fourteenth Amendment rights, and that the State was under an obligation to demonstrate, not only that the consent had been uncoerced, but that it had been given with an understanding that it could be freely and effectively withheld."

However, the Supreme Court disagreed, holding that an individual's subjective understanding of his right to refuse consent was merely a factor, among many, that a court could properly consider when assessing voluntariness. Accordingly, a free and voluntary provision of consent is not in any way dependent upon an awareness of the right to withhold that consent.

The Court opined that the Ninth Circuit's approach would undermine effective law enforcement. The Court stated that investigative officers who lacked probable cause to search but suspected criminal activity might be deprived of "the only means of obtaining important and reliable evidence." Even in situations where probable cause to arrest or search exists, consent searches, in the view of the Court, would still be useful. "If the search is conducted and proves fruitless, that, in itself, may convince the police that an arrest with its possible stigma and embarrassment is unnecessary, or that a far more extensive search pursuant to a warrant is not justified."

The Court reasoned further that adoption of a subjective awareness standard would "create serious doubt whether consent searches could continue to be conducted." In circumstances "where there was no evidence of any coercion, explicit or implicit, the prosecution would nevertheless be unable to demonstrate that the subject of the search in fact, had known of his right to refuse consent." The Court decried the "near impossibility" of the prosecution satisfying its evidentiary burden in situations where a defendant failed to testify that he was aware of his right to reject a consent request.

The Court also rejected the argument that subjective awareness is required since the provision of consent is, in effect, a waiver of an individual's Fourth Amendment protections. The Court responded that the "knowing and intelligent waiver" standard is not applicable in every instance where a constitutional right is being relinquished. Rather, the Court explained, this standard attaches only to those rights that help ensure that the defendant receives a fair trial.

> There is a vast difference between those rights that protect a fair criminal trial and the rights guaranteed under the Fourth Amendment. Nothing, either in the purposes behind

requiring a "knowing" and "intelligent" waiver of trial rights, or in the practical application of such a requirement suggests that it ought to be extended to the constitutional guarantee against unreasonable searches and seizures.

A strict standard of waiver has been applied to those rights guaranteed to a criminal defendant to insure that he will be accorded the greatest possible opportunity to utilize every facet of the constitutional model of a fair criminal trial. Any trial conducted in derogation of that model leaves open the possibility that the trial reached an unfair result precisely because all the protections specified in the Constitution were not provided. . . .

The protections of the Fourth Amendment are of a wholly different order, and have nothing whatever to do with promoting the fair ascertainment of truth at a criminal trial. Rather, as Mr. Justice Frankfurter's opinion for the Court put it in *Wolf v. Colorado*, 338 U.S. 25, 338 U.S. 27, the Fourth Amendment protects the "security of one's privacy against arbitrary intrusion by the police. . . ."

(b) Custodial Status

The custodial status of the individual providing consent is another factor that a court may consider when assessing voluntariness. As detailed in this section, the Supreme Court has found that an individual seized within the meaning of the Fourth Amendment is capable of freely and voluntarily providing consent to search.

Ohio v. Robinette[3] involved a police search of a vehicle that had been stopped for a traffic violation after consent to search had allegedly been provided by the driver. The Supreme Court addressed "whether the Fourth Amendment requires that a lawfully seized defendant must be advised that he is 'free to go' before his consent to search will be recognized as voluntary." Answering this question in the negative, the Court, referencing *Schneckloth*'s rejection of a similar bright-line requirement (knowledge of the right to withhold consent), held that a per se rule requiring the "free to go" admonition was unnecessary. The Court added that it was "unrealistic to require police officers to always inform detainees that they are free to go before a consent to search may be deemed voluntary."

Whereas *Robinette* involved an individual who was merely detained, *United States v. Watson*[4] involved an individual who provided consent after having been arrested. In Watson, the defendant, after having been arrested in a restaurant for possession of stolen mail, was removed from the establishment and questioned outside after the provision of *Miranda* warnings. During the ensuing interrogation, the defendant consented to a search of his vehicle that resulted in the recovery of evidence and formed the basis for his ultimate conviction.

The Court found that neither the defendant's arrest status nor the officer's failure to inform him of his right to refuse consent rendered the consent involuntary. The following excerpt from *Watson* is instructive. The passage not only succinctly discusses the various factors underlying the Court's judgment, but it also exemplifies how the totality of the circumstances standard is commonly applied when consent questions are presented.

> We are satisfied in addition that the remaining factors relied upon by the Court of Appeals to invalidate Watson's consent are inadequate to demonstrate that, in the totality of the circumstances, Watson's consent was not his own "essentially free and unconstrained choice" because his "will ha(d) been overborne and his capacity for self-determination

---

[3]519 U.S. 33 (1996).
[4]423 U.S. 411 (1976).

critically impaired" (citation omitted). There was no overt act or threat of force against Watson proved or claimed. There were no promises made to him and no indication of more subtle forms of coercion that might flaw his judgment. He had been arrested and was in custody, but his consent was given while on a public street, not in the confines of the police station. Moreover, the fact of custody alone has never been enough in itself to demonstrate a coerced confession or consent to search. Similarly, under *Schneckloth*, the absence of proof that Watson knew he could withhold his consent, though it may be a factor in the overall judgment, is not to be given controlling significance. There is no indication in this record that Watson was a newcomer to the law, mentally deficient, or unable in the face of a custodial arrest to exercise a free choice. He was given *Miranda* warnings and was further cautioned that the results of the search of his car could be used against him. He persisted in his consent.

(c) Police Misrepresentations

Assume a scenario where the identity of the officer requesting consent to search is unknown to the party to whom the request has been made (e.g., the officer is dressed in plain clothes, no badge or other identifying markers are displayed, etc.). Can valid consent be obtained even when deceptive conduct is employed?

In short, the employment of deceitful tactics will not necessarily render the provision of consent involuntary. Consider *Hoffa v. United States*.[5] There, an associate of the defendant was working for the government in an undercover capacity. This fact, however, was unbeknownst to the defendant. By virtue of the defendant's consent, the informant gained access to the defendant's hotel suite (and was routinely in his presence at various other locations as well) where he heard the defendant make several incriminating statements. Over the defendant's objection, the informant was allowed to testify to the defendant's comments.

The Court found that the intercepted remarks were the product, not of an unconstitutional government intrusion into the defendant's hotel room, but of the defendant's misplaced trust in his associate:

> Partin [the informant] did not enter the suite by force or by stealth. He was not a surreptitious eavesdropper. Partin was in the suite by invitation, and every conversation which he heard was either directed to him or knowingly carried on in his presence. The petitioner, in a word, was not relying on the security of the hotel room; he was relying upon his misplaced confidence that Partin would not reveal his wrongdoing.

Notice in *Hoffa* that the government employed a deceptive technique in order to gain entry to the defendant's hotel suite. Had the police in *Hoffa* attempted to gain entry while wearing their official blue uniforms, it is highly doubtful that consent would have been obtained. Yet what the government could not do openly it could do cunningly. Is this fair? Whether it is or not, what *Hoffa* teaches is that an individual must be careful whom they admit to their premises. Such an individual assumes the risk that the person whom they admit is not who he represents himself to be and may reveal the confidences that he overhears. Now you may have a greater understanding as to why law enforcement so frequently employs undercover agents!

---

[5]385 U.S. 293 (1966).

Supreme Court jurisprudence in this particular subset of consent searches is still in its developmental stages. As can easily be imagined, there are endless forms of deceptive techniques that officers can employ that present challenging constitutional questions. Imagine a scenario in which the police falsely represent the purpose underlying a request to search. What happens if the police falsely represent to a homeowner that they would like to search his home for stolen auto parts but, in reality, seek incriminating evidence of a different kind? Does this type of misrepresentation defeat a valid consent claim? Professor Wayne R. LaFave opines that the determinative factor in such circumstances might depend upon the extremity of the misrepresentation: "[W]hen the police misrepresentation of purpose is so extreme that it deprives the individual of the ability to make a fair assessment of the need to surrender his privacy . . . the consent should not be considered valid."[6] Of course, the Supreme Court will have the final word on this subject.

(d) Coercive Police Activity

The Supreme Court has found the provision of consent to be ineffective in circumstances where the police have engaged in conduct that is unduly coercive. Assume a scenario where, unlike *Hoffa*, there is no mistaking the fact that the identity of the individual seeking consent is a law enforcement officer. However, when seeking to obtain consent the officer makes certain critical and significant representations of material facts (representations that may or may not be truthful). Can such conduct, particularly if relied upon, serve to invalidate the consent provided?

The Supreme Court addressed such a situation in *Bumper v. North Carolina*.[7] The defendant lived with his grandmother in rural North Carolina. One day, several officers approached the residence. One of the officers informed the grandmother that he had a search warrant for her residence. After she responded "Go ahead," an ensuing search of the home uncovered a rifle that was subsequently admitted into evidence at the defendant's rape trial. As a justification for the search, the government did not rely upon the validity of a search warrant, but rather upon the grandmother's provision of consent.

In holding that the consent was invalid, the Court reasoned that the government's representation that they possessed a warrant (irrespective of the truth of the representation) necessarily defeated their consent argument. As explained by the Court, "When a law enforcement officer claims authority to search a home under a warrant, he announces in effect that the occupant has no right to resist the search. The situation is instinct with coercion — albeit colorably lawful coercion. Where there is coercion there cannot be consent."

Coercive police conduct was also on display in *Amos v. United States*.[8] There, "deputy collectors of internal revenue" arrived at the home of the defendant and informed his wife (the defendant was not at the residence at the time of the officers' arrival) "that they were revenue officers and had come to search the premises 'for violations of the revenue law.'" The defendant's wife allowed the collectors to enter and the officers subsequently found quantities of "illicitly distilled whiskey" within the home. The collectors had neither an arrest nor a search warrant.

---

[6]Wayne R. LaFave et al., *Criminal Procedure* 284 (2009).
[7]391 U.S. 543 (1968).
[8]255 U.S. 313 (1921).

The Court found that the wife's acquiescence to the demands of the revenue officers was the product of government coercion, thereby precluding consideration of a competing constitutional waiver claim. As stated by Justice Clarke:

> The contention that the constitutional rights of defendant were waived when his wife admitted to his home the government officers, who came, without warrant, demanding admission to make search of it under government authority, cannot be entertained. We need not consider whether it is possible for a wife, in the absence of her husband, thus to waive his constitutional rights, for it is perfectly clear that, under the implied coercion here presented, no such waiver was intended or effected.

(3) Reasonableness of a Consent Search

Even when a consent search is authorized, the ensuing search must still comport with the Fourth Amendment's reasonableness clause. In other words, the ensuing search must be interpreted and performed reasonably (e.g., scope, manner of execution). In making this assessment, the courts employ an objective person standard. How a reasonable objective individual under the circumstances would have understood the consent provided is the applicable test. Thus, an owner of an automobile who consents to have his vehicle searched probably did not consent to have his vehicle dismantled. Similarly, a homeowner who consents to a search of his residence probably did not authorize the destruction of the roof, the walls, or any other aspects of the home.

F   A   Q

Q: Aside from the limitations inherent in the objective reasonableness standard, can an individual place further restrictions upon the scope of the police search? Also, can consent be withdrawn once it has been authorized?

A: Yes to both questions. Since it is the individual who is authorizing the search, that person can also impose limitations. An individual may, for example, restrict a consensual search of an automobile to its passenger compartment. Or a person can confine a search of her home to the first and second floors but exclude the kitchen area as well as the basement. Also, a person may withdraw consent after it has been provided. Therefore, an individual who has consented to the search of his home may revoke that consent and terminate any additional police probing performed in reliance upon that consent.

(4) Third-Party Consent

Many households have more than one occupant. Married couples or single parents often live under the same roof with their children. University students may share a dwelling with other individuals. Sometimes the police in the midst of an investigation will approach a household and obtain consent to search from one of its occupants but recover evidence that implicates another resident within the dwelling. To some it might seem that the recovered evidence should be inadmissible since the implicated resident did not personally consent to the search.

In *Georgia v. Randolph*,[9] the Supreme Court summarized the rule generally applicable to these situations: "The Fourth Amendment recognizes a valid warrantless entry and search of premises when police obtain the voluntary consent of an occupant who shares, or is reasonably believed to share, authority over the area in common with a co-occupant who later objects to the use of evidence so obtained." Let's dissect this rule before branching off into other related issues that arise from this context.

(a) Consent When Other Occupant Is Absent

First, "an occupant who shares" a dwelling with another may consent to a search of those "area[s] in common with a co-occupant." Imagine that Tom and Mary are siblings who share a two-bedroom, one-bathroom apartment. Tom and Mary sleep in separate bedrooms but share the unit's bathroom. If an officer approaches Tom at his residence (Mary is not present) and requests consent to search, Tom may consent to a search of *only* those areas that he shares in common with Mary (e.g., family room, kitchen, bathroom). Conversely, Tom's consent is invalid as to those areas that are not commonly shared (e.g., Mary's separate bedroom).

Consider *United States v. Matlock*.[10] After the police arrested the defendant the officers went to the house where the defendant resided. Upon arrival at the residence, the officers were admitted to the house by one of the other residents who provided consent to search the premises. Thereafter, incriminating evidence was discovered.

The Supreme Court held this third-party consent was valid. The Court reached this decision even though the officers — seemingly quite purposefully — sought the consent from an individual other than the person whom they had just arrested. As the Court stated, "[W]hen the prosecution seeks to justify a warrantless search by proof of voluntary consent, it is not limited to proof that consent was given by the defendant, but may" demonstrate that valid third-party consent was obtained by one who commonly possessed the property at issue or who had a meaningful relationship with that particular property. The Court expounded that valid third-party consent is not dependent upon the "law of property." Instead, the authority stems from the shared use of property by individuals who together have "access or control" over that property. In such situations, the Court declared that it is reasonable to find that a co-inhabitant may permit another to search the common areas of the property and that all who share the property necessarily "assume the risk" that such authorization may, in fact, be granted.

(b) Consent When Other Occupant Is Present

In *Matlock*, the defendant was not present when the consent was granted. Such was not the case in *Georgia v. Randolph*.[11] In *Randolph*, officers were in the presence of two individuals, a husband and wife (though they were married they had separated) at the couple's marital residence. After the wife indicated that there were illegal narcotics in the house, an officer initially requested consent to search from the husband. He refused. The officer then sought and received permission to search from the wife. Thereafter, evidence of illegal narcotics was recovered.

---

[9]547 U.S. 103 (2006).
[10]415 U.S. 164 (1974).
[11]547 U.S. 103 (2006).

The issue before the Court was "whether one occupant may give law enforcement effective consent to search shared premises, as against a co-tenant who is present and states a refusal to permit the search." The Court answered this question in the negative, holding that the husband's refusal to grant consent when he was in the physical presence of the officers trumped the consent provided by his wife.

The holding in *Randolph* is extremely narrow. Remember, *Matlock* involved a consensual search of a residence after permission had been obtained by a nondefendant household member outside the defendant's presence. *Illinois v. Rodriguez,*[12] discussed in the following subsection, involved a search performed by officers who obtained consent from a woman whom they reasonably, though erroneously, believed resided at that location. At the time the consent was provided the defendant was asleep elsewhere within the apartment. The Court in *Rodriguez* upheld the search on the basis of the officer's reasonable mistake.

Emphasizing the narrowness of its holding, the Court in *Randolph* drew the following distinctions between *Randolph* and *Matlock* and *Rodriguez*:

> Although the *Matlock* defendant was not present with the opportunity to object, he was in a squad car not far away; the *Rodriguez* defendant was actually asleep in the apartment, and the police might have roused him with a knock on the door before they entered with only the consent of an apparent co-tenant. If those cases are not to be undercut by today's holding, we have to admit that we are drawing a fine line; if a potential defendant with self-interest in objecting is in fact at the door and objects, the co-tenant's permission does not suffice for a reasonable search, whereas the potential objector, nearby but not invited to take part in the threshold colloquy, loses out.

(c) Reasonable Mistake Regarding Authority to Grant Consent

As noted previously, valid consent can be also obtained from a tenant who is "reasonably believed to share" the premises with another individual. This was precisely the factual scenario in *Illinois v. Rodriguez.*[13] There the majority held that the Fourth Amendment does not require that an officer's factual determinations be accurate, only that her conclusions be reasonable. Therefore, a police officer who obtains consent to search a dwelling from an individual who does not, in fact, have a reasonable expectation of privacy in the residence could be upheld so long as

---

Sidebar

MISTAKE OF LEGAL AUTHORITY

In *Stoner v. California,*[14] officers searched a hotel room belonging to an individual the police were investigating. The officers received consent to search from a hotel clerk. The Court held, inter alia, that officers could not rely upon the reasonable mistake doctrine when the officers were mistaken about the clerk's legal authority to provide consent. The clerk neither possessed such legal authority nor was provided such authority by the room's occupant. As stated by the Court: "Even if it be assumed that a state law which gave a hotel proprietor blanket authority to authorize the police to search the rooms of the hotel's guests could survive constitutional challenge, there is no intimation in the California cases cited by the respondent that California has any such law. Nor is there any substance to the claim that the search was reasonable because the police, relying upon the night clerk's expressions of consent, had a reasonable basis for the belief that the clerk had authority to consent to the search. Our decisions make clear that the rights protected by the Fourth Amendment are not to be eroded by strained applications of the law of agency or by unrealistic doctrines of 'apparent authority.'"

---

[14]376 U.S. 483 (1964).

---

[12]497 U.S. 177 (1990).
[13]*Id.*

the officer's belief was objectively reasonable. In so holding, the Court stated that the standard by which an officer's assessment would be judged is whether "the facts available to the officer at the moment . . . 'warrant a man of reasonable caution in the belief' that the consenting party had authority over the premises."

SUMMARY

- The police can perform a warrantless search if lawful consent is obtained. However, the ensuing search must still comport with the Fourth Amendment's reasonableness clause.

- An individual can provide consent to search in situations where probable cause to believe evidence will be found in a given location is lacking.

- To be valid, the consent must have been provided voluntarily. The government bears the burden of demonstrating voluntariness.

- Whether an individual was aware of his right to refuse consent, whether an individual was in custody, and whether the government employed deception are merely factors that a court may consider in assessing voluntariness.

- Valid consent may be obtained from someone who shares the premises with another individual. However, that individual's consensual authority extends only to those areas that are commonly shared.

- A co-inhabitant who provides consent to search may not trump the interests of another cotenant who is present and objects to a search.

- Valid consent to search may be obtained from a third party even if that individual does not have authority to grant the requested consent. If the officer was reasonable in her belief that an individual was authorized to provide consent, the consent granted will be upheld.

CONNECTIONS

Relationship to Searches, Seizures, and the Warrant Clause (Chapter 4) and Executing the Warrant (Chapter 5)

Whereas a warrant requires a judicial finding of probable cause, the provision of consent allows officers to perform a warrantless search even in situations where probable cause is lacking.

Relationship to Fourth Amendment Violations and Their Associated Remedies (Chapter 15)

Like any other government search performed during a criminal investigation, a search or seizure that exceeds the boundaries of the consent provided is subject to suppression pursuant to the exclusionary rule.

Relationship to the Privilege Against Self-Incrimination: General Principles (Chapter 16) and the *Miranda* Rule (Chapter 18)

Whether a court is considering a challenge to a claim of consent or the propriety of a confession pursuant to the Fifth Amendment, a court will typically consider a myriad of factors, including whether the subject was aware of his rights and whether deception was employed.

Searches and Seizures on Less than Probable Cause — *Terry v. Ohio*

11

There are certain law school classes and Supreme Court cases that are inextricably linked. Civil Procedure has, among other cases,

Pennoyer v. Neff[1] as well as *International Shoe Co. v. Washington.*[2] Constitutional Law I is replete with such cases, including but hardly limited to, *Marbury v. Madison*[3] and *McCulloch v. Maryland.*[4] And Investigative Criminal Procedure has a full stable of prominent cases as well, with *Miranda v. Arizona*[5] serving as, perhaps, the course's signature case. The *Miranda* decision will be discussed in Chapter 18. This chapter, however, discusses in depth another such signature case: *Terry v. Ohio.*[6]

A. ENCOUNTERS AND ARRESTS

1. Arrests
2. Encounters

B. *TERRY v. OHIO*

1. General Judicial Observations
2. Facts
3. The Court's Holding and Reasoning

---

[1]95 U.S. 714 (1878).
[2]326 U.S. 310 (1945).
[3]5 U.S. (1 Cranch) 137 (1803).
[4]17 U.S. (4 Wheat.) 316 (1819).
[5]384 U.S. 436 (1966).
[6]392 U.S. 1 (1968).

C. INFORMATION SOURCE — INFORMANTS

1. Known Tipsters
2. Anonymous Tipsters

Most of the first eight chapters of this book were spent reviewing the various particularities of the Fourth Amendment. With respect to the topic of unreasonable seizures, this discussion has largely focused upon the arrest and probable cause concepts. However, as will be detailed in this chapter, a seizure can occur within the meaning of the Fourth Amendment short of an arrest and without a finding of probable cause. In a nutshell, this is what the *Terry* decision is all about, and its significance should not be understated. As stated in *Terry* by Chief Justice Earl Warren who wrote the majority opinion:

> Reflective of the tensions involved are the practical and constitutional arguments pressed with great vigor on both sides of the public debate over the power of the police to "stop and frisk" — as it is sometimes euphemistically termed — suspicious persons.

On the one hand, it is frequently argued that, in dealing with the rapidly unfolding and often dangerous situations on city streets, the police are in need of an escalating set of flexible responses, graduated in relation to the amount of information they possess. For this purpose, it is urged that distinctions should be made between a "stop" and an "arrest" (or a "seizure" of a person), and between a "frisk" and a "search." . . .

On the other side, the argument is made that the authority of the police must be strictly circumscribed by the law of arrest and search as it has developed to date in the traditional jurisprudence of the Fourth Amendment. . . . The heart of the Fourth Amendment, the argument runs, is a severe requirement of specific justification for any intrusion upon protected personal security, coupled with a highly developed system of judicial controls to enforce upon the agents of the State the commands of the Constitution.

And underlying much of this debate were racial concerns and the potential impact of this case upon minority communities — in particular the African-American populace — where complaints of police harassment, as noted by the Court, were a recurrent theme.

A. Encounters and Arrests

As a threshold matter, it will be useful to review two important concepts prior to discussing *Terry* — encounters and arrests. A discussion of these concepts will help you better appreciate the later discussion of *Terry*. Let's begin by discussing the concept of an arrest.

(1) Arrests

The Supreme Court in *California v. Hodari D*[7] described an arrest as "the quintessential 'seizure of the person' under the Fourth Amendment jurisprudence." Despite this designation, the concept of arrest remains somewhat nebulous. The Court in *Hodari D* went on to say that "[a]n arrest requires *either* physical force . . . *or,* where that is absent, *submission* to the assertion of authority." Thus, before an arrest can be found, either an officer must have physically touched the subject, "however slight," or the individual must have submitted to a verbal or nonverbal, nonphysical command of the officers.

In *Hodari D*, for example, the defendant had discarded illegal narcotics while being chased by the police. The Court concluded that the defendant, at the time of the narcotics drop, had not been seized within the meaning of the Fourth Amendment because there had been neither a physical touching nor a submission to police authority.

However, the requirements delineated in *Hodari D* are merely threshold standards. In other words, fulfillment of the standards enunciated in *Hodari D* is not determinative of whether an arrest has occurred. Individuals — like me — who have experienced being stopped by the police for traffic violations have certainly submitted to a show of governmental authority. Yet in most instances involving a police stop for a traffic infraction an arrest has not occurred. Therefore, additional factual findings will often be required before an arrest can be said to have occurred.

So what else is required? Well, it certainly requires the establishment of probable cause to believe that a crime has been committed. That is mandatory. However, an arrest does not require that an officer utter the phrase "You're under arrest" as is so often seen on television and in the movies. In fact, the subjective intentions of the officer are irrelevant in making this assessment. In other words, whether or not the officer intended through his conduct to perform an arrest has no bearing on whether an arrest has occurred. Rather, an assessment of the subject's freedom of movement is viewed through an objective lens. As stated by the Fifth Circuit, "Police detention constitutes an 'arrest,' such that it must be accompanied by probable cause, if a reasonable person in the suspect's position would understand the situation to be a restraint on freedom of the kind that the law typically associates with a formal arrest."[8]

The courts have employed a variety of factors when assessing whether an arrest has occurred. The Sixth Circuit has stated that the factors it considers include "the transportation of the detainee to another location, significant restraints on the detainee's freedom of movement involving physical confinement or other coercion preventing the detainee from leaving police custody, and the use of weapons or bodily force," as well as provision of *Miranda* warnings.[9] Another critical factor — which will become more apparent during the discussion of *Terry* — is the duration of the detainment. The longer the detainment the more the stop resembles an arrest. As stated by the Second Circuit, "If police officers 'restrain an individual in a manner that, though not technically an arrest, is nonetheless so intrusive as to be "tantamount" to an arrest,' probable cause is also required."[10]

---

[7]499 U.S. 621 (1991).
[8]*Freeman v. Gore*, 483 F.3d 404, 413 (5th Cir. 2007).
[9]*United States v. Lopez-Arias*, 344 F.3d 623, 627 (6th Cir. 2003), (quoting *United States v. Richardson*, 949 F.2d 851, 857 (6th Cir. 1991)).
[10]*Gilles v. Repicky*, 511 F.3d 239, 245 (2d Cir. 2007).

(2) Encounters

Obviously, arrests constitute a type of governmental seizure. But sometimes there are police-pedestrian contacts that do not involve any level of detention. Such contacts are referred to as encounters. Because they are deemed to be consensual interactions, such encounters do not implicate any Fourth Amendment concerns. In contrast with an individual who is under arrest, an individual who is engaged in a voluntary encounter is deemed to be free to terminate the interaction at any time.

The Supreme Court in *Florida v. Bostick*[11] described the governing standard as "whether a reasonable person would have felt free to decline the officers' requests or otherwise terminate the encounter." If so, then the police-pedestrian contact is deemed to be an encounter. If not, then the individual is seized within the meaning of the Fourth Amendment. The *Bostick* Court added that this determinative standard applies irrespective of the location of the encounter, whether it "take[s] place on trains, planes, and city streets."

Because such contacts are considered consensual in nature, police officers are entitled to approach an individual irrespective of whether that officer has any suspicion whatsoever of wrongdoing. Accordingly, a police officer devoid of any level of suspicion may approach a pedestrian with the singular purpose of asking incriminating questions or obtaining consent to search. Perhaps to some the notion of an officer, dressed in uniform and armed with a weapon, engaging in such a practice is troubling. However, as the Supreme Court stated in *Bostick*, this practice "has been endorsed by the Court any number of times." The Court continued: "[T]his Court is not empowered to forbid law enforcement practices simply because it considers them distasteful. The Fourth Amendment proscribes unreasonable searches and seizures; it does not proscribe voluntary cooperation."

So arrests — the prototypical seizure — involve at a minimum a submission to governmental authority or a physical touching. Findings such as prolonged detention, whether significant restraints on freedom have been imposed, and whether the individual has been transported to another location are also factors that may be relevant to the determination of whether an arrest has occurred. On the flip side, encounters are consensual interactions between the police and the citizenry where there are no restraints upon individual movement. The next section turns its attention to *Terry v. Ohio*, which addressed whether a seizure for Fourth Amendment purposes may occur that falls short of an arrest. As you will see, the answer to that question is yes.

B. *Terry v. Ohio*

(1) General Judicial Observations

As noted, the *Terry* case was a watershed moment in criminal procedure jurisprudence. Prior to the heart of the opinion, which discussed the rationale of *Terry*, the Court made the following observations:

> Street encounters between citizens and police officers are incredibly rich in diversity. They range from wholly friendly exchanges of pleasantries or mutually useful information to

---

[11]501 U.S. 429 (1991).

hostile confrontations of armed men involving arrests or injuries, or loss of life. Moreover, hostile confrontations are not all of a piece. Some of them begin in a friendly enough manner, only to take a different turn upon the injection of some unexpected element into the conversation. Encounters are initiated by the police for a wide variety of purposes, some of which are wholly unrelated to a desire to prosecute for crime.

This comment is especially apt in light of the preceding discussion about arrests, which implicate the Fourth Amendment, and encounters, which do not. The passage acknowledges the seemingly endless diversity of scenarios in which the police personally interact with pedestrians and, by implication, the inevitable judicial ferreting of constitutional claims that these scenarios so often produce. Indeed, this passage is all the more appropriate given the arguable gray factual area that presented itself in *Terry*.

(2) Facts

Martin McFadden was a detective with the Cleveland Police Department. One afternoon while patrolling in downtown Cleveland, he noticed two individuals, one of whom was defendant John Terry. McFadden observed Terry and another man, Richard Chilton, standing on a corner. He observed both men take turns walking along a street, peering into a store window, and then returning to the location where the other male was standing. McFadden testified that each individual engaged in this process five or six times, totaling approximately 12 trips in the aggregate. Eventually, a third male joined them but then left and headed westward along a certain street. Terry and Chilton eventually left the corner and continued westward along the same street traveled by the third male.

At a suppression hearing, McFadden testified that at the time of the incident he had been a police officer for 39 years and a detective for 35 years. He explained "that he had been assigned to patrol this vicinity of downtown Cleveland for shoplifters and pickpockets for 30 years . . . [and] that he had developed routine habits of observation over the years and . . . they didn't look right to me at the time." Given his suspicions, McFadden followed Terry and Chilton and saw them stop in front of the store in question and talk to the third male with whom they had been conferring at the corner. The detective, who was dressed in plain clothes, then approached the men. After he informed them of his identity, the detective requested that the men identify themselves.

After receiving an incoherent response, "McFadden grabbed . . . Terry, spun him around so that they were facing the other two, with Terry between McFadden and the others, and patted down the outside of his clothing." McFadden felt a pistol inside the left breast pocket of Terry's overcoat, which he initially was unable to retrieve. The detective then "ordered" the men to enter the store, where McFadden removed the coat from Terry's person and retrieved the weapon. After ordering all three men to face the wall and raise their hands, McFadden patted down Chilton and the third individual. McFadden retrieved another revolver from a pocket of Chilton's overcoat. McFadden testified "that he only patted the men down to see whether they had weapons, and that he did not put his hands beneath the outer garments of either Terry or Chilton until he felt their guns."

After losing their motion to suppress the weapons, Terry and Chilton were found guilty by a court of carrying a concealed weapon. The Supreme Court eventually granted certiorari to decide whether Terry's Fourth Amendment rights were violated by the admission into evidence of the revolvers. The Court answered this question in the negative and affirmed Terry's conviction.

(3) The Court's Holding and Reasoning

Students of Criminal Procedure should pay special note to the following statement of the Court. In resolving the question before it, the Court described its "first task" as "establish[ing] at what point in this encounter the Fourth Amendment becomes relevant. That is, we must decide whether and when Officer McFadden 'seized' Terry and whether and when he conducted a 'search.'"

When individuals are arrested and charged with a crime, it is hardly unusual for defendants to challenge the validity of their seizure. In so doing, defendants will often point to a particular moment during the police-pedestrian encounter and assert that some level of suspicion (e.g., in the arrest context, probable cause) was required before the police could constitutionally engage in the challenged conduct. The government will often respond in one of two ways: either that the seizure (e.g., the arrest) was, in fact, supported by the requisite suspicion level and then detail all the reasons why that suspicion level was satisfied, or they will assert that a seizure had not occurred at the moment cited by the defendant, thus obviating the need for any heightened factual findings.

This "first task" of the Court should, often, be the first task for Criminal Procedure students whenever you encounter a fact pattern on an exam in which a defendant's seizure or a government search is challenged. Why is that? The Fourth Amendment protects the individual only against searches and seizures that are unreasonable. Reasonable searches and seizures are, therefore, permissible. If you are a government attorney, you want to establish that the challenged conduct was reasonable. One way to do that is to prove that there was no seizure or no search. If there was no seizure or search, then the Constitution is not implicated, rendering the police conduct reasonable. At best — in the contexts of seizures — there would have been nothing more than an encounter.

If you are an attorney representing the defendant, you want to establish that the police-pedestrian interaction was more than a mere encounter. If you can establish that there had been a government seizure, then the court must undertake a Fourth Amendment analysis to ascertain whether the government, in effectuating the seizure and any subsequent search, infringed upon a constitutional protection enjoyed by the defendant. Ideally, the defendant would prefer to argue that the government failed to satisfy the loftiest of seizure standards — probable cause — when it effectuated the seizure and search in question. Conversely, in defending its conduct the government would prefer to hold itself to a lesser standard of proof.

In *Terry*, the Court addressed whether it was per se unreasonable for a policeman, in the absence of probable cause to arrest, to seize a person and perform a limited weapons search of such an individual.

The Court "emphatically reject[ed]" the suggestion that the Fourth Amendment did not encompass the seizure and search activities (albeit comparatively more circumscribed) observed in *Terry*. The Court considered it "quite plain" that seizures can occur short of a "trip to the station house and prosecution for crime — arrests in traditional terminology." With respect to the search question, the Court rejected as "simply fantastic" the suggestion that an officer's exploration of a subject's outer garments was somehow not a search within the meaning of the Amendment.

Given the applicability of the Fourth Amendment, was the government required to satisfy a probable cause standard? The Court answered this question in the negative. In reaching this conclusion, the Court reasoned that "the sounder course" was to ask whether the particular government intrusion was reasonable. Thus, by delegating such government activity for a review for reasonableness, the Court separated this category of searches and seizures in its entirety from the warrant clause. The Court reasoned, in part, that the type of conduct at issue in *Terry* could not practically be subjected to the warrant requirement given the "necessarily swift action" required by officers in such instances.

Sidebar

DEFINITION OF "SEIZURE"

The *Terry* Court defined a seizure for purposes of a Fourth Amendment analysis as "whenever a police officer accosts an individual and restrains his freedom to walk away." It further added that "[o]nly when the officer, by means of physical force or show of authority, has in some way restrained the liberty of a citizen may we conclude that a 'seizure' has occurred."

The Court concluded that the Fourth Amendment was implicated by Detective McFadden's stop and frisk activities. In reviewing the reasonableness of the detective's conduct, the Court set forth the following balancing inquiries that continue to govern the propriety of *Terry*-level seizures and frisks. The Court declared that "it is necessary 'first to focus upon the governmental interest which allegedly justifies official intrusion upon the constitutionally protected interests of the private citizen.'" Second, a court must examine "the nature and quality of the intrusion on individual rights which must be accepted if police officers are to be conceded the right to search for weapons in situations where probable cause to arrest for crime is lacking."

Therefore, in assessing reasonableness, a court should focus not only upon the reasons proffered in support of the government's intrusion, but also upon the individual liberty interests affected by this practice.

As mentioned, the Court employed the above balancing test, weighing the governmental need for the approach against the "nature and quality of the intrusion on individual rights." The Court noted two government interests in these limited intrusions. One is the interest in preventing crime and the second is the interest in officer safety. These were sufficient interests justifying the intrusions of the type performed by Detective McFadden. As noted by the Court, "When an officer is justified in believing that the individual whose suspicious behavior he is investigating at close range is armed and presently dangerous . . . , it would appear to be clearly unreasonable to deny the officer the power to take necessary measures to determine whether the person is in fact carrying a weapon and to neutralize the threat of physical harm."

Sidebar

FIRST PRONG — GOVERNING STANDARDS

As for the first prong of this test — whether the officer's initial intrusion upon the individual was justified — the Court enunciated the following governing standard. The Court held that an officer's intrusion is justified if he is "able to point to specific and articulable facts which, taken together with rational inferences from those facts, reasonably warrant that intrusion." The Court further held that the test is objective; namely, "would the facts available to the officer at the moment of the seizure or the search 'warrant a man of reasonable caution in the belief' that the action taken was appropriate?"

As for the second prong — the nature and quality of the intrusion — the Court characterized even such limited intrusions as "severe . . . intrusions upon cherished personal security." Nevertheless, the Court rejected the suggestion that probable cause was required before the police could perform such limited searches. The Court noted that the type of search at issue was limited to the search for weapons and is comparatively brief, which differs from the intrusions attendant to an arrest. In the end, the Court concluded that so long as an officer reasonably believes that the person he is investigating is armed and dangerous, a limited search for weapons is justified.

Justice Harlan in his concurrence provided some helpful clarity to the majority's opinion. He made explicit what he believed was implicit in the majority opinion. He expressly stated that before a search for weapons can be justified, the officer must initially be justified in seizing the individual. It is not enough that an officer reasonably suspect that an individual is armed and dangerous. Instead, the search must be preceded by a justified seizure of the individual. As Justice Harlan stated:

> Officer McFadden's right to interrupt Terry's freedom of movement and invade his privacy arose only because circumstances warranted forcing an encounter with Terry in an effort to prevent or investigate a crime. Once that forced encounter was justified, however, the officer's right to take suitable measures for his own safety followed automatically.

The Court upheld the actions of Detective McFadden. In so holding, the Court established what has become known as the reasonable suspicion standard. An officer who reasonably suspects that an individual has committed a crime or, as in *Terry*, is about to commit a crime, may perform an investigatory stop. If the officer further reasonably suspects that the individual is armed and dangerous, a patdown or frisk of that individual is also justified.

C. Information Source — Informants

(1) Known Tipsters

In assessing whether an officer possessed reasonable suspicion to support the type of limited intrusions approved in *Terry*, a court must determine whether the information available to the officer reasonably warranted the challenged conduct. Sometimes the source of the information stems from the personal observations of the officers. Such was the case in *Terry*. In *Terry*, the detective personally observed the suspect's movements and heard the garbled responses.

However, what if the source of information is someone other than a law enforcement officer? Can a *Terry* stop and frisk be justified when the source of information is someone other than the investigating agent? In short, the answer is yes.

Adams v. Williams[12] addressed this very issue. There, an officer who was in a patrol vehicle at approximately 2:15 A.M. in a "high-crime area" was approached by an individual with whom the officer had been acquainted. This informant told the officer that another individual who possessed narcotics and had "a gun at his waist" was sitting in a nearby vehicle. The officer, in turn, approached the vehicle, "tapped on the window," and requested that the defendant open the door. Rather than opening the door, the defendant opened the window. The officer then "reached into the car and removed a fully loaded revolver" from the defendant's waistband. The Court noted that the officer, at the time of search, had not seen any weapons.

---

[12]407 U.S. 143 (1972).

In upholding the officer's conduct, the Supreme Court rejected the defendant's contention that "reasonable cause for a stop and frisk can only be based on the officer's personal observation rather than on information supplied by another person." The Court noted that unlike an anonymous tip, the information in this instance was provided by a known source of informational intelligence. In addition, the majority reasoned that the truth or falsity of the information provided could be swiftly ascertained by the responding officer and that the provision of false information subjected the informant to possible criminal sanctions under Connecticut law.

Nevertheless, the Court acknowledged that the information provided in this case would have been insufficient to support an arrest or search warrant. As you may recall, courts when assessing warrant applications consider both the basis of the informant's knowledge as well as his credibility as part of its totality of the circumstances review. This task becomes a bit more demanding when the tip emanates from an unknown source. Consider the case discussions in the following section.

(2) Anonymous Tipsters

In assessing the sufficiency of the tip for *Terry* purposes the Court in *Adams v. Williams* applied a less demanding, more forgiving standard than applied in the probable cause assessment context. As noted by the Supreme Court in *Alabama v. White*:

> Reasonable suspicion is a less demanding standard than probable cause not only in the sense that reasonable suspicion can be established with information that is different in quantity or content than that required to establish probable cause, but also in the sense that reasonable suspicion can arise from information that is less reliable than that required to show probable cause. *Adams v. Williams* . . . demonstrates as much. . . . Reasonable suspicion, like probable cause, is dependent upon both the content of information possessed by police and its degree of reliability. . . . The [*Illinois v. Gates*] Court applied [the] totality-of-the-circumstances approach . . . taking into account the facts known to the officers from personal observation, and giving the anonymous tip the weight it deserved in light of its indicia of reliability as established through independent police work. The same approach applies in the reasonable-suspicion context, the only difference being the level of suspicion that must be established.

Alabama v. White[13] and *Florida v. J.L.*[14] are two contrasting cases involving *Terry* claims and anonymous informants that you will likely study in your Criminal Procedure class. In each case, the information leading to the *Terry* stop and frisk was provided by an anonymous source. In *White*, the Court upheld the *Terry* stop, though the Court acknowledged that it was a "close case." In *J.L.*, the *Terry* stop was not upheld. A swing factor in each case was the tipster's ability or inability to provide the officers with predictive information relevant to the defendant's future conduct.

In *J.L.*, an anonymous caller to the Miami police department indicated that an African-American male, who was dressed in a plaid shirt and was currently located at a certain bus stop, was in possession of a firearm. Sometime thereafter, officers arrived at the scene and observed a black male in a plaid shirt standing in the company of two other African-American males at the indicated bus stop. One of

---

[13]496 U.S. 325 (1990).
[14]529 U.S. 266 (2000).

the responding officers approached the male in the plaid shirt, frisked him, and seized a gun from his person.

The Court in *Florida v. J.L.* noted that "there are situations in which an anonymous tip, suitably corroborated, exhibits 'sufficient indicia of reliability to provide reasonable suspicion to make the investigatory stop.'" However, the Court found that *J.L.* was not one of those situations. In distinguishing this case from *White* the Court in *J.L.* stated, in pertinent part:

> In *White* the police received an anonymous tip asserting that a woman was carrying cocaine and predicting that she would leave an apartment building at a specified time, get into a car matching a particular description, and drive to a named motel. . . . Only after police observation showed that the informant had accurately predicted the woman's movements . . . did it become reasonable to think the tipster had inside knowledge about the suspect and therefore to credit his assertion about the cocaine. . . . Knowledge about a person's future movements indicates some familiarity with that person's affairs, but having such knowledge does not necessarily imply that the informant knows, in particular, whether that person is carrying hidden contraband. . . .
>
> The tip in the instant case lacked the moderate indicia of reliability present in *White* and essential to the Court's decision in that case. The anonymous call concerning J.L. provided no predictive information and therefore left the police without means to test the informant's knowledge or credibility. . . . All the police had to go on in this case was the bare report of an unknown, unaccountable informant who neither explained how he knew about the gun nor supplied any basis for believing he had inside information about J.L.

In general, tips provided by known tipsters are entitled to greater deference than those that emanate from unknown sources. Despite the lower quantum of proof required to satisfy the *Terry* threshold, some showing that the tipster is honest and that the information is reliable must still be made. And this threshold is easier to satisfy when, as in *White*, the government can demonstrate that the information derived from a known source. Still, tips provided anonymously may suffice for *Terry* purposes.

F   A   Q

Q: What if an anonymous tipster provided information about a grave threat — a threat much graver than that presented in *Florida v. J.L.*? Does the Court require the same level of demonstrated reliability from informants in such situations?

A: To date, that question has not been addressed by the Court. However, the Court in *J.L.* did discuss this situation in dicta. The Court left for another day whether a lower standard might suffice for tips that allege threats "so great as to justify a search even without a showing of reliability." The Court added, "We do not say, for example, that a report of a person carrying a bomb need bear the indicia of reliability we demand for a report of a person carrying a firearm before the police can constitutionally conduct a frisk."

SUMMARY

■ An encounter does not involve any level of government detention and does not implicate the Fourth Amendment.

■ An arrest is a seizure within the meaning of the Fourth Amendment and requires either the application of physical force by a government official or submission to the assertion of authority.

■ A person is seized within the meaning of the Fourth Amendment "whenever a police officer accosts an individual and restrains his freedom to walk away."

■ An officer may seize a person within the meaning of the Fourth Amendment if the officer reasonably suspects that the individual has committed or is about to commit a crime. An officer may frisk a person for weapons if he reasonably suspects that the person is armed and dangerous.

■ To justify the initial intrusion, an officer must be "able to point to specific and articulable facts which, taken together with rational inferences from those facts, reasonably warrant that intrusion." This test is assessed from the perspective of a reasonable person.

■ *Terry* stops can be upheld when the information leading to the seizure was initially obtained from either known or anonymous sources. Though a court must assess the basis of the informant's knowledge as well as his credibility, the standard is not as high as when assessing probable cause.

CONNECTIONS

Relationship to Searches and the Reasonableness Inquiry (Chapter 3), Searches, Seizures, and the Warrant Clause (Chapter 4), and Executing the Warrant (Chapter 5)

Presumptively, a warrant must be obtained prior to performing a search or seizure. *Terry* stops and frisks are an exception to the warrant requirement. In addition, a search performed pursuant to a warrant and a *Terry* search and seizure are assessed pursuant to the reasonableness clause.

Relationship to Searches and Seizures: Exceptions to the Warrant Requirement and Residential Arrests (Chapter 6)

The reasonableness clause of the Fourth Amendment governs both the legitimacy of *Terry*-level searches and seizures as well as the manner in which officers actually effectuate an arrest based upon probable cause.

Relationship to Searches Incident to Arrest (Chapter 7), the Automobile Exception (Chapter 8), and the Plain View Doctrine (Chapter 9)

An officer who performs a search pursuant to *Terry* might observe additional evidence that provides the officer with probable cause to conduct a more extensive search. Thus, an officer who performs a limited protective sweep of a house might observe in plain sight additional evidence of crime that would then justify a more extensive search of the home. Similarly, an officer who performs a *Terry* stop may discover additional evidence that provides the basis for a more expansive search pursuant to either the search incident to arrest doctrine or the automobile exception.

Relationship to Fourth Amendment Violations and Their Associated Remedies (Chapter 15)

Like any other government search or seizure performed during a criminal investigation, a search or seizure that exceeds the scope authorized by *Terry* is subject to suppression pursuant to the exclusionary rule.

Terry Stops and Frisks — Contextual Applications and Derivative Lessons

12

I remember when I was a law student one of my professors remarked, "Though each year I get older my students remain the same age." Now

O V E R V I E W

that I am a professor, having taught for several years, I can better appreciate his comment! I mention that because I am frequently afraid that certain remarks I make in class reference a time period so distant that my students are unable to appreciate my communication. The title of the following subsection is bringing back those same fears!

PLANES, BUSES, AND AUTOMOBILES

Years ago there was an excellent movie titled *Planes, Trains and Automobiles* starring Steve Martin and John Candy. This subsection title is simply a play on the movie title. I hope you caught the attempted humor! If not . . . oh well, another year older.

Terry v. Ohio involved the stop and frisk of an individual on a public street. However, since the 1968 *Terry* decision, the Court has applied the *Terry* concept in a varying array of contexts. To date, the Supreme Court has yet to issue a significant proclamation regarding the *Terry* doctrine in the railroad context. However, the Court has applied it in the context of airplane sites, buses, and automobiles. And the study of *Terry* in each of these contexts — contexts you will in all likelihood discuss in your Criminal Procedure class — provides important lessons about investigative detentions and searches.

This chapter will examine these various contexts, discuss their important derivative lessons, and reveal the significant expanse of the *Terry* doctrine. It will begin with a review of the free to leave test in the context of airport encounters.

The study of *Terry* in this context is important not only for its lessons in regard to airport encounters but also for its derivative instructiveness regarding the application of *Terry* in most non-airport situations. Thereafter, *Terry* will be examined in the context of bus encounters. As you will learn, a variant of the *Terry* doctrine is applied during police-citizen encounters aboard buses. This chapter will then examine how the Court has applied *Terry* in the context of automobile stops — a significant source point of police investigative activity. It will then conclude with a review of *Terry* as applied in the context of unprovoked flight from the presence of police officers.

A. APPLICATION OF THE FREE TO LEAVE TEST — AIRPORT CASES

    1. *United States v. Mendenhall*
    2. *Florida v. Royer*
    3. *Mendenhall* and *Royer* Applied: *Terry* Stops at the Workplace

B. VARIATION OF THE FREE TO LEAVE TEST — BUS CASES

C. EXPANDED APPLICATION OF *TERRY* — AUTOMOBILE CASES

    1. *Terry*-Level Seizures of Automobile Occupants
    2. *Terry* Frisks of an Automobile

D. UNPROVOKED FLIGHT AND HIGH-CRIME AREAS

A. Application of the Free to Leave Test — Airport Cases

In this section, two cases will be discussed, *United States v. Mendenhall*[1] and *Florida v. Royer*.[2] The lesson about these cases has little, if anything, to do with the location of the *Terry* stops — airports. Instead, the value of *Mendenhall* and *Royer* lies in their lessons about the free to leave test. The cases provide excellent insight into how the free to leave test has been applied by the Court when it attempts to ascertain whether a police-citizen interaction was an encounter, a stop requiring reasonable suspicion, or an arrest. Remember, a person is considered to be seized for Fourth Amendment purposes if a reasonable person under the circumstances would not feel free to leave.

    Mendenhall and *Royer* present facts with significant similarities. Yet despite the common features, the Court produces divergent opinions. In one case, two members of the majority found that the defendant was not seized (she was free to leave), while in the other the Court found that the defendant was seized (she was not free to leave) and that the evidence against her should have been suppressed. Indeed, a judicial determination of precisely when, if at all, a *Terry*-level seizure has occurred can be critical. And *Mendenhall* and *Royer* provide excellent examples of how the presence

---

[1]446 U.S. 544 (1980).
[2]460 U.S. 491 (1983).

or absence of certain facts can spell ultimate success or doom for a defendant challenging his stop on *Terry* grounds.

(1) *United States v. Mendenhall*

In *Mendenhall*,[3] a female passenger (defendant) who disembarked from an airplane that arrived in Detroit from Los Angeles was approached by agents with the Drug Enforcement Administration who, based upon her profile, suspected her of narcotics trafficking. The defendant, upon request, produced and handed to the agents her airline ticket and her driver's license. While the license bore the defendant's name, the airline ticket did not. After some additional questioning both items were returned to the defendant. The defendant was then asked to accompany the agents to a nearby room, to which she consented. Once there, the defendant also consented to a search of her person and her handbag. A search of her person uncovered heroin.

Chapter 11 discussed the concepts of encounters, arrests, and stops based upon reasonable suspicion. Typically, if the prosecution can prove that evidence was seized during an encounter, the government will succeed against a defendant's suppression motion. If, on the other hand, the court finds that the evidence was seized subsequent to a seizure, then the government will often have to justify the stop (prove the requisite level of suspicion) as a prerequisite to surviving the suppression motion.

Notice in *Mendenhall* that the heroin was seized after she had consented to accompany the agents to a nearby room in the airport and to a subsequent search. In fact, a majority of the Court, in an opinion by Justice Stewart, decided the case on the basis of consent. However, two members of the majority — Justices Stewart and Rehnquist — went a step further and also assessed the propriety of the government's conduct prior to the provision of consent. This was an important question, though one not decided by a majority of the Court. As noted, if the defendant in these circumstances can successfully argue that she was seized prior to her arrival in the room, then it would be incumbent upon the government to present facts sufficient to justify the initial detention.

Justices Stewart and Rehnquist found that the initial confrontation between the agents and the defendant was nothing more than an encounter. In reaching this conclusion, they enunciated a "free to leave" test, which has since been adopted by the Court as an appropriate test to govern *Terry* claims generally. Specifically, the Justices stated that a Fourth Amendment seizure occurs whenever the totality of the circumstances indicates that an individual would not reasonably believe that he was free to leave. They then expounded upon this conclusion by delineating circumstances suggestive of a Fourth Amendment seizure. As you read the following paragraph, take note of the multitude of evaluative factors delineated therein. It is a lesson in factual evaluation that is applicable to virtually any situation presenting a *Terry* claim.

> Examples of circumstances that might indicate a seizure, even where the person did not attempt to leave, would be the threatening presence of several officers, the display of a weapon by an officer, some physical touching of the person of the citizen, or the use of language or tone of voice indicating that compliance with the officer's request might be compelled (citations omitted). In the absence of some such evidence, otherwise

---

[3]446 U.S. 544 (1980).

inoffensive contact between a member of the public and the police cannot, as a matter of law, amount to a seizure of that person.

On the facts of this case, no "seizure" of the respondent occurred. The events took place in the public concourse. The agents wore no uniforms and displayed no weapons. They did not summon the respondent to their presence, but instead approached her and identified themselves as federal agents. They requested, but did not demand to see the respondent's identification and ticket. Such conduct without more, did not amount to an intrusion upon any constitutionally protected interest. The respondent was not seized simply by reason of the fact that the agents approached her, asked her if she would show them her ticket and identification, and posed to her a few questions. Nor was it enough to establish a seizure that the person asking the questions was a law enforcement official (citations omitted). In short, nothing in the record suggests that the respondent had any objective reason to believe that she was not free to end the conversation in the concourse and proceed on her way, and for that reason we conclude that the agents' initial approach to her was not a seizure.

Our conclusion that no seizure occurred is not affected by the fact that the respondent was not expressly told by the agents that she was free to decline to cooperate with their inquiry, for the voluntariness of her responses does not depend upon her having been so informed.

If you were approached by agents in an airport under the circumstances presented in *Mendenhall*, would you feel free to leave? Can the defendant's continued acquiescence to the agents' requests be a signal that neither she nor others in such circumstances truly feel free to terminate such encounters? The following case, *Florida v. Royer*,[4] presents similar facts but reaches a different conclusion.

(2) *Florida v. Royer*

In *Royer*, the defendant was observed by an undercover narcotics detective at Miami International Airport. The detectives approached the defendant given that his profile apparently fit that associated with drug couriers. In response to their request, the defendant provided the detectives with his airline ticket and his driver's license. The requested items bore different names. When asked about the discrepancy, Royer provided an explanation and "became noticeably more nervous during this conversation." The defendant was then asked to accompany them to a nearby room. Unlike in *Mendenhall*, the agents retained the defendant's license and ticket. One of the detectives also retrieved the defendant's previously checked luggage and brought it to the room where they had gathered. The detective had not obtained the defendant's consent prior to the luggage retrieval. One of the suitcases was eventually searched (after obtaining the defendant's consent to search) and illegal narcotics were recovered.

A plurality of the justices found that the defendant had been illegally detained. In so holding, they acknowledged that individuals could be detained short of probable cause. In language that remains central to any *Terry* analysis, the justices cautioned that "an investigative detention must be temporary and last no longer than is necessary to effectuate the purpose of the stop. Similarly, the investigative methods employed should be the least intrusive means reasonably available to verify or dispel the officer's suspicion in a short period of time." Though the plurality found it permissible for the agents to request to see the defendant's driver's license and ticket,

---

[4]460 U.S. 491 (1983).

they also found that the defendant was subsequently seized during his encounter with the police. Specifically, the plurality determined that a seizure occurred after the detectives had revealed their identity, informed the defendant that he was under investigation, asked him to accompany them to a nearby room, and failed to return the requested documentation or inform him that he was free to leave. This seizure occurred, according to the plurality, prior to the time consent was obtained to search the suitcase. The following detailed rationale was set forth in support for their conclusion:

> By the time Royer was informed that the officers wished to examine his luggage, he had identified himself when approached by the officers and had attempted to explain the discrepancy between the name shown on his identification and the name under which he had purchased his ticket and identified his luggage. The officers were not satisfied, for they informed him they were narcotics agents and had reason to believe that he was carrying illegal drugs. They requested him to accompany them to the police room. Royer went with them. He found himself in a small room — a large closet — equipped with a desk and two chairs. He was alone with two police officers who again told him that they thought he was carrying narcotics. He also found that the officers, without his consent, had retrieved his checked luggage from the airlines. What had begun as a consensual inquiry in a public place had escalated into an investigatory procedure in a police interrogation room, where the police, unsatisfied with previous explanations, sought to confirm their suspicions. The officers had Royer's ticket, they had his identification, and they had seized his luggage. Royer was never informed that he was free to board his plane if he so chose, and he reasonably believed that he was being detained. At least as of that moment, any consensual aspects of the encounter had evaporated. . . .

Among the most critical facts that distinguish *Royer* from *Mendenhall* were the government's failure to return the ticket and driver's license and the nonconsensual retrieval of the previously checked luggage. In your opinion, do these facts sufficiently distinguish *Royer* from *Mendenhall*? Whether these facts are or are not

---

Sidebar

REFINEMENT OF THE "LEAST INTRUSIVE MEANS REASONABLY AVAILABLE" TEST

The *Royer* plurality emphasized a point that the Supreme Court, in subsequent cases, has de-emphasized if not retreated from altogether. The Court, as part of its "investigative methods employed should be the least intrusive means reasonably available" analysis, noted that a more practical investigative alternative was available to the government officers. Specifically, the plurality observed that the police could have employed trained dogs. Just two years after *Royer* the Court retreated from the apparent strictures that this holding arguably imposed. In a pair of cases — *United States v. Sharpe*[5] and *United States v. Montoya de Hernandez*[6] — the Court emphasized that an evaluation of a challenged detention or search is not dependent upon the availability of another less intrusive alternative. Rather, the key inquiry is "whether the police diligently pursued a means of investigation that was likely to confirm or dispel their suspicions quickly, during which time it was necessary to detain the defendant." In cautioning against "unrealistic second-guessing," the Supreme Court in *Sharpe* stated, "A creative judge engaged in *post hoc* evaluation of police conduct can almost always imagine some alternative means by which the objectives of the police might have been accomplished. But '[t]he fact that the protection of the public might, in the abstract, have been accomplished by "less intrusive" means does not, itself, render the search unreasonable.'"

[5]470 U.S. 675 (1985).
[6]473 U.S. 531 (1985).

sufficiently distinguishable, what these cases highlight is the delicate task facing courts — and students taking a criminal procedure examination — when assessing whether a given police-citizen encounter constitutes a seizure implicating Fourth Amendment concerns.

(3) *Mendenhall* and *Royer* Applied: *Terry* Stops at the Workplace

The Overview section of this chapter stated that the airport line of cases are instructive, in part, for the lessons they teach regarding how *Terry* is commonly applied in an array of non-airport settings. The case of *INS v. Delgado*,[7] decided one year after *Florida v. Royer*, is precisely one such situation.

In *Delgado*, agents with the Immigration and Naturalization Service "conducted a survey of the work force" at a particular pleating company in an attempt to locate illegal aliens. Several agents participated in the operation, with some located close to the building's exits, while others were "dispersed throughout the factory." All the agents were armed, carried communication devices, and displayed their badges. After the workers were approached, the agents would identify themselves and ask from one to three questions regarding the employee's citizenship. Credible replies resulted in the cessation of further questioning. However, less than satisfactory responses resulted in a request for the production of immigration documents. The Court noted that during the inquisitorial process, "employees continued with their work and were free to walk around within the factory."

Whether the agent-worker contact amounted to a seizure or was merely an encounter was the Court's focus. Citing *Mendenhall* and *Royer*, the Court recognized "that an initially consensual encounter between a police officer and a citizen can be transformed into a seizure or detention within the meaning of the Fourth Amendment, 'if, in view of all the circumstances surrounding the incident, a reasonable person would have believed that he was not free to leave.'" The Court concluded that the defendant-workers had not been seized.

In reaching this result, the Court stated that mere questioning about an individual's identity does not, by itself, trigger Fourth Amendment safeguards. Additional conduct by the government must be demonstrated before a seizure within the meaning of the Constitution can be found. The Court found unpersuasive the argument that the positioning of agents at various locations at the factory created an atmosphere whereby the workers would not feel free to leave. The Court reasoned that the workers' freedom to leave was already restricted on account of their obligations to their employer. The majority further noted that during the course of questioning the workers continued to work and move about the factory with only minimal interruption. The Court also concluded — to the dismay of many of my students — that the "obvious purpose" for the positioning of the agents by the exits was not to intimidate workers from leaving but merely to ensure that all workers were questioned.

---

[7] 466 U.S. 210 (1984).

B. Variation of the Free to Leave Test — Bus Cases

As noted, a seizure for Fourth Amendment purposes occurs when a reasonable person would not feel free to leave. However, a refinement of this test applies in the context of a bus encounter.

In a pair of cases — *Florida v. Bostick*[8] and *United States v. Drayton*[9] — the Supreme Court held that the traditional "free to leave" test was inapplicable in the context of police-citizen encounters aboard buses. The Court noted that the free to leave test was an inappropriate standard given that bus passengers "may not want to get off a bus" given the possibility of it departing prior to their reentry. Instead, the appropriate test "is whether a reasonable person would feel free to decline the officer's requests or otherwise terminate the encounter."

In *Drayton*, the Court found that a seizure had not occurred. In my experience teaching this case, many students — though not all — find this result rather remarkable given the factual scenario presented. There, the defendants were aboard a Greyhound bus that had made a scheduled stop. After the driver departed the bus to do some paperwork, three officers boarded "as part of a routine drug and weapons interdiction effort." The officers were in plain clothes and possessed "concealed weapons and visible badges." With one officer situated in the driver's seat at the front of the bus and a second officer stationary at its rear, a third officer, starting at the bus's rear, approached each passenger and asked them some questions. As he walked "toward the front of the bus," the officer inquired about each passenger's travel plans and "sought to match passengers with luggage in the overhead racks." When making these inquiries, the officer would stand adjacent to or just behind the passenger with whom he was speaking.

With respect to the defendants (Drayton and Brown, who were seated in aisle and window seats, respectively), the officer followed the described protocol and obtained consent to search. Narcotics were found on the person of each defendant. Finding that the defendants had not been seized, the Court provided the following rationale:

> The officers gave the passengers no reason to believe that they were required to answer the officers' questions. When Officer Lang approached respondents, he did not brandish a weapon or make any intimidating movements. He left the aisle free so that respondents could exit. He spoke to passengers one by one and in a polite, quiet voice. Nothing he said would suggest to a reasonable person that he or she was barred from leaving the bus or otherwise terminating the encounter.
>
> There was no application of force, no intimidating movement, no overwhelming show of force, no brandishing of weapons, no blocking of exits, no threat, no command, not even an authoritative tone of voice. It is beyond question that had this encounter occurred on the street, it would be constitutional. The fact that an encounter takes place on a bus does not on its own transform standard police questioning of citizens into an illegal seizure (citation omitted).

Do you accept the Court's analogy of this encounter to a police-citizen encounter on the street? Do the confines of a bus sufficiently distinguish this police-citizen encounter from one that occurs in an outside venue? Many of my students do not

---

[8]501 U.S. 429 (1991).
[9]536 U.S. 194 (2002).

accept the Court's analogy. Consider the following additional rationales set forth by the Court:

> [Defendants] make much of the fact that [the officer] displayed his badge. . . . Officers are often required to wear uniforms and in many circumstances this is cause for assurance, not discomfort. . . . That most law enforcement officers are armed is a fact well known to the public. The presence of a holstered firearm thus is unlikely to contribute to the coerciveness of the encounter absent active brandishing of the weapon. . . .
>
> And of more importance, bus passengers answer officers' questions and otherwise cooperate not because of coercion but because the passengers know that their participation enhances their own safety and the safety of those around them. "While most citizens will respond to a police request, the fact that people do so, and do so without being told they are free not to respond, hardly eliminates the consensual nature of the response" (citation omitted).

If you were a passenger on a bus, would your cooperation, if any, be motivated by a desire to enhance your own safety as well as the safety of others? The three justices in dissent dismissed the majority's viewpoint, characterizing this contention as bearing "an air of unreality."

C. Expanded Application of *Terry* — Automobile Cases

The *Terry* doctrine allows an officer to stop an individual if there is reasonable suspicion to believe that a crime has been committed. It further authorizes a frisk of an individual if an officer reasonably suspects that the person may be armed and dangerous. *Terry*, of course, involved the stop and frisk of an actual human being. As this section explains, the *Terry* doctrine has been expanded to allow officers to order the movement of individuals — even those not suspected of any criminal activity — and to perform limited searches of automobiles.

(1) *Terry*-Level Seizures of Automobile Occupants

When an officer effectuates a traffic stop, the Supreme Court held in *Delaware v. Prouse*[10] that for Fourth Amendment purposes the driver has been seized. This result may seem rather unremarkable. After all, an officer has effectuated a stop — albeit a brief stop — of a traveling vehicle. And, certainly, the driver would not feel free to leave the scene in such instances.

But some important questions emanate from this holding. One such question is whether passengers, in addition to drivers, are seized when a traffic stop is effectuated. Another question that will be discussed in much greater length in Chapter 15 concerns the issue of standing. Specifically, that chapter will address, among other issues, whether all the occupants within a stopped vehicle have standing to challenge the introduction of government-seized evidence during a vehicular stop.

In *Brendlin v. California*,[11] the Supreme Court addressed both of these issues. The Court answered, wisely, that all occupants within a stopped vehicle are detained

---

[10]440 U.S. 648 (1979).
[11]551 U.S. 249 (2007).

for Fourth Amendment purposes and have standing to challenge the constitutionality of the seizure. The Court reasoned that all occupants of a stopped vehicle would reasonably feel that they were not free to depart the scene. It stated that the travels of all the occupants within a stopped vehicle are equally curtailed and that any attempt by a passenger to leave would raise the suspicions of the investigating officer. It would be reasonable for passengers to assume, according to the Court, that an officer would "not let people move around in ways that could jeopardize his safety." The Court further observed that the result in *Brendlin* was foretold by dicta appearing in prior Court decisions. In *Prouse*, for example, the Court declared, "[S]topping an automobile and detaining its occupants constitute a 'seizure' within the meaning of [the Fourth and Fourteenth] Amendments, even though the purpose of the stop is limited and the resulting detention quite brief."

In a pair of cases — *Pennsylvania v. Mimms*[12] and *Maryland v. Wilson*[13] — the Supreme Court held that it is reasonable within the Fourth Amendment for an officer, as a matter of right, to order the driver of a vehicle as well as any passengers to exit the car whenever a vehicle is lawfully stopped. Thus, whether stopped for a felonious crime or a mere traffic infraction, an officer has an absolute right to order that the occupants of a vehicle exit for reasons of officer safety. This right exists irrespective of whether the officer has any reason to suspect that an individual is armed and dangerous.

A contrary rule, in the view of the Court, would expose officers to greater safety risks. Aside from the possibility of roadside assaults, the *Mimms* Court added that officers are also exposed to the possibility of "accidental injury from passing traffic." Given this reality, an "officer prudently may prefer to ask the driver of the vehicle to step out of the car and off onto the shoulder of the road where the inquiry may be pursued with greater safety to both." And, according to the Court in *Wilson*, the presence of passengers only heightens these safety risks given the increased numbers of individuals present at the scene.

On the other hand, the Court in *Mimms* and *Wilson* found that the additional intrusion that would accompany this requirement would be *de minimus*. As stated in *Mimms*:

> The driver is being asked to expose to view very little more of his person than is already exposed. The police have already lawfully decided that the driver shall be briefly detained; the only question is whether he shall spend that period sitting in the driver's seat of his car or standing alongside it. Not only is the insistence of the police on the latter choice not a "serious intrusion upon the sanctity of the person," but it hardly rises to the level of a "petty indignity."

With respect to passengers, the *Wilson* Court added that since "the passengers are already [lawfully] stopped . . . [t]he only change in their circumstances which will result from ordering them out of the car is that they will be outside of, rather than inside of, the stopped car." Therefore, any infringement upon individual liberty imposed by the rule would be "minimal."

---

[12]434 U.S. 106 (1977).
[13]519 U.S. 408 (1997).

Sidebar

TERRY-LEVEL SEIZURE OF HOUSE OCCUPANTS

The same rationale that permits officers to direct the movements of the occupants of an automobile has been applied in the home context as well. In *Michigan v. Summers*,[14] the Supreme Court had occasion to consider whether officers in the midst of executing a search warrant for narcotics could detain the occupant-owner of a residence who was present during the warrant's execution. Answering this question in the affirmative, the Court emphasized the less intrusive nature of the seizure at issue in *Summers*. It noted, for example, that the liberty infringement in *Summers* was less than the infringement occasioned by the search warrant itself, that the seizure occurred within the occupant's home, that many individuals in these circumstances would prefer to remain within their home during the warrant's execution, and that overall intrusiveness of the seizure in *Summers* was less than for custodial arrests. The Court further noted the governmental interests in flight prevention and officer safety. Observing that "no special danger [of evidence destruction or officer safety] to the police [was] suggested by the evidence in this record," the Court found that such dangers often present themselves in search warrants for narcotics. In addition, the Court reasoned that the prior judicial determination that there was probable cause to believe that contraband would be found within the home also served to justify the detention of occupants connected to that residence.

In the end, the Court adopted the following rule: "If the evidence that a citizen's residence is harboring contraband is sufficient to persuade a judicial officer that an invasion of the citizen's privacy is justified, it is constitutionally reasonable to require that citizen to remain while officers of the law execute a valid warrant to search his home. Thus, for Fourth Amendment purposes, we hold that a warrant to search for contraband founded on probable cause implicitly carries with it the limited authority to detain the occupants of the premises while a proper search is conducted."

---

[14]452 U.S. 692 (1981).

(2) *Terry* Frisks of an Automobile

Terry permits a frisk of an individual if the officer has reasonable suspicion that the individual is armed and dangerous. But are there circumstances where an officer can conduct a *Terry* frisk of a vehicle? If so, is the *Terry* search limited to a patdown of the vehicle's exterior? Now that would look a bit strange! The Supreme Court addressed this issue in *Michigan v. Long*.[15] In that case, officers observed a vehicle traveling at an excessive speed swerve into a ditch. Upon arriving at the scene, the officers met the driver at the rear of the vehicle. After requesting the defendant's driver's license and registration, the officers followed the defendant as he turned and approached his driver's side door (which was open at the time of the officers' arrival). As they approached, the officers observed a large hunting knife on the driver's-side floorboard. They then subjected the defendant to a protective *Terry* frisk of his person. The frisk did not reveal the presence of any weapons.

Thereafter, the officers conducted a search of the passenger compartment, whereupon they discovered marijuana under an armrest on the front seat. The Supreme Court addressed the "important question of the authority of a police officer to protect himself by conducting a *Terry*-type search of the passenger compartment

---

[15]463 U.S. 1032 (1983).

TERRY SEIZURES AND FRISKS: PART ONE — HOUSES

Given the stated purpose that underlies *Terry* frisks — namely, officer safety — it is not surprising that the Court extended this principle to the search of homes. In *Maryland v. Buie*,[16] the Court held that an officer may conduct a "protective sweep" of a home if the officer has a reasonable belief "that the area swept harbored an individual posing a danger to the officer or others." It declared that a protective premises sweep must be incident to an arrest, swift, and narrow in scope. Noting that the objective underlying such sweeps is officer and public safety, the Court stated that such sweeps allow inspecting officers to cursorily search only those areas large enough that an individual may be harbored. Citing *Terry* and *Long*, the Court reasoned that officers performing an arrest within a home have an "analogous interest . . . in taking steps to assure themselves that the house in which a suspect is being, or has just been, arrested is not harboring other persons who are dangerous and who could unexpectedly launch an attack. The risk of danger in the context of an arrest in the home is as great as, if not greater than, it is in an on-the-street or roadside investigatory encounter." In contrast to an arrest or search warrant, which typically grants an officer broad access to a home, and a search incident to arrest, which allows for a search of only the immediate area of an arrestee, a "protective sweep" arguably falls somewhere in between these two extremes. It potentially grants an officer access to rooms that extend well beyond the immediate grab area of the arrestee, but restricts the areas that can be searched to those large enough to harbor an individual.

---

[16]494 U.S. 325 (1990).

of a motor vehicle during the lawful investigatory stop of the occupant of the vehicle." Rejecting the defendant's claim that *Terry* was limited to a protective search of the individual, the Court held that the principles of *Terry* can extend to searches of the automobile itself. Specifically, the Court held that an officer may search the passenger compartment of a vehicle if the officer has a reasonable belief that a suspect is dangerous and that he may gain immediate access to weapons. Though a search of the passenger compartment is allowed, a search is permitted of only those areas where a weapon may be placed or concealed. The Court concluded that in this case the search of the vehicle was reasonable.

D. Unprovoked Flight and High-Crime Areas

I often tell my students that when I was prosecuting I would frequently receive investigative reports that would include statements such as "the defendant while in our presence appeared

TERRY SEIZURES AND FRISKS: PART TWO — EFFECTS

In *United States v. Place*,[17] the Supreme Court addressed "whether the Fourth Amendment prohibits law enforcement authorities from temporarily detaining personal luggage for exposure to a trained narcotics detection dog on the basis of reasonable suspicion that the luggage contains narcotics." Though the Court found that the specific search at issue exceeded the permissible bounds of *Terry*, the Court held "that when an officer's observations lead him reasonably to believe that a traveler is carrying luggage that contains narcotics, the principles of *Terry* and its progeny would permit the officer to detain the luggage briefly to investigate the circumstances that aroused his suspicion, provided that the investigative detention is properly limited in scope."

---

[17]462 U.S. 696 (1983).

to be nervous." Or "the defendant fled the scene upon our arrival." Or perhaps it was claimed that the defendant appeared nervous or acted evasively while in a comparatively high-crime area. Maybe the defendant was nervous or did indeed flee upon noticing the police. Or perhaps the defendant engaged in evasive conduct while in a high-crime section of town. But there might be innocent explanations for such behavior. Moreover, what difference, if any, should it make if evasive conduct occurred in a low- or high-crime area? And what constitutes a "high-crime" area anyway? When assessing *Terry* claims and presented with such evidence, what is the appropriate weight that a court should assign these and other comparable factors when making *Terry* assessments?

Illinois v. Wardlow[18] was a case that involved unprovoked flight in a purported high-crime area. Though only five members of the *Wardlow* Court ultimately concluded that the facts presented warranted the investigatory stop, a central lesson that should be gleaned from this chapter is that the quantum of proof required to support an investigatory stop pursuant to *Terry* is not very steep.

In *Wardlow*, officers with the Chicago Police Department were traveling in an area known for its drug trafficking. As they were driving, they observed the defendant, who was standing next to a nearby building holding a bag. After observing the officers, the defendant then fled. The officers pursued the defendant and eventually effectuated a stop. An ensuing protective search revealed the presence of a loaded firearm in the bag that the defendant had been carrying.

The Court stated that a person's mere presence in a high-crime area, though a relevant criterion, will not standing alone justify a *Terry* stop. Here, however, the majority found an additional fact — the defendant's unprovoked flight — that ultimately justified the investigatory stop. The Court reasoned that such flight, while not conclusive of criminal activity, "is certainly suggestive of such." The majority further distinguished this conduct from a citizen's mere refusal to cooperate with the police during a police-citizen encounter. The Court declared that an individual's refusal to cooperate does not provide a sufficient basis to justify a *Terry*-level seizure. Unprovoked flight, according to the Court, "is not 'going about one's business'; in fact, it is just the opposite."

The Court acknowledged that innocent persons will inevitably be wrongfully subjected to *Terry* stops. Yet the Court stressed that the police, when confronted with ambiguous conduct, are entitled to resolve the ambiguity by conducting a *Terry*-level seizure.

The dissenting justices concurred with the majority that flight in conjunction with other factors may serve to justify a stop on *Terry* grounds. However, the dissent disagreed that such circumstances existed in this instance. In considerable detail, the dissent recognized that there are a myriad of reasons — both innocent and less-innocent reasons — why an individual may flee a scene. And they added that these reasons are particularly present for many minorities and for those who reside in high-crime areas. Such individuals, the dissent stated, might consider contact with law enforcement to be fraught with personal risk, irrespective of any separate criminal incident. In the end, it was the dissent's view that the majority's reliance upon the purported high-crime character of a neighborhood not only failed to support the finding that reasonable suspicion existed, but, in fact, served to undercut that conclusion. The dissent asserted that since "many factors providing innocent motivations for unprovoked flight are concentrated in high crime areas, the character of the neighborhood

---

[18]528 U.S. 119 (2000).

arguably makes an inference of guilt less appropriate, rather than more so. Like unprovoked flight itself, presence in a high-crime neighborhood is a fact too generic and susceptible to innocent explanation to satisfy the reasonable suspicion inquiry."

SUMMARY

- An array of factors is typically considered by a court when assessing whether an individual was seized within the meaning of the Fourth Amendment. A key inquiry in determining whether an individual was free to leave is "whether the police diligently pursued a means of investigation that was likely to confirm or dispel their suspicions quickly, during which time it was necessary to detain the defendant."

- During police-citizen encounters on buses, the central issue is not whether the citizen-passenger was free to leave, but "whether a reasonable person would feel free to decline the officer's requests or otherwise terminate the encounter."

- In the automobile context, both the driver and the vehicle's passengers are seized during a traffic stop. Moreover, an officer may, pursuant to *Terry*, order the driver and the passengers to exit the vehicle. An officer may also search the passenger compartment of the vehicle if the officer reasonably suspects that a suspect is dangerous and that he may gain immediate access to weapons.

- An officer may perform a *Terry* frisk of the passenger compartment of a vehicle if the officer has a reasonable belief that a suspect is dangerous and that he may gain immediate access to weapons.

- An officer may perform a *Terry* frisk of a house if the officer has a reasonable belief that other persons who may pose a danger might be found within the home.

- An officer may detain an individual's luggage that the officer reasonably suspects contains narcotics or illegal contraband in order to conduct additional investigation provided the detention is temporary and sufficiently limited in scope.

- Unprovoked flight, without more, cannot justify a *Terry* stop. However, when combined with other factors such as presence in a high-crime area, a *Terry* stop may be justified.

CONNECTIONS

Relationship to Searches Incident to Arrest (Chapter 7)

Whereas an officer who effectuates an arrest may search an individual (and, in the automobile context, the passenger compartment of an automobile) incident thereto, an officer who performs a *Terry* stop may perform a search (of either an individual or a vehicle) that is comparatively more limited. A *Terry* search may be performed only if the officer reasonably suspects that the individual seized possesses a weapon (or, in the automobile context, reasonably suspects that a weapon might be found within the vehicle that could be immediately accessible to the suspect).

Relationship to the Automobile Exception (Chapter 8)

An officer who performs an automobile search pursuant to *Terry* may only search those areas of the vehicle that the officer reasonably suspects might contain a weapon. An officer who performs a search pursuant to the automobile exception can search anywhere in the vehicle where there is probable cause to believe evidence of crime might be found.

Relationship to Administrative and Special Needs Searches and Seizures (Chapter 14)

The reasonable suspicion standard has also been applied in certain administrative search contexts. For example, a school official may perform a search of a student's closed containers (e.g., purse, backpack, etc.) if the official reasonably suspects that student of violating a school code (e.g., against school policy to possess cigarettes, etc.).

Relationship to Fourth Amendment Violations and Their Associated Remedies (Chapter 15)

Like any other government search or seizure performed during a criminal investigation, a search or seizure that exceeds the scope authorized by *Terry* is subject to suppression pursuant to the exclusionary rule.

Terry Stops and Frisks — Relevant Considerations

13

Chapter 2 stated that among the very first tasks that a criminal procedure student should undertake when an examination fact pattern presents a

O V E R V I E W

challenge to an alleged seizure is to determine whether the Fourth Amendment was implicated by the government conduct. If so, then the student should proceed to ascertain at what moment the claimant was either seized pursuant to *Terry* or arrested. A student should pursue the same evaluative process when assessing whether a challenged search was constitutional. If the Fourth Amendment was implicated, then the student should proceed to assess whether the government search required a finding of reasonable suspicion or probable cause. The preceding material in Chapters 11 and 12 detailed many of the factors relevant to these questions. This chapter will attempt to synthesize these factors as well as discuss some additional factors that are ordinarily considered when making these assessments.

A. *TERRY* SEIZURES AND SEARCHES: DURATION OF INVESTIGATIVE CONDUCT/MANNER OF EXECUTION

 1. *Terry* Seizures: Duration of Police-Citizen Encounter
 2. *Terry* Seizures: Manner of Execution
 3. *Terry* Searches: Duration/Manner of Execution
 4. *Terry* Searches: Probationers

A. *Terry* Seizures and Searches: Duration of Investigative Conduct/Manner of Execution

As noted, shortly after *Terry* was decided the Supreme Court essentially abandoned the "least intrusive means reasonably available" evaluative test for *Terry* seizures and searches. In its stead, the Court adopted a more lenient standard that asks whether the police, in pursuing their investigation, diligently attempted to confirm or dispel their suspicions. Two factors relevant to this evaluative process — the duration of the investigation and the manner in which the investigation was executed — are often critical to this inquiry. As you will see, these factors are frequently considered in conjunction.

(1) *Terry* Seizures: Duration of Police-Citizen Encounter

In the context of *Terry*-level seizures, the duration of the police-citizen encounter is a central inquiry. The reason for this is that the longer the encounter, the more the encounter resembles a *Terry* stop. And the longer the *Terry* stop, the more that stop resembles an arrest. Yet the Court has not established any definitive time limits demarking encounters, stops, and arrests. This is not terribly surprising given the impracticality of engaging in such abstract line-drawing. But does this failure inevitably produce inconsistent results? Consider the following two cases that involve *Terry* stops of drastically different lengths.

In *Illinois v. Caballes*,[1] the defendant was stopped by an officer for speeding along a highway. During the stop, a second officer pulled up to the scene, exited his car, and walked a trained narcotics-detection dog around the exterior of the defendant's car. This took place while the first officer was writing a warning ticket. As a result of the dog's alert, a search of the trunk ensued and revealed the presence of illegal narcotics. The duration of these events did not exceed ten minutes.

The Supreme Court observed that "[a] seizure that is justified solely by the interest in issuing a warning ticket to the driver can become unlawful if it is prolonged beyond the time reasonably required to complete that mission." In upholding the *Terry* seizure, the Court accepted the lower court's finding that "the duration of the stop . . . was entirely justified by the traffic offense and the ordinary inquiries incident to such a stop."

Compare *Caballes* with *United States v. Montoya de Hernandez*.[2] In *Montoya de Hernandez*, the defendant was detained after departing from an airplane on suspicion that she was transporting illegal narcotics through a method referred to as "balloon swallowing." The defendant had been flying internationally from Bogota, Colombia, to Los Angeles. After a lengthy detainment by custom officials a court order was obtained ordering a rectal exam. The exam revealed within her rectum balloons that were later determined to contain illegal narcotics. Though this was a case involving a border search, where the Court has determined that individuals have a lesser expectation of privacy, the Court upheld the detainment (which lasted approximately 24 hours) on *Terry* grounds. The Court observed that the length of the detention

---

[1]543 U.S. 405 (2005).
[2]473 U.S. 531 (1985).

"undoubtedly exceeds any other detention we have approved under" the *Terry* reasonable suspicion standard.

(2) *Terry* Seizures: Manner of Execution

It bears reemphasis that an identifying characteristic of *Terry* stops is their comparative brevity. Notwithstanding the result in *Montoya de Hernandez*, the *Terry* stop (including the accompanying time span) upheld in *Caballes* is more reflective of normative *Terry*-level seizures. In fact, *Caballes* is in general instructive for the lessons it provides regarding the proper approach to Fourth Amendment seizure and search problems.

Aside from the aforementioned duration issue, *Caballes* presented a second claim that the defendant insisted rendered the governmental seizure unreasonable. It was urged that the police exceeded the grounds permissible for a valid *Terry* stop when it commenced its narcotics investigation during a routine traffic stop. It was argued that the *Terry* stop authorized only an investigation of the traffic violation. Thus, by exceeding this boundary, the defendant argued that the *Terry* seizure was unreasonable.

The Court initially noted an important general principle applicable to all *Terry* stops: that "a seizure that is lawful at its inception can violate the Fourth Amendment if its manner of execution unreasonably infringes interests protected by the Constitution." The Court then stated—as noted in the previous subsection—that "[a] seizure that is justified solely by the interest in issuing a warning ticket to the driver can become unlawful if it is prolonged beyond the time reasonably required to complete *that* mission" (emphasis added). Indeed, the Illinois Supreme Court found that the employment of the dog sniff rendered the initial lawful stop of the vehicle unlawful. The court reasoned that "the use of the dog converted the citizen-police encounter from a lawful traffic stop into a drug investigation, and because the shift in purpose was not supported by any reasonable suspicion that respondent possessed narcotics, it was unlawful."

But the Supreme Court disagreed, reasoning that the government's method of execution—the employment of a drug-sniffing dog during a traffic stop—did not implicate an interest protected by the Constitution. As Justice Ginsburg stated in her dissent, "The Court so rules, holding that a dog sniff does not render a seizure that is reasonable in time unreasonable in scope." The majority found that the dog sniff at issue could only reveal the presence of illegal substances—an interest that is not constitutionally protected. As the Court stated, "In our view, conducting a dog sniff would not change the character of a traffic stop that is lawful at its inception and otherwise executed in a reasonable manner, unless the dog sniff itself infringed respondent's constitutionally protected interest in privacy." The Court contrasted this case with *Kyllo v. United States*. In *Kyllo*, the Court struck down the government's use of a thermal imaging device since that instrument could reveal the existence of innocent activities within the home. In contrast, the dog sniff in *Caballes* could only reveal the presence of illegal activity.

The method of execution factor was also at issue in *Hiibel v. Sixth Judicial Dist. Court of Nevada*.[3] There, a Nevada statute authorized officers during the course of a

---

[3] 542 U.S. 177 (2004).

lawful stop to demand the identity of a seized individual. The defendant in that case argued, inter alia, that the statute violated his rights under the Fourth Amendment. In upholding the statute, the Court observed that *Terry* stops are of limited duration, allowing an "officer to stop the person for a brief time and take additional steps to investigate further." It added, "The officer's action must be 'justified at its inception, and . . . reasonably related in scope to the circumstances which justified the interference in the first place.'"

The Court found a reasonable relation between a *Terry* stop and the identity request. In so holding, the Court assessed the statute's reasonableness by balancing the state's interest in law enforcement against the individual's interests under the Fourth Amendment:

> The Nevada statute satisfies that standard. The request for identity has an immediate relation to the purpose, rationale, and practical demands of a *Terry* stop. The threat of criminal sanction helps ensure that the request for identity does not become a legal nullity. On the other hand, the Nevada statute does not alter the nature of the stop itself: it does not change its duration (citation omitted) or its location. . . .

As in *Caballes*, the *Hiibel* Court concluded that the challenged conduct did not extend the duration of the stop and was not inconsistent with the underlying nature of the detention. The *Hiibel* Court added that the "reasonably related in scope" requirement prevented an officer from arresting an individual under the Nevada statute if the identity request was "not reasonably related to the circumstances justifying the [*Terry*] stop." In that regard, the Court concluded that the government's "request was a commonsense inquiry, not an effort to obtain an arrest for failure to identify after a *Terry* stop yielded insufficient evidence."

(a) Suspect Movements Ordered by Law Enforcement: Examples of Permissible Movements

Earlier in this chapter we learned that the longer the period of detention, the more that detention resembles an arrest. An analogous observation can be made regarding suspect movements that are initiated by government personnel: the more extensive and involved the suspect movement, the more likely the detention resembles an arrest.

Remember in *Terry*, the officer commanded a movement of not only the defendant, Terry, but also his companions. In *Terry*, the officer approached the defendant and his two associates while they were standing in front of a store that the officer had suspected the men of planning to rob. In the words of the Court:

> When the men "mumbled something" in response to his inquiries, Officer McFadden grabbed petitioner Terry, spun him around so that they were facing the other two, with Terry between McFadden and the others, and patted down the outside of his clothing. In the left breast pocket of Terry's overcoat Officer McFadden felt a pistol. He reached inside the overcoat pocket, but was unable to remove the gun. At this point, keeping Terry between himself and the others, the officer ordered all three men to enter Zucker's store. As they went in, he removed Terry's overcoat completely, removed a .38-caliber revolver from the pocket and ordered all three men to face the wall with their hands raised. Officer McFadden proceeded to pat down the outer clothing of Chilton and the third man, Katz. He discovered another revolver in the outer pocket of Chilton's overcoat, but no weapons were found on Katz.

Thus, the frisk of Terry was not completed until after the defendant had been moved to a location within Zucker's store. The frisk of the other men was performed entirely after the men had been moved. Despite the forced move, the frisk of Terry was upheld (only Terry's stop and frisk were at issue). Notice the Court's language in the following passage. The Court plainly upheld not only the stop outside the store and the frisk of Terry's outer clothing but also the continuation of the frisk (when the officer retrieved the weapon), which was not completed until Terry had been ordered to move to another location.

The scope of the search in this case presents no serious problem in light of these standards. Officer McFadden patted down the outer clothing of petitioner and his two companions. He did not place his hands in their pockets or under the outer surface of their garments until he had felt weapons, and then he merely reached for and removed the guns. He never did invade Katz' person beyond the outer surfaces of his clothes, since he discovered nothing in his patdown which might have been a weapon. Officer McFadden confined his search strictly to what was minimally necessary to learn whether the men were armed and to disarm them once he discovered the weapons. He did not conduct a general exploratory search for whatever evidence of criminal activity he might find.

This discussion reveals that *Terry* authorizes not only a stop and frisk based upon suspicion that falls short of probable cause, but it also permits limited government-ordered movements of the suspect. This chapter will next review examples of impermissible suspect movements before discussing additional factors relevant to whether a government seizure or search necessitates a finding of reasonable suspicion or probable cause.

Sidebar

OTHER INSTANCES OF PERMISSIBLE *TERRY* MOVEMENTS

This limited authority to order the movements of suspects has been upheld in other contexts as well. In *Pennsylvania v. Mimms* and *Maryland v. Wilson*, the Court upheld an officer's authority to order a driver and any passengers to exit a vehicle. In *Michigan v. Summers*, the Court upheld the detention of a homeowner during the execution of a search warrant. In *Summers*, the defendant had been outside his home when he was initially encountered by the police. Once the officers gained entry into the home, one of the officers requested another officer "previously stationed along the side of the house, to bring the defendant, still on the porch, into the house." This forced movement was upheld by the Supreme Court. *Mimms, Wilson*, and *Summers* are discussed in greater length in Chapter 12 (*Mimms, Wilson*, and *Summers*) and Chapter 5 (*Summers*).

(b) Suspect Movements Ordered by Law Enforcement: Examples of Impermissible Movements

Yet, compare *Terry* to *Kaupp v. Texas*.[4] There, officers were investigating the defendant's involvement in a murder. Early one morning (3 A.M.), officers entered the defendant's home, woke him while he was in his bedroom, and transported him to police headquarters after placing him in handcuffs. After removing his handcuffs and providing him with *Miranda* warnings, the defendant was interrogated, whereupon he made incriminating statements.

The Supreme Court found that the defendant's seizure required the establishment of probable cause, which the State had failed to demonstrate. In reaching this

---

[4]538 U.S. 626 (2003).

OTHER INSTANCES OF IMPERMISSIBLE *TERRY* MOVEMENTS

In *Florida v. Royer* (discussed at length in Chapter 12), the defendant was approached by narcotics officers in an airport and later accompanied the officers to a nearby room located within the concourse. In holding that the defendant's detainment required proof beyond mere reasonable suspicion, the Court relied upon a number of factors, including the defendant's forced move to the alternate location. The Court observed, "[T]here are undoubtedly reasons of safety and security that would justify moving a suspect from one location to another during an investigatory detention, such as from an airport concourse to a more private area (citation omitted). There is no indication in this case that such reasons prompted the officers to transfer the site of the encounter from the concourse to the interrogation room. It appears, rather, that the primary interest of the officers was not in having an extended conversation with Royer but in the contents of his luggage, a matter which the officers did not pursue orally with Royer until after the encounter was relocated to the police room. The record does not reflect any facts which would support a finding that the legitimate law enforcement purposes which justified the detention in the first instance were furthered by removing Royer to the police room prior to the officer's attempt to gain his consent to a search of his luggage."

result, the Court distinguished this police conduct from *Terry*-level seizures and relied heavily upon the fact that the defendant had been forcibly removed from his home and transported to police headquarters.

> Although certain seizures may be justified on something less than probable cause, we have never sustained against Fourth Amendment challenges the involuntary removal of a suspect from his home to a police station and his detention there for investigative purposes absent probable cause or judicial authorization. Such involuntary transport to a police station for questioning is sufficiently like arrest to invoke the traditional rule that arrests may constitutionally be made only on probable cause.

(c) Use of Handcuffs

As noted, the defendant in *Kaupp* was handcuffed prior to his transportation to the police station. Can officers employ handcuffs yet effectuate a seizure that requires only the establishment of reasonable suspicion? Yes. When officer safety is an issue, courts have upheld the use of handcuffs during the course of a *Terry* stop. In *Kaupp*, however, the Court considered this fact as among the indicators that the defendant had been arrested.

(d) Fingerprints

Though the issue has not been squarely addressed, the Supreme Court in *Hayes v. Florida*[5] stated, in dicta, that there exists "support in our cases for the view that the Fourth Amendment would permit seizures for the purpose of fingerprinting, if there is reasonable suspicion that the suspect has committed a criminal act, if there is a reasonable basis for believing that fingerprinting will establish or negate the suspect's connection with that crime, and if the procedure is carried out with dispatch." The Court suggested that a legislatively enacted procedure authorizing judicially approved seizures for purposes of fingerprinting might survive Fourth Amendment scrutiny as might a brief warrantless detention "in the field."

(3) *Terry* Searches: Duration/Manner of Execution

As with *Terry*-level seizures, searches or frisks performed on the basis of reasonable suspicion are intrusions upon Fourth Amendment liberties that are comparatively

---

[5]470 U.S. 811 (1985).

more limited in duration and scope. A *Terry* frisk is justified by the need for officers to protect themselves or others. But this rationale justifies only a limited weapons search. It is a search that implicates Fourth Amendment interests, but it is a "strictly circumscribed" search for evidence that is potentially harmful. Thus, a frisk for non-threatening forms of evidence is impermissible under *Terry* and is subject to suppression.

The typical method in which the *Terry* frisk is performed upon an individual is through a patdown of the suspect's outer clothing. Under *Terry*, an officer performing a patdown must be able to immediately determine that the object he felt was a weapon. This is precisely what happened in *Terry*. There, the officer patted down the defendant's outer clothing and felt an object that he immediately ascertained was a firearm. It follows that an officer who is unable to immediately ascertain the nature of the item felt may not continue to feel or manipulate the object in order to determine its nature.

Though *Terry* frisks are not wedded to this singular methodology (see *Adams v. Williams*, Chapter 11, where an officer retrieved a firearm from the waist area of a defendant who was seated in a vehicle), this form of individual search was the type expressly approved by the Court in *Terry* and in subsequent cases.

Nevertheless, the recovery of non-endangering contraband may still be admissible under this doctrine. Compare *Terry* with *Minnesota v. Dickerson*.[6] In *Dickerson*, an officer observed the defendant leaving a building that was associated with narcotics distribution. Based upon this information as well as the defendant's subsequent evasive conduct, the officer pursued the defendant, eventually stopping him and performing a *Terry*-level frisk. Though the frisk failed to uncover any weapons, the officer testified:

> [A]s I pat-searched the front of his body, I felt a lump, a small lump, in the front pocket. I examined it with my fingers and it slid and it felt to be a lump of crack cocaine in cellophane.

The Court held that the recovery of the narcotics was not authorized pursuant to *Terry*. It reiterated the protection rationale that underlies such searches and held that, in this instance, the search exceeded the permissible limits under *Terry*. The Court found that the officer's "continued exploration of" the object — which occurred after the officer had determined that the item was not a weapon — required justification beyond that allowed by *Terry*. On the other hand, had the officer been able to immediately determine the incriminating nature of the item, the narcotics would have been admissible. The Court analogized this circumstance to the observance and recovery of incriminating evidence pursuant to a plain-view sighting. Thus, evidence of a nonthreatening nature that an officer feels pursuant to a lawful *Terry* stop and frisk may be recovered if the officer can immediately determine the incriminating nature of the evidence in question.

Note the analog between *Terry*-level stops and frisks. The validity of a *Terry* stop is determined by, among other factors, the duration of the encounter. *Terry* searches or frisks are measured, in part, by the immediacy of the officer's determination of the item's incriminating nature. Neither *Terry* stops nor searches authorize an officer to

---

[6]508 U.S. 366 (1993).

prolong a detention or a search beyond what is necessary to confirm or deny his suspicions. With this in mind, consider the next section.

F   A   Q

Q: What about *Terry* searches of effects, such as automobiles and luggage (not found in moving vehicles), and searches for dangerous individuals during protective house sweeps? How does a court consider duration and manner of execution in these instances?

A: In the automobile context, *Terry* authorizes a search limited to the driver's person as well as those locations within the vehicle's passenger compartment that may house a weapon. More extensive searches of the vehicle, as well as searches performed subsequent to the vehicle's transportation to an alternate location, will likely require a separate justification. Regarding searches of other personal effects (e.g., luggage, purses, etc.), an officer who possesses reasonable suspicion that a particular effect may contain contraband may temporarily seize the item and conduct a brief minimally intrusive investigation (e.g., dog sniffs). Finally, an officer conducting a sweep of a residence for individuals who may pose a danger may only perform a cursory search of those areas that might harbor an individual. The sweep, according to *Maryland v. Buie*, must "last no longer than is necessary to dispel the reasonable suspicion of danger and in any event no longer than it takes to complete the arrest and depart the premises."

(4) *Terry* Searches: Probationers

Normally, an officer who seeks to search a residence must either demonstrate probable cause to believe the premises contain evidence of crime or establish consent to search. I say "normally" because the Supreme Court has established that a residential search on less than probable cause may yet be Fourth Amendment compliant if the subject of the search is an individual serving a probationary sentence. In *United States v. Knights*,[7] the Court reasoned that probationers, like those who are incarcerated, possess lesser privacy interests than those who are not subject to criminal sanctions. Probationers, therefore, might properly be subject to special conditions that would offend constitutional norms if applied to ordinary citizens.

In *Knights*, the defendant's probation agreement with the state authorized a search of his residence in the absence of probable cause. Yet the Court did not address the obvious consent to search issue that such an agreement would present. Instead the Court balanced the government's interest in crime control and rehabilitation against the lesser privacy interests possessed by probationers and concluded that the residential search at issue supported by no more than reasonable suspicion was reasonable.

There is one final note regarding this case that is worthy of mention. The opinion states that the search was of the defendant's apartment. There is nothing in the opinion that suggests the government search was anything less than a search of

---

[7]534 U.S. 112 (2001).

the entire premises. A staple of *Terry* searches or frisks is that they are circumscribed intrusions. More extensive intrusions require consent or the establishment of probable cause. The full-scale search approved in *Knights* stands in stark contrast to every other instance where *Terry* has been applied in the criminal investigative context.

SUMMARY

- When assessing a *Terry* claim a court asks whether the police, in pursuing their investigation, diligently attempted to confirm or dispel their suspicions.

- Among the factors relevant to this evaluative process are the length of time that the defendant was detained and the manner in which the investigation was executed.

- A forcible movement of a suspect does not necessarily offend *Terry*.

- An officer may sometimes handcuff or fingerprint a suspect within the bounds of *Terry*.

- Though a *Terry* frisk is authorized only if the officer reasonably suspects that the individual is armed and dangerous, an officer may properly seize evidence that is nonthreatening if the officer can immediately ascertain during the frisk that the evidence in question is incriminating.

- A search of a residence based upon reasonable suspicion may be justified if the subject of the search is serving a probationary sentence.

- Whereas *Terry* authorizes limited searches and seizures based upon reasonable suspicion, the next chapter discusses administrative searches that authorize even more extensive searches based upon reasonable suspicion or sometimes no suspicion whatsoever.

CONNECTIONS

Relationship to Searches Incident to Arrest (Chapter 7) and the Automobile Exception (Chapter 8)

Terry frisks of individuals and automobiles are characterized by their comparative brevity. Generally, searches of individuals performed incident to arrest and searches of vehicles pursuant to the automobile exception are more extensive.

Relationship to the Plain View Doctrine (Chapter 9)

If during a valid *Terry* stop and frisk the officer observes in plain view (or touches during a frisk) evidence that the officer can immediately determine is criminal in nature, the officer may seize the evidence.

Relationship to Fourth Amendment Violations and Their Associated Remedies (Chapter 15)

Like any other government search or seizure performed during a criminal investigation, a search or seizure that exceeds the scope authorized by *Terry* is subject to suppression pursuant to the exclusionary rule.

Administrative and Special Needs Searches and Seizures

14

Almost invariably during the course of the semester, one or more students in my Criminal Procedure course will volunteer that they have been

O V E R V I E W

previously arrested, subjected to a police roadblock, and/or been required to submit a blood or urine sample pursuant to a government request. What is common among these events is that they involve either a search or seizure that is government initiated. What may not be common is the standard that governs the propriety of the government's conduct.

The preceding chapters have focused upon government searches and seizures performed during the course of a criminal investigation. That shouldn't be too surprising given that this book is a treatise on *criminal* procedure! However, sometimes the government engages in activities that implicate Fourth Amendment concerns, yet are subject to an alternative, more deferential standard than that typically applicable in the criminal venue. Such situations are presented when the government engages in either administrative searches or seizures or searches and seizures based upon "special needs" of the government.

For example, sometimes a state may want to conduct a residential or commercial search in order to further an administrative interest (e.g., ensure compliance with health codes). Alternatively, a government may seek to perform a search designed to further, not an administrative objective, but a "special need" of the government (a legitimate noncriminal interest; e.g., promoting a healthy learning environment for schoolchildren). It is in these contexts that three broad categories of government searches and seizures will be examined: government searches of houses, government searches of businesses, and government searches and seizures of individuals and their effects.

As you study the material presented in this chapter, you will find that the searches and seizures, when justified on administrative or "special needs" grounds, are almost always performed in the absence of a warrant, are adjudged pursuant to the reasonableness clause (including a balancing test) of the Fourth Amendment, further a government interest that is distinct from its interest in criminal law enforcement, and are subject to a more forgiving standard than probable cause.

A. ADMINISTRATIVE INSPECTIONS

1. Residential Inspections
2. Business Inspections

B. "SPECIAL NEEDS" SEARCHES OF INDIVIDUALS AND THEIR EFFECTS

1. Drug, Alcohol, and Criminal Roadblocks and Checkpoints
2. Searches of Students
3. Searches of Current and Prospective Public Employees, Their Effects, and Pregnant Women in Public Hospitals
4. Border Searches
5. Probationers and Parolees

A. Administrative Inspections

(1) Residential Inspections

Camara v. Municipal Court[1] involved a constitutional challenge to a San Francisco code that authorized warrantless residential searches by health inspectors. Specifically, those challenging the law argued that the housing code "is contrary to the Fourth and Fourteenth Amendments in that it authorizes municipal officials to enter a private dwelling without a search warrant and without probable cause to believe that a violation of the Housing Code exists therein."

Noting the "very tangible interest" that an individual retains in the "sanctity" of his home, the Court held that the government must, indeed, procure a search warrant prior to engaging in this type of residential inspection. The Court found that the Fourth Amendment's warrant requirement addressed not only criminal searches but also situations—such as that presented in *Camara*—where the objective of the search was noncriminal in nature. The Court declared that to permit warrantless searches

> is to leave the occupant subject to the discretion of the official in the field. This is precisely the discretion to invade private property which we have consistently circumscribed by a requirement that a disinterested party warrant the need to search (citation omitted). We simply cannot say that the protections provided by the warrant procedure are not needed in this context; broad statutory safeguards are no substitute for individualized review. . . .

---

[1]387 U.S. 523 (1967).

Aside from this holding, *Camara* is also significant for another finding regarding the concept of probable cause. In stark contrast to criminal investigative procedure (which focuses, in large part, upon the privacy rights of the *individual*), the Court found that an administrative warrant could issue in this context provided it satisfied the Fourth Amendment's reasonableness clause. In other words, the government need not establish that probable cause existed that a *particular* home was in violation of the housing code. Instead, a warrant could issue so long as the desired administrative search was deemed to be reasonable under the circumstances. Thus, the Court did not dispense with the probable cause requirement but rather redefined the concept in this administrative context. It noted that the probable cause standard needed for a home inspection warrant could be obtained

> if reasonable legislative or administrative standards for conducting an area inspection are satisfied with respect to a particular dwelling. Such standards, which will vary with the municipal program being enforced, may be based upon the passage of time, the nature of the building . . . or the condition of the particular dwelling. . . . If a valid public interest justifies the intrusion contemplated, then there is probable cause to issue a suitably restricted search warrant.

Thus, the existence of probable cause was assessed on a "city-wide" level and was not dependent upon the identification of particular dwellings that were likely noncompliant with the subject housing code. In performing this reasonableness assessment, the Court employed a balancing test. Indeed, as you will soon discover, this balancing test is one that the Court has employed repeatedly in the administrative/"special needs" context. Specifically, it weighed the government's need to perform the housing inspection "against the invasion which the search entails."[2] After assessing various factors, the Court found that the inspection scheme at issue was, in fact, reasonable.

(2) Business Inspections

As in *Camara*, the Supreme Court in *See v. City of Seattle*[3] held that the Fourth Amendment also protects a commercial property owner from warrantless intrusions by government officials. The Court stated that a "businessman, like the occupant of a residence, has a constitutional right to go about his business free from unreasonable official entries upon his private commercial property." However, the Court recognized that circumstances may arise that allow the government greater access to businesses than to residences. Though "administrative entry, without consent, upon the portions of commercial premises which are not open to the public" requires a warrant, the Court did not mean to "imply that business premises may not reasonably be inspected in many more situations than private homes, nor do we question such accepted regulatory techniques as licensing programs which require inspections prior to operating a business or marketing a product." Precisely identifying when such situations presented themselves required a "case-by-case" assessment.

---

[2]You may recall in Chapter 11, during the discussion of *Terry v. Ohio* and the reasonable suspicion standard, that the Court assessed the propriety of the government's conduct pursuant to the Fourth Amendment's reasonableness clause and employed a similar balancing test in upholding the officer's conduct. *Camara*, decided in 1966, was the first Supreme Court case to employ this balancing test. *Terry* was decided two years later in 1968.
[3]387 U.S. 541 (1967).

WHY THE JUNKYARD BUSINESS WAS DEEMED BY THE COURT IN *BURGER* TO BE A CLOSELY REGULATED BUSINESS

The Supreme Court in *Burger* explained why it considered the junkyard business at issue to be part of a closely regulated industry:

> The automobile junkyard business . . . is simply a new branch of an industry that has existed, and has been closely regulated, for many years. The automobile junkyard is closely akin to the secondhand shop or the general junkyard. Both share the purpose of recycling salvageable articles and components of items no longer usable in their original form. As such, vehicle dismantlers represent a modern, specialized version of a traditional activity. In New York, general junkyards and secondhand shops long have been subject to regulation. One New York court has explained: "Vehicle dismantlers are part of the junk industry, as well as part of the auto industry. . . . Prior to the enactment of section 415-a of the Vehicle and Traffic Law, auto dismantlers were subject to regulatory provisions governing the licensing and operation of junkyards. These regulations included provisions mandating the keeping of detailed records of purchases and sales, and the making of such records available at reasonable times to designated officials including police officers, by junk dealers . . . and by dealers in secondhand articles. . . ."

The New York court added that the aforementioned provisions have been in place in excess of 140 years.

One such case where the Court upheld a warrantless search of a commercial establishment was in *New York v. Burger*.[4] At issue was the constitutionality of a New York statute that authorized warrantless inspections of junkyards that sold automobile parts. In *Burger*, several plain-clothed police officers arrived at a junkyard in order to perform the statutorily authorized inspection. The statute required that the owner of a junkyard retain a business license and a record reflecting the automobiles and parts in his possession. After being informed by the owner that he possessed neither of these documents, the officers inspected the premises and uncovered evidence suggesting that the business owner was in possession of stolen automotive components. Subsequently, the owner was criminally charged with several counts of possession of stolen property and a single count of unregistered operation as a vehicle dismantler.

The Court acknowledged that residential and business owners alike enjoy Fourth Amendment protections. However, the Court observed that an owner's expectation of privacy in commercial premises is lessened or reduced, especially when that commercial property is part of a closely regulated business. The Court explained that an operator of a business subject to extensive regulation goes into such a venture with open eyes. He is fully aware that, by participating in this industry, his business will be subjected to extensive governmental regulation. In such circumstances, warrantless intrusions upon closely regulated establishments "may well be reasonable within the meaning of the Fourth Amendment."

However, merely being a participant in a closely regulated industry does not alone justify warrantless government intrusions. Rather, the Court detailed three additional prerequisites. First, the government must articulate a "'substantial' government interest" (in *Burger*, it was combating auto theft). Second, "warrantless inspections must be 'necessary to further [the] regulatory scheme.'" The Court found that since junkyards were a "major market for stolen vehicles and vehicle parts," the government could rationally find that warrantless inspections, and the surprise upon junkyard owners that they entail, could help further this legitimate objective. And third, the statutory "inspection program" should amount to a "constitutionally adequate substitute for a warrant." In this regard, the statute must inform or notify the owner that his property will be subjected to periodic inspections and that the search — as in a prototypical search warrant — "must be 'carefully limited in time, place and scope.'" The *Burger* Court found that this final requirement

---

[4]482 U.S. 691 (1987).

was satisfied as well. It observed that the statute notified the junkyard owner that regular inspections would occur and detailed the time, place, and contours of the government search. As noted by the Court:

> The officers are allowed to conduct an inspection only "during [the] regular and usual business hours" (citations omitted). The inspections can be made only of vehicle-dismantling and related industries. And the permissible scope of these searches is narrowly defined: the inspectors may examine the records, as well as "any vehicles or parts of vehicles which are subject to the record keeping requirements of this section and which are on the premises" (citation omitted).

As noted, if a government seeks to justify a warrantless search on administrative or "special needs" grounds, it is essential that the government articulate a legitimate, noncriminal purpose for the search. In this regard, the results of a particular search are a nondeterminative factor. Thus, for example, a purported administrative or "special needs" search will not be rendered invalid simply due to the fact that evidence suggestive of criminal activity was uncovered. Needless to say, however, the more a search resembles a criminal search (whether in terms of outcome or procedure), the more difficult it will be for the government to justify it on administrative/"special needs" grounds.

For instance, in *Burger* it was argued that the administrative statute at issue was simply a pretext for a criminal search; that the objectives of the administrative statute were identical to those underlying a criminal search. Indeed, the New York Court of Appeals agreed with this assessment, citing, inter alia, that the inspecting officials were none other than police officers.

The Supreme Court in *Burger*, however, disagreed. The Court acknowledged that the administrative and criminal laws may share the ultimate objective of eradicating a particular societal problem. However, the Court noted that they differed in terms of their "subsidiary purposes" as well as their methodologies for addressing the issue. On the one hand, the Court explained, the criminal laws are designed to punish those who commit auto theft and possess stolen property. Administrative regulations, however, are enacted "to ensure that vehicle dismantlers are legitimate businesspersons and that stolen vehicles and vehicle parts passing through automobile junkyards can be identified."

The Court also dismissed the significance that police officers—as enforcers of the penal laws—were authorized by the statute to perform the administrative junkyard search. Noting the various functions performed by law enforcement officers as well as the resource limitations encountered by many states, the Court concluded that an administrative scheme "is not rendered illegal by the fact that the inspecting officer has the power to arrest individuals for violations other than those created by the scheme itself."

B. "Special Needs" Searches of Individuals and Their Effects

There are an array of "special needs" searches and seizures that are directed at individuals as well as their effects. This subsection will address the various contexts in which these issues have arisen, including but not limited to: searches and seizures of individuals at roadblocks and checkpoints, searches of students, searches of public employees, seizures and searches of individuals and effects at borders, and searches of probationers and parolees.

(1) Drug, Alcohol, and Criminal Roadblocks and Checkpoints

A suitable topic with which to commence the discussion of "special needs" is with an area of the law that a great many students have experienced firsthand. Over the years, a sizeable number of students in my Criminal Procedure course have volunteered that they have been subjected to some form of government roadblock or checkpoint. So I suspect that it came as no surprise to them that this practice has been upheld by the Supreme Court. However, the Supreme Court has placed some important limitations upon the propriety of this practice and has in no way granted the government a free pass to implement such schemes.

The case that follows, *City of Indianapolis v. Edmond*,[5] is illustrative. In short, *Edmond* teaches that while a demonstrated need for such roadblocks — distinct from the government's general interest in crime control — is often critical to finding such programs constitutional (this was central to the outcome in *Edmond*, which struck down the scheme at issue), such programs may yet survive constitutional scrutiny even if their primary purpose relates to the government's criminal law enforcement interests. It is also worth mentioning that such government checkpoint stops should be of limited duration if they are to be deemed reasonable within the meaning of the Fourth Amendment.

Edmond involved an effort by the city of Indianapolis to interdict illegal narcotics through the establishment of six roadblocks during a certain time period in 1998. In essence, at each checkpoint an officer would approach the stopped vehicle and request the driver's license and registration. Each checkpoint was preceded by a sign warning drivers that they were approaching a narcotics checkpoint. During the stop, the officer would look for indicators suggestive of impairment, perform "an open-view examination of the vehicle from the outside," and have a dog trained to detect narcotics walk around the car's exterior. The officers would not search a stopped car absent consent or an appropriate level of suspicion, and the officer would stop each car in sequence. Each stop lasted approximately two to three minutes, unless further investigation was necessary.

The Court held that the Indianapolis checkpoint violated the Fourth Amendment's prohibition against unreasonable searches and seizures. The Court noted, inter alia, that Fourth Amendment reasonableness normally demands that a search or seizure be supported by some level of suspicion of criminal wrongdoing. However, the Court noted that exceptions to this requirement exist, such as when the government has established a valid "special need" or administrative interest. The Court observed that *Delaware v. Prouse*[6] (see Sidebar) — where the Court found that a suspicionless stop of a driver in order to perform a license and registration check was unconstitutional — had suggested, in dictum, that the government's interest in roadway safety might justify a license and registration checkpoint that required all vehicles to stop. As stated in *Prouse*:

> This holding does not preclude the State of Delaware or other States from developing methods for spot checks that involve less intrusion or that do not involve the unconstrained exercise of discretion. Questioning of all oncoming traffic at roadblock-type stops is one possible alternative.

---

[5]531 U.S. 32 (2000).
[6]440 U.S. 648 (1979).

But the checkpoint scheme at issue in *Edmond* could not, in the Court's view, be legitimized on this basis. In invalidating the checkpoint, the Court reached several conclusions. First, it held that a checkpoint effectuated a seizure within the meaning of the Fourth Amendment. Second, it found that the government's use of a drug-sniffing dog did not constitute a Fourth Amendment search, given that the information disclosed by the sniffs was limited to the presence of illegal narcotics.

Third, and most significantly, the Court found that the program's primary purpose — the interdiction of illegal narcotics — was indistinguishable from the government's general interest in crime control. "When law enforcement authorities pursue primarily general crime control purposes at checkpoints such as here, however, stops can only be justified by some quantum of individualized suspicion." The Court was not persuaded that the gravity of the drug problem and the government's interest in highway safety and license and registration verification justified dispensing with the individualized suspicion requirement.

The dissent asserted that the majority had created "a new non-law-enforcement primary purpose test." In their view, the constitutionality of checkpoint programs, such as that challenged in *Edmond*, would be dependent upon a finding that its primary purpose was noncriminal. The

> **Sidebar**
>
> ### DELAWARE v. PROUSE — LICENSE AND REGISTRATION CHECKS
>
> In *Prouse*, the Supreme Court found that the Fourth Amendment prohibited police from effectuating traffic stops of individual drivers — without any suspicion of wrongdoing — for the sole purpose of checking the driver's license and registration. The case involved a stop by a Delaware police officer who discovered marijuana within a vehicle that he had stopped on the public roads. The officer testified that he had no suspicion of wrongdoing prior to the stop and that his underlying motivation was to perform a license and registration check. After performing the relevant balancing test, the Court found that this practice was unconstitutional. The Court analogized the Delaware practice of stopping random motorists to the roving border patrol stops disapproved of in *United States v. Brignoni-Ponce*[7] (this case will be discussed later in this chapter in the section pertaining to borders), and found that the program neither contributed meaningfully to roadway safety nor sufficiently constrained the discretion of the police.
>
> ---
> [7]422 U.S. 873 (1975).

majority flatly rejected this contention. It noted that earlier Court decisions upholding roadblocks[8] (see Sidebar discussing *Sitz*) never asserted that the primary purpose underlying the challenged roadblocks was noncriminal. In fact, the *Edmond* majority declared that checkpoint programs could be justified even in instances where the primary purpose of the program relates to the government's interest in crime control.

> Of course, there are circumstances that may justify a law enforcement checkpoint where the primary purpose would otherwise, but for some emergency, relate to ordinary crime control. For example, . . . the Fourth Amendment would almost certainly permit an appropriately tailored roadblock set up to thwart an imminent terrorist attack or to catch a dangerous criminal who is likely to flee by way of a particular route (citation omitted). The exigencies created by these scenarios are far removed from the circumstances under which authorities might simply stop cars as a matter of course to see if there just happens to be a felon leaving the jurisdiction. While we do not limit the purposes that may justify a checkpoint program to any rigid set of categories, we decline to approve a program whose primary purpose is ultimately indistinguishable from the general interest in crime control.

---
[8]*Michigan State Police v. Sitz*, 496 U.S. 444 (1990); *United States v. Martinez-Fuerte*, 428 U.S. 543 (1976).

MICHIGAN STATE POLICE v. SITZ[9] — SOBRIETY CHECKPOINTS

In *Sitz*, the Supreme Court upheld the establishment of temporary checkpoints designed to examine drivers for evidence of intoxication. Various checkpoints were established that required that all vehicles passing through be stopped. Each stop averaged approximately 25 seconds. If evidence of intoxication was detected, the motorist would be directed to another location where a license and registration check would be performed as well as possible sobriety tests. After balancing the individual's privacy expectations against the government's interest in eradicating drunk driving, the Court found the balance favored the state. The Court determined that the discretion of the police was appropriately limited given that they were required to stop every car that approached the checkpoint, as opposed to selective vehicles, and that the stops were brief and were "indistinguishable from the checkpoint stops we upheld in [United States v.] *Martinez-Fuerte*." The *Martinez-Fuerte* case will be discussed in more detail later in this chapter in the section pertaining to borders.

---

[9]496 U.S. 444 (1990).

The declaration in *Edmond* that the Constitution does not categorically preclude a state from implementing a checkpoint scheme with a motive that is primarily criminal in nature was tested in *Illinois v. Lidster*.[10]

Lidster was arrested and convicted for driving under the influence of alcohol. Evidence leading to his arrest and conviction was obtained by virtue of a highway checkpoint set up by a local police department in Illinois. As a result of a hit-and-run accident on a highway that resulted in a civilian death, the police established a checkpoint "[a]bout one week later at about the same time of night and at about the same place" as the earlier incident. The cars approaching the roadblock formed a line. When in the presence of the officer, the occupants were asked whether they had information relevant to the hit-and-run incident and were given a flyer that requested any relevant information. Lidster challenged the constitutionality of the checkpoint.

Finding the checkpoint constitutional, the Court distinguished this case from *Edmond*. Unlike the checkpoint in *Edmond*, the scheme in *Lidster* was not designed to investigate the criminal activities of the individuals seized, but was intended to seek citizen assistance in the criminal investigation of other unknown individuals. Drawing another contrast with *Edmond*, the Court stated that the concept of reasonable suspicion has "little role to play" in the checkpoint situation at issue in *Lidster*. The Court analogized the *Lidster* roadblock to police efforts to maintain "crowd control or public safety" where a finding of individualized suspicion is an unnecessary precondition.

As part of its reasonableness balancing, the Court in *Lidster* found that "the stop advanced [a] grave public concern [a homicide investigation] to a significant degree," that the roadblock sufficiently limited officer discretion in its execution, and that the stops amounted to only a minimal intrusion on individual liberties. Regarding the latter point, the Court noted that the stops were systematic, lasted "a very few minutes at most," and likely produced little anxiety or alarm.

(2) Searches of Students

(a) Searches of Individual Students

An appreciable percentage of my Criminal Procedure students, though numerically less notable than in the roadblock/checkpoint context, acknowledge having

---

[10]540 U.S. 419 (2004).

been subjected to school-initiated searches while in grade school. Perhaps my class-room observations can be explained, at least in part, by the permissive Supreme Court jurisprudence in this area. For the most part, the search and seizure activities of school administrators, when considered by the High Court, have been upheld. However, as will be discussed in this section, this authority is not without boundaries.

Imagine that you are a public high school principal or administrator. Your ultimate objective is to educate the students at your school so that they will be prepared for life irrespective of the vocation, if any, they elect to pursue. Therefore, as part of your overall plan, you devise a comprehensive curriculum and you hire and train the best teachers available. However, you are also aware that your educational mission will be severely compromised if you are unable to sufficiently discipline students who are disruptive to the school's mission. So you establish certain rules, which include no smoking, no drugs or cigarettes, and no firearms or firecrackers, just to name a few. Drafting the policies is the easy part. Enforcing them is another. Can school officials search their students? If so, what is the standard of proof required before a search can be performed? Under what circumstances can a search be under-taken and what, if any, limitations are placed upon the school officials?

The Supreme Court has provided guidance in regards to these questions, though this area of the law is still evolving. Consider *New Jersey v. T.L.O.,*[11] where the Court upheld a search by a school official of a student who was reasonably suspected of possessing an item prohibited under school rules. Specifically, an assistant vice principal reasonably suspected that a student possessed cigarettes in contravention of school policy. After some conversation with the student, the school official proceeded to search the student's purse and discovered cigarettes. A further search uncovered marijuana and additional items associated with marijuana use and distribution. The police were subsequently notified of the school official's findings and delinquency proceedings commenced. The student challenged the search of her purse on Fourth Amendment grounds.

The Supreme Court held that the search of the student's purse was reasonable. Preliminarily, the Court found that the Fourth Amendment governed the search at issue. It declared that students did, indeed, have protections guaranteed by the Fourth Amendment and that school officials are, accordingly, limited by its safe-guards. However, the Court also concluded that school officials possessed greater leeway in performing student searches than the government enjoys when performing searches of individuals pursuant to criminal investigations.

The Court observed that the Fourth Amendment demands that searches be rea-sonable. However, what is reasonable is dependent upon the context of the search. In performing this assessment, the Court employed the balancing test enunciated in *Camara v. Municipal Court.* The Court noted that "[o]n one side of the balance are arrayed the individual's legitimate expectations of privacy and personal security; on the other, the government's need for effective methods to deal with breaches of public order." In this case, the Court balanced the school's need to maintain order and a proper educational atmosphere within the school against the student's legit-imate expectation of privacy. After balancing these respective interests, the Court held that neither a warrant nor probable cause to believe that the law had been violated was necessary before a student search could be performed. Rather, such searches would be upheld so long as they were performed reasonably.

---

[11]469 U.S. 325 (1985).

The Court, citing *Terry v. Ohio*, held that what was reasonable would be determined by the following two-part inquiry:

> [F]irst, one must consider "whether the . . . action was justified at its inception" [*Terry v. Ohio*, 392 U.S. 1 (1968)]; second, one must determine whether the search as actually conducted "was reasonably related in scope to the circumstances which justified the interference in the first place" (footnote omitted). Under ordinary circumstances, a search of a student by a teacher or other school official (footnote omitted) will be "justified at its inception" when there are reasonable grounds for suspecting that the search will turn up evidence that the student has violated or is violating either the law or the rules of the school (footnote omitted). Such a search will be permissible in its scope when the measures adopted are reasonably related to the objectives of the search and not excessively intrusive in light of the age and sex of the student and the nature of the infraction.

F   A   Q

Q: Has the Supreme Court addressed the applicability of the Fourth Amendment to government searches of school property such as lockers?

A: To date, the Supreme Court has yet to address this situation. As noted by the Supreme Court in *T.L.O.*: "We do not address the question, not presented by this case, whether a schoolchild has a legitimate expectation of privacy in lockers, desks, or other school property provided for the storage of school supplies. Nor do we express any opinion on the standards (if any) governing searches of such areas by school officials or by other public authorities acting at the request of school officials."

In *Safford Unified School District v. Redding*,[12] the Supreme Court addressed another related issue in the school search context — how extensively (or intrusively) a school official may search a student suspected of wrongdoing. Specifically, the Court addressed "whether a 13-year-old student's Fourth Amendment right was violated when she was subjected to a search of her bra and underpants by school officials acting on reasonable suspicion that she had brought forbidden prescription and over-the-counter drugs to school."

The Court held that the search violated the Constitution. In *Redding*, school officials reasonably suspected that a female student possessed narcotics in violation of school policy. The Court found that the information possessed by school officials justified a search of the student's backpack and outer clothing. However, it rejected the school's contention that it was within its authority to perform a more extensive search of the student. In this instance, school officials required the student to "remove her clothes down to her underwear, and then 'pull out' her bra and the elastic band on her underpants."[13] The Court declared that this type of search required a heightened level of justification. Reasonableness under the Fourth Amendment, the Court explained, does not categorically prohibit such intrusive

---

[12]557 U.S. 364 (2009).
[13]The search was performed in the presence of two school officials who, to some extent, were able to observe the student.

searches. But, per *T.L.O.*, it does require that the scope of any such search be reasonable given the nature of the suspected offense as well as the age and gender of the
student.

The Court noted that the narcotics at issue were "nondangerous" and that only a
small quantity of the drugs were suspected of being possessed and distributed. It also
found that there was no reason to suspect that the student was hiding the narcotics in
intimate bodily locations. These facts, according to the Court, were "fatal" to a finding of reasonableness under the circumstances. The Court explained that it sought to

> make it clear that the *T.L.O.* concern to limit a school search to reasonable scope requires
> the support of reasonable suspicion of danger or of resort to underwear for hiding
> evidence of wrongdoing before a search can reasonably make the quantum leap from
> outer clothes and backpacks to exposure of intimate parts. The meaning of such a search,
> and the degradation its subject may reasonably feel, place a search that intrusive in a
> category of its own demanding its own specific suspicions.

(b) Searches of Student Groups

T.L.O. and *Redding* involved the search of an individual student. What about
searches involving entire sets of students? Are school searches that target groups
of students permissible? If so, are "reasonable grounds" (or reasonable suspicion)
of wrongdoing a necessary prerequisite?

The Supreme Court has twice addressed this issue and upheld the searches in
each instance. *Vernonia School Dist. 47J v. Acton*[14] involved an effort by school officials to combat a drug problem via a program designed to test all students who
elected to participate in the extracurricular athletic activities at the school. School
officials had previously identified athletes at the school as "leaders of [its] drug
culture."

Given its concern over the increasingly adverse impact that narcotics were having upon its student population and overall environment at the institution, the
school instituted a narcotics testing policy. Specifically, the drug testing program
was designed "to prevent student athletes from using drugs, to protect their health
and safety, and to provide drug users with assistance programs." Any student wishing
to participate in interscholastic sports was required to consent in writing to the drug
testing. The student-athletes were then tested at the start of the season, followed by
weekly tests of 10 percent (randomly selected) of the relevant student group.

The testing was in the form of a urinalysis and the specimen was tested for
various narcotics. The procedure followed to gather the specimen varied slightly
depending upon the gender of the student. Both male and female students provided
their respective specimens in a school locker room while accompanied by an adult
monitor. Unlike male students who "produce[d] a sample at a urinal, remaining fully
clothed with his back to the monitor," female students provided their specimens
within "an enclosed bathroom stall." This collection process allowed for the moni-
tors to listen for sounds consistent with urination and for the possible viewing of the
male subjects, but did not allow for a similar observation of the females. A positive
test generated a second test in order to confirm the initial conclusion. A negative test
did not generate a repeat test.

---

[14]515 U.S. 646 (1995).

The Court assessed the constitutionality of the testing program pursuant to the reasonableness clause of the Fourth Amendment. As in *T.L.O.*, the Court engaged in a balancing test, weighing the aforementioned interests of the school against the intrusion that the testing program had upon the students. Citing *T.L.O.* the Court found that a warrant was unnecessary in this instance. In contrast to *T.L.O.*, however, the Court declined to impose a reasonable suspicion requirement prior to the implementation of the testing program.

The Court held that the suspicionless testing program instituted by the school complied with the Fourth Amendment. The Court emphasized not only that public school students have a reduced privacy expectation, but that athletes who engage in interscholastic sports have a privacy expectation that is even further reduced. The Court noted that students who elect to participate in extracurricular sports do so voluntarily. A student who wished to avoid testing could simply choose not to participate.

The Court then addressed whether the legitimate expectation of privacy of the student-athletes — although limited — was nevertheless violated given the manner in which the testing was conducted and the test results were handled. It was satisfied on both fronts. Regarding the manner of testing, the Court noted, among other things, that the students were not required to undress and that any viewing of students that may have occurred by school officials was limited to the male athletes and only then from behind. The Court also noted that the samples submitted were tested

Sidebar

WHY PUBLIC SCHOOL CHILDREN HAVE A REDUCED EXPECTATION OF PRIVACY

The Supreme Court in *Vernonia* provided the following explanation regarding why public school students and students who engage in after-school athletics have a reduced expectation of privacy:

> For their own good and that of their classmates, public school children are routinely required to submit to various physical examinations, and to be vaccinated against various diseases. According to the American Academy of Pediatrics, most public schools "provide vision and hearing screening and dental and dermatological checks. . . . Others also mandate scoliosis screening at appropriate grade levels" (citation omitted). In the 1991-1992 school year, all 50 States required public school students to be vaccinated against diphtheria, measles, rubella, and polio (citation omitted). Particularly with regard to medical examinations and procedures, therefore, "students within the school environment have a lesser expectation of privacy than members of the population generally" (citation omitted).

> Legitimate privacy expectations are even less with regard to student athletes. School sports are not for the bashful. They require "suiting up" before each practice or event, and showering and changing afterwards. Public school locker rooms, the usual sites for these activities, are not notable for the privacy they afford. The locker rooms in *Vernonia* are typical: No individual dressing rooms are provided; shower heads are lined up along a wall, unseparated by any sort of partition or curtain; not even all the toilet stalls have doors. As the United States Court of Appeals for the Seventh Circuit has noted, there is "an element of 'communal undress' inherent in athletic participation" (citation omitted).

> There is an additional respect in which school athletes have a reduced expectation of privacy. By choosing to "go out for the team," they voluntarily subject themselves to a degree of regulation even higher than that imposed on students generally. In Vernonia's public schools, they must submit to a preseason physical exam (reference to Appendix omitted), they must acquire adequate insurance coverage or sign an insurance waiver, maintain a minimum grade point average, and comply with any "rules of conduct, dress, training hours and related matters as may be established for each sport by the head coach and athletic director with the principal's approval" (reference to Record omitted). Somewhat like adults who choose to participate in a "closely regulated industry," students who voluntarily participate in school athletics have reason to expect intrusions upon normal rights and privileges, including privacy (citation omitted).

only for drugs and not for other personal information (e.g., other health issues, pregnancy, etc.), and that disclosure was limited to selected school officials and not to law enforcement.

Next, the Court turned its attention to the government's interest in performing the tests. Referencing *Skinner v. Railway Labor Executives' Association* and *National Treasury Employees Union v. Von Raab*,[15] which upheld federal drug testing programs of select railroad employees and customs officials, the *Vernonia* Court noted that those cases found the government interest in drug testing to be "compelling." However, the *Vernonia* Court stressed that the term "compelling" should not be construed literally or as imposing a minimum threshold. Rather, the Court held that the government can successfully justify its search program if it can establish that the nature of its concern is simply "important enough." Here, the Court had little difficulty concluding that the school's interest in deterring drug use satisfied this standard. The Court found that the school's drug testing program addressed "an immediate crisis," and constituted an effective approach to addressing the school's concerns.

The second and most recent Supreme Court pronouncement in this area of testing student groups came in *Board of Education of Independent School District No. 92 of Pottawatomie County v. Earls*.[16] I enjoy teaching this particular case because the facts are less compelling than in *Vernonia* — due, in part, to the greater universe of students subjected to drug testing in *Earls* — and it always generates an array of very interesting student perspectives. At the outset, I will tell you that the Court in *Earls*, by a 5-4 vote, upheld the drug testing program.

Earls involved a school district in Oklahoma that required all middle and high school students who participated in *any* extracurricular activity (not just athletic activities) to submit to drug testing.[17] In certain respects the testing procedure resembled that in *Vernonia*. Each student was required to submit to a urinalysis prior to participating in the school activity, to periodic random tests performed thereafter, and to subsequent tests if school officials developed reasonable suspicion regarding drug use. The collected samples were tested only for the presence of illegal narcotics.

The Supreme Court relied heavily upon *Vernonia* and rejected the Fourth Amendment challenge to the testing program. It had been argued that the school district "failed to identify a special need for testing students who participate in extracurricular activities, and that the [drug testing program] neither addresses a proven problem nor promises to bring any benefit to students or the school."

In upholding the program, the Court found that the testing scheme implicated Fourth Amendment interests, but that neither a warrant nor probable cause was required prior to testing. The Court then proceeded with a reasonableness analysis, balancing the government's asserted legitimate need for testing against the intrusion upon individual privacy interests.

The Court found that the testing program was reasonable. With respect to individual privacy, the Court stated that student expectations are lessened in the school context, adding that the testing program at issue pertained to extracurricular activities, which are voluntary exercises. It also found that the testing procedures

---

[15]These cases will be discussed later in this chapter.

[16]536 U.S. 822 (2002).

[17]The Court stated that the following student groups were subject to drug testing: those who engage in "competitive extracurricular activities sanctioned by the Oklahoma Secondary Schools Activities Association, such as the Academic Team, Future Farmers of America, Future Homemakers of America, band, choir, pom pom, cheerleading, and athletics."

respected personal dignity. In contrast to *Vernonia*, all students—male and female—provided their urine samples without any observation whatsoever from school officials. Thus, the Court found that "the method here is even less problematic" than in *Vernonia*. It further noted that the test results were released only to school personnel and not to law enforcement.

Regarding the government's interest in testing, the Court found that the school district had demonstrated that it had "legitimate concerns in preventing, deterring, and detecting drug use." The Court made reference not only to the evidence suggestive of narcotic use at the school but also to the nationwide problem of narcotics use among students, which, according to the Court, "makes the war against drugs a pressing concern in every school." The Court also found that the testing program was a "reasonably effective" approach to addressing this problem. It rejected the argument that testing should be restricted only to those student groups (e.g., the student-athletes in *Vernonia*) "most likely to use drugs." Rather, it stated that the constitutionality of such testing programs should be evaluated "in the context of the public school's custodial responsibilities." It found that the program at issue in *Earls* "effectively serves the School District's interest in protecting the safety and health of its students."

(3) Searches of Current and Prospective Public Employees, Their Effects, and Pregnant Women in Public Hospitals

The Supreme Court has also had occasion to assess the propriety of government drug/alcohol testing programs in various noneducational settings. This subsection will review four Supreme Court cases that address the constitutionality of such government testing programs for certain public employees, for candidates for public office, and for expectant mothers. As you will see, the Court has reached mixed results. More recently, the Court addressed the constitutionality of a government search of an effect—a pager—that was used by a public employee. That case, *City of Ontario v. Quon*, will also be discussed later in this chapter.

(a) Drug Testing of Current and Potential Public Employees

On the same day, the Supreme Court decided both *Skinner v. Railway Labor Executives' Association*[18] and *National Treasury Employees Union v. Von Raab*.[19] This pair of cases upheld warrantless government drug testing programs that tested select government employees for the presence of illegal narcotics. *Skinner* addressed the constitutionality of regulations promulgated by the Federal Railroad Administration requiring that certain employees involved in major train accidents submit blood, breath, and urine tests in order to detect the presence of alcohol and illegal narcotics. To determine whether the tests were reasonable within the meaning of the Fourth Amendment, the Court balanced the program's "intrusion on the individual's Fourth Amendment interests against its promotion of legitimate governmental interests."[20]

With respect to individual liberties, the Court found the blood, breath, and urine tests to be only slightly intrusive. It reasoned, in part, that any "transportation and like restrictions" attributable to the tests were "minimal" given that most workplace environments impose "significant restrictions" upon employee movement.

---

[18]489 U.S. 602 (1989).
[19]489 U.S. 656 (1989).
[20]489 U.S. at 619, citing *Delaware v. Prouse*, 440 U.S. 648, 654 (1979).

WHY A WARRANT WAS UNNECESSARY IN *SKINNER*

In dispensing with the need for a warrant, the *Skinner* Court provided the following detailed explanation:

> An essential purpose of a warrant requirement is to protect privacy interests by assuring citizens subject to a search or seizure that such intrusions are not the random or arbitrary acts of government agents. A warrant assures the citizen that the intrusion is authorized by law, and that it is narrowly limited in its objectives and scope (citation omitted). A warrant also provides the detached scrutiny of a neutral magistrate, and thus ensures an objective determination whether an intrusion is justified in any given case (citation omitted). In the present context, however, a warrant would do little to further these aims. Both the circumstances justifying toxicological testing and the permissible limits of such intrusions are defined narrowly and specifically in the regulations that authorize them, and doubtless are well known to covered employees (citation omitted). Indeed, in light of the standardized nature of the tests and the minimal discretion vested in those charged with administering the program, there are virtually no facts for a neutral magistrate to evaluate (citation omitted).
>
> We have recognized, moreover, that the Government's interest in dispensing with the warrant requirement is at its strongest when, as here, "the burden of obtaining a warrant is likely to frustrate the governmental purpose behind the search" (citation omitted). As the FRA recognized, alcohol and other drugs are eliminated from the bloodstream at a constant rate (citation omitted), and blood and breath samples taken to measure whether these substances were in the bloodstream when a triggering event occurred must be obtained as soon as possible. . . .
>
> The Government's need to rely on private railroads to set the testing process in motion also indicates that insistence on a warrant requirement would impede the achievement of the Government's objective. Railroad supervisors, like school officials (citation omitted), and hospital administrators (citation omitted), are not in the business of investigating violations of the criminal laws or enforcing administrative codes, and otherwise have little occasion to become familiar with the intricacies of this Court's Fourth Amendment jurisprudence.

Thus the Court determined that any additional infringements upon employee movement caused by the tests would be insignificant.

Citing *Schmerber v. California*,[21] the Court further found that the blood tests were an insignificant intrusion upon individual privacy given that such "tests are a commonplace in these days of periodic physical examinations and experience with them teaches that the quantity of blood extracted is minimal, and that for most people the procedure involves virtually no risk, trauma, or pain." Similarly, breath tests are "even less intrusive" since no skin penetration is involved and no significant facts outside an individual's blood alcohol level are revealed. The Court reached the same conclusion with respect to the urine tests, albeit with greater difficulty. The Court made two points in this regard. First, it explained that the procedures employed to collect the sample were sufficiently respectful of individual privacy. Second, and of even greater significance, the Court found that the employees had a lessened privacy interest given "their participation in an industry that is regulated pervasively to ensure safety, a goal dependent, in substantial part, on the health and fitness of covered employees."

On the other hand, the Court found the government's interest in suspicionless testing to be "compelling." The Court explained that "[e]mployees subject to the tests discharge duties fraught with such risks of injury to others that even a momentary lapse of attention can have disastrous consequences." It further found that the

---

[21]384 U.S. 757 (1966) (upholding a state's right to extract blood from a motorist suspected of driving while under the influence of alcohol).

testing program—including the unpredictable nature of its timing—constituted an "effective means" of furthering this interest.

Von Raab involved a program implemented by the U.S. Customs Service, which mandated that employees seeking a transfer or a promotion to positions involving drug interdiction, firearm possession, or the handling of classified material be subjected to drug screening. Individuals were required to provide a urine sample, which was tested for the presence of various narcotics. The Supreme Court upheld the program as applied to individuals seeking positions involving drug interdiction and firearm possession. However, it remanded the case with respect to the classified documents positions.

THE FUNCTIONS OF THE U.S. CUSTOMS SERVICE

The Supreme Court in *Von Raab* provided the following overview of the work performed by the U.S. Customs Service:

> The United States Customs Service, a bureau of the Department of the Treasury, is the federal agency responsible for processing persons, carriers, cargo, and mail into the United States, collecting revenue from imports, and enforcing customs and related laws (citation omitted). An important responsibility of the Service is the interdiction and seizure of contraband, including illegal drugs (citation omitted). In 1987 alone, Customs agents seized drugs with a retail value of nearly $9 billion (citation omitted). In the routine discharge of their duties, many Customs employees have direct contact with those who traffic in drugs for profit. Drug import operations, often directed by sophisticated criminal syndicates, may be effected by violence or its threat. As a necessary response, many Customs operatives carry and use firearms in connection with their official duties.

The Court found that the warrant requirement was inapplicable for drug testing in this context. It reasoned that the government's interest in deterring narcotics use in certain work-sensitive positions and preventing the elevation of drug users to sensitive positions was compelling and constituted a legitimate "special need." To require a warrant in this context, according to the Court, would unduly compromise the mission of the Customs Service. The Court added that the inapplicability of the warrant requirement is buttressed by the fact that employees who apply for such positions are fully aware of the Service's drug testing program.

It also concluded that suspicionless testing of employees seeking positions involving drug interdiction and firearm possession was appropriate given the vital border protection and safety functions performed by the Customs Service. The Court further recognized the difficulty associated with identifying drug use in the workplace, particularly in the context presented here where the employees are not subject to the "day-to-day scrutiny that is the norm in more traditional office environments." In addition, the Court found that "the almost unique mission of the Service gives the Government a compelling interest" in safeguarding against the use of drugs by employees in certain positions, "for such use creates risks of bribery and blackmail against which the Government is entitled to guard."

The Court also factored the diminished privacy expectations of the covered employees. Individuals in these positions, the Court explained, should reasonably expect that the government would be interested in information regarding their physical fitness and personal integrity.

(b) Drug Testing of Elected Officials

In contrast to the successful programs approved in *Skinner* and *Von Raab*, the Supreme Court struck down a drug testing program in *Chandler v. Miller*.[22] In

---

[22]520 U.S. 305 (1997).

Chandler, the state of Georgia required that candidates for a host of elected positions[23] submit to a urinalysis test to detect the presence of illegal narcotics. In order to be placed on the election ballot, a candidate had to certify that he had submitted "a urinalysis drug test within 30 days prior to qualifying for nomination or election and that the results were negative." A candidate could provide a urine sample at either of two locations: a state-approved laboratory or his personal physician's office. A certificate would then be prepared by an approved laboratory indicating the results of the drug test.

Finding that Georgia had "effectively limited the invasiveness of the testing procedure," the Court focused its attention upon whether the government had articulated a constitutionally satisfactory "special need." The Court found that the state had failed to make such a demonstration. It rejected Georgia's plea that the testing scheme was justified given the adverse effect of narcotic use upon an official's judgment, integrity, job performance, and public confidence. The Court noted that Georgia had failed to present any evidence suggestive of a drug problem among the targeted class. It acknowledged that identification of a concrete problem is not a prerequisite in order for such programs to be upheld. However, the Court commented that such a showing would have helped "shore up" the asserted need for testing in *Chandler*. Contrasting this case with *Von Raab*, the Court observed that the targeted population in *Chandler* did not engage in "high-risk, safety-sensitive tasks." And, unlike *Von Raab* where daily scrutiny of the subject group was "not feasible," the selected individuals in *Chandler* were "subject[ed] to relentless scrutiny — by their peers, the public and the press." To uphold the *Chandler* program would be, in the Court's view, sustaining it for "symbolic" reasons.

(c) Drug Testing of Pregnant Women

The Court was similarly skeptical of the drug testing program at issue in *Ferguson v. City of Charleston*.[24] There, the Court considered the constitutionality of a program administered by a South Carolina hospital[25] that required pregnant women who were patients at the hospital and who were suspected cocaine users to be tested for the presence of the drug. The program also included a chain of custody provision, certain police notification and arrest procedures, and a warning provision that informed patients about possible criminal prosecution in the event of a positive test.

The Court held that the program was unconstitutional. In contrast to the programs in *Von Raab, Skinner, Chandler,* and *Vernonia*, the *Ferguson* Court found the hospital's testing program to be "far more" invasive of personal privacy. It noted that the aforementioned cases presented

> no misunderstanding about the purpose of the test or the potential use of the test results, and there were protections against the dissemination of the results to third parties. The

---

[23]The Court in *Chandler* listed the following positions: "Governor, Lieutenant Governor, Secretary of State, Attorney General, State School Superintendent, Commissioner of Insurance, Commissioner of Agriculture, Commissioner of Labor, Justices of the Supreme Court, Judges of the Court of Appeals, judges of the superior courts, district attorneys, members of the General Assembly, and members of the Public Service Commission."
[24]532 U.S. 67 (2001).
[25]The policy at issue was developed by a "task force" that "included representatives of [the hospital], the police, the County Substance Abuse Commission and the Department of Social Services."

Sidebar

THE *FERGUSON* COURT'S DESCRIPTION OF THE DRUG TESTING PROGRAM

In striking down the program, the Court was troubled by the extensive police involvement and the accompanying threat of prosecution. The Court provided the following relevant description:

> The threat of law enforcement involvement was set forth in two protocols, the first dealing with the identification of drug use during pregnancy, and the second with identification of drug use after labor. Under the latter protocol, the police were to be notified without delay and the patient promptly arrested. Under the former, after the initial positive drug test, the police were to be notified (and the patient arrested) only if the patient tested positive for cocaine a second time or if she missed an appointment with a substance abuse counselor. In 1990, however, the policy was modified at the behest of the solicitor's office to give the patient who tested positive during labor, like the patient who tested positive during a prenatal care visit, an opportunity to avoid arrest by consenting to substance abuse treatment.
>
> The last six pages of the policy contained forms for the patients to sign, as well as procedures for the police to follow when a patient was arrested. The policy also prescribed in detail the precise offenses with which a woman could be charged, depending on the stage of her pregnancy. If the pregnancy was 27 weeks or less, the patient was to be charged with simple possession. If it was 28 weeks or more, she was to be charged with possession and distribution to a person under the age of 18 — in this case, the fetus. If she delivered "while testing positive for illegal drugs," she was also to be charged with unlawful neglect of a child. Under the policy, the police were instructed to interrogate the arrestee in order "to ascertain the identity of the subject who provided illegal drugs to the suspect." Other than the provisions describing the substance abuse treatment to be offered to women who tested positive, the policy made no mention of any change in the prenatal care of such patients, nor did it prescribe any special treatment for the newborns.

use of an adverse test result to disqualify one from eligibility for a particular benefit, such as a promotion or an opportunity to participate in an extracurricular activity, involves a less serious intrusion on privacy than the unauthorized dissemination of such results to third parties. The reasonable expectation of privacy enjoyed by the typical patient undergoing diagnostic tests in a hospital is that the results of those tests will not be shared with nonmedical personnel without her consent.

However, the most significant distinction lay in the asserted special need for the testing. In *Von Raab, Skinner,* and *Vernonia*, the Court observed that the need for testing was sufficiently divorced from the state's interest in criminal law enforcement.

This was not the case in *Ferguson*. The Court found that a "central" component to the program was the "coerc[ive]" use of law enforcement to pressure patients into substance abuse treatment. The Court rejected the government's contention that its asserted special need — the advancement of the health of the mother and child — was distinct from the state's interest in enforcing its criminal laws. Distinguishing between the policy's "ultimate" intentions — to promote the health of the mother and child — and the policy's "immediate" objective — to gather evidence that could be used in future criminal litigation — the Court asserted that the "extensive involvement of law enforcement officials at every stage of the policy" coupled with the threat of prosecution cast this program outside "the closely guarded category of 'special needs.'"

(d) Public Employer Search of Public Employee's Government-Issued Pager

In *City of Ontario v. Quon*,[26] the Supreme Court considered whether a government employer could, consistent with the Fourth Amendment, review the text messages of one of its employees when the pager that was issued to, and used by, the public employee had been purchased by the employer. The Court found, in the circumstances presented in *Quon*, that the government search was reasonable.

Police Sergeant Jeff Quon was employed by the City of Ontario (California) and was given a pager that had been purchased by the City and was capable of performing text messaging functions. Employees, including Quon, were instructed that the pagers were to be used for work-related purposes and that the devices had a monthly numerical character restriction. They were also informed that the City of Ontario "reserves the right to monitor and log all network activity including e-mail and Internet use, with or without notices. Users should have no expectation of privacy or confidentiality when using these resources." The City informed Quon and the other recipients of the City pagers that text messages (which were not explicitly encompassed by the aforementioned computer policy) and e-mails would be treated in the same fashion.

On several occasions, Quon exceeded the text message monthly character limit. Although Quon reimbursed the City for his overages, the City elected to audit his text messages. A review indicated that Quon had been using his pager, in part, to send and receive personal-use (and sometimes sexually explicit) text messages. Quon was ultimately disciplined for his actions.

Quon filed suit against the City arguing, in part, that the government review of his text messages violated the Fourth Amendment. In a narrowly tailored decision, the Court found that the actions of the City were reasonable. In reaching this result, the Court made certain assumptions, including that Quon had a reasonable expectation of privacy in his text messages and that the government did, in fact, perform a search when it subsequently reviewed the messages from the pager. Given these assumptions, the Court proceeded to find that the City's review did not contravene the Fourth Amendment. Since the search was work-related (to determine whether the character limit was sufficient for the City's employees in performing their duties) and the breadth of the search was limited and nonintrusive (the City reviewed the texts for only two months and off-duty text messages were not reviewed), the Court concluded that the search was reasonable.

(4) Border Searches

In the border context, the Court has upheld searches and seizures in the absence of a warrant, on less than probable cause and, in many instances, in the complete absence of any suspicion of wrongdoing. A review of the law in this area will begin with an examination of the foundational case on this subject, *United States v. Ramsey*.[27]

Ramsey involved a heroin-by-mail enterprise, whereby individuals in Thailand would send heroin to various parts of the District of Columbia. A U.S. Customs official, on one occasion, seized and opened several such envelopes after having

---

[26]130 S. Ct. 2619 (2010).
[27]431 U.S. 606 (1977).

developed reason to believe that the envelopes contained contraband. The Supreme Court upheld the search and seizure, finding that the government's conduct was reasonable given its interest in protecting its border. The Court stated "[t]hat searches made at the border, pursuant to the long-standing right of the sovereign to protect itself by stopping and examining persons and property crossing into this country, are reasonable simply by virtue of the fact that they occur at the border." It added that border searches

> have been considered to be "reasonable" by the single fact that the person or item in question had entered into our country from outside. There has never been any additional requirement that the reasonableness of a border search depended on the existence of probable cause. This longstanding recognition that searches at our borders without probable cause and without a warrant are nonetheless "reasonable" has a history as old as the Fourth Amendment itself.

Thus, the government's right to "control . . . who and what may enter the country" is the central justification underlying the border search and seizure exception. The Court noted that during oral argument it was conceded that border officials could open, with neither a warrant nor any suspicion, envelopes possessed by someone attempting to cross the border into this country. The Court stated that this right to search is no less compromised when the envelopes are mailed across the border as opposed to being physically transported.

After *Ramsey* several questions remained unresolved. One of these questions concerned the scope of a permissible border search. In this regard, the Court has distinguished between border searches of humans and searches of effects. In short, the Court is more permissive of extensive, suspicionless border searches when the subject of the search is an effect as opposed to a human. The next subsection discusses the relevant Supreme Court authority on this subject.

(a) How Extensive a Search Is Permissible?

In *United States v. Montoya de Hernandez*,[28] the Supreme Court considered whether the Fourth Amendment's reasonableness standard was violated when Customs officials detained a woman whom they reasonably suspected to be "a 'balloon swallower,' one who attempts to smuggle narcotics into this country hidden in her alimentary canal," for approximately 16 hours after she had arrived in the United States on a commercial airliner from Colombia. The Court found that there was no Fourth Amendment violation.

The Court stated that individuals who attempt to enter this country have a lessened expectation of privacy. The fact that such individuals present themselves "at the border for admission and subject [themselves] to the criminal enforcement powers of the Federal Government" contributes to this reduced expectation.

Weighed against this limited privacy right was the "heav[y]" interest of the government. The Court found that the government was entitled to perform what it termed "routine" searches of entrants to this country in the absence of a warrant and in the absence of any suspicion. It further held that more extensive detentions — those that exceed the parameters of a "routine" search — can be justified if the government can establish that they reasonably suspect the individual of "smuggling

---

[28]473 U.S. 531 (1985).

contraband in her alimentary canal." The Court found that Customs officials reasonably suspected that the defendant was smuggling narcotics via her alimentary canal and that her detention was, therefore, reasonable. Regarding other forms of nonroutine searches, such as "strip, body cavity, or involuntary x-ray searches," the Court expressed no opinion as to requisite standard of proof necessary since such searches were not at issue.

In contrast to *Montoya de Hernandez*, the Supreme Court in *United States v. Flores-Montano*[29] considered the propriety of a border search and seizure that involved not a person but an effect. *Flores-Montano* involved a suspicionless search of an automobile by Customs officials at an international border in southern California. After the vehicle had been initially inspected by a Customs officer, the vehicle was taken to a "secondary inspection station." At that location, another Customs official examined the gas tank. Eventually, "a mechanic under contract with Customs" removed the tank and, in a process that took between 15 and 25 minutes, proceeded to dismantle the component. As a result, "37 kilograms of marijuana bricks" were recovered.

The Court upheld the search. It recognized that in *Montoya de Hernandez* the Court distinguished between searches that were "routine" and others that were more extensive. But the Court in *Flores-Montano* held that such distinctions are inapposite in the context of vehicular searches at the border.

It noted the government's "paramount" interest in border patrol and held that this interest overcame the reduced privacy interests presented in this case. The Court observed that it has "long recognized" that automobiles may be searched when they attempt to cross the border into the United States. Given such, the Court found it difficult to comprehend how the invasiveness associated with the search of a gas tank could exceed the invasiveness of a search of a passenger compartment. The Court also found that the search at issue was "brief" and did not produce any vehicular damage. The Court did acknowledge, however, the possibility that a future case (e.g., a car search case involving extensive damage) at the border could present itself and require a different outcome.

(b) Definition of a "Border"

Now to the question of what constitutes a border. Certainly, when an individual attempts to walk or drive into the country from Mexico or Canada the boundary line separating the United States from these countries is a border. I grew up in Michigan approximately 30 minutes from Windsor, Ontario. Whenever I traveled to and from Canada via a tunnel or a bridge, I was met by government agents patrolling the border. Any searches performed at these stops clearly qualified as border searches. Similarly, if an individual attempts to enter this country via a vessel and docks along the U.S. coastline, this, too, constitutes a border. Borders also include locations that are the functional equivalent of an actual border. Thus, an international traveler who enters this country via an airplane arrives at the functional equivalent of an actual border. This is true whether the airport is located along the coastline or in the heart of the country.

The Supreme Court has considered the question of what constitutes a border in a couple of additional contexts as well. *United States v. Martinez-Fuerte*[30] addressed

---

[29]541 U.S. 149 (2004).
[30]428 U.S. 543 (1976).

the constitutionality of a government seizure at a fixed checkpoint in California located 66 miles north of the Mexican border. The case involved three separate prosecutions of individuals who approached the checkpoint in a vehicle and then, in the absence of any suspicion of wrongdoing, were directed to a secondary inspection post where evidence of criminal activity was eventually uncovered.

The Court rejected the constitutional challenge to the stop, finding that the government's seizures comported with the Fourth Amendment. Balancing the requisite interests, the Court found that the government had a "great" interest in making routine inland traffic checkpoint stops "because the flow of illegal aliens cannot be controlled effectively at the border." The Court added that requiring reasonable suspicion prior to making such stops "would be impractical because the flow of traffic tends to be too heavy to allow the particularized study of a given car that would enable it to be identified as a possible carrier of illegal aliens."

On the other hand, the Court found that the infringement upon privacy was "quite limited" given that the stops were of short duration and were accompanied by brief questioning and a limited visual search of the vehicle. The Court added that motorists stopped at these checkpoints "are not taken by surprise as they know, or may obtain knowledge of, the location of the checkpoints and will not be stopped elsewhere." The Court also noted that the checkpoint program limited officer discretion regarding which vehicles may be stopped. In contrast to random vehicular stops, officers at fixed checkpoints "may stop only those cars passing the checkpoint," which leaves "less room for abusive or harassing stops of individuals." Regarding the selection of drivers for secondary inspections, the Court found that border agents "must have wide discretion" in this regard, and that the Constitution does not forbid such referrals even when "made largely on the basis of apparent Mexican ancestry."

F   A   Q

Q: Can roving border patrol seizures and searches be performed in the absence of any suspicion?

A: No. In short, searches and seizures performed in this context are governed by the same Fourth Amendment standards that apply in the criminal context. In *Almeida-Sanchez v. United States*,[31] a Border Patrol agent, acting pursuant to a federal statute, stopped and subsequently searched a vehicle traveling along a California highway approximately 25 miles north of the Mexican border without either probable cause or reasonable suspicion. Illegal narcotics were found within the vehicle. The Court held that, absent probable cause or consent, the suspicionless search of the vehicle contravened the Fourth Amendment. The Court rejected the government's contention that the problems associated with patrolling the border, however "serious," justify diverging from traditional Fourth Amendment principles in this context. And in *United States v. Brignoni-Ponce*,[32] the Supreme Court considered the propriety of a vehicular stop by roving Border Patrol agents along a California highway near the Mexican border. The agents stopped the vehicle solely on account of the Mexican ancestry of its occupants. The Court held that the stop violated the Fourth Amendment. In so holding, the

---

[31]413 U.S. 266 (1973).
[32]422 U.S. 873 (1975).

Court found that officers must possess reasonable suspicion of criminal activity before such random stops can be deemed to be reasonable. "To approve roving patrol stops of all vehicles in the border area, without any suspicion that a particular vehicle is carrying illegal immigrants, would subject the residents of these and other areas to potentially unlimited interference with their use of the highways, solely at the discretion of Border Patrol officers." The Court further held that Mexican ancestry alone justifies "neither a reasonable belief that they were aliens, nor a reasonable belief that the car concealed other aliens who were illegally in the country."

Whereas *Martinez-Fuerte* involved a government *seizure* at a fixed interior checkpoint, *United States v. Ortiz*[33] addressed the constitutionality of a warrantless and suspicionless government *search* of a vehicle at such a site (the checkpoint was situated over 60 miles north of the Mexican border). This time the Court reached a different result, concluding that probable cause or consent is required before the government may search a private vehicle.

The Court analogized searches at fixed interior checkpoints to searches performed pursuant to roving patrols. It declared that automobile searches constitute "a substantial invasion of privacy" and that, in this context, government discretion regarding the selection of vehicles to be searched is not meaningfully restricted.

(5) Probationers and Parolees

Though the Supreme Court has distinguished between government searches of parolees and probationers, substantively there is little differentiation. Nevertheless, the law is still evolving in this area, so stay tuned. The first two cases discussed in this section — *Griffin v. Wisconsin* and *United States v. Knights* — address searches of probationers. The final case — *Samson v. California* — addresses searches of parolees.

(a) Searches of Probationers

In *Griffin v. Wisconsin*,[34] the Supreme Court upheld as reasonable under the Fourth Amendment a warrantless search of a probationer's home by probation officers. A Wisconsin statute authorized the residential searches of probationers provided that "reasonable grounds" existed that contraband might be found therein. The Court found that the Fourth Amendment governed the government search at issue, but stated that probationers, like parolees, enjoy liberty protections that are more limited than what is commonly enjoyed by citizens of this country.

Noting the rehabilitative and community safety objectives (the "special needs") that underlie the Wisconsin probation system, the Court concluded that the imposition of a warrant requirement would "interfere to an appreciable degree with the probation system" (which requires that a probation officer assess the probationer's compliance with his conditions), would cause unnecessary investigative delays for probation officers, and would adversely impact the deterrent effect that warrantless searches might otherwise provide.

The Court also found that the impracticability of a warrant requirement justified dispensing with the probable cause requirement as well. The Court was satisfied that

[33]422 U.S. 891 (1975).
[34]483 U.S. 868 (1987).

the "reasonable grounds" standard delineated in the statute was sufficient. It declared that this lesser standard was necessary in order to allow probation officers sufficient latitude to advance the system's rehabilitative and community protective policies.

In *United States v. Knights*,[35] the Court essentially extended *Griffin*. The holding in *Griffin*—allowing warrantless residential searches based upon "reasonable grounds" that contraband might be found therein—was a "special needs" finding. It was based upon the Court's finding that the "special needs" of the Wisconsin probationary system were furthered by this type of government practice. However, *Knights* extended *Griffin* beyond the "special needs" context and into the criminal needs arena. *Knights* involved a probationer whose residence was searched without a warrant after the government developed reasonable suspicion that he had committed another, separate crime. The Court upheld the warrantless search.

The Court assessed the practice in accordance with the Fourth Amendment's reasonableness clause and balanced the individual's liberty interests against the interests of the government. Regarding the former interest, the Court reiterated the principle enunciated in *Griffin* that probationers possess a lesser expectation of privacy. The Court cited the "search condition" included in the subject probation order, which required that the probationer "[s]ubmit his . . . person, property, place of residence, vehicle, personal effects, to search at anytime, with or without a search warrant, warrant of arrest or reasonable cause by any probation officer or law enforcement officer." This condition, according to the Court, "inform[ed] both sides of that balance."

It also noted the government's "dual concern" regarding probationers—rehabilitation and the greater likelihood that those on probation will commit crimes than "ordinary member[s] of the community." After balancing the respective interests, the Court concluded that "[w]hen an officer has reasonable suspicion that a probationer subject to a search condition is engaged in criminal activity, there is enough likelihood that criminal conduct is occurring that an intrusion on the probationer's significantly diminished privacy interests is reasonable."

Notice that the search in *Knights* was seemingly quite extensive. Nothing in the opinion's relatively brief factual description suggests that the search was anything but a full-fledged search of the home. Yet the Court dispensed with the warrant and probable cause requirements and justified the search based simply upon a reasonableness balancing test. While a balancing test is standard fare in the administrative search/ "special needs" context, such balancing is not employed with the same frequency in the criminal sphere, particularly in the context of full-scale searches. Therefore, the balancing observed in *Knights* and *Terry v. Ohio* are situational and should not be interpreted as an invitation to employ balancing whenever a criminal search and seizure issue presents itself.

TERRY v. OHIO BALANCING

If this balancing of the government's criminal investigative interests against the invasion upon individual liberty interests sounds familiar, it is because this is precisely what the Court did in *Terry v. Ohio*.[36] That case did not involve "special needs" balancing, but was a balancing performed in the criminal context. There, the Court balanced the government's interest in "effective crime prevention and detection" as well as its interest in safeguarding its investigating officers against "the nature and quality of the intrusion" upon the individual.

---

[36]392 U.S. 1 (1968).

---

[35]534 U.S. 112 (2001).

(b) Searches of Parolees

The same considerations resurfaced in *Samson v. California*.[37] In *Samson*, the defendant, a parolee, was walking down a street when an officer approached him, searched his person, and discovered illegal narcotics. The officer had neither a warrant nor any suspicion of wrongdoing. A California statute provided that parolees could be searched without a warrant by a parole officer or other police officer irrespective of any suspicion of wrongdoing.

The Supreme Court upheld the search. The Court declared that parolees actually have a privacy expectation that is beneath that enjoyed not only by ordinary citizens but also by probationers given that "parole is more akin to imprisonment than probation is to imprisonment." It noted that a parolee in California may serve his term either in custody or on release subject to certain conditions, including the one at issue in *Samson*. In addition, the Court reasoned that since the parolee agreed to the subject search condition, he "did not have an expectation of privacy that society would recognize as legitimate."

As in *Knights*, the Court found the government's interest in supervising parolees to be "substantial," given the greater propensity of parolees to engage in criminal activity. It also recognized that the government's interest in combating recidivism and promoting societal reintegration justifies greater "privacy intrusions that would not otherwise be tolerated under the Fourth Amendment." Given these substantial interests, and the lessened privacy expectations of parolees, the Court found that warrantless, suspicionless searches of parolees are not prohibited under the Fourth Amendment.

SUMMARY

■ Administrative and "special needs" searches are assessed pursuant to the reasonableness clause of the Fourth Amendment. The interest (administrative or "special need") of the government in performing the search is weighed against the intrusion upon the individual that the search entails.

■ A warrant must be obtained prior to performing an administrative search of a home and it may be required prior to searching a business. However, where a commercial entity is heavily regulated, where the government has substantial noncriminal interest in performing the search, where the warrantless inspection is necessary to further that interest, and where the inspection program constitutes a "constitutionally adequate substitute for a warrant," then a warrantless search of a commercial enterprise is more likely to be upheld.

■ Individuals have a greater expectation of privacy within their homes than do business owners in their commercial properties.

■ License and registration roadside checkpoints, as well as alcohol checkpoints, that are warrantless and suspicionless may survive constitutional scrutiny if officer discretion is sufficiently restrained and the intrusiveness of the stop is limited. However, stops that are indistinguishable from traditional law enforcement stops require compliance with standard Fourth Amendment principles.

---

[37]547 U.S. 843 (2006).

- School officials may perform searches of individual students if they have reasonable suspicion of criminal activity or that a school rule has been infringed. More intrusive strip searches are allowed only if there is reasonable suspicion of danger or that the prohibited item is being concealed in a private bodily location.

- Individualized suspicion is not required in order to drug test student groups. Thus, drug testing of students who participate in extracurricular activities has been upheld. Though it may be helpful if the school can establish a linkage between a particular student group and narcotics usage, it is not a prerequisite for a constitutionally valid testing program.

- Public employees may be subjected to warrantless drug testing in the absence of individualized suspicion. The Supreme Court has upheld such testing when the subject employees have a reduced expectation of privacy in their employment and when the government has established an overriding "special need" to perform the test.

- Warrantless searches and seizures at the border are constitutionally permissible. Routine border searches of individuals may be performed in the absence of probable cause or reasonable suspicion. Such searches may be performed simply by virtue of the fact that a person (who has a lessened expectation of privacy at the border) is attempting to enter the country. Nonroutine border searches of individuals require reasonable suspicion. The Court does not distinguish between routine and nonroutine searches of motor vehicles at the border.

- Actual borders (e.g., the border between the United States and Mexico) and their functional equivalents (e.g., an international traveler who arrives via airplane to an airport located inland) are encompassed within the term "border." Fixed checkpoints established further inland can constitute a border as well. Vehicular stops at such locations can be made absent any suspicion. However, the Supreme Court has held that vehicular searches at such fixed checkpoints require either probable cause or consent. Seizures and searches performed by roving patrols are governed by traditional Fourth Amendment analyses.

- Probationers and parolees have a privacy expectation that is reduced in comparison to ordinary citizens. Thus, warrantless searches (for probationers) have been approved when the government has established "reasonable grounds" of wrongdoing and (for parolees) in the absence of any suspicion of wrongdoing.

CONNECTIONS

Relationship to Executing the Warrant (Chapter 5)

Administrative searches of a home require the prior attainment of a search warrant. Warrants may also be required in the search of a business.

Relationship to the Various Exceptions to the Warrant Requirement (Chapters 6-11)

Like the many exceptions to the warrant requirement, administrative and "special needs" searches are routinely performed in the absence of a warrant.

Relationship to Searches and Seizures on Less than Probable Cause — *Terry v. Ohio* (Chapter 11)

Terry stops and frisks are warrantless intrusions that are deemed to be reasonable under the Fourth Amendment. They are also performed based upon a quantum of proof that is less than probable cause. Likewise, all "special needs" searches and virtually all administrative-type searches that have been upheld have been performed in the absence of a warrant and have been justified on suspicion levels less than probable cause (sometimes no suspicion whatsoever). Moreover, these types of searches have been justified pursuant to the reasonableness clause of the Fourth Amendment.

Fourth Amendment Violations and Their Associated Remedies

15

This chapter discusses the exclusionary rule remedy for violations of the Fourth Amendment. Today the exclusionary rule is a prophylactic

O V E R V I E W

measure that is applicable in both state and federal systems. In essence, it provides that evidence seized as a direct product of a Fourth Amendment breach as well as any fruits derived therefrom ("the fruit of the poisonous tree" doctrine) are inadmissible as substantive evidence by the government. Note: There is an exclusionary rule for Fifth and Sixth Amendment breaches, but this will be discussed in later chapters.

A. PRE-*MAPP* HISTORICAL REVIEW OF THE EXCLUSIONARY RULE

B. *MAPP v. OHIO*: THE CONSTITUTIONALITY OF AND PRIMARY RATIONALES FOR THE EXCLUSIONARY RULE

  1. Standing
  2. *Rakas v. Illinois* and the Reformulation of the Standing Inquiry
  3. Post-*Rakas* Applications: Interpretation of the Legitimate Expectation of Privacy Standard

C. LIMITS ON THE REACH OF THE EXCLUSIONARY RULE

  1. Absence of Direct Causal Links: Independent Source, Inevitable Discovery, and the Absence of Causal Connection
  2. Existence of Direct Causal Links: Attenuated Circumstances and the Good Faith Rule

A. Pre-*Mapp* Historical Review of the Exclusionary Rule

Though the exclusionary rule has settled harmoniously in the state and federal systems, the rule's historical evolution was comparatively more jagged. In 1914, the Supreme Court held in *Weeks v. United States*[1] that evidence obtained by federal agents was inadmissible in a federal prosecution when such evidence was obtained by virtue of an unconstitutional residential search in violation of the Fourth Amendment. Perhaps the most forceful rationale advanced by the *Weeks* Court for its holding was a judicial-integrity-type argument. The Court rather pointedly stated, "The tendency of those who evaluate the criminal laws of the country to obtain conviction by means of unlawful seizures and enforced confessions . . . should find not sanction in the judgments of the courts, which are charged at all times with the support of the Constitution, and to which people of all conditions have a right to appeal for the maintenance of such fundamental rights." As will be seen, however, reliance upon this argument as a primary justification later gave way to another rationale; namely, the need to deter law enforcement from purposefully engaging in conduct that violates the Constitution.

It is important to note that the holding in *Weeks* extended neither to state court matters nor to actions performed by nonfederal officers. After all, as originally referenced in Chapter 1 (Incorporation), it was not until the 1960s that the Fourth Amendment exclusionary rule (as well as other aspects of the Amendment) was made applicable to the states. As a consequence, *Weeks* did not extend to federal or state court prosecutions involving, for example, unreasonable residential searches performed by state officers. It also did not encompass Fourth Amendment violations by federal officials in matters pending in state courts. *Weeks* reached only Fourth Amendment violations committed by federal officers in matters tried in federal court.

Chapter 1 discussed the contentious debate over incorporation. And this debate was firmly on display in *Wolf v. Colorado*.[3] *Wolf* held that Fourteenth Amendment due process is offended when evidence, otherwise inadmissible in a federal criminal case on Fourth Amendment grounds, is admitted at a state court trial. The Court, as a preliminary matter, stated that it has never deemed the Fourteenth Amendment due process clause to be "shorthand for the first eight amendments of the Constitution." But it also recognized that the contours of the due process clause are neither fixed nor capable of predetermination.

Sidebar

THE UNRAVELING OF THE LIMITATIONS IN *WEEKS*: *ELKINS v. UNITED STATES*

The propriety of using illegally obtained evidence by state officers in federal prosecutions was reconsidered by the Supreme Court in *Elkins v. United States*.[2] In *Elkins*, the Supreme Court considered whether "articles obtained as the result of an unreasonable search and seizure by state officers, without involvement of federal officers, [could] be introduced in evidence against a defendant [in federal court]. In a word, we re-examine here the validity of what has come to be called the silver platter doctrine." The Court struck down the doctrine, holding "that evidence obtained by state officers during a search which, if conducted by federal officers, would have violated the defendant's immunity from unreasonable searches and seizures under the Fourth Amendment, is inadmissible."

[2]364 U.S. 206 (1960).

[1]232 U.S. 383 (1914).
[3]338 U.S. 25 (1949).

It considered application of the clause to be a "gradual and empiric process of 'inclusion and exclusion.'"

Wolf is significant, in part, due to its application of the Fourth Amendment proscriptions against unreasonable searches and seizures to the states. But *Wolf* was also notable for what it failed to hold. The Court held that due process did not require that a state impose an exclusionary penalty for such constitutional violations. It seemingly discounted the constitutionality of the exclusionary rule, stating that the exclusionary principle approved in *Weeks* did emanate from the Fourth Amendment's plain text but was an implied remedy. The Court acknowledged that the exclusionary rule "may be an effective way of deterring unreasonable searches." However, the Court stated that "most of the English-speaking world does not regard as vital to such protection the exclusion of evidence thus obtained" and therefore "hesitate[d] to treat this remedy as an essential ingredient of the right."

Nevertheless, in subsequent years the Court chipped away at this latter finding. Consider *Rochin v. California*,[4] where officers, after entering the defendant's residence without a warrant and failing to physically extract two capsules containing morphine that they had observed the defendant swallow, handcuffed the defendant, took him to a hospital, and directed a doctor to obtain the items from the defendant's person. The doctor, in turn, "forced an emetic solution into" the defendant's stomach that produced the swallowed capsules. Finding that due process required that the evidence be excluded, the Court explained:

> [W]e are compelled to conclude that the proceedings by which this conviction was obtained do more than offend some fastidious squeamishness or private sentimentalism about combatting crime too energetically. This is conduct that shocks the conscience. Illegally breaking into the privacy of the petitioner, the struggle to open his mouth and remove what was there, the forcible extraction of his stomach's contents — this course of proceeding by agents of government to obtain evidence is bound to offend even hardened sensibilities. They are methods too close to the rack and the screw to permit of constitutional differentiation.

The Court continued:

> Due process of law, as a historic and generative principle, precludes defining, and thereby confining, these standards of conduct more precisely than to say that convictions cannot be brought about by methods that offend "a sense of justice" (citation omitted). It would be a stultification of the responsibility which the course of constitutional history has cast upon this Court to hold that in order to convict a man the police cannot extract by force what is in his mind but can extract what is in his stomach.

B. *Mapp v. Ohio*: The Constitutionality of and Primary Rationales for the Exclusionary Rule

Though subsequent Supreme Court decisions seemed to limit *Rochin*,[5] *Wolf*'s holding regarding the inapplicability of the exclusionary rule was finally overturned

---

[4]342 U.S. 165 (1952).
[5]*Irvine v. California*, 347 U.S. 128 (1954) (exclusion of statements not required when officers entered defendant's home to install a hidden listening device, and subsequently reentered in order to move the

by the Supreme Court in *Mapp v. Ohio*.[6] In applying the exclusionary rule to the states, the Court in *Mapp* set forth two rationales for its extension.

First, the Court reasoned that the exclusionary rule operates as a deterrent to flagrant government abuse of Fourth Amendment rights. Consider the Court's forceful comment that follows. The Court not only considered the exclusionary remedy as a necessary deterrent to unconstitutional government search and seizure practices, but it also viewed the rule as constitutional in nature.

> Were it otherwise, then just as without the *Weeks* rule the assurance against unreasonable federal searches and seizures would be "a form of words," valueless and undeserving of mention in a perpetual charter of inestimable human liberties, so too, without that rule the freedom from state invasions of privacy would be so ephemeral and so neatly severed from its conceptual nexus with the freedom from all brutish means of coercing evidence as not to merit this Court's high regard as a freedom "implicit in the concept of ordered liberty." . . . The right to privacy, when conceded operatively enforceable against the States, was not susceptible of destruction by avulsion of the sanction upon which its protection and enjoyment had always been deemed dependent. . . . Therefore, in extending the substantive protections of due process to all constitutionally unreasonable searches — state or federal — it was logically and constitutionally necessary that the exclusion doctrine — an essential part of the right to privacy — be also insisted upon as an essential ingredient of the right newly recognized by the *Wolf* case. In short, the admission of the new constitutional right by *Wolf* could not consistently tolerate denial of its most important constitutional privilege, namely, the exclusion of the evidence which an accused had been forced to give by reason of the unlawful seizure. To hold otherwise is to grant the right but in reality to withhold its privilege and enjoyment. Only last year the Court itself recognized that the purpose of the exclusionary rule "is to deter — to compel respect for the constitutional guaranty in the only effectively available way — by removing the incentive to disregard it."

That the rule was imbedded within the Constitution, in the Court's view, was not only a "logical dictate of prior cases, but it also [made] very good sense." Yet, despite such unambiguous declarations, the Court in subsequent cases retreated from this constitutional finding. This change in approach will be reviewed later in this chapter.

The Court also asserted a second rationale for the exclusionary penalty, namely the previously referenced judicial integrity argument. In that regard the Court was equally forceful, declaring that "[n]othing can destroy a government more quickly than its failure to observe its own laws, or worse, its disregard of the charter of its own existence." In conclusion, the Court stated that its decision "gives to the individual no more than that which the Constitution guarantees him, to the police officer no less than that to which honest law enforcement is entitled, and, to the courts, that judicial integrity so necessary in the true administration of justice."

Mapp is replete with such powerful judicial proclamations. Yet, as with the Court's finding regarding the constitutional nature of the exclusionary rule, the Court would similarly turn its back upon this aspect of its holding. Cases decided by the Supreme Court beginning in the 1970s, such as *United States v. Calandra*,[7]

---

device to alternate locations); *Breithaupt v. Abram*, 352 U.S. 432 (1957) (exclusion of blood extracted from defendant who was rendered unconscious after an accident did not shock the conscience so as to require exclusion).
[6]367 U.S. 643 (1961).
[7]414 U.S. 338 (1974) (finding that "allowing a grand jury witness to invoke the exclusionary rule would unduly interfere with the effective and expeditious discharge of the grand jury's duties").

United States v. Leon,[8] *Nix v. Williams,*[9] *Arizona v. Evans,*[10] *Herring v. United States,*[11] and *Davis v. United States,*[12] strongly attest to this fact. Those cases, among others, unequivocally reflect the Court's current view that the primary rationale for the exclusionary rule is exclusive: deterrence. And if the deterrence policy is not furthered by exclusion, then the Court has shown a disinclination to require the remedy. *Leon, Evans, Herring,* and *Davis* will be discussed later in this chapter.

(1) Standing

During my Criminal Procedure class I invariably tell my students that for those who plan to pursue a career in criminal litigation the issue of standing is of vital importance. Prosecutors enjoy enormous power. They get to decide, for example, whom to arrest, what to charge, and with whom to plea bargain. Defense attorneys, on the other hand, have comparatively fewer weapons in their arsenal. Typically they have little influence over the various arrest and indictment decisions exercised by their prosecutorial counterparts. And while a defense attorney may initiate plea bargain discussions, a prosecutor is not under any legal or ethical obligation to entertain any such discussions. Instead, the role of the defense attorney is more reactionary. The attorney typically reacts to the arrest, charging, and plea bargaining decisions instigated by the government.

One of the weapons that a defense attorney does enjoy is the power to file pretrial motions. While a defense attorney may have little or no influence over the indictment decisions of the government, he or she may be able to influence the course of the litigation through the filing of pretrial motions. In this regard, pretrial motions challenging the admission of evidence are rather typical, particularly in federal court litigation.

Accordingly, prosecutors must respond to such motions with great frequency. Before addressing the merits of the suppression motion, however, prosecutors should always — and I mean always — address the threshold issue of standing. This principle — as well as the Supreme Court's refined phraseology associated with this concept — will be explored in greater depth in this section. But suffice it to say, a defendant can challenge the introduction of the evidence against him only if he has standing. In the absence of standing, a court will not entertain a defendant's suppression motion.

In short, a defendant today may establish standing to contest the admission of evidence against him if the government's action breached his personal Fourth Amendment rights. Thus, for example, if a defendant can establish that he was seized in violation of the Constitution or that evidence was seized from an area where he had a reasonable expectation of privacy, then the defendant will have standing to contest the admission of evidence that flows from that breach.

Imagine the following scenario. Police officers, with neither probable cause nor a search warrant, arrive at Tom's residence to search a vehicle that Tom owns and is located in his driveway. When the police arrive at the residence, defendant Phil, who

---

[8]468 U.S. 897 (1984).
[9]467 U.S. 431 (1984) (finding that suppression of evidence that would have been inevitably discovered "would do nothing whatever to promote the integrity of the trial process, but would inflict a wholly unacceptable burden on the administration of criminal justice").
[10]514 U.S. 1 (1995).
[11]129 S. Ct. 695 (2009).
[12]131 S. Ct. 2419 (2011).

just happened to have met Tom for the first time earlier that same day, is seated in the vehicle's front passenger seat. An ensuing search of the vehicle reveals the presence of an illegal firearm that links defendant Phil with a recent armed bank robbery committed within the jurisdiction. Does Phil have standing to contest the government's use of the weapon obtained during its illegal search of Tom's vehicle?

Well, this was the question (involving an analogous factual pattern) addressed by the Supreme Court in *Jones v. United States*.[13] In holding that the defendant could contest a police search of an apartment (which he testified, inter alia, was not his but belonged to a friend) that uncovered illegal narcotics, the Court established a rule of "automatic standing." The rule provided that whenever the possession of evidence necessary to establish standing is also an essential element of a charged offense, "automatic standing" is conferred upon the defendant against whom the evidence is directed. On the one hand, the government argued in *Jones* that the defendant did not have standing to contest the search because he claimed not to be in possession of the seized narcotics and insisted that he was merely a guest or an invitee of the residence. On the other hand, the government, as part of its case against the defendant, was attempting to demonstrate that the defendant possessed the very same narcotics. The Court found that the government should not be allowed to advantage itself of such "contradictory" positions. As the Court explained:

> Petitioner's conviction flows from his possession of the narcotics at the time of the search. Yet the fruits of that search, upon which the conviction depends, were admitted into evidence on the ground that petitioner did not have possession of the narcotics at that time. The prosecution here thus subjected the defendant to the penalties meted out to one in lawless possession while refusing him the remedies designed for one in that situation. It is not consonant with the amenities, to put it mildly, of the administration of criminal justice to sanction such squarely contradictory assertions of power by the Government. The possession on the basis of which petitioner is to be and was convicted suffices to give him standing. . . .

Jones also held that standing could be established by "anyone legitimately on premises where a search occurs . . . when its fruits are proposed to be used against him." The Court noted that the hearing testimony established that the defendant was "present in the apartment" with the owner's consent. The defendant's mere presence at the searched location was sufficient to confer upon the defendant a sufficient interest in the premises so as to confer standing.[14] As will be seen later in this section, this rather liberal construction of the standing concept would later give way to a more restricted interpretation.

At the time of *Jones*, defendants were often faced with a quandary. The problem they confronted concerned the government's potential use of their suppression hearing testimony against them at their subsequent criminal trial. Thus, for example, a defendant charged with a narcotics crime who testified at a suppression hearing that he possessed the narcotics in question and/or lived at the residence where the drugs

---

[13]362 U.S. 257 (1960).

[14]The Court noted that the lower courts had adopted a more narrow construction of the possessory interest necessary in order to confer standing. In describing this "prevailing view," the Court stated: "They have denied standing to 'guests' and 'invitees' (citations omitted) and employees, who, though in 'control' or 'occupancy,' lacked 'possession' (citations omitted). The necessary quantum of interest has been distinguished as being, variously, 'ownership in or right to possession of the premises' (citations omitted), the interest of a "lessee or licensee" (citation omitted), or of one with 'dominion' (citations omitted)."

were found was faced with the prospect that such admissions could be used against him at his trial. So what was a defendant to do? Should he refrain from testifying at the hearing and, essentially, offer no contest to the admission of the narcotics at his trial? Or should he contest the validity of the search, testify to his proximity to the drugs and/or the search location, and (assuming he loses the suppression motion) have that testimony used against him at trial? Not an enviable position!

The Supreme Court remedied this dilemma eight years later in *Simmons v. United States*.[15] There, the Court held that the government was prohibited from introducing as substantive evidence at a defendant's criminal trial testimony that he provided during a suppression hearing. Commenting upon the aforementioned dilemma, the Court stated:

> For a defendant who wishes to establish standing must do so at the risk that the words which he utters may later be used to incriminate him. Those courts which have allowed the admission of testimony given to establish standing have reasoned that there is no violation of the Fifth Amendment's Self-Incrimination Clause because the testimony was voluntary. . . . However, the assumption which underlies this reasoning is that the defendant has a choice: he may refuse to testify and give up the benefit. When this assumption is applied to a situation in which the "benefit" to be gained is that afforded by another provision of the Bill of Rights, an undeniable tension is created. Thus, in this case Garrett was obliged either to give up what he believed . . . to be a valid Fourth Amendment claim or . . . waive his Fifth Amendment privilege against self-incrimination. [W]e find it intolerable that one constitutional right should have to be surrendered in order to assert another. We therefore hold that when a defendant testifies in support of a motion to suppress evidence on Fourth Amendment grounds, his testimony may not thereafter be admitted against him at trial on the issue of guilt unless he makes no objection.

(2) *Rakas v. Illinois* and the Reformulation of the Standing Inquiry

Rakas v. Illinois[16] is most notable for its reformulation of the traditional standing approach to the Fourth Amendment, its curtailment of *Jones*, and its narrowing of the class of individuals eligible to pursue Fourth Amendment challenges.

In *Rakas*, the Court questioned whether the issue of standing should be considered separately "from the merits of a defendant's Fourth Amendment claim." The Court answered this question in the negative, concluding that the standing issue should be viewed as part and parcel of a substantive Fourth Amendment analysis. Specifically, the Court held that a court should make a single inquiry: namely, "whether or not the proponent of the motion to suppress had *his own* Fourth Amendment rights infringed by the search and seizure which he seeks to challenge" (emphasis added). In other words, the Court declared that Fourth Amendment interests cannot be asserted vicariously. Rather, such constitutional protections are personal in nature. As the Court declared, "A person who is aggrieved by an illegal search and seizure only through the introduction of damaging evidence secured by a search of a third person's premises or property has not had any of his Fourth Amendment rights infringed (citation omitted). And since the exclusionary rule is an attempt to effectuate the guarantees of the Fourth Amendment (citation omitted) it is proper to permit only defendants whose Fourth Amendment rights have been violated to benefit from the rule's protections."

---

[15]390 U.S. 377 (1968).
[16]439 U.S. 128 (1978).

Thus, per *Rakas*, the issue of standing should be considered within the general framework of a substantive Fourth Amendment review. The Court asserted that "[t]he inquiry under either approach is the same," but insisted that its reformulated test produced a "better analysis." As the Court stated:

> [T]he question is whether the challenged search or seizure violated the Fourth Amendment rights of a criminal defendant who seeks to exclude the evidence obtained during it. That inquiry in turn requires a determination of whether the disputed search and seizure has infringed an interest of the defendant which the Fourth Amendment was designed to protect. We are under no illusion that by dispensing with the rubric of standing used in *Jones* we have rendered any simpler the determination of whether the proponent of a motion to suppress is entitled to contest the legality of a search and seizure. But by frankly recognizing that this aspect of the analysis belongs more properly under the heading of substantive Fourth Amendment doctrine than under the heading of standing, we think the decision of this issue will rest on sounder logical footing.

F   A   Q

Q: In light of *Rakas*, should the concept of standing still be considered?

A: Yes. *Rakas* is certainly correct when it states that analysis under either approach would produce the same end result. However, considering the issue of standing as a separate inquiry preliminary to any substantive Fourth Amendment review is a cleaner, preferable analytical approach to such constitutional challenges. The *Rakas* approach is suggestive, if nothing else, of an immediate consideration of the merits of the Fourth Amendment claim. Yet the need for a substantive review is obviated if the defendant fails to establish that he has standing to even present the claim. Thus, if a defendant files a motion to suppress drugs found in his neighbor's house, and if the government can establish that the defendant does not have a reasonable expectation of privacy in that residence, then the court can dismiss the defendant's petition without ever addressing the merits of the officers' conduct, however contemptible the government's conduct might be. If, on the other hand, the government fails in this attempt, then the court should proceed to address the merits of the defendant's claim.

(a) Adoption of the Legitimate Expectation of Privacy Standard

In reaching this result, the *Rakas* Court considered, and rejected, two proffered theories of standing. One was "the so-called 'target' theory." This theory would allow an individual to pursue a Fourth Amendment challenge so long as he was a target of the government investigation. Thus, an individual asserting a Fourth Amendment claim would have standing to pursue such a claim even if the only constitutional interest infringed belonged to a third party.

Rejecting this theory, the Court stated that allowing the vicarious assertion of Fourth Amendment claims overlooks not only the personal nature of the right, but also the authority it vests in individuals to enforce constitutional safeguards when they have "not had any of [their own] Fourth Amendment rights infringed." To this point, the Court added that "since the exclusionary rule is an attempt to effectuate the guarantees of the Fourth Amendment (citation omitted), it is proper

Sidebar

"TARGET" THEORY REJECTED: *UNITED STATES v. PAYNER*

Two years after *Rakas*, the Supreme Court had opportunity to, once again, consider and reject a proposed "target" theory of standing. In *United States v. Payner*,[17] the Court refused to suppress evidence found by the government, and admitted against the defendant, during a search of a third party's briefcase. The unconstitutional search was performed with the specific design of obtaining evidence against the defendant. In fact, the district court in *Payner* observed that "the Government affirmatively counsels its agents that the Fourth Amendment standing limitation permits them to purposefully conduct an unconstitutional search and seizure of one individual in order to obtain evidence against third parties. . . ." The *Payner* decision rested, primarily, upon two bases: the private nature of the Fourth Amendment right and the insufficiency of the deterrence rationale as a justification for a contrary result. "No court should condone the unconstitutional and possibly criminal behavior of those who planned and executed this 'briefcase caper.' . . . But our cases also show that these unexceptional principles do not command the exclusion of evidence in every case of illegality. Instead, they must be weighed against the considerable harm that would flow from indiscriminate application of an exclusionary rule. . . . Our Fourth Amendment decisions have established beyond any doubt that the interest in deterring illegal searches does not justify the exclusion of tainted evidence at the instance of a party who was not the victim of the challenged practices."

---

[17]447 U.S. 727 (1980).

to permit only defendants whose Fourth Amendment rights have been violated to benefit from the rule's protections." The Court also commented upon the "practical difficulties" associated with a "target" theory, stating that the task of identifying the targets of a particular investigation could be cumbersome and result in "a more widespread invocation of the exclusionary rule during criminal trials." In the Court's view, a "target" theory would also impose substantial societal costs by excluding relevant evidence and impairing the "search for truth at trial." It added in a footnote that the exclusionary rule's deterrent rationale was an insufficient justification for extending the right to present Fourth Amendment challenges to mere targets.

The Court also addressed another basis for standing identified in *Jones* — that anyone "legitimately on the premises" where the search was performed could challenge the constitutional legitimacy of that search. *Rakas* rejected this formulation, claiming it to be too liberal a test, and substituted in its stead a new, more narrow, standard: namely, that an individual may present and pursue a Fourth Amendment challenge if he can establish that he personally has a legitimate privacy expectation in the area where the search was performed. While the Court acknowledged that the "legitimately on the premises" inquiry may have some relevance to an expectation of privacy inquiry, the majority believed that the more expansive *Jones* test would lead to some less desirable outcomes. For example, "a casual visitor who has never seen, or been permitted to visit, the basement of another's house" would be permitted under *Jones* "to object to a search of the basement if the visitor happened to be in the kitchen of the house at the time of a search." Under the new *Rakas* standard, such a visitor would likely be unable to maintain a Fourth Amendment challenge.

Rakas did not overrule *Jones* (it would be overruled, but later). But it interpreted *Jones* in a manner consistent with the new *Rakas* paradigm. The Court declared that

Jones stood "for the unremarkable proposition that a person can have a legally sufficient interest in a place other than his own home so that the Fourth Amendment protects him from unreasonable governmental intrusion into that place." Relying upon *Katz v. United States*,[18] the Court explained that in *Jones* the defendant could assert a Fourth Amendment claim since he had a legitimate privacy expectation in the apartment unit that was searched despite the fact that he did not have a property interest in that residence.

(3) Post-*Rakas* Applications: Interpretation of the Legitimate Expectation of Privacy Standard

(a) Automatic Standing

Two years after *Rakas*, the Supreme Court discarded the Jones "automatic standing" principle in *United States v. Salvucci*.[19] Relying largely upon *Rakas*, the *Salvucci* Court declared:

> We need not belabor the question of whether the "vice" of prosecutorial contradiction could alone support a rule countenancing the exclusion of probative evidence on the grounds that someone other than the defendant was denied a Fourth Amendment right. The simple answer is that the decisions of this Court, especially our most recent decision in *Rakas v. Illinois* (citation omitted), clearly establish that a prosecutor may simultaneously maintain that a defendant criminally possessed the seized good, but was not subject to a Fourth Amendment deprivation, without legal contradiction. To conclude that a prosecutor engaged in self-contradiction in *Jones*, the Court necessarily relied on the unexamined assumption that a defendant's possession of a seized good sufficient to establish criminal culpability was also sufficient to establish Fourth Amendment "standing." This assumption, however, even if correct at the time, is no longer so.

Thus, after *Salvucci*, the mere charge of a possessory offense involving evidence seized during a government search no longer conferred "automatic standing" upon the individual so charged.

(b) Property Ownership

Another case decided the same day as *Salvucci* further illustrates this point. In *Rawlings v. Kentucky*,[20] the Court held that mere ownership of property did not confer standing to contest a government search of the area where the property was found. Though a relevant factor, the Court stated that ownership of property without more does not establish that an individual has a reasonable expectation of privacy in the place where the government performed the search. Given the holding in *Rakas*, this makes sense. In *Rawlings*, the defendant had placed a vial among other containers in another individual's purse. A search of that purse uncovered the narcotics and the defendant was ultimately charged with possession. In the Court's view, though the defendant was alleged to have possessed the narcotics, he did not have a reasonable expectation of privacy in the place of the search, the purse.

---

[18]389 U.S. 347 (1967).
[19]448 U.S. 83 (1980).
[20]448 U.S. 98 (1980).

CONTESTING A "SEIZURE" UNDER THE FOURTH AMENDMENT

A seizure of one's person, whether by virtue of an arrest (requiring probable cause) or a *Terry* stop (requiring reasonable suspicion), confers upon that individual the automatic right to contest his seizure on Fourth Amendment grounds. A seized individual is never deprived of the right to present this type of constitutional challenge. What is debatable, however, is whether a seizure occurred at all. In *Brendlin v. California*,[21] the Supreme Court resolved one such dispute involving the right of passengers within a vehicle to contest their seizure pursuant to a traffic stop. The Court held that a traffic stop constitutes a seizure of not only the driver but the passengers as well. It found that a "traffic stop necessarily curtails the travel a passenger has chosen just as much as it halts the driver, diverting both from the stream of traffic to the side of the road. . . ."

With respect to seizures of property (requiring meaningful government interference with the subject property; see Chapter 2), an individual's ownership or possessory interest in the item is often, though not always, sufficient to confer standing to present a Fourth Amendment claim alleging an improper seizure. Note that the right to contest a seizure is distinct from the right to contest a search. The importance of this distinction should not be underestimated. As noted, a passenger in a vehicle has standing to contest his seizure when that vehicle is stopped. This does not necessarily translate into a right to contest a search of that vehicle.

---

[21]551 U.S. 249 (2007).

Whether or not you agree with that assessment, what is clear is that mere ownership of a piece of property — whether a vial, such as in *Rawlings*, a television set, a bicycle, etc. — does not necessarily translate into having an expectation of privacy in the location where that object is stored. Consider the following. If A owned a bicycle, and loaned that bike to B who, in turn, took it to and placed it within his (B's) residence, A would not have standing to object to the search of B's residence merely because the bicycle, which A owned, was located therein. Though A would have a possessory interest in the bicycle, this fact alone would not confer upon him a reasonable expectation of privacy within B's residence.

(c) Conspiracy Membership

In 1993, the Supreme Court in *United States v. Padilla*[22] rejected a theory of coconspirator standing that had been adopted by the Ninth Circuit. That theory allowed individuals to assert Fourth Amendment claims if their "participation in an operation or arrangement . . . indicate[d] joint control and supervision of the place searched." The Court rejected the theory, reiterating that suppression of evidence can only be pursued by defendants who can establish that their personal Fourth Amendment rights — as opposed to the rights of third parties — had been infringed.

(d) Residential Guests

In 1990, the Supreme Court found, in *Minnesota v. Olson*,[23] that individuals who were overnight guests in another individual's residence had a legitimate expectation

---

[22]508 U.S. 77 (1993).
[23]495 U.S. 91 (1990).

of privacy therein and could, therefore, challenge the legitimacy of a search on Fourth Amendment grounds. The Court reasoned, in part, that the subjective expectations of privacy that overnight guests possess in such circumstances are reasonable. As stated by the Court:

> To hold that an overnight guest has a legitimate expectation of privacy in his host's home merely recognizes the everyday expectations of privacy that we all share. Staying overnight in another's home is a longstanding social custom that serves functions recognized as valuable by society. We stay in others' homes when we travel to a strange city for business or pleasure, when we visit our parents, children, or more distant relatives out of town, when we are in between jobs or homes, or when we house-sit for a friend. . . . [W]e think that society recognizes that a houseguest has a legitimate expectation of privacy in his host's home.

The Court signaled in *Minnesota v. Carter*[24] that visitors might possess a legitimate expectation of privacy in the home of another even if they are not overnight guests. In *Carter*, the defendants were inside the apartment residence of another individual, bagging cocaine, when they were observed from the outside by a police officer. Though a majority of the Court (Kennedy, O'Connor, Rehnquist, Scalia, and Thomas) held that the defendants in that case did not have a reasonable expectation of privacy,[25] a different majority (Kennedy, Breyer, Stevens, Ginsburg, and Souter) opined that social guests may have a legitimate privacy interest in the home of another despite the fact that they are not staying overnight. The law in this area is clearly still in development, especially given that the Court's membership has changed since the decision in *Carter*. But four members of the Court (Breyer, Stevens, Ginsburg, and Souter) appeared willing to extend standing to residential guests whether they are present for business or leisure purposes. And while Kennedy was comparatively more measured in his support for this principle, he, too, signaled a willingness to liberalize the standing concept as enunciated in *Olson*.

> As we recognized in . . . *Olson* (citation omitted) where these social expectations exist— as in the case of an overnight guest — they are sufficient to create a legitimate expectation of privacy, even in the absence of any property right to exclude others. In this respect, the dissent must be correct that reasonable expectations of the owner are shared, to some extent, by the guest. This analysis suggests that, as a general rule, social guests will have an expectation of privacy in their host's home. That is not the case before us, however.
>
> In this case respondents have established nothing more than a fleeting and insubstantial connection with Thompson's home. For all that appears in the record, respondents used Thompson's house simply as a convenient processing station, their purpose involving nothing more than the mechanical act of chopping and packing a substance for distribution. There is no suggestion that respondents engaged in confidential communications with Thompson about their transaction. Respondents had not been to Thompson's apartment before, and they left it even before their arrest.

---

[24]525 U.S. 83 (1998).
[25]Rehnquist and O'Connor cited to the limited duration of the defendants' visit, the commercial purpose underlying their presence, and the absence of a preexisting association with the lessor as their basis for concluding that the defendants could not pursue a Fourth Amendment claim. Scalia and Thomas would restrict standing to the residents of a home as well as to overnight guests. In their view, extending standing to overnight guests constitutes "the absolute limit of what [the Fourth Amendment] text and tradition permit. . . ."

C. Limits on the Reach of the Exclusionary Rule

In the Overview to this chapter, I stated that evidence obtained by virtue of a Fourth Amendment breach is subject to exclusion if it was the direct byproduct of the government's unconstitutional conduct. However, this generally stated principle, while true, requires further refinement. Not all evidence that is the direct byproduct of unconstitutional conduct will, in fact, be excluded. In light of recent case law, two additional factors are seemingly necessary. First, there must be a meaningful, substantial connection between the government breach and the evidence that is seized. And, second, the underlying deterrent benefits to the exclusionary rule must outweigh the social costs associated with exclusion.

Accordingly, there are circumstances when a constitutional breach precedes the recovery of evidence but, due to the complete absence of any causal connection, the subsequently recovered evidence is admissible. Consider the following subsection.

(1) Absence of Direct Causal Links: Independent Source, Inevitable Discovery, and the Absence of Causal Connection

(a) Independent Source Doctrine

Sometimes evidence is seized subsequent to illegal government conduct, yet is admissible as substantive evidence of guilt. One doctrine that provides for such admissibility is the independent source doctrine. This doctrine allows for the substantive use of evidence acquired after an unconstitutional search or seizure if the government can demonstrate that it had a source for that evidence that is independent of its tainted conduct. In situations where two or more sources for evidence exist and one is unconstitutional, the evidence will be admissible provided that the remaining source is independent of the tainted source. The following two cases illustrate this point.

(b) *Segura v. United States* and *Murray v. United States*

In *Segura v. United States*,[26] the Supreme Court framed the question before it as "whether, because of an earlier illegal entry, the Fourth Amendment requires suppression of evidence seized later from a private residence pursuant to a valid search warrant which was issued on information obtained by the police before the entry into the residence." The Court answered that question in the negative.

In *Segura*, the police had ample probable cause to believe that cocaine trafficking had been taking place within a particular residence as well as probable cause to arrest individuals located within the premises. However, the initial government entry was without a warrant or any legitimizing exigency. The Court found that this initial entry, though illegal, was irrelevant to the question of whether the subsequently seized evidence was admissible. It concluded that because "the evidence discovered during the subsequent search of the apartment the following day [was] pursuant to the valid search warrant issued wholly on information known to the officers before the entry into the apartment," the recovered evidence "need not [be] suppressed as 'fruit' of the illegal entry because the warrant and the information on which it was based were

---

[26]468 U.S. 796 (1984).

unrelated to the entry and therefore constituted an independent source for the evidence. . . ." Stressing the independence of the warrant affidavit, the Court emphasized that "[n]one of the information" was "related in any way" to the government entry, and that the two events were "wholly unconnected."

This independent source doctrine enunciated in *Segura* was followed by the Supreme Court in *Murray v. United States.*[27] In *Murray*, agents had entered a warehouse without a warrant or any apparent exigency and observed marijuana in plain view. The agents did not seize the narcotics at that time, but instead sought and obtained (approximately eight hours thereafter) a search warrant for the warehouse. The warrant application made no mention of the previous warrantless entry. The marijuana was seized after the warrant was executed.

The Court noted that it held in *Segura*[28] "that the evidence found for the first time during the execution of the valid and untainted search warrant was admissible because it was discovered pursuant to an 'independent source.'" *Murray* addressed a similar problem, describing the central inquiry before the Court as "whether the search pursuant to warrant was in fact a genuinely independent source of the information and tangible evidence at issue." The Court recognized that the marijuana was observed by government officials during the initial entry into the warehouse as well as during the subsequent entry pursuant to the warrant. However, if the subsequent discovery was, in fact, independent of the initial entry, then, the Court concluded, "there is no reason why the independent source doctrine should not apply." The Court remanded the case to the district court with instructions to make this determination.

(c) Inevitable Discovery Doctrine

Murray also made reference to another concept related to the independent source rule — the inevitable discovery doctrine. This doctrine provides that evidence discovered pursuant to a constitutional breach may still be admissible if that evidence would have been inevitably discovered by the police. That is, if the government can demonstrate, by a preponderance of the evidence, that the natural sequence of events — independent of the tainted government conduct — would have resulted in the recovery of the subject evidence, then the exclusionary principle will not be imposed. Explaining the relationship between the two concepts, the *Murray* Court stated:

> This "inevitable discovery" doctrine obviously assumes the validity of the independent source doctrine as applied to evidence initially acquired unlawfully. . . . The inevitable discovery doctrine, with its distinct requirements, is in reality an extrapolation from the independent source doctrine: Since the tainted evidence would be admissible if in fact discovered through an independent source, it should be admissible if it inevitably would have been discovered.

The following example will help demonstrate the inevitable discovery doctrine. Assume Officer conducts a valid traffic stop (speeding) of a vehicle containing Driver and no passengers. Dispatch informs Officer that Driver has an outstanding warrant for a bank robbery. Officer, in turn, arrests Driver and performs a valid search

---

[27]487 U.S. 533 (1988).
[28]468 U.S. 796 (1984).

incident to arrest. However, Officer also searches the trunk, without probable cause, thus exceeding the permissible boundaries of the search incident to arrest doctrine. A search of the trunk reveals the presence of illegal narcotics. While Driver would have standing to assert that his Fourth Amendment rights were violated and have a legitimate basis to suggest that the evidence should be suppressed, the government will likely prevail if it can demonstrate that the evidence would have been inevitably discovered since the car would have been towed and subsequently inventoried at the police station.

(d) Absence of Causal Connection Between Constitutional Breach and Evidence Seized

The rationale underlying the independent source and inevitable discovery exceptions to the exclusionary rule is that the seizure of the evidence at issue was obtained (or would have been obtained) in a manner entirely separate and distinct from the tainted government conduct. Thus, in such situations the evidence seized was not a direct product of the constitutional breach. Consider the following section where the Court has found that evidence seized after a constitutional violation is admissible, not on account of an independent source or inevitable discovery, but given the absence of a direct link between the government breach and the seized evidence.

(e) *Hudson v. Michigan*: Knock and Announce Violation

Hudson v. Michigan[29] is notable not only because it is representative of a series of cases (not involving an independent source or inevitable discovery) where the Supreme Court has refused to require exclusion where a direct link between the constitutional breach and the evidence seized was not found, but also because meaningful portions of the Court's opinion stressed the substantial social costs that accompany exclusion. To many, this case serves as an indicator that the future of the exclusionary rule might be in doubt.

Hudson involved policemen who discovered illegal narcotics and firearms during the execution of a search warrant in Michigan. The issue in the case did not center on the validity of the warrant itself, but upon the improper manner in which that warrant had been executed and what, if any, evidentiary penalties should be imposed. When the police arrived at the subject residence, they announced their presence and waited "perhaps 'three to five seconds'" prior to entering. The government stipulated that their conduct constituted a violation of the knock and announce rule. Given this breach, the Court focused exclusively upon the remedial question.

The Court noted that the exclusionary rule requires the establishment of a direct linkage between the constitutional breach and the evidence seized. But the Court cautioned that the establishment of this linkage does not automatically mandate exclusion. In *Hudson*, however, the Court found that evidence of a direct linkage was not present. In other words, the knock and announce violation was not a "but-for" cause of the police recovering the guns and drugs from within the residence because "the police would have executed the warrant they had obtained, and would have discovered the gun and drugs inside the house."

---

[29]547 U.S. 586 (2006).

Thus, in the Court's view, the manner in which an otherwise valid warrant had been executed was unrelated to the evidence that was subsequently recovered. Justice Kennedy provided the crucial fifth vote and wrote a separate concurrence. In it he attempted to assuage concerns expressed by the dissent[30] of the potential weakening of the exclusionary remedy. He declared:

> The Court's decision should not be interpreted as suggesting that violations of the requirement are trivial or beyond the law's concern. Second, the continued operation of the exclusionary rule, as settled and defined by our precedents, is not in doubt. Today's decision determines only that in the specific context of the knock-and-announce requirement, a violation is not sufficiently related to the later discovery of evidence to justify suppression.

Rather than simply disposing of the case on direct linkage grounds, the Court proceeded with an alternative analysis. And it is this alternative analysis that concerns those who advocate a vigorous exclusionary rule. Assuming the existence of such a linkage, the Court asserted that sometimes the exclusionary penalty is an inappropriate remedy on account of attenuation. The Court noted that attenuation can occur when the direct linkage is either "remote" or when "the interest protected by the constitutional guarantee that has been violated would not be served by suppression of the evidence obtained." The Court stated that the interests served by the knock and announce rule — the safeguarding and protection of human health, property, privacy, and dignity — are not furthered by the exclusionary rule. The Court noted that these underlying interests do not include an individual's "interest in preventing the government from seeing or taking evidence described in a warrant." Thus, assuming the establishment of a direct linkage, suppression may be inappropriate when the interests underlying the exclusionary rule and the constitutional safeguard are sufficiently distinct.

The Court added that the costs associated with exclusion can sometimes be too substantial to impose such a drastic remedy. In that regard, the Court commented that the exclusionary rule is a remedy of "last resort," that the "rule generates 'substantial social costs' which sometimes include setting the guilty free and the dangerous at large," and that the rule imposes a "costly toll upon truth-seeking and law enforcement objectives." It later explained that exclusion should be imposed only when "its deterrence benefits outweigh its substantial social costs."[31] The Court feared that imposing an exclusionary penalty for knock and announce violations "would generate a constant flood of alleged failures" of the knock and announce requirement, and that it might discourage police officers from timely entering premises for which they have judicial authorization to proceed with a search.

The Court also opined that exclusion was unnecessary to encourage police to comply with the rule. It noted the availability of civil actions and civil rights actions

---

[30]Justice Breyer wrote on behalf of four members of the Court. He stated, in pertinent part: "[T]he Court destroys the strongest legal incentive to comply with the Constitution's knock-and-announce requirement. And the Court does so without significant support in precedent. At least I can find no such support in the many Fourth Amendment cases the Court has decided in the near century since it first set forth the exclusionary principle in *Weeks v. United States* [232 U.S. 383 (1914)].

"Today's opinion is thus doubly troubling. It represents a significant departure from the Court's precedents. And it weakens, perhaps destroys, much of the practical value of the Constitution's knock-and-announce protection."

[31]Justice Breyer, in his dissent, stated that "[t]he majority's 'substantial social costs' argument is an argument against the Fourth Amendment's exclusionary principle itself. And it is an argument that this Court, until now, has consistently rejected."

under 18 U.S.C. 1983, as well as what the Court described as "the increasing professionalism of police forces, including a new emphasis on internal police discipline."

(2) Existence of Direct Causal Links: Attenuated Circumstances and the Good Faith Rule

Sometimes evidence that is recovered is, indeed, the direct byproduct of the government's unconstitutional conduct. However, due to the dissipation of the government taint, an insubstantial connection between the constitutional infringement and the recovered evidence, and certain policy rationales the Supreme Court has held that the exclusionary penalty is inapplicable.

(a) Attenuated Circumstances Doctrine

The attenuated circumstances doctrine recognizes that there is a linkage between the government's constitutional breach and the seized evidence. However, when a court concludes that the taint from the challenged illegality has sufficiently dissipated, a court may find that the seized evidence is not subject to exclusion. In other words, if factors are present that put some meaningful distance between the constitutional breach and the evidence that is subsequently recovered, then the exclusionary rule may not apply.

Wong Sun v. United States. A case you are likely to discuss in your Criminal Procedures class is *Wong Sun v. United States.*[34] There, officers illegally arrested an individual (Toy) in his living quarters. Moments thereafter, Toy made statements that led the officers to another individual (Yee). After the officers unlawfully entered the residence of Yee, heroin and statements from Yee were obtained. These statements led the officers to another individual (Wong Sun) who was arrested. Several days after Wong Sun's arraignment and release on his personal recognizance, he returned to the police station and made incriminating statements.

The Court found that the police unconstitutionally arrested Toy in his living quarters. Accordingly, the Court found that his statements should be excluded. It also found that the narcotics found in Yee's residence were inadmissible against Toy since they were the fruits of the original illegality. As stated by the Court,

Sidebar

NEW YORK v. HARRIS: EVIDENCE ADMISSIBLE THOUGH FOUND AFTER *PAYTON* VIOLATION

Hudson cited to *New York v. Harris.*[32] In *Harris,* the defendant was inside his residence at the time of his arrest. Though probable cause existed that the defendant had engaged in criminal activity, the manner in which the police effectuated his arrest violated the rule established in *Payton v. New York,*[33] which requires the attainment of a warrant or consent to enter prior to effectuating an arrest of a subject within his residence. At issue was the admissibility of a confession subsequently obtained from the defendant at the police station after he had waived his *Miranda* rights. The Court declined to exclude the confession. In so holding, the Court found that the defendant's police station confession was not the byproduct of an unlawful detention. The majority noted that probable cause existed for his arrest. The Court further reasoned that suppression would not further the policies that underlie the rule in *Payton,* which are concerned with preserving and respecting "the physical integrity" of a residence, as opposed to providing suspects, for whom probable cause to arrest exists, "protection for statements made outside their premises."

[32]495 U.S. 14 (1990).
[33]445 U.S. 573 (1980).

[34]371 U.S. 471 (1963).

Sidebar

BROWN v. ILLINOIS: AN EXAMPLE OF INSUFFICIENT ATTENUATION

Compare *Wong Sun* with *Brown v. Illinois*.[35] In *Brown*, the defendant was arrested in the absence of probable cause in his home and was transported to the police station where he made two voluntary confessions after being provided with, and waiving, his rights pursuant to *Miranda v. Arizona*.[36] The first statement was provided 90 minutes after his arrest and the second was rendered seven hours thereafter. Finding that the exclusionary rule required that the statements be excluded, the Court concluded that the taint of the government's illegality was not attenuated by the provision of *Miranda* warnings. However, the Court refused to adopt a per se rule to that effect, instead identifying the provision of *Miranda* warnings as a factor among many a court may consider when considering attenuation. "While we therefore reject the per se rule . . . , we also decline to adopt any alternative per se or 'but for' rule. . . . The question whether a confession is the product of a free will under *Wong Sun* must be answered on the facts of each case. No single fact is dispositive. The workings of the human mind are too complex, and the possibilities of misconduct too diverse, to permit protection of the Fourth Amendment to turn on such a talismanic test. The *Miranda* warnings are an important factor . . . [b]ut they are not the only factor to be considered. The temporal proximity of the arrest and the confession, the presence of intervening circumstances and, particularly, the purpose and flagrancy of the official misconduct are all relevant."[37]

---

[35]422 U.S. 590 (1975).
[36]384 U.S. 436 (1966). This case will be discussed at length in Chapter 18. This constitutional protection entitles an individual who is in "custody" (and an arrest constitutes "custody" for *Miranda* purposes) to be informed of two rights regarding his custodial interrogation: his right to an attorney and his right to remain silent.
[37]For additional authority holding that *Miranda* warnings alone will not dissipate the taint stemming from an arrest without probable cause, see *Kaupp v. Texas*, 538 U.S. 626 (2003) (per curiam) (holding that statements obtained after an arrest without probable cause should be excluded, despite the provision of *Miranda* warnings, given that an insubstantial time period passed between the illegal arrest of the defendant in his residence and his confession, and the absence of any "meaningful intervening event[s]"); *Taylor v. Alabama*, 457 U.S. 687 (1982); *Dunaway v. New York*, 442 U.S. 200 (1979).

We need not hold that all evidence is "fruit of the poisonous tree" simply because it would not have come to light but for the illegal actions of the police. Rather, the more apt question in such a case is "whether, granting establishment of the primary illegality, the evidence to which instant objection is made has been come at by exploitation of that illegality or instead by means sufficiently distinguishable to be purged of the primary taint" (citation omitted). We think it clear that the narcotics were "come at by the exploitation of that illegality" and hence that they may not be used against Toy.

That part of the decision is not what makes this case noteworthy. This case is notable, in part, for what follows. The Court found that the arrest of Wong Sun was also unconstitutional. And though the incriminating statements he uttered at the police station occurred subsequent to his illegal arrest, the Court held that his statements were admissible. The Court reasoned that since Wong Sun "had been released on his own recognizance after a lawful arraignment, and had returned voluntarily several days later to make the statement . . . the connection between the arrest and the statement had 'become so attenuated as to dissipate the taint.'"

There is no question that but for Wong Sun's arrest, it is highly unlikely he would have voluntarily elected to waltz into the police station and render a confession. Clearly, his confession was the byproduct of his illegal arrest. Yet the Court did not suppress the statements. The Court's finding that Wong Sun's decision to provide a confession was voluntary (and thus sufficiently purged from the earlier government taint) was certainly influenced by the fact that several days had passed between the date of his illegal arrest and the date of his confession.

United States v. Ceccolini. The Court also found that attenuating circumstances existed in *United States v. Ceccolini.*[38] There, the Court refused to suppress the testimony of a witness whose grand jury and trial testimony was allegedly linked to an unconstitutional search of an envelope. The Court rejected the government's contention that live witness testimony should be immune from exclusion at trial irrespective of the strength of its linkage to illegally obtained evidence. However, the Court did suggest that attenuation is more prone to occur in the context of testimonial as opposed to physical evidence. In this instance, not only was the purported fruit of the constitutional violation the testimony of someone other than the defendant, but witnesses, as opposed to tangible objects, have free wills that can be exercised independent of tainted government conduct. As explained by the Court:

> Witnesses can, and often do, come forward and offer evidence entirely of their own volition. And evaluated properly, the degree of free will necessary to dissipate the taint will very likely be found more often in the case of live-witness testimony than other kinds of evidence. The time, place and manner of the initial questioning of the witness may be such that any statements are truly the product of detached reflection and a desire to be cooperative on the part of the witness. And the illegality which led to the discovery of the witness very often will not play any meaningful part in the witness' willingness to testify.

The Court added that application of the exclusionary rule to live witness testimony could result in the exclusion of relevant testimony that bears no relation to the challenged government conduct. Accordingly, application of the exclusionary rule in such instances would do little to further its underlying purposes.

Rawlings v. Kentucky. Two years after *Ceccolini*, the Court, once again, found attenuating circumstances in *Rawlings v. Kentucky.*[39] *Rawlings* involved a situation where an individual, who was detained by the police within a residence, subsequently uttered statements admitting to his ownership of narcotics previously found within the home. As in *Wong Sun* and *Ceccolini*, *Rawlings* found the exclusionary rule inapplicable on account of attenuated circumstances. Referencing the evaluative criteria employed in *Brown v. Illinois*,[40] the Court noted that the defendant "received *Miranda* warnings only moments before he made his incriminating statements," that the "congenial atmosphere" during the period of detention "outweigh[ed]" the relatively brief time span between the defendant's detention and his admissions, that the defendant's utterances were spontaneous and were the product of his free will, and that the actions of the officers were insufficiently flagrant under the circumstances.

(b) Good Faith Doctrine

Leon v. United States. The good faith doctrine is another exception to the exclusionary rule. This doctrine, enunciated by the Supreme Court in *Leon v. United States*,[41] allows for the admission of evidence seized pursuant to a defective search warrant in

---

[38]435 U.S. 268 (1978).
[39]448 U.S. 98 (1980).
[40]422 U.S. 590 (1975).
[41]468 U.S. 897 (1984).

instances where the warrant is relied upon by a "reasonably well trained" executing officer. After the government had executed a search warrant that, on its face, appeared to be valid, a district court found that the facts presented in support of the warrant application were insufficient to constitute probable cause. The Court concluded that the exclusionary remedy was inappropriate in such circumstances.

In reaching this conclusion, the Court found that the costs associated with exclusion were too substantial. The Court reasoned that the underlying purpose of the exclusionary rule — the deterrence of unlawful police conduct — would not be furthered by excluding evidence obtained by officers who were executing a warrant that they reasonably believed was valid. Here the origin of the error lied with the judiciary, not with law enforcement. To impose an exclusionary penalty in such instances would not further the principal purpose of the rule.[42] As the Court explained:

> First, the exclusionary rule is designed to deter police misconduct rather than to punish the errors of judges and magistrates. Second, there exists no evidence suggesting that judges and magistrates are inclined to ignore or subvert the Fourth Amendment or that lawlessness among these actors requires application of the extreme sanction of exclusion. Third, and most important, we discern no basis, and are offered none, for believing that exclusion of evidence seized pursuant to a warrant will have a significant deterrent effect on the issuing judge or magistrate. . . . Judges and magistrates are not adjuncts to the law enforcement team; as neutral judicial officers, they have no stake in the outcome of particular criminal prosecutions. The threat of exclusion thus cannot be expected significantly to deter them. Imposition of the exclusionary sanction is not necessary meaningfully to inform judicial officers of their errors, and we cannot conclude that admitting evidence obtained pursuant to a warrant while at the same time declaring that the warrant was somehow defective will in any way reduce judicial officers' professional incentives to comply with the Fourth Amendment, encourage them to repeat their mistakes, or lead to the granting of all colorable warrant requests.

F   A   Q

Q: I understand that warrantless searches and seizures are subject to challenges by the defense that probable cause did not exist. May a defendant challenge a probable cause determination after a warrant has been issued by a magistrate?

A: Yes. One way is to attack the sufficiency of the evidence submitted in support of a magistrate's probable cause determination. *Leon* was such a case. In that case, the defendant established that the information presented in support of the warrant was insufficient to establish probable cause. But the court there held that, despite the insufficiency, the officer was reasonable in relying upon the magistrate's probable cause determination. A second approach is to attack the truthfulness of the information contained in the warrant affidavit. In *Franks v. Delaware*,[43] the Supreme Court held that if a defendant can "make a substantial

---

[42]In *Massachusetts v. Sheppard*, 468 U.S. 981 (1984), the Supreme Court held that it was objectively reasonable for officers to rely upon a search warrant approved by a magistrate despite the fact that the warrant application submitted by the government authorized a search for evidence (controlled substances) for which probable cause did not exist. The Court reasoned, in part, that the magistrate had assured the government detective that he had made the necessary corrections to the warrant application and that the warrant was, therefore, in proper form.
[43]438 U.S. 154 (1978).

preliminary showing" that the affiant knowingly or recklessly included false information, material to the issue of probable cause, in the warrant affidavit, then the defendant is entitled to a hearing on the matter. If the defendant can then establish by a preponderance of the evidence that false information was knowingly or recklessly included in the affidavit and that, after setting aside the false information, probable cause to search does not exist, "the search warrant must be voided and the fruits of the search excluded to the same extent as if probable cause was lacking on the face of the affidavit." Thus, it is not enough to allege and establish that false information was included in the affidavit. It is also not enough to establish that the affiant was negligent in including such information. Rather, the defendant must show intentional or reckless inclusion and that the remaining properly included information does not amount to probable cause.

The Court stressed that for the exception to apply the officer's reliance upon the warrant's validity must be "objectively reasonable." It then proceeded to identify certain instances where objective reasonableness could not be found.

First, "if the magistrate or judge in issuing a warrant was misled by information in an affidavit that the affiant knew was false or would have known was false except for his reckless disregard of the truth." This makes sense. If the affiant (usually an officer or law enforcement official) either knew or was reckless in not knowing that the information sworn to before the Court was false, then the government cannot avail itself of the good faith exception.

Second, the good faith exception will not apply "where the issuing magistrate wholly abandoned his judicial role." An issuing magistrate is required to be neutral and detached. Thus, if facts and circumstances suggest that a magistrate has abandoned this role during the warrant application and review process, then the *Leon* good faith exception will not apply.

Third, the exception is inapplicable in situations where an official could not reasonably conclude that the information contained in the search warrant application amounted to probable cause. For example, if the affidavit in *Leon* did not provide facts that were "close" (as in *Leon*), but contained facts that no reasonable police officer could conclude established probable cause, then the good faith principle could not be relied upon. Finally, the Court indicated that a warrant that is facially deficient would not satisfy *Leon*. The Court cited as examples a warrant that fails to particularly describe either the location of the place to be searched or the items sought to be seized therein.

Sidebar

GROH v. RAMIREZ: AN EXAMPLE OF LEON'S FACIAL DEFICIENCY EXCEPTION

Groh v. Ramirez[44] involved a warrant that was issued to search a residence for certain weaponry and related parts. Though the warrant application described with particularity the place to be searched and the items to be seized, "the warrant itself was less specific." Specifically, the warrant neither included a description of the items to be seized nor incorporated by reference the accompanying application. The Court found that the warrant was invalid and was not cured by the accompanying application, which, as noted, detailed the sought-for items and was not incorporated by the warrant. Rejecting the contention that the search was reasonable despite the omission, the Court concluded that the "warrant did not simply omit a few items from a list of many to be seized, or misdescribe a few of several items. Nor did it make what fairly could be characterized as a mere technical mistake or typographical error. Rather, in the space set aside for a description of the items to be seized, the warrant stated that the items consisted of a 'single dwelling residence . . . blue in color.' In other words, the warrant did not describe the items to be seized *at all*. In this respect the warrant was so obviously deficient that we must regard the search as 'warrantless' within the meaning of our case law."

[44]540 U.S. 551 (2004).

Illinois v. Krull; Arizona v. Evans; Herring v. United States; and *Davis v. United States. Leon* represents much more than merely another exception to the exclusionary rule to memorize for your final examination. In fact, supporters of a robust exclusionary rule fear that the case has broad implications and will eventually lead — if it has not already — to a significantly weakened exclusionary principle. More precisely, they worry that the Court will expand *Leon* and validate all kinds of *warrantless* searches and seizures that, though erroneous, were performed in good faith. As you ponder this concern, consider the following cases.

Seven years after *Leon*, the Court applied the *Leon* rationale in *Illinois v. Krull*.[45] *Krull* involved a search of an automobile wrecking yard that uncovered evidence of a crime. The search was performed pursuant to an Illinois statute that was later determined to be unconstitutional. The Supreme Court, however, upheld the search, finding that the officer's reliance upon the statute was objectively reasonable and that the deterrent rationale that underlies the exclusionary rule would not be furthered in this context. The Court commented that legislators, unlike law enforcement officers, are not the focus of the exclusionary rule and, citing *Leon*, declared that it had "no basis for believing that legislators are inclined to subvert their oaths and the Fourth Amendment. . . ."

As in *Leon, Arizona v. Evans*[46] involved a police search performed as a result of an error attributable to the judicial branch. Specifically, an officer performed a routine traffic stop and arrested the driver after a computer check indicated that he had an outstanding misdemeanor warrant. However, this information was erroneous given that the warrant had been quashed. A subsequent search of the vehicle revealed the presence of marijuana.

Citing *Leon*, the Court found that there was a "categorical exception to the exclusionary rule for clerical errors of court employees." It reasoned that application of the exclusionary rule to this type of judicial branch error would not further the rule's deterrence rationale. Such an "extreme sanction," according to the Court, would do nothing to deter such clerical errors, which were found to have occurred infrequently.

Note that *Leon, Krull,* and *Evans* all involved errors committed by either the judiciary (*Leon* and *Evans*) or the legislature (*Krull*). In each case, the Court reasoned that application of the exclusionary rule would do nothing to further the rule's principal purpose — to deter unlawful police conduct. But what should happen if the error that leads to the recovery of incriminating evidence is attributable not to either the judicial or legislative branches of government, but to the police itself? Should evidence seized under such circumstances be suppressed?

These questions were addressed by the Supreme Court in *Herring v. United States*.[47] After receiving information from police department 2 that the defendant had an outstanding arrest warrant, an officer from police department 1 effectuated a traffic stop of the defendant's vehicle, arrested him, and found illegal narcotics on his person and a pistol in his vehicle. As it turned out, the arrest warrant had been recalled a few months earlier but the recall had not been entered by police department 2 in their computer database. The Supreme Court found that the logic of

---

[45]480 U.S. 340 (1987).
[46]514 U.S. 1 (1995).
[47]555 U.S. 135 (2009).

Leon, Krull, and *Evans* extended to this situation and that the evidence seized was not subject to suppression.

In reaching this conclusion, the Court reasoned that the exclusionary rule was a rule of "last resort" and that it should be applied only when an "appreciable deterrence" of Fourth Amendment violations can be achieved. It found that application of the exclusionary rule in this context would not contribute to this deterrence objective. The Court noted that "the abuses that gave rise to the exclusionary rule featured intentional conduct that was patently unconstitutional." In contrast, the constitutional infringement at issue in *Herring* was, in the view of the Court, merely negligent. In fact, the Court commented that it has never imposed the exclusionary penalty in an instance "where the police conduct was no more intentional or culpable than this."

Ultimately, whether *Herring* provides a platform from which the exclusionary rule's applicability is significantly curtailed remains to be seen. In language that may be at the heart of this future debate,[48] the Court held that illegal acts "that arise from nonrecurring and attenuated negligence is thus far removed from the core concerns that led us to adopt the rule in the first place." In *Herring*, the negligence was considered nonrecurring given the absence of any indicia that this type of computer database problem was widespread. And the negligence was deemed attenuated from the tainted arrest given that it was attributable to a police department distinct from the police group that effectuated the arrest.

Herring, thus, leaves many wondering. Is the holding in *Herring* limited to fact patterns involving nonrecurring and attenuated negligence? If so, then perhaps the exclusionary rule will be vigorously applied in the context of erroneous warrantless searches and seizures. Or will *Herring* be interpreted more broadly and encompass warrantless searches and seizures that are the product of police negligence irrespective of recurrence rate and attenuation issues?

In *Davis v. United States*,[49] the Supreme Court further pressed the themes expressed in *Herring* and, arguably at least, suggests that further dwindling of the exclusionary rule may be forthcoming. In *Davis*, the defendant was a passenger in a car that was lawfully stopped for a traffic violation. Both the driver and the defendant were arrested — the driver for driving while intoxicated and the defendant for providing a false name to the police. After both individuals were secured within separate police vehicles, the officers searched the passenger compartment of the subject vehicle and found a firearm in a jacket belonging to the defendant. The defendant was later charged with felon in possession of a firearm.

At the time of the search, the decision in *Arizona v. Gant* (see Chapter 7) had yet to be rendered (that decision would come later while the defendant's case was on appeal). Had the search at issue occurred post-*Gant*, the constitutional validity of the officers' search would have certainly been debatable. However, the defendant acknowledged that the search performed by the *Davis* officers complied with then-existing Eleventh Circuit precedent.

At issue was whether the exclusionary rule should apply when law enforcement executes a search that at the time of its performance is constitutionally compliant, but is later determined to be unconstitutional. The Court found that, under the

---

[48]For an excellent discussion about the impact of *Herring v. United States*, see Tom Goldstein, *The Surpassing Significance of Herring*, SCOTUSblog, http://www.scotusblog.com/blog/2009/01/14/the-surpassing-significance-of-herring/.

[49]131 S. Ct. 2419 (2011).

circumstances presented in *Davis*, the firearm was not subject to the exclusionary rule. The Court reasoned that since the officers reasonably relied on existing precedent, suppression would not further the deterrence rationale that underlies the exclusionary principle. As the Court stated:

> About all that exclusion would deter in this case is conscientious police work. . . . An officer who conducts a search in reliance on binding appellate precedent does no more than act as a reasonable officer would and should act under the circumstances. The deterrent effect of exclusion in such a case can only be to discourage an officer from doing his duty.

It also reemphasized several notable principles enunciated in *Herring*. The Court reiterated that the exclusionary rule contemplates only those Fourth Amendment violations that are the product of police behavior that can be characterized as deliberate, reckless, or grossly negligent. It is in those instances, the Court declared, where the high costs associated with exclusion are outweighed by the value of police deterrence. On the other hand, "when the police act with an objectively 'reasonable good faith belief' that their conduct is lawful (citation omitted) or when their conduct involves only simple 'isolated' negligence (citation omitted) the 'deterrence rationale loses much of its force,' and exclusion cannot 'pay its way.'"

The Court also rejected an argument that principles of retroactivity mandated the application of the exclusionary rule. The majority recognized that since *Gant* announced a new rule, the substantive new rule of that case applied to the defendant. However, the Court held that while the defendant could, per *Gant*, seek a remedy, it does not necessarily follow that the imposition of an exclusionary penalty is automatic. The Court noted that whether the exclusionary rule is applicable in a given factual circumstance is subject to limitations. The good faith exception, like the inevitable discovery doctrine, is a limitation upon this type of remedy, and since the officers in *Davis* acted in good faith, the exclusionary penalty, according to the Court, was an inappropriate sanction.

F   A   Q

Q: Can evidence seized in violation of the Fourth Amendment be used at trial for non-substantive purposes? Can such evidence be used in a noncriminal trial context?

A: Yes to both questions. The Supreme Court has held that during a criminal trial a defendant can be impeached with evidence obtained in violation of the Fourth Amendment. Assuming a proper foundation (e.g., testifying defendant opens the door to questions pertaining to the illegally seized evidence), a prosecutor may employ such evidence to impeach the defendant's credibility. However, this authority to impeach does not extend to defense witnesses. The Court has also held that such evidence can be used at sentencings, during grand jury sessions, and during parole revocation proceedings.

Evidence obtained in violation of the Fourth Amendment can also be used in various noncriminal contexts. The Court has found that such evidence can be used in civil tax and deportation cases and in proceedings where the government seeks the forfeiture of property. In the context of habeas corpus petitions, the Court has reached different results regarding Fourth and Fifth Amendment claims. With respect to Fourth Amendment matters, the Court in *Stone v. Powell*[50] held that a state prisoner who contends that evidence was introduced against him at trial in contravention of the Fourth Amendment is not entitled to a habeas remedy when he has been afforded a "full and fair" opportunity to litigate that claim. On the other hand, the Court in *Withrow v. Williams*[51] held that habeas petitioners presenting *Miranda* claims — what the Court referred to as a rule that "safeguards 'a fundamental trial right'" — may have federal court review of such matters.

SUMMARY

- After the decision in *Weeks*, the exclusionary rule applied only to actions involving federal officers in federal court prosecutions. It was not until *Mapp v. Ohio* that the exclusionary principle became applicable to the states.

- Though two justifications have historically been cited in support of the exclusionary rule — deterrence of unlawful police behavior and judicial integrity — only the former is primarily relied upon today.

- Today, an individual has standing to maintain a Fourth Amendment claim if the government's action breached his personal Fourth Amendment rights. Examples include if an individual can establish that he has a reasonable expectation of privacy in the area searched or if he was personally seized by the government. Thus, an individual does not necessarily have standing to contest a search simply due to the fact that he has an ownership or possessory interest in an item, that he was legitimately on the premises at the time of the search, that he was a target of an investigation, or that he was a member of a criminal conspiracy.

- Standing to contest a search is not limited to the permanent occupants of a particular residence, but can also include overnight guests as well as other individuals. Generally speaking, the fewer contacts an individual has with a home, the more difficult it will be for that individual to establish standing.

- The Independent Source doctrine is an exception to the exclusionary rule, which holds that evidence obtained subsequent to an illegal government search is admissible as substantive evidence if the government can demonstrate that it had a source for that evidence that is independent of its tainted conduct.

- The Inevitable Discovery doctrine provides that evidence discovered pursuant to a constitutional breach may still be admissible if that evidence would have been inevitably discovered by the police.

- The Supreme Court has also held that evidence seized after a constitutional violation is admissible, not on account of an independent source or inevitable discovery, but when a direct link between the government breach and the seized evidence is absent. In *Hudson v. Michigan*, the Court found that there was not a direct link between the knock and announce constitutional violation and the seizure of evidence within the searched premises.

---

[50]428 U.S. 465 (1976).
[51]507 U.S. 680 (1993).

■ Evidence seized after a constitutional infringement is also admissible, despite the existence of a direct link, if the original taint from the government conduct has become attenuated. Among the factors that a court may consider is the time lapse between the constitutional infraction and the attainment of the evidence at issue.

■ The Good Faith exception allows for the admission of evidence seized pursuant to a defective search warrant where the warrant was reasonably relied upon by a "reasonably well trained" executing officer. The rule has been extended to situations involving officer reliance upon judicial errors, legislative errors, errors committed by other police departments, and errors attributable to a reasonable reliance upon judicial precedent.

■ Unconstitutionally seized evidence can also be used at sentencings, before the grand jury, at parole revocation hearings, and to impeach a defendant's trial testimony (though not the trial testimony of defense witnesses). Such evidence can also be used in noncriminal contexts, such as civil tax and deportation hearings. In addition, individuals may pursue habeas corpus petitions that allege *Miranda* violations.

CONNECTIONS

Relationship to Incorporation (Chapter 1)

In *Mapp v. Ohio*, the Supreme Court made the exclusionary rule penalty applicable to the states.

Relationship to Involuntary Confessions and the Due Process Clause Cases (Chapter 17)

The exclusionary rule applies to violations of the Fourth Amendment, the Fifth and Fourteenth Amendment due process clauses, and the Fifth Amendment privilege against self-incrimination (*Miranda* and non-*Miranda*). The fruit of the poisonous tree doctrine applies to Fourth Amendment violations, but is subject to exceptions. In the Fifth Amendment realm, the applicability of the fruits doctrine is dependent upon the particular guarantee that is infringed.

Relationship to Sixth Amendment Right to Counsel and Deliberate Police Elicitations (Chapter 19)

Evidence obtained in violation of the Sixth Amendment right to counsel is subject to exclusion, as are the fruits derived therefrom. However, such evidence may be used for impeachment purposes. Evidence (and its fruits, subject to various exceptions) seized in violation of the Fourth Amendment is also subject to suppression. Similarly, such evidence may be employed to impeach the testimony of the defendant, though not defense witnesses.

Relationship to Identifications, the Sixth Amendment, and the Due Process Clause (Chapter 20)

Out-of-court identifications made in violation of the Sixth Amendment are subject to automatic exclusion. Subsequent in-court identifications are also subject to exclusion, unless the proponent can demonstrate that the later identification is not tainted by the former violation. Out-of-court identifications that are made pursuant to unnecessarily suggestive procedures are subject to exclusion. However, such identifications do not violate due process if the identifications are otherwise reliable. By analogy, evidence seized in violation of the Fourth Amendment is subject to exclusion (as are its fruits). However, such evidence may be admissible if, inter alia, there is an independent source for the evidence or if attenuated circumstances exist.

The Privilege Against Self-Incrimination — General Principles

16

Whether through the media or some other forum, individuals who have resided an appreciable number of years in America have, in all likelihood, at some point become acquainted with the following phrase: "I plead the Fifth." What is meant when those words are uttered?

What the speaker is, of course, referencing is the Fifth Amendment to the Constitution and, more particularly, the Fifth Amendment privilege against self-incrimination. For purposes of this chapter, the pertinent part of that Amendment provides that "[n]o person . . . shall be compelled in any criminal case to be a witness against himself." With the 1964 Supreme Court decision in *Malloy v. Hogan*,[1] this constitutional right was incorporated to the states via the due process clause of the Fourteenth Amendment.

The Supreme Court in *United States v. White* elaborated upon the purposes underlying this constitutional privilege:

> It grows out of the high sentiment and regard of our jurisprudence for conducting criminal trials and investigatory proceedings upon a plane of dignity, humanity and impartiality. It is designed to prevent the use of legal process to force from the lips of the accused individual the evidence necessary to convict him or to force him to produce and authenticate any personal documents or effects that might incriminate him. Physical torture and other less violent but equally reprehensible modes of compelling the production of incriminating evidence are thereby avoided. The prosecutors are forced to search for independent evidence instead of relying upon proof extracted from individuals by force of law. The immediate and potential evils of compulsory self-disclosure transcend any difficulties that

---

[1] 378 U.S. 1 (1964).

the exercise of the privilege may impose on society in the detection and prosecution of crime. While the privilege is subject to abuse and misuse, it is firmly embedded in our constitutional and legal frameworks as a bulwark against iniquitous methods of prosecution. It protects the individual from any disclosure, in the form of oral testimony, documents or chattels, sought by legal process against him as a witness.[2]

This chapter is designed to explain the essential components of this privilege. In so doing it will discuss, inter alia, who can assert the privilege, the compulsion requirement, the criminal case mandate, the testimonial communication requirement, and when the privilege may be waived.

A. WHO CAN ASSERT THE PRIVILEGE?

B. THE COMPULSION REQUIREMENT

1. The Absence of Compulsion
2. The Existence of Compulsion
3. Permissible Compulsion

C. THE CRIMINAL CASE REQUIREMENT

D. THE TESTIMONIAL REQUIREMENT

E. WAIVER OF THE FIFTH AMENDMENT PRIVILEGE

A. Who Can Assert the Privilege?

The Fifth Amendment privilege against self-incrimination is personal in nature and can be asserted only by individuals. As declared by the Court in *United States v. White*, "The constitutional privilege against self-incrimination is essentially a personal one, applying only to natural individuals."[3] The privilege, therefore, can be asserted by none other than the actual holder of the privilege. In *Fisher v. United States*,[4] for example, the Supreme Court rejected the contention that attorneys in receipt of tax preparation documents provided to them by their taxpayer clients could refuse to comply with a summons requesting the production of such documents by relying upon the Fifth Amendment privilege held by each taxpayer. The Court held that only the taxpayers themselves could assert the privilege.

This means that entities such as corporations and partnerships do not enjoy Fifth Amendment protection.[5] Moreover, where a corporation is subpoenaed for the production of documents, a custodian of those documents cannot assert a personal Fifth Amendment privilege since the documents he possesses are being

---

[2]322 U.S. 694, 699 (1944).
[3]322 U.S. at 698.
[4]425 U.S. 391 (1976).
[5]The Supreme Court, in *United States v. Doe*, 465 U.S. 605 (1984), held that a sole proprietorship did, in fact, enjoy Fifth Amendment protection against compelled self-incrimination.

held in a representative, as opposed to personal, capacity.[6] However, such a custodian may assert the Fifth Amendment privilege if verbal testimony is sought with respect to the corporate documents. As stated by the Supreme Court in *Curcio v. United States*,[7] "forcing the custodian to testify orally as to the whereabouts of nonproduced records requires him to disclose the contents of his own mind. He might be compelled to convict himself out of his own mouth."

B. The Compulsion Requirement

The privilege can be asserted only when the government actually *compels* a person to provide testimony that he reasonably believes could be used against him in a criminal proceeding. Thus, government compulsion is an absolute precondition to triggering this Fifth Amendment interest. It stands to reason that an individual who, for example, *voluntarily* elects to testify at his criminal trial or *voluntarily* creates a document (e.g., a diary) cannot successfully assert that the contents of the verbal or physical evidence were compelled within the meaning of the Fifth Amendment.

(1) The Absence of Compulsion

Government prosecutors routinely encounter individuals who they believe can assist them in an investigation, but who are entitled to assert the protections of the Fifth Amendment. Yet, despite this apparent constitutional roadblock, the government routinely — and legally — performs such interviews and obtains critical testimonial information from these subjects. How is this accomplished without violating the Fifth Amendment?

In *Kastigar v. United States*,[8] the Supreme Court held that the government could compel testimonial evidence from an individual provided that he was given immunity that prohibits governmental use of the compelled testimony as well as any derivative fruits. Rejecting the contention that a broader form of immunity — "transactional immunity," which completely bars prosecution for offenses related to the compelled testimony — is necessary to protect an individual's Fifth Amendment interests, the Court held that "use immunity" afforded sufficient protection. As stated by the Court: "[T]he use of compelled testimony, as well as evidence derived directly and indirectly therefrom, affords this protection. It prohibits the prosecutorial authorities from using the compelled testimony in any respect, and it therefore insures that the testimony cannot lead to the infliction of criminal penalties on the witness." Thus, an individual who, for example, is subpoenaed to testify before a grand jury or at trial may not refuse to answer on Fifth Amendment grounds if the witness is provided with this more limited form of use immunity.

---

[6]*Braswell v. United States*, 487 U.S. 99 (1988).
[7]354 U.S. 118 (1957).
[8]406 U.S. 441 (1972).

S i d e b a r

USE OF COMPELLED TESTIMONY FOR IMPEACHMENT PURPOSES

The grant of use immunity prohibits not only the substantive use of any such testimonial evidence but also the use of such evidence for impeachment purposes. However, this immunity grant does not prohibit the government from subsequently using such immunized statements as the basis for a subsequent perjury prosecution. As stated by Justice Brennan in his concurrence in *United States v. Apfelbaum*, 445 U.S. 115 (1980):

> When the Government compels testimony via a grant of immunity, it is constitutionally required to place the victim in a position similar to the one he would have occupied had he exercised his Fifth Amendment privilege. . . . This does not, however, bar a prosecution for perjury committed in the course of immunized testimony, even though such a prosecution will obviously place the witness in a worse position than he would have been in had he invoked the privilege. The perjury exception seems to have two sources. First, it stems from the aforementioned fact that, prior to the immunity grant, the witness had no Fifth Amendment right to answer falsely, and, second, it flows from the simple reality that affording the witness a right to lie with impunity would render the entire immunity transaction futile.

(2) The Existence of Compulsion

Where sufficient government compulsion is present, an individual may be entitled to assert the Fifth Amendment privilege. For example, when a person is sought to testify before either the grand jury or at trial, that individual is served with either a grand jury or trial subpoena. It is a legal order, typically issued by a judge, private attorney (e.g., a criminal defense attorney), or government lawyer, that requires a person to appear and provide testimony or to produce certain specified documents. Failure to comply with a subpoena can result in *criminal* sanctions. Thus, subpoenas are a type of compulsive activity that can trigger Fifth Amendment protections.

Thus, a non-immunized individual served with a subpoena may refuse to comply with its terms, provided that the information sought could reasonably be used against the subpoenaed target in a criminal action. This is why prosecutors cannot demand that defendants testify at their own trials. In fact, prosecutors must refrain from making any comment during the course of a trial regarding a defendant's failure to testify.[9] Moreover, a court, upon request, must instruct the jury that it may not draw an adverse inference from a defendant's refusal to present himself as a witness. The Court, in *Carter v. Kentucky*,[10] stated that jurors are too often tempted, on their own volition, to draw such an adverse inference. The Court commented that "[t]oo many, even those who should be better advised, view this privilege as a shelter for wrongdoers. They too readily assume that those who invoke it are . . . guilty of crime. . . ." While a court "can [not] prevent jurors from speculating about why a defendant stands mute in the face of a criminal accusation," it must provide the requested jury instruction in order to lessen this danger.

```
F    A    Q
```

Q: Does the Fifth Amendment privilege against self-incrimination apply during sentencing proceedings?

A: Yes. The Supreme Court, in *Mitchell v. United States*, 526 U.S. 314 (1999), held that the sentencing phase of a trial "is part of the criminal case" and therefore a judge is prohibited from drawing an adverse inference from a defendant's silence at his sentencing proceeding.

---

[9]*Griffin v. California*, 380 U.S. 609 (1965).
[10]450 U.S. 288 (1981).

Compulsion has also been found in situations where a government has threatened individuals with *noncriminal* sanctions. Consider *Garrity v. New Jersey*,[11] where the Court addressed the constitutionality of a statute that authorized the removal of certain public employees from their positions in the event they refused to testify regarding certain matters in a criminal trial. The *Garrity* Court struck down the statute, declaring "[t]he choice given petitioners was either to forfeit their jobs or to incriminate themselves. The option to lose their means of livelihood or to pay the penalty of self-incrimination is the antithesis of free choice to speak out or to remain silent." In *Lefkowitz v. Turley*,[12] the Court held that a New York statute that required public contracts to contain a provision requiring contractors to testify to matters concerning their performance or risk contract termination violated the Fifth Amendment. The Court stated that "answers elicited upon the threat of the loss of employment are compelled and inadmissible in evidence. Hence, if answers are to be required in such circumstances States must offer to the witness whatever immunity is required to supplant the privilege, and may not insist that the employee or contractor waive such immunity." And in *Lefkowitz v. Cunningham*,[13] the Supreme Court found a violation of the privilege against self-incrimination, where a New York statute required the removal from office of political party officials who, when subpoenaed, refused to testify to matters regarding their conduct in office.

(3) Permissible Compulsion

However, the Fifth Amendment does not require that a person be free from any and all government pressures that may ultimately produce an incriminating statement. As stated by Justice Stevens in his dissent in *Lefkowitz v. Cunningham*,[14] "It is often incorrectly assumed that whenever an individual right is sufficiently important to receive constitutional protection, that protection implicitly guarantees that the exercise of the right shall be cost free. Nothing could be further from the truth."

For example, the Supreme Court has recognized that individuals who testify in their own defense at trial[15] or who must testify before a panel in order to be considered for clemency[16] do not suffer an infringement of their Fifth Amendment privilege against self-incrimination. As stated by the Court in *Ohio Adult Parole Authority v. Woodard*,[17] the decision to testify in such circumstances is not sufficiently compelling to bring it within the protection afforded by the Fifth Amendment.

> Long ago we held that a defendant who took the stand in his own defense could not claim the privilege against self incrimination when the prosecution sought to cross-examine him (citations omitted). A defendant who takes the stand in his own behalf may be impeached by proof of prior convictions without violation of the Fifth Amendment privilege (citation omitted). A defendant whose motion for acquittal at the close of the government's case is denied must then elect whether to stand on his motion or to put on a defense, with the accompanying risk that in doing so he will augment the government's case against him (citation omitted). In each of these situations, there are undoubted pressures—generated

---

[11]385 U.S. 493 (1967).
[12]414 U.S. 70 (1973).
[13]431 U.S. 801 (1977).
[14]*Id.*
[15]*Brown v. Walker*, 161 U.S. 591 (1896).
[16]*Ohio Adult Parole Authority v. Woodard*, 523 U.S. 272 (1998).
[17]*Id.*

by the strength of the government's case against him—pushing the criminal defendant to testify. But it has never been suggested that such pressures constitute "compulsion" for Fifth Amendment purposes. . . .

Here, respondent has the same choice of providing information to the Authority—at the risk of damaging his case for clemency or for postconviction relief—or of remaining silent. But this pressure to speak in the hope of improving his chance of being granted clemency does not make the interview compelled.

The Court also failed to find a Fifth Amendment violation in *Minnesota v. Murphy*,[18] where a probationer, who reasonably perceived a threat of probation revocation, answered questions posed by his probation officer regarding certain uncharged criminal activity. Finding the compulsion under these circumstances "indistinguishable from that felt by any witness who is required to appear and give testimony," the Court noted that the probation condition at issue

> proscribed only false statements; it said nothing about his freedom to decline to answer particular questions, and certainly contained no suggestion that his probation was conditional on his waiving his Fifth Amendment privilege with respect to further criminal prosecution.

Also, in *McKune v. Lile*[19] the Court held that a Kansas prison treatment program geared toward inmates who had been convicted of sexual assault crimes did not violate the Fifth Amendment. Participants in the program were required to admit, in detail, their commission of prior sexual criminal offenses, irrespective of whether they had been previously charged for such conduct. The information they provided could be used against them in future criminal trials. In addition, failure to participate in the program could adversely impact the inmate's living conditions within the prison. Specifically, in *McKune*, the respondent/inmate was informed that his refusal to participate in the prison program would reduce

> his privilege status . . . from Level III to Level I. As part of this reduction, respondent's visitation rights, earnings, work opportunities, ability to send money to family, canteen expenditures, access to a personal television, and other privileges automatically would be curtailed. In addition, respondent would be transferred to a maximum-security unit, where his movement would be more limited, he would be moved from a two-person to a four-person cell, and he would be in a potentially more dangerous environment.

The Court concluded that the prison program did not impermissibly compel testimonial information. Rather, the Court deemed the decision to participate in the program and provide such testimony to be elective, albeit in a setting accompanied by pressures. The Court reasoned, in part, that stressful choices are an inherent characteristic of the criminal justice process and that such choices, even when made by an incarcerated individual, do not always "give . . . rise to a self-incrimination claim." As the Court declared, "It is well settled that the government need not make the exercise of the Fifth Amendment privilege cost free." In a strongly worded dissent, Justice Stevens, writing for four members of the Court, declared that until the decision in *McKune*, the Court had never "held that a person who has made a

---

[18]465 U.S. 420 (1984).
[19]536 U.S. 24 (2002).

valid assertion of the privilege may nevertheless be ordered to incriminate himself and sanctioned for disobeying such an order. This is truly a watershed case."

C. The Criminal Case Requirement

An individual can properly assert his Fifth Amendment privilege against self-incrimination whenever he reasonably believes that the testimonial evidence tendered could be used against him in a domestic criminal prosecution. As the Supreme Court stated in *Kastigar v. United States*, the Fifth Amendment

> can be asserted in any proceeding, civil or criminal, administrative or judicial, investigatory or adjudicatory, and it protects against any disclosures that the witness reasonably believes could be used in a criminal prosecution or could lead to other evidence that might be so used.[20]

Thus, a valid Fifth Amendment claim can be raised during the course of a criminal investigation and trial as well as at proceedings that are entirely noncriminal in nature. For example, in the *Kastigar, Turley*, and *Cunningham* cases discussed earlier in this chapter, the Supreme Court found that the Fifth Amendment was implicated when individuals were required to provide testimony before criminal grand juries. Similarly, in *United States v. Kordel*,[21] the Court held that a corporate officer who submitted answers to interrogatories was also entitled to Fifth Amendment protection. "Without question, he could have invoked his Fifth Amendment privilege against compulsory self-incrimination. Surely [the corporate officer] was not barred from asserting his privilege simply because the corporation had no privilege of its own, or because the proceeding in which the Government sought information was civil, rather than criminal, in character." So long as the individual witness has a reasonable basis for believing that the testimony called for could be used against him in a criminal case, the Fifth Amendment privilege can be successfully raised.

F   A   Q

Q: Can the Fifth Amendment privilege against self-incrimination be asserted if a reasonable basis exists to believe that the testimony provided could be used against the witness in a civil case or in a foreign prosecution?

A: No. The Supreme Court has held that the privilege is inapplicable in such settings. In *United States v. Balsys*,[22] Balsys refused to answer questions posed to him during a deposition regarding, inter alia, his immigration to the United States several years earlier, given that his responses could possibly incriminate him in a foreign prosecution. In rejecting his Fifth Amendment argument, the Court preliminarily noted that "Balsys agrees that the risk that his testimony might subject him to deportation is not a sufficient ground for asserting the privilege, given the civil character of a deportation proceeding." But the Court added that should he be able to demonstrate "that any testimony he might give in the deportation

---

[20]406 U.S. 441 (1972).
[21]397 U.S. 1 (1970).
[22]524 U.S. 666 (1998).

investigation could be used in a criminal proceeding against him brought by the Government of either the United States or one of the States, he would be entitled to invoke the privilege." Given that Balsys asserted a fear of prosecution by the governments of Lithuania and Israel, the Court found that he failed to meet this standard.

Sidebar

WHEN STATEMENTS OBTAINED ARE NOT ADMITTED AT TRIAL

Is there an infringement of the Fifth Amendment self-incrimination clause when the government procures statements in contravention of the *Miranda* rule, yet fails to admit the statements criminally? This issue was addressed by the Supreme Court in *Chavez v. Martinez*[23] in the context of a civil rights action brought under 42 U.S.C. 1983. Though a majority of the Court agreed that the Fifth Amendment is not violated under such circumstances, the Justices disagreed as to the underlying rationale. Four Justices (Thomas, Roberts, O'Connor, and Scalia) found that there was no constitutional violation given that "Martinez was never prosecuted for a crime, let alone compelled to be a witness against himself in a criminal case." Two other Justices (Souter and Breyer) agreed that "the core of the Fifth Amendment" does not provide for civil compensatory relief. However, they concluded that sometimes "complimentary protection" of a constitutional right is necessary. After weighing the costs and benefits, the two Justices concluded that Martinez did not make a "powerful showing" demonstrating why a civil remedy is necessary to aid the Fifth Amendment guarantee.

---

[23]538 U.S. 760 (2003).

Whether a person's fear of future prosecutorial use of his testimonial statements is reasonable is assessed one question at a time. Thus, an individual who asserts the Fifth Amendment cannot simply refuse to answer any and all questions directed at him. Rather, the Fifth Amendment can be successfully pleaded only to those questions where there is a reasonable fear of future use in a criminal case. In other words, the witness must elect whether to assert the privilege with respect to each question asked.

Consider also *Hiibel v. Sixth Judicial District Court of Nevada, Humboldt County*,[24] where the Supreme Court rejected a claim that a Nevada law that required an individual lawfully stopped by the police to identify themselves violates the Fifth Amendment. The Court reasoned, in part, that the defendant's refusal to reveal his identify "was not based on any articulated real and appreciable fear that his name would be used to incriminate him, or that it would furnish a link in the chain of evidence needed to prosecute him." Though the Court did not entirely dismiss the possibility of a valid Fifth Amendment claim in such circumstances, it believed that generally the act of identifying oneself is highly unlikely to constitute an incriminating act.

D. The Testimonial Requirement

The Fifth Amendment protects only those communications that are deemed to be "testimonial." Naturally, this raises the question, what is meant by the term "testimonial"? In *Doe v. United States*,[25] the Supreme Court declared that "in order to be testimonial, an accused's communication must itself, explicitly or

---

[24]542 U.S. 177 (2004).
[25]487 U.S. 201 (1988).

implicitly, relate a factual assertion or disclose information. Only then is a person compelled to be a 'witness' against himself." Thus, a witness who is compelled to provide verbal testimony or physical evidence may be entitled to Fifth Amendment protection in the event such disclosure requires him to speak or disclose factual knowledge or information that he possesses.

The Supreme Court has provided some guidance regarding the meaning of this term. And, in a great many instances, the Court has upheld the challenged government conduct, finding that the evidence obtained is non-testimonial. *Doe v. United States*,[26] which held that the Fifth Amendment privilege against self-incrimination did not bar the government from compelling the signature from the target of an investigation upon a consent form that authorized foreign banks to release certain financial records in the target's name, provided a useful summary of this line of cases:

> [A] suspect may be compelled to furnish a blood sample,[27] to provide a handwriting exemplar,[28] or a voice exemplar,[29] to stand in a lineup,[30] and to wear particular clothing.[31]

These decisions are grounded on the proposition that "the privilege protects an accused only from being compelled to testify against himself, or otherwise provide the State with evidence of a testimonial or communicative nature."[32] The Court accordingly held that the privilege was not implicated in each of those cases, because the suspect was not required "to disclose any knowledge he might have," or "to speak his guilt" (citations omitted). It is the "extortion of information from the accused,"[33] the attempt to force him "to disclose the contents of his own mind,"[34] that implicates the Self-Incrimination Clause.[35]

Therefore, whether or not a statement is testimonial depends upon whether the challenged government activity requires an individual to reveal "the contents of his own mind." If "yes," then the information disclosed is deemed to be testimonial. If "no," then the government's conduct requires non-testimonial evidence and can withstand a Fifth Amendment challenge.

An interesting case that had both testimonial and non-testimonial aspects is *Pennsylvania v. Muniz*.[37] In that case, the defendant was arrested on suspicion of drunk driving. After his arrival at a

Sidebar

THE EXCLUSIONARY RULE

Testimonial evidence obtained in violation of the Fifth Amendment privilege against self-incrimination is subject to exclusion. The same is true with respect to any derivative fruit. Consider *United States v. Hubbell*,[36] where the Supreme Court dismissed an indictment that was based upon testimonial documents that were compelled via a subpoena (after the provision of use immunity), but were later improperly used by the government to secure an indictment against the defendant. The Court found that the Fifth Amendment privilege against self-incrimination was violated and that dismissal of the fruit of that violation — the indictment — was warranted given the government's inability to demonstrate that the indictment was based upon information independent of the subpoenaed documents.

[36]530 U.S. 27 (2000).

[26]487 U.S. 201 (1988).
[27]*Schmerber v. California*, 384 U.S. 756, 757 (1966).
[28]*Gilbert v. California*, 388 U.S. 263, 266-267 (1967).
[29]*United States v. Dionisio*, 410 U.S. 1 (1973).
[30]*United States v. Wade*, 388 U.S. 218, 221-222 (1967).
[31]*Holt v. United States*, 218 U.S. 245, 252-253 (1910).
[32]*Schmerber*, 384 U.S. at 761.
[33]*Couch v. United States*, 409 U.S. 322, 328 (1973).
[34]*Curcio v. United States*, 354 U.S. 118 (1957).
[35]*Doe*, 487 U.S. 201, 210-211 (1988).
[37]496 U.S. 582 (1990).

booking center, a police officer posed several questions to the defendant. The first set of questions inquired about the defendant's name, his residential location, and various personal characteristics (e.g., height, weight, age, etc.). The defendant's responses were slurred. Thereafter, he was asked whether he knew the date of his sixth birthday. After an initial inaudible response, the defendant ultimately responded, "No, I don't."

The Court held that the defendant's responses to questions about his name, address, height, weight, eye color, date of birth, and current age were non-testimonial. The Court stated that the incriminating aspect of the defendant's responses to these questions was his slurred speech. As with blood samples, voice exemplars, and lineup participations, the Court concluded that the defendant's slurred speech was non-testimonial given that it revealed real and physical evidence as opposed to an assertive fact or belief. As stated by the Court, "Requiring a suspect to reveal the physical manner in which he articulates words, like requiring him to reveal the physical properties of the sound produced by his voice (citation omitted), does not, without more, compel him to provide a 'testimonial' response for purposes of the privilege."

But the Court reached a different conclusion regarding the defendant's response to the birth date question. Whereas the defendant's slurred speech constituted real and physical evidence of his speech delivery, his birth date response was testimonial due to its "content." Noting that verbal statements are, in general, testimonial in nature given that information or facts are typically asserted in such circumstances, the Court declared:

> Whenever a suspect is asked for a response requiring him to communicate an express or implied assertion of fact or belief, the suspect confronts the "trilemma" of truth, falsity, or silence, and hence the response (whether based on truth or falsity) contains a testimonial component.

The Court added that if the defendant

> knew the date of his sixth birthday and [he] for whatever reason, could not remember or calculate that date, he was confronted with the trilemma. By hypothesis, the inherently coercive environment created by the custodial interrogation precluded the option of remaining silent (citation omitted). [The defendant] was left with the choice of incriminating himself by admitting that he did not then know the date of his sixth birthday or answering untruthfully by reporting a date that he did not then believe to be accurate (an incorrect guess would be incriminating as well as untruthful). The content of his truthful answer supported an inference that his mental faculties were impaired, because his assertion (he did not know the date of his sixth birthday) was different from the assertion (he knew the date was [correct date]) that the trier of fact might reasonably have expected a lucid person to provide. Hence, the incriminating inference of impaired mental faculties stemmed, not just from the fact that [the defendant] slurred his response, but also from a testimonial aspect of that response.

Sometimes the mere act of producing physical evidence can constitute a testimonial communication. The Court in *Fisher v. United States*[38] explained that when an individual complies with a subpoena request to produce documents, his

---

[38] 425 U.S. 391 (1976).

compliance "tacitly concedes the existence of the papers demanded and their possession or control by the [subpoenaed individual]. It also would indicate the [subpoenaed individual's] belief that the papers are those described in the subpoena."

Thus, whether the act of producing the documents is testimonial is, therefore, an inquiry "distinct from the question whether the unprotected contents of the documents themselves are incriminating."[39] And the answer to the act of production question is dependent upon the government's awareness, prior to the issuance of the subpoena, of the existence and location of the documents. If the government was previously unaware, then the act of production has communicative significance. By producing the requested information, the subpoenaed individual is, in effect, communicating to the government not only that the documents exist but that he is in possession of this material. On the other hand, if the government did, in fact, possess such previous knowledge, then no such communicative aspects are present.[40]

E. Waiver of the Fifth Amendment Privilege

A witness is entitled to waive his Fifth Amendment privilege, and such a waiver can occur either explicitly or implicitly. Voluntary decisions on the part of the witness may serve to waive the privilege. For example, the Fifth Amendment privilege against self-incrimination affords a defendant the right not to testify at his criminal trial. A defendant who elects to testify at trial, more often than not, has made a knowing and voluntary decision to waive this privilege and to subject himself to questioning.

Similarly, an individual who voluntarily decides to converse with his probation officer about uncharged criminal conduct implicitly waives his right to raise a Fifth Amendment challenge as to that interrogation. As stated by the Supreme Court in *Minnesota v. Murphy*, "Thus it is that a witness confronted with questions that the government should reasonably expect to elicit incriminating evidence ordinarily must assert the privilege, rather than answer, if he desires not to incriminate himself. . . . [I]f he chooses to answer, his choice is considered to be voluntary, since he was free to claim the privilege and would suffer no penalty as the result of his decision to do so."

SUMMARY

- The Fifth Amendment privilege against self-incrimination provides, in pertinent part, that "[n]o person . . . shall be compelled in any criminal case to be a witness against himself."

- Only natural individuals (not corporations or partnerships) can assert the Fifth Amendment privilege against self-incrimination.

- The privilege applies only when the testimonial evidence at issue has been compelled by the government.

---

[39] *United States v. Hubbell*, 530 U.S. 27, 37 (2000).
[40] As explained by the Supreme Court in *United States v. Hubbell*: "[W]e have . . . made it clear that the act of producing documents in response to a subpoena may have a compelled testimonial aspect. We have held that 'the act of production' itself may implicitly communicate 'statements of fact.' By 'producing documents in compliance with a subpoena, the witness would admit that the papers existed, were in his possession or control, and were authentic.'"

■ The privilege cannot be properly asserted when the witness has been provided use immunity with respect to such testimony. Testimony obtained by virtue of this method cannot be used either substantively or for purposes of impeachment.

■ An individual is entitled to the Fifth Amendment privilege against self-incrimination whenever he reasonably believes that testimonial information he provides might be subsequently used against him in a domestic criminal case.

■ A "testimonial" communication is when an accused's communication "explicitly or implicitly, relate[s] a factual assertion or disclose[s] information."

■ Central to determining whether a statement is testimonial is to consider whether the challenged government activity requires that the subject reveal "the contents of his own mind." If "yes," then the individual can rely upon the Fifth Amendment privilege. If "no," then the government's request is non-testimonial and can withstand a Fifth Amendment challenge.

■ Sometimes the mere act of producing documents can constitute a testimonial communication. If the government was previously unaware of the existence of the subpoenaed documents, then the act of production has communicative significance. By producing the subpoenaed records, the producer of those documents is, in effect, communicating to the government that such documents not only exist but that he is in possession of this material.

■ An individual may waive his Fifth Amendment privilege. For example, an individual who elects to testify at his own trial waives the privilege with respect to those matters within the scope of his direct examination.

CONNECTIONS

Relationship to Incorporation (Chapter 1)
The Fifth Amendment privilege against self-incrimination is now fully incorporated to the states via the Fourteenth Amendment Due Process Clause.

Relationship to Involuntary Confessions and the Due Process Clause Cases (Chapter 17), and Sixth Amendment Right to Counsel and Deliberate Police Elicitations (Chapter 19)
An individual can waive his Fifth Amendment *Miranda* rights as well as his Sixth Amendment right to counsel. As in these other contexts, an individual can also waive his non-*Miranda* Fifth Amendment privilege against self-incrimination.

Relationship to Fourth Amendment Violations and Their Associated Remedies (Chapter 15), Involuntary Confessions and the Due Process Clause Cases (Chapter 17), and The Sixth Amendment Right to Counsel — General Principles (Chapter 19)

The exclusionary rule applies to violations of the Fourth Amendment, the Fifth and Fourteenth Amendment due process clauses, the Fifth Amendment privilege against self-incrimination (*Miranda* and non-*Miranda*), and the Sixth Amendment right to counsel. The fruit of the poisonous tree doctrine applies to Fourth and Sixth Amendment violations, but is subject to exceptions. In the Fifth Amendment realm, the applicability of the fruits doctrine is dependent upon the particular guarantee that is infringed.

Involuntary Confessions and the Due Process Clause Cases

17

The historical prelude to *Miranda v. Arizona*[1] is certainly less well known than the infamous incantations that emanated from that decision.

OVERVIEW

However, the historical value should not in any way be discounted. As detailed in this chapter, in the years prior to *Miranda* the Supreme Court decided confession challenges by determining whether or not the subject statements were obtained voluntarily. And in deciding these cases, the Court assessed these challenges primarily pursuant to the due process clauses of the Fifth and Fourteenth Amendments.

This chapter will succinctly discuss this history and detail how judicial frustration with this voluntariness test contributed significantly to the development of the *Miranda* rule. However, this chapter should not be viewed as merely a historical rehashing of due process law cases from an earlier era. It also represents a description of the law in its current form. Indeed, Fifth and Fourteenth Amendment due process claims challenging the voluntariness of a statement can still be brought today. This type of constitutional challenge is distinct from the *Miranda*-type challenge that is based upon the Fifth Amendment privilege against self-incrimination.

---

[1]384 U.S. 436 (1966).

A. VOLUNTARINESS REVIEW AND THE FIFTH AND FOURTEENTH AMENDMENT DUE PROCESS CLAUSES

1. The Emergence of the Due Process Voluntariness Review
2. The Years Immediately Preceding *Miranda v. Arizona*
3. Due Process Voluntariness Challenges: Current Standards

A. Voluntariness Review and the Fifth and Fourteenth Amendment Due Process Clauses

(1) The Emergence of the Due Process Voluntariness Review

Prior to 1897, the common law governed the admissibility of confessions in federal and state courts. During much of this time period, the admissibility of a confession required a finding of voluntariness, which was determined by assessing the reliability of the suspect's confession in light of the interrogation tactics employed by government officials. This concern for reliability reflected the court's concern with criminal convictions being based upon false confessions.

However, reliance upon these two factors as a basis for ascertaining a statement's voluntary character began to change significantly in 1897. In *Bram v. United States*,[2] the Supreme Court, citing a string of English and American authorities, held that a confession obtained from the defendant murder suspect was involuntary and violated the Fifth Amendment privilege against self-incrimination. This was the first time that the Court linked the concept of voluntariness to the Constitution[3] and, in so doing, distanced — though it did not completely abrogate — the concept of reliability from the voluntariness equation. In reaching its conclusion, the Court referenced the effect of the interrogation tactics employed upon the defendant's free will to decide whether to make a statement. Indeed, *Bram*'s shift in emphasis away from reliability and toward the free will of the individual to utter statements *arguably* prohibited virtually any interrogation tactic that influenced an individual's decision to talk.[4]

Irrespective of the merits of this contention, and despite the shift in analytical emphasis, *Bram* did not represent a wholesale change in the analytical approach to confession issues. First, remember the time period. When *Bram* was decided in 1897, the Fifth Amendment privilege against self-incrimination had yet to be incorporated to the states. That would not happen for another 67 years. Moreover, the federal courts themselves were slow to embrace this new constitutional approach to assessing involuntariness claims.

Thus, the shift away from the traditional common law standards to a constitutionally based analytical framework was gradual. In the state court context, this shift

---

[2]168 U.S. 532 (1897).
[3]The Court commented: "In criminal trials, in the courts of the United States, wherever a question arises whether a confession is incompetent because not voluntary, the issue is controlled by that portion of the Fifth Amendment to the Constitution of the United States commanding that no person 'shall be compelled in any criminal case to be a witness against himself.'"
[4]The Court commented, "As said in the passage from *Russell on Crimes* already quoted: 'The law cannot measure the force of the influence used, or decide upon its effect upon the mind of the prisoner, and therefore excludes the declaration if any degree of influence has been exerted.' In the case before us we find that an influence was exerted, and, as any doubt as to whether the confession was voluntary must be determined in favor of the accused, we cannot escape the conclusion that error was committed by the trial court in admitting the confession under the circumstances disclosed by the record."

finally came to fruition in the 1936 case *Brown v. Mississippi*.[5] There, the Court found that confessions that were procured by "state authorities" by virtue of methods that the Court described as "extreme[ly] brutal" violated the due process clause of the Fourteenth Amendment. Specifically, in *Brown*, police officials employed an array of extremely coercive tactics to obtain confessions from African-American murder defendants. So repulsive were the methods employed by the police in that case, the Court commented that it would be hard to fathom tactics that could be deemed any more abhorrent. The Court easily and unanimously found that "the use of the confessions thus obtained as the basis for conviction and sentence was a clear denial of due process."

The adoption of a due process framework for assessing voluntariness claims was eventually followed at the federal level as well. This post-*Brown* development signified a shift away from the use (albeit quite limited) of the privilege against self-incrimination clause as a basis for assessing Fifth Amendment involuntariness claims.[6] "While *Bram* was decided before *Brown* and its progeny," declared the Court in *Dickerson v. United States*,[7] "for the middle third of the 20th century our cases based the rule against admitting coerced confessions primarily, if not exclusively, on notions of due process. We applied the due process voluntariness test in 'some 30 different cases decided during the era that intervened between *Brown* and *Escobedo v. Illinois*, 378 U.S. 478 [(1964)].'" Today, the due process clause is still employed as the primary constitutional basis to exclude non-*Miranda* statements that are obtained involuntarily.[8]

As less egregious factual constructs presented themselves before the Court, however, the Court struggled with its application of the due process clause during the years between *Brown* and the historic decision in 1966, *Miranda v. Arizona*. At times, the Court decided these cases with a lens focused largely, if not exclusively, upon the propriety of police conduct.[9] This was certainly the

> ## Sidebar
>
> ### FIFTH AND FOURTEENTH AMENDMENT DUE PROCESS CLAUSES
>
> The due process clause of the Fifth Amendment provides that "[n]o person shall . . . be deprived of life, liberty, or property, without due process of law." The Fourteenth Amendment due process clause states that "[n]o State shall . . . deprive any person of life, liberty, or property, without due process of law."

---

[5]297 U.S. 278 (1936).

[6]Part of the slow federal response could be attributable to Rule 5(a) of the Federal Rules of Criminal Procedure, and a pair of Supreme Court decisions rendered in 1943 and 1957, respectively: *McNabb v. United States*, 318 U.S. 332 (1943), and *Mallory v. United States*, 354 U.S. 449 (1957). As stated by the Supreme Court in *Miranda v. Arizona*, 384 U.S. 436 (1966), "Because of the adoption by Congress of Rule 5(a) of the Federal Rules of Criminal Procedure, and this Court's effectuation of that Rule in [*McNabb* and *Mallory*], we have had little occasion in the past quarter century to reach the constitutional issues in dealing with federal interrogations. These supervisory rules, requiring production of an arrested person before a commissioner 'without unnecessary delay' and excluding evidence obtained in default of that statutory obligation, were nonetheless responsive to the same considerations of Fifth Amendment policy that unavoidably face us now as to the States." The *McNabb-Mallory* Rule, as it is known today, allows for statements obtained from suspects to be excluded if such statements were obtained while they were delayed unnecessarily from appearing before a magistrate for arraignment. The decision in *Miranda* has greatly muted the significance of this doctrine, which is applicable only in the federal system.

[7]530 U.S. 428 (2000).

[8]*Id.* at 434 ("We have never abandoned this due process jurisprudence, and thus continue to exclude confessions that were obtained involuntarily").

[9]See *Chambers v. Florida*, 309 U.S. 277 (1940) (finding a violation of Fourteenth Amendment due process when African-American individuals were subjected to five days of custodial interrogation, including an all-night interrogation, where "the haunting fear of mob violence was around them in an atmosphere charged with excitement and public indignation"); *Ashcraft v. Tennessee*, 322 U.S. 143 (1944) (finding that Fourteenth Amendment due process was violated when several police officers "in relays" interrogated the

case in *Brown*. Yet in other instances the Court cast a wider net, considering in its calculus various individual traits.[10]

Of particular frustration to the Court, though, was ascertaining what actually transpired during police interrogations, particularly when they occurred within the confines of a police station. In *Ashcraft v. Tennessee*,[11] two murder defendants alleged that their Fourteenth Amendment due process rights were violated given that their convictions were based upon confessions involuntarily obtained during extended jailhouse interrogations. With respect to defendant Ashcraft's confession, the Court found a due process violation. In reaching this conclusion, the Court noted that not only was the defendant, while seated in a chair in a room within the county jail, continuously interrogated by "relays" of police officers for 36 hours, but that he had also been deprived of any opportunity to rest or communicate with others during this period.

The Court was able to render its decision based upon facts that were not in dispute. However, the Court was unable to resolve other critical questions of fact regarding defendant Ashcraft's interrogation and made the following rather pointed observations:

> In reaching our conclusion as to the validity of Ashcraft's confession we do not resolve any of the disputed questions of fact relating to the details of what transpired within the confession chamber of the jail or whether Ashcraft actually did confess. Such disputes . . . are an inescapable consequence of secret inquisitorial practices. And always evidence concerning the inner details of secret inquisitions is weighted against an accused, particularly where, as here, he is charged with a brutal crime, or where, as in many other cases, his supposed offense bears relation to an unpopular economic, political, or religious cause.

(2) The Years Immediately Preceding *Miranda v. Arizona*

Indeed, the sentiments expressed in *Ashcraft* regarding the "secret inquisitorial practices" of the police were of ongoing concern to members of the Court in the years immediately preceding the historic decision in *Miranda v. Arizona*. It appeared increasingly clear that the voluntariness model was particularly ineffectual in the

---

defendant (who was denied any opportunity to rest or communicate with others) for 36 hours while he was seated in a chair in a room located within the county jail); *Harris v. South Carolina*, 338 U.S. 68 (1949) (finding that Fourteenth Amendment due process was violated when a defendant arrested for theft was, inter alia, interrogated for an unrelated murder in relays for several hours at a time over three days in a very hot room in a county jail, was held incommunicado during the course of the interrogation, and was never advised of various rights under South Carolina law, such as the right to remain silent; *Arizona v. Fulminante*, 499 U.S. 279 (1991) (a post-*Miranda* case) (affirming state supreme court finding that Fifth and Fourteenth Amendment due process was violated when a defendant confessed to a murder to an undercover agent who posed as a fellow inmate who had offered to protect the defendant from harm posed by other inmates provided the defendant told him the truth about the murder for which the defendant was still under investigation).
[10]See *Haley v. Ohio*, 332 U.S. 596 (1948) (holding that the Fourteenth Amendment due process was violated when the police interrogated a 15-year-old boy for a prolonged period and who was held incommunicado in excess of three days); *Spano v. New York*, 360 U.S. 315 (1959) (relying, in part, upon the defendant's limited education, lengthy mental instability, and the fact that he was foreign born, the Court invalidated a confession pursuant to the Fourteenth Amendment due process clause that was obtained after approximately eight hours of questioning by several police officers who refused the defendant's repeated requests to contact his attorney); *Blackburn v. Alabama*, 361 U.S. 199 (1960) (citing the defendant's mental incompetence as a decisive factor, the Court found that Fourteenth Amendment due process was violated when a confession was obtained after eight to nine hours of police interrogation).
[11]322 U.S. 143 (1944).

context of custodial interrogations and the Supreme Court in the 1960s appeared poised to alter the analytical landscape.

This change was evidenced in a pair of cases decided by the Supreme Court in 1964: *Massiah v. United States*[12] and *Escobedo v. Illinois*.[13] Both cases were decided on Sixth Amendment grounds (the Sixth Amendment will be discussed in greater depth in Chapter 19). But brief mention of each case, in particular *Escobedo*, is worthy at this point because both decisions were decided in the years immediately preceding *Miranda v. Arizona* and are reflective of the Court's readiness to extend constitutional safeguards to individuals interrogated by the police.

Massiah involved the surreptitious interrogation of an indicted individual who had been released on bail (therefore he was not in police custody) at the time of the governmental questioning. The defendant challenged the government's use of his statements, arguing that their admission violated his Fifth and Sixth Amendment rights to counsel. The Court excluded the statements, finding that where the police "deliberately elicited" incriminating statements from the defendant "after he had been indicted and in the absence of his counsel," the Sixth Amendment right to counsel is violated.

In contrast to *Massiah*, *Escobedo* involved a pre-indictment interrogation. There, the defendant, who had been arrested for murder and transported to a police station, was denied the opportunity to consult with his attorney (despite his repeated requests), was not informed of his right to remain silent, and was led to believe by the police that he would be released if he implicated another individual in the murder. Citing *Massiah*, the Court in *Escobedo* found that the Sixth Amendment counsel right was also applicable to the pre-indictment scenario presented in that case.

Two observations regarding *Escobedo* should be noted. First, extending a right to counsel to pre-indictment settings—where, unquestionably, the vast majority of interrogations occurs—had potentially significant implications. On the one hand, a broadly applied constitutional right to counsel posed a rather obvious investigative hindrance. The presence of counsel during pre-indictment interrogations would undoubtedly hinder the ability of police to obtain crucial evidentiary information. Yet an expansive counsel right at this stage could be largely curative and might effectively address the Court's concerns regarding the propriety of stationhouse interrogations.

In the end, *Escobedo* arguably split the difference. Its holding was narrowly phrased, limiting the reach of the *Massiah* Sixth Amendment counsel right to the factual context before the Court. Specifically, it found that in pre-indictment settings, an individual retains a Sixth Amendment counsel right when "the investigation is no longer a general inquiry into an unsolved crime but has begun to focus on a particular suspect, the suspect has been taken into police custody, the police carry out a process of interrogations that lends itself to eliciting incriminating statements, the suspect has requested and been denied an opportunity to consult with his lawyer, and the police have not effectively warned him of his absolute constitutional right to remain silent. . . ."

Decided a mere two years prior to the landmark *Miranda* decision, *Massiah* and *Escobedo* reflected the willingness of a majority of the Court to extend the reach of the

---

[12]377 U.S. 201 (1964) (holding that the Sixth Amendment right to counsel was violated when the government deliberately elicited statements from an indicted individual who was represented by counsel).
[13]378 U.S. 478 (1964).

**INCORPORATION OF THE FIFTH
AMENDMENT TO THE STATES**

In the same year that the Court decided
Massiah and *Escobedo*, the Court decided
another significant case that was an important
precedent to *Miranda*. In *Malloy v. Hogan*,[14] the
Court held that the Fourteenth Amendment fully
incorporated to the states the Fifth Amendment
privilege against self-incrimination. In so
holding, the Court emphasized, in part, the
importance of an individual's free will
determination regarding whether to speak to
government authorities: "The Fourteenth
Amendment secures against state invasion the
same privilege that the Fifth Amendment
guarantees against federal infringement — the
right of a person to remain silent unless he
chooses to speak in the unfettered exercise of
his own free will. . . ."

[14]378 U.S. 1 (1964).

constitution within the sphere of police interrogation. They reflected the Court's dual concern with individual determination (the right of the individual to decide whether to speak) and with the propriety of police interrogation practices. These concerns were amply on display in *Miranda v. Arizona.*

(3) Due Process Voluntariness Challenges: Current Standards

As noted, Fifth and Fourteenth Amendment due process challenges are a viable constitutional avenue to challenge the voluntariness of a confession. The courts employ a totality of the circumstances standard when assessing voluntariness claims brought pursuant to these clauses. "The due process test takes into consideration 'the totality of all the surrounding circumstances — both the characteristics of the accused and the details of the interrogation.'"[15] The Supreme Court has also held that a due process violation cannot be found in the absence of any coercive police activity. Therefore, while a court engaged in a totality of the circumstances review may properly consider individual characteristics and how those traits might bear upon an individual's capacity to resist the police interrogation methods at issue, such traits standing alone, no matter how compelling, will not give rise to a viable due process claim. As the Court stated in *Colorado v. Connelly*, "[C]oercive police activity is a necessary predicate to the finding that a confession is not 'voluntary' within the meaning of the Due Process Clause of the Fourteenth Amendment."[16]

SUMMARY

- Judicial frustration with the voluntariness tests (common law and constitutional) in police-dominated contexts was a significant precursor to the *Miranda v. Arizona* decision.

- In 1964, the Fifth Amendment privilege against self-incrimination was incorporated to the states via the Fourteenth Amendment.

- The Fifth and Fourteenth Amendment due process clauses prohibit the government from obtaining statements from individuals involuntarily.

[15]*Dickerson v. United States*, 530 U.S. 428 (2000).
[16]479 U.S. 157 (1986).

■ Fifth and Fourteenth Amendment due process challenges (non-*Miranda* challenges) are reviewed pursuant to a totality of the circumstances standard, considering both the characteristics of the accused as well as the details of the interrogation. Coercive police activity is a necessary prerequisite to finding that a statement was obtained involuntarily in violation of the due process clause.

CONNECTIONS

Relationship to Incorporation (Chapter 1)

The Fifth Amendment Privilege Against Self-Incrimination is now fully incorporated to the states via the Fourteenth Amendment due process clause.

Relationship to the *Miranda* Rule (Chapter 18)

Claims alleging involuntary statements can be reviewed pursuant to the Fifth and Fourteenth Amendment due process clauses as well as the Fifth Amendment *Miranda* rule. Without a finding of coercive police activity there cannot be a due process violation. A *Miranda* violation can be found without such a finding.

The *Miranda* Rule

OVERVIEW

This chapter will review the infamous case of *Miranda v. Arizona*. The right to remain silent and the right to an attorney — which are at the heart of the Fifth Amendment *Miranda* rule — have been referenced so much in American society that, as the Supreme Court said in *Dickerson v. United States*, "the warnings have become part of our national culture."

This chapter will discuss and explain not only the *Miranda* decision, but also its component parts, including its exclusionary rules. Though the gist of the *Miranda* rights might be comparatively easy to remember, this chapter will reveal that the rule itself is both complex and constantly evolving.

C. THE *MIRANDA* EXCLUSIONARY RULE AND THE FRUIT OF THE POISONOUS TREE DOCTRINE

1. The *Miranda* Exclusionary Rule
2. The Fruit of the Poisonous Tree Doctrine

A. *Miranda v. Arizona*

In *Miranda v. Arizona*,[1] the Court considered whether custodial statements obtained from various defendants who were held incommunicado in a "police-dominated atmosphere" and who were not fully informed of their constitutional rights violated the Fifth Amendment privilege against self-incrimination. The *Miranda* Court answered this question in the affirmative.

The *Miranda* opinion is replete with references to the Court's concerns regarding the propriety of police interrogation strategies and individual free will.

Regarding the former, it noted that police manuals provide instruction regarding successful interrogation methodologies. The manuals, the Court observed, emphasized the importance of subject isolation and unfamiliar surroundings and suggested various strategies to obtain psychological advantage over their subjects. The Court acknowledged that the interrogation practices at issue in *Miranda* did not necessarily present instances of involuntarily obtained statements "in traditional terms." Nevertheless, the Court stressed that its concern for compelled self-incrimination in the custodial contexts presented in *Miranda* was "not lessened in the slightest." It observed that statements obtained in such environments "exacts a heavy toll on individual liberty and trades on the weakness of individuals. . . ."

The Court similarly stressed how personal characteristics may adversely influence a subject's susceptibility to what the Court referred to as the "menacing . . . interrogation procedures" employed by the police. As examples, the Court noted that one defendant was an "indigent Mexican defendant" who "was seriously disturbed with pronounced sexual fantasies," and that another "was an indigent Los Angeles Negro who had dropped out of school in the sixth grade." In the Court's view, these dual concerns created a compulsive, intimidating atmosphere. Thus, the Court concluded that "adequate protection devices" must be imposed

S i d e b a r

MEMORANDUM FROM JUSTICE WILLIAM BRENNAN TO CHIEF JUSTICE EARL WARREN

In this memorandum, Justice Brennan expresses his views to Chief Justice Warren regarding language that should be included in the *Miranda* opinion. Brennan's suggestion on this first page of his memorandum was adopted by the Court and was part of the first sentence of the *Miranda* opinion.

Supreme Court of the United States
Washington 25, D. C.

CHAMBERS OF
JUSTICE WM J. BRENNAN, JR.   May 11, 1966

RE: Nos. 759, 760, 761 and 584.

Dear Chief:

    I am writing out my suggestions addressed to your *Miranda* opinion with the thought that we might discuss them at your convenience. I feel guilty about the extent of the suggestions but this will be one of the most important opinions of our time and I know that you will want the fullest expression of my views.

    I have one major suggestion. It goes to the basic thrust of the approach to be taken. In your very first sentence you state that the root problem is "the role society must assume, consistent with the federal Constitution, in prosecuting individuals for crime." I would suggest that the root issue is "the restraints society must observe, consistent with the federal Constitution, in prosecuting individuals for crime."

Justice Brennan's Memorandum
Papers of Earl Warren, Manuscript Division,
Library of Congress, Washington, D.C.

---

[1] 384 U.S. 436 (1966).

to combat the compulsive atmosphere that is an integral part of such custodial settings. And while the Court did not forbid the development of viable federal and state alternatives, it was the protective safeguards announced by the Court — the so-called *Miranda* rights — that have become the most infamous aspect of the *Miranda* decision.

The *Miranda* rights are constitutional protections that must be recited to a suspect prior to the commencement of custodial interrogation. Specifically, the Court declared:

> [An individual] must be warned prior to any questioning that he has the right to remain silent, that anything he says can be used against him in a court of law, that he has the right to the presence of an attorney, and that if he cannot afford an attorney one will be appointed for him prior to any questioning if he so desires.

Statements obtained by virtue of custodial interrogation in the absence of *Miranda* warnings are deemed to be compelled within the meaning of the Fifth Amendment. The Court further explained that a custodial suspect may waive his *Miranda* rights if done knowingly, intelligently, and voluntarily.

F A Q

Q: Do *Miranda* rights apply to misdemeanor arrests?

A: Yes. In *Berkemer v. McCarty*, 468 U.S. 420 (1984), the Supreme Court held that *Miranda* protections must be provided irrespective of whether the crime is a felony or something less serious. The Court reasoned, in part, that it would be unreasonable to expect police to ascertain the nature of the crime prior to deciding the manner in which they would proceed to question the suspect.

It must be emphasized that *Miranda* warnings are required only when a suspect is in "custody"[2] and only when such an individual is "interrogated." Each of these terms will be discussed at greater length later in this chapter. But it is important to understand that *Miranda* warnings need not be provided in the event the police question an individual who is not in their custodial care. Thus, an officer who merely approaches an individual and commences a conversation, or who merely detains (within the meaning of *Terry v. Ohio*) and interrogates an individual need not recite the *Miranda* safeguards. Similarly, *Miranda* warnings need not be provided to an individual who is in custody but is not interrogated. Thus, an individual who is arrested but is not asked questions by the police is not entitled to the provision of *Miranda* warnings.

As noted, an individual may elect to waive his constitutional protections, but such a waiver is valid only if it is done voluntarily, knowingly, and intelligently. Proof that an individual expressly indicated a willingness to talk in the absence of counsel might, according to the Court, constitute a valid waiver. However, the Court added that a waiver will not be presumed from a suspect's silence, because a confession was

---

[2]Elaborating upon the meaning of the term "custody," the Court explained that it envisions an individual who is "in custody at the station or otherwise deprived of his freedom of action in any significant way. . . . "

ultimately obtained, or because the suspect elected to answer select questions prior to the invocation of rights.[3]

Though the so-called *Miranda* warnings are undoubtedly the most infamous aspect of the case, they are arguably not the most transformative. For starters, *Miranda* represented a significant shift in terms of constitutional review. As you may recall, *Escobedo*, relying upon the Sixth Amendment right to counsel clause, excluded the confession obtained from an unindicted individual who was in police custody. Like *Escobedo*, *Miranda* involved the interrogation of individuals who were in police custody but had not been indicted. However, in terms of constitutional analysis, *Miranda* broke new ground. Rather than rely upon the right to counsel clause of the Sixth Amendment, the Court in *Miranda* rested its decision upon the privilege against self-incrimination clause in the Fifth Amendment. Indeed, the decision in *Miranda* paved the way for the Court's eventual retreat from the *Escobedo*-type analysis in the pre-indictment interrogation context. Just eight years after *Miranda*, the Supreme Court, in *Kirby v. Illinois*,[4] a case involving a photographic lineup display, limited the reach of the Sixth Amendment right to counsel clause. *Kirby* held that the Sixth Amendment right to counsel provision applies once adversary judicial proceedings have commenced, which, in essence, refers to the post-indictment/arraignment phase of the criminal justice process.[5] Thus, today pre-indictment/arraignment interrogation questions, such as those presented in *Miranda* and *Escobedo*, are subject to Fifth Amendment scrutiny. Post-indictment/arraignment interrogation contests are primarily assessed pursuant to the Sixth Amendment.

Miranda was also notable for what it failed to do. As noted, in the years leading up to *Miranda* the Court expressed ongoing concern about the voluntariness of confessions obtained during stationhouse interrogations. How to remedy this was the central question. At one extreme, the Court could have found embedded in the Constitution an absolute counsel right during any and all custodial interrogations. Or it might have prohibited custodial interrogations altogether. But such sweeping mandates would have undoubtedly hamstrung the police investigative function. To obtain confessions in such circumstances would have been, at the very least, exceedingly difficult. Whatever their shortcomings, the police play a central role in the maintenance of an orderly society and must have sufficient discretionary authority to properly execute their investigative function.

In the end, the *Miranda* decision avoided the more extreme remedial solutions in favor of a more nuanced approach. *Miranda* did nothing more than institute a warning system, which required the police to briefly inform custodial suspects of certain constitutional protections, and it mandated respect for safeguards only if the suspect elected to exercise his rights. Given its custodial requirement, *Miranda* has no applicability whatsoever to police interrogation of suspects who are not in police custody. And within the custodial context, *Miranda* does little, if anything, to curb the police interrogation tactics about which the Court had expressed serious misgivings. Thus, the police today retain the latitude to employ a vast array of interrogation practices in custodial and non-custodial situations. The mandates required by *Miranda* allow the police to satisfy their Fifth Amendment obligations in literally

---

[3]As described later in this chapter, the Court has since retreated, at least in part, from this declaration regarding waiver.
[4]406 U.S. 682 (1972).
[5]The Sixth Amendment will be discussed at greater length in Chapters 19 and 20.

seconds. Upon recitation of the required warnings and a valid waiver, the police enjoy enormous discretion regarding the interrogation strategies and techniques they elect to employ. Moreover, the *Miranda* Court placed enormous responsibility for enforcing these constitutional safeguards upon the interrogated individual. And in recent years that individual responsibility has only increased. It is the individual suspect who must insist that his constitutional rights be respected, and he must make this election while in the midst of police custody and its inherent coercive pressures.

F   A   Q

Q: If the police fail to comply with *Miranda* but the statements obtained are otherwise voluntary, are the statements admissible?

A: No. Two years after *Miranda* was issued, Congress passed 18 U.S.C. 3501, which, in essence, attempted to overrule *Miranda*. At its core, the statute provided that a statement's admissibility is dependent, not upon whether the police complied with the requirements delineated in *Miranda*, but on whether it was voluntarily obtained. Whether the interrogated suspect was informed of his right to remain silent and his right to counsel were merely factors, among others, to be considered in the voluntariness calculus. In *Dickerson v. United States*[6] the Court considered whether Congress could, through this statute, overrule *Miranda*. The Court answered this question in the negative, finding that *Miranda* was a constitutional rule and, thus, could not be overruled by statute. The Court noted, inter alia, that *Miranda* itself applied to state court proceedings, that *Miranda* in subsequent years had been applied to state court cases, and that the *Miranda* decision itself contains numerous statements indicative of the Court's understanding that the announced rule was constitutional in nature.

(1) The Custody Requirement

As noted, *Miranda* rights need not be provided unless the suspect is within the custody of the police. Naturally this raises the question, what is meant by the term "custody"?

The Supreme Court has held that an individual is in custody, and therefore potentially eligible for the recitation of *Miranda* warnings, when he is either formally arrested or in circumstances tantamount to a formal arrest. Certainly the easiest custodial questions present themselves when the police, by all accounts, effectuate a formal arrest. For instance, when the police physically restrain a suspect, inform the suspect of his arrest, place him in handcuffs, and transport the individual via a police vehicle to a stationhouse, rarely do such scenarios present challenging *Miranda* issues. However, more difficult cases arise when the behavior of the police is more ambiguous. What if, for example, a suspect has not been formally arrested, has not been placed in handcuffs, and is interrogated within his own home or at a location other than a police station?

---

[6]530 U.S. 428 (2000).

F   A   Q

> **Q: Is a person in custody for purposes of the *Miranda* rule when he has been stopped pursuant to an ordinary traffic violation?**
>
> A: Generally the answer is no. While the ordinary traffic stop certainly qualifies as a seizure within the meaning of the Fourth Amendment, such seizures do not typically rise to the level of custody within the meaning of the *Miranda* rule. In *Berkemer v. McCarty*,[7] the Court analogized such stops to *Terry*-level seizures. The Court noted that the "duration and atmosphere" of ordinary traffic stops are comparable to the *Terry*-level detentions. Indeed, the Court added that motorists' expectations are that they will be stopped for a brief period, will have to address a few inquiries, and then will be allowed to depart. The nature of the typical traffic stop, according to the Court, stands in contrast to the more prolonged detentions associated with arrests. Nevertheless, traffic stops can ripen into custodial arrests, thus triggering *Miranda* protections.

The Supreme Court stated in *Berkemer v. McCarty* that "the only relevant inquiry is how a reasonable man in the suspect's position would have understood his situation." This inquiry, as later explained by the Court in *Thompson v. Keohane*,[8] involves two steps. First, it must determine "the circumstances surrounding the interrogation," and second, in light of "those circumstances, would a reasonable person have felt he or she was not at liberty to terminate the interrogation and leave."

When undertaking this two-step evaluation, the courts will consider the totality of the circumstances presented in a given situation. Rarely is a custodial question determined on the basis of any single consideration. Rather, it is far more typical for courts to decide this question on the basis of an array of factors. Commonly considered criteria include, but are hardly limited to, the location of the interrogation (e.g., a suspect's residence, a squad car, a police station, etc.), whether weapons were displayed, whether the suspect was handcuffed, whether the contact was initiated by the government or the suspect, whether or not the suspect was informed of his arrest status and of his freedom to depart, the duration of the detainment, and any suspect movements.

Though the list of evaluative criteria is of indefinable length, one factor was deemed irrelevant by the Supreme Court. In *Stansbury v. California*,[9] the Court held that the subjective impressions — whether possessed by the officer or the suspect — of the custodial status of the interrogated individual were irrelevant to the custodial inquiry. In *Stansbury*, officers investigating a murder went to the defendant's house and knocked on the door, which was opened by the defendant. The officers asked the defendant whether he would agree to accompany them to the police station to answer some questions related to a homicide. The defendant agreed and accompanied the officers in a police vehicle. While at the police station, the defendant was questioned about the murder without being provided with *Miranda*

---

[7]468 U.S. 420 (1984).
[8]516 U.S. 99 (1995).
[9]511 U.S. 318 (1994).

warnings. At the time of the commencement of the interrogation, the officers did not consider the defendant a prime suspect. However, their impression changed during the course of the interrogation after the defendant made a comment that raised the suspicions of the officers.

On appeal, the California Supreme Court found that the defendant was in custody — and was therefore entitled to *Miranda* warnings — once the officers' suspicions focused upon the defendant. Accordingly, the defendant's comments rendered prior to the triggering event — the moment when the interrogating officer's suspicions shifted to the defendant — were admissible, given the inapplicability of the *Miranda* rule during that phase of custodial questioning. The Supreme Court, however, disagreed with this analysis, concluding that the court's consideration of the officers' subjective impressions regarding the suspect's custodial status was improper. Rather, the Court stressed, an individual's custodial status for purposes of *Miranda* should be based upon an objective assessment of the circumstances surrounding the interrogation.

However, the Court did not entirely discount the relevance of an officer's subjective thoughts. According to the Court, an officer's subjective impressions become relevant to the reasonableness inquiry once those impressions have actually been communicated to the interviewee. Once communicated, the interviewee's subjective impressions regarding his arrest status is impacted by the substance of the words spoken. If, for example, an officer conveys to an interviewee that they consider him a suspect, that individual may, in turn, feel more restricted in his freedom of movement. Conversely, an officer who informs an interviewee that he is not a suspect may cause that individual to reasonably believe that he is not in custody.

Consider also the case of *Yarborough v. Alvarado*.[10] There, the police, who were investigating a murder and robbery, informed the parents of a 17-year-old male that they wanted to talk with their son. The parents, in turn, drove their son (hereinafter "defendant") to the police station. There, the defendant was questioned, without the provision of *Miranda* warnings, in a room in the stationhouse while his parents remained in the lobby. Though he initially denied any knowledge of a homicide, the defendant eventually changed course and made some incriminating remarks, which he later sought to suppress. He argued that his statements should have been suppressed given that he was in custody and was interrogated in the absence of *Miranda* warnings.

The trial court found that the defendant was not in custody for *Miranda* purposes. On habeas review, the federal district court agreed with the trial court's conclusion. But the Ninth Circuit disagreed, finding that the defendant was in custody and was entitled to *Miranda* warnings. It found that it was "simply unreasonable to conclude that a reasonable 17-year-old, with no prior history of arrest or police interviews, would have felt that he was at liberty to terminate the interrogation and leave."

The Supreme Court, however, reversed, holding that the state court's application of clearly established federal precedent on the custodial question was reasonable. The Court repeatedly emphasized that the custody inquiry is an objective test and that the subjective viewpoint of the arresting officer is irrelevant to the custody calculus. It declared that "the Court of Appeals ignored the argument that the custody inquiry states an objective rule designed to give clear guidance to the police, while

---

[10]541 U.S. 652 (2004).

consideration of a suspect's individual characteristics — including his age — could be viewed as creating a subjective inquiry." The clarity that comes with an objective test, according to the Court, "ensur[es] that the police do not need to make guesses as to [the circumstances] at issue before deciding how they may interrogate the suspect."

Despite such proclamations, I hesitate to entirely dismiss the relevance of subjective considerations from the reasonableness inquiry. First, as noted, *Yarborough*, which was decided by a narrow 5-4 majority, was a habeas case, in which the Court was required to simply assess whether the state court reasonably applied clearly established federal law when it found that the defendant was not in custody for purposes of *Miranda*. In fact, the Court did not definitively state that consideration of a suspect's age was per se irrelevant to this calculus. Rather, it merely found that the state court's refusal to consider the suspect's age was not "an unreasonable application of clearly established law." Second, *Stansbury* declared that an officer's subjective impressions regarding a suspect's custodial status becomes relevant once they are communicated to that suspect. The reasonableness of that suspect's subjective impression regarding his custodial status (in light of the officer's communicated statements) is undoubtedly impacted by his personal characteristics (e.g., age, mental status, language capacity). Moreover, the line of demarcation between subjective and objective criteria is difficult to draw. As stated by the *Yarborough* Court: "To be sure, the line between permissible objective facts and impermissible subjective experiences can be indistinct in some cases. It is possible to subsume a subjective factor into an objective test by making the latter more specific in its formulation."

Consider also *J.D.B. v. North Carolina*,[11] decided by the Supreme Court in 2011. There, the Court considered whether the age of a juvenile is relevant to a *Miranda* custody analysis. The Court answered this question in the affirmative. In *J.D.B.*, a 13-year-old was removed from his classroom by a uniformed police officer and questioned in a different room at school regarding some residential burglaries. Present within the room were two school officials and two police officers. The interrogation, which lasted a minimum of 30 minutes and produced some incriminating statements, was not preceded by the administration of *Miranda* warnings. In fact, at no time during the session were *Miranda* warnings provided.

The Court acknowledged that the test governing the custody analysis is objective in nature. However, in instances where the minor status of the child is plainly apparent to the interrogating officers (or any reasonable interrogating officer), the Court determined that the age of the juvenile suspect is an appropriate consideration for evaluating custody. In other words, the Court determined that it would be inappropriate, given these circumstances, to assess custody from the perspective of a reasonable adult. As the Court commented:

> In some circumstances, a child's age "would have affected how a reasonable person" in the suspect's position "would perceive his or her freedom to leave." *Stansbury*, 511 U.S., at 325. That is, a reasonable child subjected to police questioning will sometimes feel pressured to submit when a reasonable adult would feel free to go. We think it clear that courts can account for that reality without doing any damage to the objective nature of the custody analysis.

---

[11]131 S. Ct. 2394 (2011).

The Court continued:

> Were the court precluded from taking *J.D.B.*'s youth into account, it would be forced to evaluate the circumstances present here through the eyes of a reasonable person of average years. In other words, how would a reasonable adult understand his situation, after being removed from a seventh-grade social studies class by a uniformed school resource officer; being encouraged by his assistant principal to "do the right thing"; and being warned by a police investigator of the prospect of juvenile detention and separation from his guardian and primary caretaker? To describe such an inquiry is to demonstrate its absurdity. Neither officers nor courts can reasonably evaluate the effect of objective circumstances that, by their nature, are specific to children without accounting for the age of the child subjected to those circumstances.

(2) Custodial Findings — Alternative Contexts

As noted, at the time that *Miranda* was decided, the Court was largely preoccupied with the interrogation practices of officers in police-dominated atmospheres. Yet in the years since *Miranda*, the Court has found custody for *Miranda* purposes in settings beyond the four walls of the police station. And it has even failed to find custody when the interrogation occurs in a police-dominated environment.

(a) Police Station Interviews

In *Yarborough v. Alvarado*[12] (a habeas case discussed earlier in this chapter), the Court found that a 17-year-old suspect who was questioned by police was not in custody, despite the fact that the interrogation occurred within a police station. The Court reasoned, in part, that the suspect was transported to the station not by the police but by his parents and, during the interview, he was neither threatened nor informed that he was under arrest, he was offered the opportunity to take a break from the questioning, and he was allowed to leave and return home at the conclusion of the session. In light of these factors, the Court held that the state court did not unreasonably find that the *Miranda* custody requirement was not satisfied.

Similarly, in *Oregon v. Mathiason*,[13] the Court found that the defendant, a parolee who was interrogated at a police station in regards to a residential theft, was not in custody given that his arrival at the station was voluntary, that upon his arrival the police informed him that he was not under arrest, and that he was allowed to leave the station at the conclusion of the questioning, which lasted 30 minutes. In reaching this result, the Court declared that *Miranda* warnings are not required merely because the location of the interrogation is a police station or the individual interrogated is deemed by the police to be a suspect.

The Court reached the same result in *California v. Beheler*.[14] There, the Court found that the defendant, a murder suspect who was interrogated at a police station, was not in custody for purposes of *Miranda*. Referring to *Mathiason* as a case "remarkably similar to the present case," the Court summarily found that the defendant's "freedom was not restricted in any way whatsoever," noting, in part, that the initial communication between the defendant and law enforcement was instigated

---

[12]541 U.S. 652 (2004).
[13]429 U.S. 492 (1977).
[14]463 U.S. 1121 (1983).

not by the police but by the defendant himself (who called the police to inform them of the subject homicide).

(b) Non-Police-Department Settings: Residential, Probation Department, and Prison Interrogations

The Court has found the custody requirement satisfied in residential contexts. Consider *Orozco v. Texas*,[15] where the Supreme Court held that a murder suspect who was interrogated by four officers in his bedroom at a boardinghouse at 4 A.M. was in custody for purposes of *Miranda*. Quoting *Miranda*, the *Orozco* Court declared that *Miranda* warnings are required whenever an individual is "in custody at the station or otherwise deprived of his freedom of action in any significant way." The Court noted that the officer testified that the defendant, during the bedroom interrogation, was under arrest and was not free to leave the area.

In another residential interrogation case, however, the Court reached a different result. In *Beckwith v. United States*,[16] two IRS agents interrogated the defendant, not in his bedroom during the early morning hours as in *Orozco*, but instead in his residential dining room at 8 A.M. Despite the fact that the IRS investigation was singularly focused upon the defendant and his possible criminal tax fraud activities, the Court dismissed this fact, stating that the *Miranda* custody inquiry was dependent not upon the investigative focus of the officers, but upon whether the individual interrogated had been formally taken into custody or had a significant curtailment of his freedom of action. "Although the 'focus' of an investigation may indeed have been on [the defendant] at the time of the interview in the sense that it was his tax liability which was under scrutiny, he hardly found himself in the custodial situation described by the *Miranda* Court as the basis for its holding. *Miranda* implicitly defined 'focus,' for its purposes, as 'questioning initiated by law enforcement officers *after* a person has been taken into custody or otherwise deprived of his freedom of action in any significant way.'"

The Supreme Court has also addressed the custody question in the context of an interview of a probationer by his probation officer. In *Minnesota v. Murphy*,[17] the Court found that a defendant who was on probation for a criminal offense was not entitled to have suppressed incriminating statements he made to his probation officer in her office regarding a separate criminal matter (rape and murder). The Court found that the defendant was not in custody, even though he was required, pursuant to his probation agreement, to meet with his probation officer and to be truthful during their sessions, and the probation officer was cognizant of the defendant's involvement in the rape and murder prior to questioning him about these events. The Court further explained that a probation interview differs from a custodial arrest. It noted that a "[c]ustodial arrest is said to convey to the suspect a message that he has no choice but to submit to the officer's will and to confess (citation omitted). It is unlikely that a probation interview, arranged by appointment at a mutually convenient time, would give rise to a similar impression." The Court added that the regularity of the probationer's meetings with his officer in her office

---

[15]394 U.S. 324 (1969).
[16]425 U.S. 341 (1976).
[17]465 U.S. 420 (1984).

would "insulate" him from the psychological pressures that often accompany custodial interrogation sessions.

In *Howes v. Fields*,[18] the Supreme Court rendered its most recent pronouncement regarding the issue of *Miranda* custody in the context of prison interrogations.
There, the Court held on habeas review that the Sixth Circuit had erroneously concluded that the Supreme Court had clearly established that "*Miranda* warnings must
be administered when law enforcement officers remove an inmate from the general
prison population and interrogate him regarding criminal conduct that took place
outside the jail or prison."

In *Fields*, the defendant, who was serving a term of imprisonment, was escorted
by prison officials to a conference room within the prison where he was interviewed
by two law enforcement personnel for several hours regarding a separate criminal
incident that occurred prior to his incarceration. The defendant uttered incriminating statements during this session.

The Court emphasized that it had not established the bright-line rule suggested
by the Sixth Circuit, or any bright-line rule in the prison context. In support, the Court
referenced, among other cases, *Maryland v. Shatzer*,[19] where the Court noted that it
had "*never* decided whether incarceration constitutes custody for *Miranda* purposes,
and have indeed explicitly declined to address the issue." Moreover, the Court
declared that though the measures delineated in *Miranda* were intended to combat
the coercive pressures attendant to custodial questioning,

> *Miranda* did not hold that such pressures are always present when a prisoner is taken
> aside and questioned about events outside the prison walls. Indeed, *Miranda* did not even
> establish that police questioning of a suspect at the station house is always custodial.

The *Fields* Court also reasoned that the interrogation of individuals already
incarcerated does not involve the "shock" that frequently accompanies an arrest.
In the typical arrest scenario, the Court noted, an individual's arrest, followed by his
transport to a police station and subsequent interrogation by law enforcement, constitutes a significant change in an individual's circumstances, which may render him
more susceptible to "coercive pressures." Such is not the case with individuals who
are already jailed. In addition, the Court submitted that "a prisoner, unlike a person
who has not been sentenced to a term of incarceration, is unlikely to be lured into
speaking by a longing for prompt release" and likely "knows that the law enforcement officers who question him probably lack the authority to affect the duration of
his sentence."

Finally, the Court concluded that the facts presented indicated that the
defendant was not in custody for purposes of *Miranda*. The Court acknowledged
that facts existed that were suggestive of custody. However, the Court maintained
that these facts were outweighed by others. The Court noted, inter alia, that the
defendant was informed more than once that he could leave the interrogation
room and return to his cell, that he was neither restrained nor threatened, that the
interview took place in an average-sized room, that the defendant was seemingly
comfortable, that he had been offered food and water, and that the door was open on
occasion.

---

[18]565 U.S. _____ (2012).
[19]130 S. Ct. 1213 (2010). This case will be discussed later in this chapter.

(3) The Interrogation Requirement

As noted, *Miranda* warnings are not mandated unless an individual in custody is interrogated. Thus, it is essential to understand what is meant by the term "interrogation."

The Supreme Court addressed this question in *Rhode Island v. Innis*.[20] The Court held that *Miranda* warnings must be provided whenever an individual "is subjected to either express questioning or its functional equivalent." Express questioning is comparatively easy to identify. It refers to situations where law enforcement poses questions to suspects that are plainly designed to elicit incriminating responses. More difficult questions arise, however, when the police interrogation methods are something other than express. In such situations, a court must ascertain whether the challenged conduct of the police amounted to the "functional equivalent" of express questioning.

In *Innis*, for example, the police arrested the defendant, who was suspected of having committed an armed robbery. After being advised of his *Miranda* warnings, the defendant expressed his desire to speak with an attorney. The defendant was then placed in a police vehicle for the purpose of transporting him to a police station. While en route, two officers, while in the presence of the defendant, talked to each other. One of the officers stated that there were many handicapped children in a certain area located near a school and "God forbid" that a child might discover the weapon used in the robbery and harm himself. The defendant then interjected himself and informed the officers that he wanted to show them where the weapon used in the robbery could be located. After being re-advised of his *Miranda* rights, the defendant affirmed his comprehension but stated that he "wanted to get the gun out of the way because of the kids in the area in the school." The defendant then led the police to the weapon.

The Supreme Court rejected the defendant's claim that the officers violated his *Miranda* rights when they engaged in the aforementioned conversation. The Court rather summarily found that the defendant had not been interrogated.[21] In so holding, the Court explained that the functional equivalent of interrogation occurs whenever the "words or actions on the part of the police (other than those normally attendant to arrest and custody)" cause a reasonable police officer to know that his words or actions "are reasonably likely to elicit an incriminating response from the suspect." The Court added that it is the perspective of the interrogated individual from which this assessment is undertaken. It follows then that the perspective and the underlying intent of the interrogating officer typically are without relevance to this inquiry.

However, the Court added that an officer's knowledge of the particular traits or susceptibilities of an interrogated individual remains a relevant consideration. As noted, the standard focuses upon the reasonableness of an officer's knowledge regarding the impact of his words or actions upon a suspect. Given this standard, an officer's cognizance of the peculiarities of a particular individual can affect the

---

[20]446 U.S. 291 (1980).
[21]Specifically, the Court found "that the entire conversation appears to have consisted of no more than a few off hand remarks," that the conversation was between the two officers and no response from the defendant "was invited," and the record was devoid of any evidence suggesting that the officers were cognizant of any personal trait rendering the defendant susceptible to this form of manipulation. Therefore, the Court concluded, "we cannot say that the officers should have known that it was reasonably likely that [the defendant] would so respond."

reasonableness of his knowledge base. Thus, an officer whose conversation or conduct might not ordinarily be expected to elicit an incriminating response might engage in the functional equivalent of interrogation if a reasonable officer should have known that her words or conduct might affect a particular individual in a way different from most members of the population.

(4) Exceptions to the *Miranda* Interrogation Requirement

The Supreme Court has identified some categories of custodial interrogation where police questioning is permitted without the provision of *Miranda* warnings.

(a) Undercover Interrogation

One such exception is for questioning posed by officers acting in an undercover capacity. *Illinois v. Perkins*[23] involved a defendant who was in a jail cell along with an undercover agent who was posing as a fellow inmate. When asked by the agent whether he had ever killed anyone, the defendant uttered several incriminating statements. The defendant argued that his *Miranda* rights were violated, given that he was questioned by a police officer while in police custody.

The Supreme Court rejected this argument. The Court reasoned that a primary objective of *Miranda* — "to preserve the privilege during 'incommunicado interrogation of individuals in a police-dominated atmosphere'" — is simply not present in the context of surreptitious interrogations. The Court declared that the "inherently compelling pressures" that the *Miranda* warnings were designed to combat are "not present" when a jailed individual believes that he is merely conversing with another cellmate. In contrast to interrogations with known officers, jailed individuals who converse with others similarly situated have no reason to suspect that such individuals possess any authority to influence their fate.

ARIZONA v. MAURO: NO FUNCTIONAL EQUIVALENT OF INTERROGATION

Arizona v. Mauro[22] is another instance where the police obtained an incriminating response from a custodial defendant without implicating *Miranda*. There, the defendant had been arrested for killing his son. After being advised of his *Miranda* rights, the defendant declined to answer questions citing his desire to have an attorney. The defendant was then placed in the police captain's office. The defendant's wife was interrogated in a room separate from that of her husband. After insisting that she be allowed to talk to her husband, the police eventually agreed, provided that an officer was present. During the ensuing meeting, an officer placed a tape recorder in plain view of the defendant and his wife. Incriminating statements were uttered during the meeting. The Supreme Court found that the police did not engage in interrogation within the meaning of *Miranda*. In so holding, the Court reasoned, in part, that the officer did not pose any questions regarding the crime during the meeting, that the meeting was the product of the wife's "insistent demands," and that the meeting was not part of a psychological ploy on the part of law enforcement. The Court also found that, when viewed from the perspective of the defendant, it "doubt[ed] that a suspect, told by officers that his wife will be allowed to speak to him, would feel that he was being coerced to incriminate himself in any way."

---

[22]481 U.S. 520 (1987).

(b) Public Safety

A second exception to the *Miranda* warnings requirement is the public safety exception. Under this exception, the provision of *Miranda* warnings is forgiven whenever the police reasonably believe that such questioning is necessary in

---

[23]496 U.S. 292 (1990).

S i d e b a r

***MASSIAH v. UNITED STATES*: UNDERCOVER INTERROGATION UNDER THE SIXTH AMENDMENT**

Chapter 19 will discuss interrogations that implicate an individual's Sixth Amendment rights. However, an important distinction regarding the propriety of undercover interrogation under the Fifth and Sixth Amendments is worthy of brief mention in this chapter. Whereas *Illinois v. Perkins* held that undercover interrogation of custodial suspects did not implicate *Miranda,* such activity is flatly prohibited under the Sixth Amendment. Upon the commencement of adversary proceedings, the Sixth Amendment right to counsel is triggered and any undercover interrogation performed thereafter violates an individual's constitutional protection. *Massiah v. United States*[24] is the seminal case regarding this Sixth Amendment principle and will be discussed at greater length in Chapter 19.

[24]377 U.S. 201 (1964).

order to safeguard the public and/or the police from danger. This rule was enunciated in *New York v. Quarles,*[25] which involved a confrontation between an officer and the defendant after the police received a report that an individual matching the defendant's description had recently committed a rape and possessed a firearm. After chasing the defendant in a supermarket, one of the responding officers seized the defendant, frisked him, discovered that his shoulder holster was empty, and then handcuffed him. The officer, without providing *Miranda* warnings, then inquired about the location of the firearm. The defendant's response led the officer to the discovery of the weapon.

Upholding the admissibility of the defendant's statement, the Court recognized that a social cost associated with the *Miranda* rule is that convictions might be more difficult to obtain. Individuals cognizant of their rights to remain silent and to counsel might elect to invoke these rights, thereby depriving the government of potentially useful evidence. The *Miranda* Court was willing to accept such costs.

However, the emergency situation in *Quarles* presented a more challenging—and potentially costly—set of circumstances, Aside from the exclusion of relevant statements at trial, the concealment of the firearm presented a volatile public safety hazard. To require the rendition of *Miranda* warnings in such emergency situations, the Court concluded, would place the police in an "untenable" situation. They could provide the warnings and potentially further compromise a public safety hazard or forgo the warnings in order to further public peace and risk the later substantive use of such a confession at trial. This was a choice that the Court was unwilling to impose. The Court noted that "police officers can and will distinguish almost instinctively between questions necessary to secure their own safety or the safety of the public and questions designed solely to elicit testimonial evidence from a suspect."

(c) Booking Questions

In *Pennsylvania v. Muniz,*[26] the Supreme Court exempted routine booking questions from the *Miranda* rule. In *Muniz,* officers transported the defendant to a booking center after he had been arrested on suspicion of driving while under the influence of alcohol. While there, an officer asked the defendant several biographical questions regarding his name, address, height, weight, eye color, date of birth, and current age. The Court held that such questioning, which was performed in the absence of *Miranda* warnings, is permissible. It reasoned that such questions do not satisfy the *Innis* interrogation standard given that they are not designed to elicit

[25]467 U.S. 649 (1984).
[26]496 U.S. 582 (1990).

an incriminating response. Instead, the Court found that such routine booking questions—designed to obtain "biographical data necessary to complete booking or pretrial services"—are administrative in nature and are, thus, exempted from the *Miranda* rule.

B. The Sufficiency of *Miranda* Warnings, the Waiver of Rights, and the Invocation of Rights

(1) Sufficiency of Warnings

Just as an individual subjected to custodial interrogation enjoys a Fifth Amendment right to receive *Miranda* warnings, he also possesses the authority to waive such rights. The government bears, according to the *Miranda* Court, a "heavy burden" of proof regarding the waiver of such rights. Thus, when confronted with a *Miranda* challenge, the government must demonstrate not only that the requisite warnings were provided, but that they were knowingly, intelligently, and voluntarily waived by the interrogated individual.

With respect to the sufficiency of the provided warnings, the Supreme Court does not require a verbatim recitation of the rights as delineated in the *Miranda* opinion. What is essential, however, is that the substance of the *Miranda* rights be effectively conveyed. As the Court stated in *California v. Prysock*,[27] the Supreme Court has never held, including in *Miranda* itself, that compliance with the *Miranda* requirement demands strict adherence to a scripted set of warnings. Thus, the substance of the warnings provided trumps the literal text when it comes to satisfaction of the *Miranda* requirements.

An example of this can be seen in *Florida v. Powell*.[28] There, a defendant who had been arrested and transported to a police station in Tampa was interrogated. Prior to his interrogation, he was provided with the following set of warnings:

> You have the right to remain silent. If you give up the right to remain silent, anything you say can be used against you in court. *You have the right to talk to a lawyer before answering any of our questions.* If you cannot afford to hire a lawyer, one will be appointed for you without cost and before any questioning. *You have the right to use any of these rights at any time you want during this interview.*

Following the conveyance of these rights, the defendant acknowledged his understanding, waived his rights, and made incriminating remarks.

As noted earlier in this chapter, the *Miranda* warnings include the right to an attorney. Expounding upon the meaning of this right, the *Miranda* Court explained that prior to any custodial interrogation an individual "must be clearly informed that he has the right to consult with a lawyer and to have the lawyer with him during interrogation." At issue in *Powell* was whether the defendant was adequately informed of this right.

By a 7-2 margin, the Court found that the warnings provided by the Tampa police, when considered together, reasonably conveyed the substance of the subject

---

[27]453 U.S. 355 (1981).
[28]130 S. Ct. 1195 (2010).

Miranda right: namely, that he had the right to have counsel present throughout any governmental interrogation. The Court noted that while the *Miranda* rights themselves "are invariable," greater latitude is permitted with respect to the manner by which those rights are conveyed. Thus, when assessing such sufficiency challenges, the central issue is whether the requisite *Miranda* warnings were reasonably conveyed. And the Court found that this standard was satisfied in *Powell*. The majority declared that a "commonsense reading" of the italicized sentences in the previous quote (the first and third sentences) informed the defendant of his right to have counsel present both prior to and during any police interrogations.

(2) Sufficiency of *Miranda* Waiver

A separate sufficiency question concerns the adequacy of a purported *Miranda* waiver. Assuming the government can establish that a defendant's *Miranda* rights had been reasonably conveyed, it must then demonstrate, by a preponderance of the evidence, that any resulting statements were the product of a knowing, intelligent, and voluntary waiver.

The government's proof will be assessed pursuant to a totality of the circumstances standard. When reviewing the government's proof, a court may consider a host of factors, including, but not limited to, traits pertinent to the defendant (e.g., language proficiency, educational attainment, mental capacity, youth status, criminal record, etc.), the conduct of the government interrogators (e.g., the quantity of officers present, the manner in which the *Miranda* rights were read and the waiver was obtained, whether weapons were displayed, whether deception was employed, etc.), and environmental conditions (e.g., the location of the challenged encounter, weather conditions, etc.).

However, before a waiver can be deemed valid the government is saddled with a "heavy burden" and must present at least some affirmative evidence that reflects the defendant's intent to waive his *Miranda* protections. The *Miranda* Court declared that a waiver of rights "will not be presumed simply from the silence of the accused," nor by evidence that the provision of warnings was followed by a confession. The Court further stated:

Sidebar

THE MEANING OF KNOWING, INTELLIGENT, AND VOLUNTARY

The Supreme Court, in *Moran v. Burbine*, 475 U.S. 412 (1986), elaborated upon the meaning of the terms "knowing, intelligent, and voluntary." The Court stated that in order for a *Miranda* waiver to be valid, the right relinquished must be voluntary. It explained that the choice to waive must be "the product of a free and deliberate choice," and not one that stems from police "intimidation, coercion, or deception." The Court further declared that a valid waiver requires an individual's "full awareness" of the essence of the right he is electing to forgo as well as the consequences that flow from that decision. "Only if the 'totality of the circumstances surrounding the interrogation' reveals both an uncoerced choice and the requisite level of comprehension may a court properly conclude that the *Miranda* rights have been waived."

Moreover, where in-custody interrogation is involved, there is no room for the contention that the privilege is waived if the individual answers some questions or gives some information on his own prior to invoking his right to remain silent when interrogated.

Whatever the testimony of the authorities as to waiver of rights by an accused, the fact of lengthy interrogation or incommunicado incarceration before a statement is made is strong evidence that the accused did not validly waive his rights. In these circumstances, the fact that the individual eventually made a statement is consistent with the conclusion that the compelling influence of the interrogation finally forced him to do so.

As noted, the Court made clear that an express waiver of rights would certainly suffice. A defendant who flatly declares, "I understand my *Miranda* rights, I agree to waive them and to talk with you," is certainly strong evidence of a valid waiver.

But what about situations where custodial suspects do not necessarily speak as forthrightly? Can a valid waiver be found in the absence of an explicit waiver? The Supreme Court addressed this situation in *North Carolina v. Butler*.[29] There, the Court held that evidence of a valid *Miranda* waiver can derive from evidence that is either explicit or implicit. Even when a defendant remains silent after the provision of rights, such evidence does not necessarily preclude a finding of a valid waiver. The *Butler* Court declared that a "defendant's silence, coupled with an understanding of his rights and a course of conduct indicating waiver" would also be sufficient.

Consider also the case of *Berghuis v. Thompkins*.[30] This case represents a significant shift away from the stringent requirements attendant to the finding of a valid waiver originally detailed in *Miranda*. There, a murder suspect (the defendant) was arrested and provided with a form that detailed his *Miranda* rights. The defendant complied with a police request to verbally read a portion of the *Miranda* rights form, but he refused their request to sign the form acknowledging his understanding of his rights. There was conflicting evidence regarding the suspect's verbal confirmation of his understanding of his *Miranda* rights.

Thereafter, an interrogation that ultimately lasted three hours commenced. During the interrogation, the defendant remained "largely silent," and never expressed a desire to invoke his right to remain silent or his right to counsel. After approximately 2 hours and 45 minutes of questioning, the defendant was asked about his belief in God. That question was followed by two additional questions. To each of these three questions the defendant uttered only a single word: "yes." However, it was his response to the last of the three questions that was incriminating and implicated the defendant in the murder.[31] At trial, he unsuccessfully attempted to suppress his remarks, arguing, inter alia, that he never waived his *Miranda* rights. The issue regarding the validity of his waiver eventually reached the Supreme Court via a habeas petition.

The Court rejected his contention, concluding that the defendant validly waived his right to remain silent. First, the Court found that there was "no basis" to find that he did not comprehend his *Miranda* warnings. The Court noted that there was no dispute among the parties regarding his comprehension. Next, the Court found that his responses to the line of questions regarding God constituted "'a course of conduct indicating waiver' of the right to remain silent." As the Court explained:

> If [the defendant] wanted to remain silent, he could have said nothing in response to [the officer's] questions, or he could have unambiguously invoked his *Miranda* rights and ended the interrogation. The fact that [the defendant] made a statement about three hours after receiving a *Miranda* warning does not overcome the fact that he engaged in a course of conduct indicating waiver.

---

[29]441 U.S. 369 (1979).
[30]130 S. Ct. 2250 (2010).
[31]The Court described the interrogation as follows:
> About 2 hours and 45 minutes into the interrogation, Helgert asked [the defendant], "Do you believe in God?" [The defendant] made eye contact with Helgert and said "Yes," as his eyes "well[ed] up with tears." Helgert asked, "Do you pray to God?" [The defendant] said "Yes." Helgert asked, "Do you pray to God to forgive you for shooting that boy down?" [The defendant] answered "Yes" and looked away. [The defendant] refused to make a written confession, and the interrogation ended about 15 minutes later.

Thus, the Court found that the defendant's waiver was valid given that he was provided his *Miranda* warnings, it was demonstrated that he comprehended the safeguards, and he responded to the questions posed. It further held that officers need not postpone their interrogation until a waiver has been obtained. Instead, interrogation can commence once the requisite warnings have been provided and it has been established that the suspect understands his rights.

In the end, *Berghuis* has imposed an affirmative obligation upon custodial suspects to speak up and invoke their right to remain silent if they, in fact, desire not to be interrogated and not to speak with the government. In its absence, the government remains free to interrogate a suspect. And any responsive utterance—even, apparently, a single monosyllabic word—may constitute an effective waiver of *Miranda* rights. As stated by the Court, "[A] suspect who has received and understood the *Miranda* warnings, and has not invoked his *Miranda* rights, waives the right to remain silent by making an uncoerced statement to the police." According to Justice Sotomayor, writing in dissent on behalf of Justices Stevens, Ginsburg, and Breyer, the decision in *Berghuis* constitutes a "substantial retreat from the protections" provided by *Miranda* and "turns *Miranda* upside down."

F   A   Q

Q: Does a suspect's ignorance regarding the topics of the impending interrogation or of the efforts by his attorney to contact him influence the validity of a *Miranda* waiver?

A: No to both questions. In *Colorado v. Spring*,[32] the Supreme Court held that knowledge of the possible topical areas of interrogation is irrelevant to a determination of whether a suspect's waiver of *Miranda* rights was knowing and voluntary. The Court stated that while such awareness might impact the "wisdom of a *Miranda* waiver," it does not impact the knowledge and voluntariness of the waiver itself.

The Supreme Court also held in *Moran v. Burbine*[33] that the knowledge and voluntariness of a *Miranda* waiver is not undermined by a suspect's ignorance of an attorney's efforts to contact him. The Court reasoned that a suspect's knowledge of his *Miranda* rights is not impacted by outside events of which he has no knowledge. "[W]e have never read the Constitution to require that the police supply a suspect with a flow of information to help him calibrate his self interest in deciding whether to speak or stand by his rights."

(3) Invocation of *Miranda* Rights

The preceding two subsections dealt with the issues concerning the *provision* of *Miranda* warnings and the *waiver* of those rights. An issue of critical importance— particularly given the Court's decision in *Berghuis*—is determining whether a *Miranda* right has been properly invoked. Remember, there are two *Miranda* rights—the right to counsel and the right to remain silent. What guidance has the

---

[32]479 U.S. 564 (1987).
[33]475 U.S. 412 (1986).

Supreme Court provided regarding the invocation of these rights? The next two subsections will discuss these topics.

(a) Invocation of the Right to Counsel

The Supreme Court in *Davis v. United States*[34] held that a defendant does not invoke his *Miranda* right to counsel unless his request is unambiguous. The Court explained that an individual "must articulate his desire to have counsel present sufficiently clearly that a reasonable police officer in the circumstances would understand the statement to be a request for an attorney. If the statement fails to meet the requisite level of clarity," then an officer can continue with his interrogation.

Davis involved a situation where the defendant had initially waived his *Miranda* rights, had answered several questions, and then stated "Maybe I should talk to a lawyer." Thereafter, a conversation ensued in an attempt to ascertain whether or not the defendant sought the assistance of counsel. After indicating that he did not want an attorney, the interrogation eventually continued. About an hour after the resumption of questioning, the defendant stated, "I think I want a lawyer before I say anything else." Thereafter, no additional questions were posed.

The defendant sought to suppress the statements made after he uttered "Maybe I should talk to a lawyer." The Supreme Court rejected his claim. In reaching this conclusion, the Court found that his request for counsel was equivocal, and thus insufficient to trigger his *Miranda* counsel right. The Court noted that Supreme Court precedent (additional discussion on this in the next subsection) requires the cessation of additional questioning whenever a suspect requests the presence of counsel. However, to trigger this protection, the Court explained that the counsel request must be clear and unequivocal:

> [I]f we were to require questioning to cease if a suspect makes a statement that *might* be a request for an attorney, this clarity and ease of application would be lost. Police officers would be forced to make difficult judgment calls about whether the suspect in fact wants a lawyer even though he has not said so, with the threat of suppression if they guess wrong. We therefore hold that, after a knowing and voluntary waiver of the *Miranda* rights, law enforcement officers may continue questioning until and unless the suspect clearly requests an attorney.

(b) Questioning After Invocation of the *Miranda* Right to Counsel

When a defendant has invoked his *Miranda* right to counsel, the Supreme Court has adopted a more stringent standard regarding police interrogation than that applicable in the right to silence context. Back in 1981, the Supreme Court in *Edwards v. Arizona*[35] announced a bright-line rule that forbade any additional questioning of a suspect once he had invoked his *Miranda* right to counsel. The Court declared that an individual who invoked this right could not be interrogated further until either counsel had been provided or the suspect had initiated a resumption of communications with law enforcement. Any waiver obtained after a subsequent interrogation was presumed to be involuntary.

Pursuant to *Edwards*, therefore, the resumption of custodial interrogation was permissible in only two instances: 1) if counsel was present; or 2) if the suspect

[34]512 U.S. 452 (1994).
[35]451 U.S. 477 (1981).

personally initiated communications with the police. Even in these circumstances, the government retains the burden of demonstrating a valid waiver. If, for example, a defendant initiated a resumption of talks with law enforcement, the government would bear the burden of demonstrating that the defendant, not the government, initiated the contact, that *Miranda* warnings were subsequently provided, and that any statements were the product of a knowing, intelligent, and voluntary waiver of his rights.[36]

F   A   Q

Q: Does the *Edwards* rule prohibit the reinitiation of interrogation once the suspect has met with his counsel? Also, does the *Edwards* rule prohibit the police from interrogating a suspect about crimes unrelated to the underlying arrest?

A: Yes to both questions. The Supreme Court held in *Minnick v. Mississippi*[37] that the police may not reinitiate questioning of a suspect who has requested counsel, even if the suspect has met with his attorney. Counsel must be present before questioning can be reinitiated. The Court reasoned that an attorney consultation does nothing to safeguard a suspect from the inherent coercive pressures attendant to his custodial status (which sometimes increase with time) or from subsequent sustained law enforcement attempts to obtain a waiver of his counsel right.

In *Arizona v. Roberson*,[38] the Supreme Court held that the *Edwards* rule cannot be overcome even if the officers later approach the suspect to discuss a wholly unrelated criminal offense. In other words, the *Miranda* right to counsel is not specific to the offense. Once invoked, officers are prohibited from re-approaching a suspect and interrogating him about any criminal matter.

In 2010, the Supreme Court decided *Maryland v. Shatzer*,[39] which modified— and softened—the *Edwards* rule. In *Shatzer*, the Court addressed whether the *Edwards* presumption of involuntariness survived when the police re-interrogated the defendant after an extended break in his custodial status. The Court ultimately concluded that the *Edwards* presumption no longer applied after a 14-day break in custody. In *Shatzer*, the defendant had been questioned while in prison regarding a sexual assault. After having been provided his *Miranda* warnings, the defendant exercised his right to counsel. Over two years later, the defendant was questioned again while in prison regarding the same offense. This time the defendant waived his *Miranda* rights and made an incriminating remark.

The Court recognized that underlying *Edwards* was a concern regarding the coercive influences of uninterrupted custody upon an individual's exercise of his right to counsel. As stated by the *Shatzer* Court, "It is easy to believe that a suspect may be coerced or badgered into abandoning his earlier refusal to be questioned without counsel in the paradigm *Edwards* case. That is a case in which the suspect has been arrested for a particular crime and is held in uninterrupted pretrial custody

---

[36]The hypothetical assumes that the subsequent statements were the product of re-interrogation as opposed to spontaneous declarations.
[37]498 U.S. 146 (1990).
[38]486 U.S. 675 (1988).
[39]130 S. Ct. 1213 (2010).

while that crime is being actively investigated." However, the Court concluded that where the custodial break extends to at least 14 days, the influences of concern in *Edwards* have sufficiently dissipated. The Court reasoned, in part, that after 14 days on noncustodial status an individual has had "plenty of time . . . to get reacclimated to his normal life, to consult with friends and counsel, and to shake off any residual coercive effects of his prior custody."

(c) Invocation of Right to Silence

In the years after *Davis v. United States*, an open question remained regarding whether the *Davis* unambiguous request standard should be applicable in the right to remain silent context. The Court finally answered this question — affirmatively — in *Berghuis v. Thompkins*.[40]

In *Berghuis* the Court declared, "[T]here is no principled reason to adopt different standards for determining when an accused has invoked the *Miranda* right to remain silent and the *Miranda* right to counsel." The Court reasoned that the requirement of an unambiguous invocation would produce an "objective inquiry" that would give clear guidance to interrogating officers. In the Court's view, a standard that disallows questioning in the face of ambiguous invocations would only marginally further *Miranda*'s underlying purpose of lessening the compulsive influences of custodial interrogation. Yet, the Court continued, suppression of voluntary incriminating statements "significant[ly] burden[s]" the public interest in effective law enforcement. Had the defendant made "simple, unambiguous statements" indicating a desire to remain silent or not to converse with the police, the interrogation would have ceased. Because he failed to make such requests, the Court found that the defendant did not invoke his right to remain silent.

(d) Questioning After Invocation of the *Miranda* Right to Remain Silent

Assume that a defendant has properly invoked his *Miranda* right to remain silent. Are the police forever barred from attempting to interrogate such an individual? In short, the answer is no. The police are permitted to re-interrogate a suspect who has invoked his right to remain silent provided that the police have "scrupulously honored" the exercise of this right. As you read further in this chapter, notice how the rule regarding interrogation in this context differs from the rules pronounced in *Edwards* and *Shatzer* in the right to counsel setting.

Michigan v. Mosley[41] involved a defendant who had invoked his right to remain silent. There, the defendant had been arrested, been provided with *Miranda* warnings, and expressed his desire not to talk with law enforcement. No further attempts were made to interrogate him until approximately two hours later. At that time, the defendant was re-Mirandized and questioned by a different officer about a crime unrelated to the events leading up to his arrest. This time the defendant waived his right to remain silent and made incriminating remarks.

The Court upheld the admission of the defendant's statements. Citing *Miranda*, the Court stated that whenever and however an individual indicates a desire to invoke his right to remain silent, law enforcement must respect that choice and refrain from further interrogation. The Court added that statements obtained after

---

[40]130 S. Ct. 2250 (2010).
[41]423 U.S. 96 (1975).

such an invocation would be deemed to be compelled. Despite the arguably broad sweep of this language, however, the *Mosley* Court held that *Miranda* is not violated by a resumption of interrogation provided that the defendant's initial exercise of his right to remain silent is "scrupulously honored."

Though no bright-line standards were established in *Mosley*, the Court found that the defendant's rights were properly respected in this instance. It noted that the case before the Court did not involve a situation where law enforcement failed to respect the wishes of an individual who requested the cessation of interrogation. Rather, the Court observed, the police had refrained from further questioning after the defendant's initial invocation, had waited two hours before re-approaching the defendant, and had provided a second set of *Miranda* warnings. Additionally, the subject matter of the second interrogation differed from that which motivated the initial attempt.

C. The *Miranda* Exclusionary Rule and the Fruit of the Poisonous Tree Doctrine

(1) The *Miranda* Exclusionary Rule

It was noted that in the Fourth Amendment context, the scope of the exclusionary rule principle operates to bar not only the evidence directly obtained as a result of the constitutional infraction but also any derivative fruits. Though vigorous proponents of the exclusionary principle have undoubtedly been dismayed by the various limitations the Court has placed upon the rule—especially in recent years—the exclusionary rule and its accompanying fruits doctrine, at least in principle, remain intact. Yet whatever one's opinion regarding the current status of the Fourth Amendment exclusionary rule, the scope of the principle in the *Miranda* context is unquestionably more restrictive.

As noted, statements obtained in violation of *Miranda* cannot be used substantively at trial. In the words of the *Miranda* Court, "The warnings required and the waiver necessary . . . are . . . prerequisites to the admissibility of any statement made by a defendant." In this respect, the exclusionary doctrine operates in a manner completely congruous with its operation in the Fourth Amendment context. A breach of either the Fourth Amendment or the *Miranda* standards results in the exclusion of the evidence that is immediately derived from the infraction.

(2) The Fruit of the Poisonous Tree Doctrine

In contrast to the Fourth Amendment context, the fruit of the poisonous tree doctrine in the *Miranda* context is, to put it mildly, noticeably more tailored. In fact, it can be persuasively argued that the fruits doctrine has no application whatsoever to *Miranda* claims.

(a) *Oregon v. Elstad:* Verbal Fruits

Oregon v. Elstad[43] involved a situation where a defendant's earlier unwarned confession preceded a later confession obtained after the provision of *Miranda* warnings. Specifically, the police, armed with an arrest warrant, entered the defendant's residence and interrogated him therein in the absence of *Miranda* warnings. During this interrogation, the defendant made an incriminating remark. He was later transported to the police station. While there, the police read him his *Miranda* rights, which the defendant waived. The defendant then provided the police with a more detailed account of his criminal activities. At issue was "whether an initial failure of law enforcement officers to administer the warnings required by *Miranda* (citation omitted) without more, 'taints' subsequent admissions made after a suspect has been fully advised of and has waived his *Miranda* rights." Despite the earlier *Miranda* violation, the Court refused to suppress the later confession.

The Court observed that a violation of *Miranda* creates a "presumption of compulsion." Thus, a statement that may be "patently voluntary" under general Fifth Amendment principles is subject to suppression under *Miranda* simply on account of a procedural failure (e.g., failure to administer the required warnings). Given the vast scope of the *Miranda* exclusionary principle, however, the Court reasoned that it does not follow that the fruits stemming from such procedural violations are "inherently tainted." As stated by the Court:

> It is an unwarranted extension of *Miranda* to hold that a simple failure to administer the warnings, unaccompanied by any actual coercion or other circumstances calculated to undermine the suspect's ability to exercise his free will, so taints the investigatory process that a subsequent voluntary and informed waiver is ineffective for some indeterminate period. Though *Miranda* requires that the unwarned admission must be suppressed, the admissibility of any subsequent statement should turn in these circumstances solely on whether it is knowingly and voluntarily made.

Now, it is important to remember that *Elstad* was decided prior to *Dickerson v. United States*,[44] which held that *Miranda* was a constitutional decision. This is notable given language in *Elstad* that seemingly distinguished *Miranda* from Fifth Amendment violations. The Court noted, for example, that "[t]he *Miranda* exclusionary rule . . . serves the Fifth Amendment and sweeps more broadly than the Fifth Amendment itself. It may be triggered even in the absence of a Fifth Amendment violation." And it further declared that "unwarned statements that are otherwise voluntary within the meaning of the Fifth Amendment must nevertheless be excluded from evidence under *Miranda*. Thus, in the individual case, *Miranda*'s preventive medicine provides a remedy even to the defendant who has suffered no identifiable constitutional harm."

---

[43]470 U.S. 298 (1985).
[44]530 U.S. 428 (2000).

(b) *Missouri v. Seibert:* An Exception to the *Elstad* Rule?

In *Missouri v. Seibert*,[45] the Supreme Court addressed whether statements obtained after the provision of *Miranda* warnings and a waiver were admissible when the warnings themselves were preceded by an interrogation deliberately performed in violation of *Miranda*. Specifically, in *Seibert* the police interrogated a custodial suspect without providing *Miranda* warnings, obtained incriminating statements, and then, after a 20-minute break, provided the suspect with *Miranda* warnings for the first time. After obtaining a waiver, the police then interrogated her a second time (reminding her of her pre-*Miranda* admissions), and then obtained a confession. The police affirmed that this technique was deliberate and that the admission ultimately obtained was essentially repetitive of the suspect's earlier statement.

By a narrow 5-4 majority, the Supreme Court held that the subsequent confessions were inadmissible. However, the rationale governing the Court's holding is less than clear. Justice Souter, who wrote on behalf of four members of the Court, found that this case was not governed by *Elstad*—and was, therefore, not a fruits case—but was rather an ineffective warnings case. Justice Souter wrote that the subject police protocol was designed to undermine the effectiveness of the *Miranda* warnings ultimately provided.

> Upon hearing warnings only in the aftermath of interrogation and just after making a confession, a suspect would hardly think he had a genuine right to remain silent, let alone persist in so believing once the police began to lead him over the same ground again. . . . Thus, when *Miranda* warnings are inserted in the midst of coordinated and continuing interrogation, they are likely to mislead and deprive a defendant of knowledge essential to his ability to understand the nature of his rights and the consequences of abandoning them.

Justice Breyer concurred, but viewed the case as governed by *Elstad*. He wrote that "the 'fruits' of the initial unwarned questioning [should be excluded] unless the failure to warn was in good faith."

In his concurrence, Justice Kennedy seemingly shared Justice Breyer's view that the matter was governed by *Elstad*. However, he suggested "a narrower test" than the *Miranda* effectiveness approach proposed by the plurality. In essence, his test allowed for a departure from *Elstad*, but only in a limited instance—when the police deliberately engaged in the two-step interrogation practice at issue in *Seibert*. Therefore, according to Kennedy, "[i]f the deliberate two-step strategy has been used, postwarning statements that are related to the substance of prewarning statements must be excluded," provided that law enforcement did not undertake adequate remedial measures prior to the postwarning comments.

In the end, all members of the majority agreed that the intentional two-step interrogation practice at issue (absent sufficient curative measures) renders inadmissible statements obtained as a result of this practice. However, it remains an open question whether *Seibert* should be construed as an ineffective warnings case or as exception—albeit an extremely narrow one—to the *Elstad* rule.

---

[45]542 U.S. 600 (2004).

(c) *United States v. Patane:* Physical Fruits

Whereas the alleged taint in *Elstad* was verbal in nature, the potential suppression of physical evidence was at issue in *United States v. Patane*.[46] There, the defendant made incriminating remarks regarding the location of a firearm following the provision of defective *Miranda* warnings. The firearm was subsequently retrieved. The Court held that, despite the *Miranda* failure, the firearm should not be suppressed.

Writing for three members of the Court, Justice Thomas declared, despite the holding in *Dickerson*, that the *Miranda* safeguards were "prophylactic" and suggested that a *Miranda* violation did not occur until, and unless, the subject statements were introduced at trial. He therefore concluded that the admission of the firearm "presents no risk that a defendant's coerced statements . . . will be used against him at a criminal trial" and that the suppression of the *Miranda*-defective statements constitutes an adequate remedy. Justices Kennedy and O'Connor concurred in the judgment, though they declined to adopt the reasoning of the plurality. They deemed it unnecessary to address "whether the detective's failure to give [the defendant] the full *Miranda* warnings should be characterized as a violation of the *Miranda* rule itself, or whether there is 'anything to deter' so long as the unwarned statements are not later introduced at trial." Rather, they contended that sometimes the concerns underlying *Miranda* "must be accommodated to other objectives of the criminal justice system." Here, they found that the physical evidence had "important probative value," that its exclusion could not be justified on deterrence grounds, and that its admission was even more justifiable than the verbal statements at issue in *Elstad*.

F   A   Q

Q: Does the *Miranda* exclusionary rule and fruits doctrine differ from that applicable to due process clause violations and to non-*Miranda* violations of the Fifth Amendment privilege against self-incrimination?

A: Yes. Like the *Miranda* exclusionary rule, any coerced statement or a statement that is improperly compelled is subject to exclusion and, therefore, cannot be introduced substantively at trial. In contrast to the *Miranda* rule, however, such statements cannot be used for impeachment purposes.[47] Moreover, the government is prohibited from using the derivative fruit of such violations.[48]

SUMMARY

■ The Supreme Court in *Miranda v. Arizona* held that before custodial interrogation can occur an individual must be informed of and comprehend the following warnings: that he has the right to remain silent, that anything he says can and will be

---

[46]542 U.S. 630 (2004).
[47]*New Jersey v. Portash*, 440 U.S. 450 (1979).
[48]See *Counselman v. Hitchcock*, 142 U.S. 547 (1892) (upholding appellant's refusal to testify before a grand jury given that the subject immunity statute did not prevent the government from using evidence derivatively obtained against him in a criminal proceeding).

used against him, that he has the right to an attorney, and if he cannot afford an attorney a lawyer will be appointed prior to any interrogation.

■ Any statement obtained in violation of *Miranda* is considered to be compelled within the meaning of the Fifth Amendment. Thus, any such statements are inadmissible as substantive evidence.

■ An individual must be in "custody" before the provision of *Miranda* warnings is required. A person is in "custody" when he has been formally arrested or in circumstances tantamount to a formal arrest. This inquiry is considered from the vantage point of a reasonable person in the suspect's position.

■ *Miranda* warnings are not mandated unless a custodial suspect is subjected to "interrogation," which occurs when an individual "is subjected to either express questioning or its functional equivalent."

■ The Supreme Court has recognized that some forms of custodial interrogation are permissible in the absence of *Miranda* warnings: undercover interrogation, emergency situations where the public's safety is at stake, and routine booking questions.

■ An individual who has been provided with *Miranda* warnings has the authority to waive his rights. The government must demonstrate, by a preponderance of the evidence, that any purported waiver was knowing, intelligent, and voluntary. The government's proof will be assessed pursuant to a totality of the circumstances standard.

■ Central to the waiver issue is whether the *Miranda* warnings were reasonably conveyed. The provision of such warnings need not follow a precise script.

■ Assuming reasonable conveyance, the government's proof of waiver must include at least some evidence suggestive of a suspect's intent to waive his rights. Waiver will not be presumed from mere silence. But, in effect, little more than mere silence is required.

■ After the administration of warnings, coupled with evidence indicating that the rights were validly comprehended, the government may proceed to interrogate a suspect until such time that the suspect invokes his *Miranda* rights. A suspect must clearly and explicitly communicate his invocation of his *Miranda* rights in order to halt police questioning. Moreover, any answer—however slight or brief—in response to an officer's question will constitute a waiver of that individual's *Miranda* rights.

■ An individual who seeks to invoke either his *Miranda* right to remain silent or his *Miranda* right to counsel must do so clearly and unequivocally.

■ Once a suspect invokes his *Miranda* right to counsel, the police may not subject that individual "to further interrogation . . . until counsel has been made available to him, unless the accused himself initiates further communication, exchanges or conversations with the police." Any waiver obtained after invocation of this right is presumed to be involuntary. However, this presumption no longer applies if there has been a break in custody that extends at least 14 days.

■ The *Miranda* right to counsel is non-offense-specific. Thus, an individual who invokes his *Miranda* counsel right may not be questioned about any other criminal matter.

■ Once a suspect invokes his *Miranda* right to remain silent, further interrogation is permissible only after the police have "scrupulously honored" the invocation of that right.

■ A statement obtained in violation of the *Miranda* rule cannot be used substantively in a subsequent criminal case. However, there is no or virtually no fruit of the poisonous tree doctrine with respect to *Miranda* violations.

■ Statements obtained in violation of *Miranda* can be used for impeachment purposes. This differs from the rule applicable to due process violations and to non-*Miranda* violations of the Fifth Amendment, which requires the suppression of such statements for substantive and impeachment purposes.

CONNECTIONS

Relationship to Incorporation (Chapter 1)

The Fifth Amendment Privilege Against Self-Incrimination is now fully incorporated to the states via the Fourteenth Amendment due process clause.

Relationship to The Sixth Amendment Right to Counsel — General Principles (Chapter 19)

The Fifth Amendment *Miranda* rule applies to custodial *interrogations* that occur prior to the commencement of adversarial proceedings. The Sixth Amendment right to counsel applies to statements that are *deliberately elicited* after the commencement of adversarial proceedings. Due process challenges can be brought at any stage of the litigation process. While an individual is entitled to waive his Fifth Amendment *Miranda* rights and his Sixth Amendment right to counsel, the latter right cannot be waived while being questioned surreptitiously. A *Miranda* waiver will usually suffice to waive an individual's Sixth Amendment right to counsel. The *Miranda* right to counsel is non-offense-specific. On the other hand, the Sixth Amendment right to counsel is offense-specific.

Relationship to Fourth Amendment Violations and Their Associated Remedies (Chapter 15), The Privilege Against Self-Incrimination — General Principles (Chapter 16), and The Sixth Amendment Right to Counsel — General Principles (Chapter 19)

The exclusionary rule applies to violations of the Fourth Amendment, the Fifth and Fourteenth Amendment due process clauses, and the Fifth Amendment privilege against self-incrimination (*Miranda* and non-*Miranda*). The fruit of the poisonous tree doctrine applies to Fourth Amendment violations, but is subject to exceptions. In the Fifth Amendment realm, the applicability of the fruits doctrine is dependent upon the particular guarantee that is infringed. In the *Miranda* context, the fruits doctrine is virtually, if not entirely, inapplicable.

Relationship to Involuntary Confessions and the Due Process Clause Cases (Chapter 17)

Claims alleging involuntary statements can be reviewed pursuant to the Fifth and Fourteenth Amendment due process clauses as well as the Fifth Amendment *Miranda* rule. Without a finding of coercive police activity there cannot be a due process violation. A *Miranda* violation can be found without such a finding.

Relationship to The Sixth Amendment Right to Counsel — General Principles (Chapter 19) and Identifications, the Sixth Amendment, and the Due Process Clause (Chapter 20)

The Fifth Amendment *Miranda* right to counsel attaches to custodial interrogations that occur prior to the commencement of adversarial proceedings. The Sixth Amendment right to counsel, on the other hand, attaches after the commencement of adversarial proceedings. Thus, suspect identifications (excluding photographic displays) that occur after the commencement of adversary proceedings implicate this Sixth Amendment right. The Sixth Amendment, therefore, does not attach to identification procedures that occur prior to this time. Fifth Amendment due process challenges to statements made during government interviews or to out-of-court identifications can be made at any time, irrespective of whether adversary proceedings have commenced.

The Sixth Amendment Right to Counsel — General Principles

19

OVERVIEW

In addition to the Fifth Amendment *Miranda* right to counsel, there is a Sixth Amendment right to counsel. The pertinent part of the Sixth Amendment provides:

> In all criminal prosecutions, the accused shall enjoy the right . . . to have the Assistance of Counsel for his defence.

This chapter will discuss the essential components of this constitutional right and will note the features that distinguish it from the *Miranda* right to counsel. As part of this review, it will also explain when the right can be successfully asserted, how the right can be waived, and how the exclusionary rules apply in this circumstance.

A. *MASSIAH v. UNITED STATES* AND *BREWER v. WILLIAMS*: ADVERSARY PROCEEDINGS

B. DELIBERATE ELICITATIONS

C. WAIVER

D. THE SIXTH AMENDMENT EXCLUSIONARY RULE

A. *Massiah v. United States* and *Brewer v. Williams*: Adversary Proceedings

The core of the Sixth Amendment right to counsel was established in two Supreme Court decisions: *Massiah v. United States*[1] and *Brewer v. Williams*.[2] And these core components remain intact today.

At issue in *Massiah* was the admissibility of incriminating comments uttered post-indictment by a defendant who was represented by counsel. More specifically, the defendant's comments were spoken to his codefendant while the two were seated in a parked vehicle a few days after the defendant had been released from custody pending trial. Unbeknownst to the defendant, his codefendant, who had engaged the defendant in conversation while the two men were situated within the vehicle, was cooperating with the government and had allowed a government agent to listen to the "entire conversation" via a radio transmitter that had previously been installed under the front seat of the vehicle.

The defendant challenged the admissibility of the statements on Fourth, Fifth, and Sixth Amendment grounds. In reversing his conviction, however, the Court relied solely upon the Sixth Amendment, finding that the defendant's counsel right under this Amendment was violated given that the government "deliberately elicited" incriminating comments from him "after he had been indicted and in the absence of his counsel." Thus, *Massiah* held that an individual's Sixth Amendment counsel rights are violated if, after an indictment has been returned, the government deliberately elicits statements from that individual without his counsel being present.

The meaning of this constitutional guarantee was expounded upon in *Brewer v. Williams*. *Brewer* involved the murder of a young child. The defendant, a recent escapee from a mental facility, had been arrested in connection with the child's disappearance. The defendant, who had surrendered to the police in Davenport, Iowa, was subsequently arraigned in that city. Prior to his arraignment, however, the defendant conversed over the telephone with his attorney, who advised him that the police from Des Moines would be traveling to Davenport to transport him back to Des Moines, that the police had agreed not to question the defendant, and that the defendant was to refrain from talking with the police.

During the transport to Des Moines, the defendant and the two detectives in the vehicle engaged in "a wide-ranging conversation." Cognizant of the defendant's mental status as well as his religious faith, one of the detectives delivered a "Christian burial speech." Specifically, the detective said:

> I want to give you something to think about while we're traveling down the road. . . . Number one, I want you to observe the weather conditions, it's raining, it's sleeting, it's freezing, driving is very treacherous, visibility is poor, it's going to be dark early this evening. They are predicting several inches of snow for tonight, and I feel that you yourself are the only person that knows where this little girl's body is, that you yourself have only been there once, and if you get a snow on top of it you yourself may be unable to find it. And, since we will be going right past the area on the way into Des Moines, I felt that we

---

[1]377 U.S. 201 (1964).
[2]430 U.S. 387 (1977).

could stop and locate the body, that the parents of this little girl should be entitled to a Christian burial for the little girl who was snatched away from them on Christmas [E]ve and murdered. And I feel we should stop and locate it on the way in, rather than waiting until morning and trying to come back out after a snow storm, and possibly not being able to find it at all.

The defendant eventually uttered statements that implicated himself in the child's murder.

Relying upon the Sixth and Fourteenth Amendments, the Court found that the defendant's Sixth Amendment right to the assistance of counsel had been infringed. The Court acknowledged that the "peripheral scope of this constitutional right" had, at times, divided the Court. However, the Court found that the "basic contours" of the right were clear. Specifically, the Court proclaimed that the Sixth and Fourteenth Amendment counsel right, at a minimum, means that an individual "is entitled to the help of a lawyer at or after the time that judicial proceedings have been initiated against him — 'whether by way of formal charge, preliminary hearing, indictment, information, or arraignment' (citation omitted)." And, citing the defendant's arraignment and his pre-transport confinement, the Court readily concluded that "adversary proceedings" had commenced, thus triggering Sixth Amendment safeguards.

Indeed, the Court considered *Brewer* and *Massiah* to be "indistinguishable." In that regard, the Court discounted as "irrelevant" the fact that the interrogation at issue in *Brewer* was overt and not surreptitious as in *Massiah*. In both instances, the Court found the statements obtained were deliberately elicited by the government, and because they were obtained after "adversary proceedings [had] commenced" the interrogated individual had a constitutional right to an attorney.

Thus, *Massiah* and *Brewer* set forth an important line of demarcation that separates the Fifth and Sixth Amendment rights to counsel cases. Interrogations that occur prior to the commencement of "adversary proceedings" are governed by the Fifth Amendment. The Sixth Amendment attaches to interrogations that occur after the commencement of such proceedings.

B. Deliberate Elicitations

As noted in *Massiah* and *Brewer*, the Sixth Amendment is implicated whenever the government deliberately elicits statements from an individual once "adversary proceedings" have commenced. Whereas the previous section focused primarily upon the concept of "adversary proceedings," this section devotes itself to the Supreme Court's pronouncements with respect to the term "deliberate elicitation."

You may recall from Chapter 18 that police "interrogation" is a necessary predicate to establishing a Fifth Amendment *Miranda* violation. In the Sixth Amendment context, however, a finding of "interrogation" is unnecessary. Instead, the Sixth Amendment requires a finding of "deliberate elicitation."

At first glance, the two terms might appear to be interchangeable. And that is true to a certain extent. It is clear that certain police practices are encompassed by both terms. Certainly, the most obvious example of this overlap is the traditional, standard police interrogation of suspects, where plain-clothes officers interrogate an arrested or detained individual. However, the Supreme Court has declared that the two terms are distinct. As stated by the Court in *Michigan v. Jackson*,[3] "[A]fter the initiation of adversary judicial proceedings, the Sixth Amendment provides a right to counsel at a 'critical stage,' even when there is no interrogation and no Fifth Amendment applicability." Thus, comments can be deliberately elicited, thereby implicating Sixth Amendment concerns, in the absence of any Fifth Amendment–type interrogation.

As noted in Chapter 18, the Supreme Court in *Rhode Island v. Innis*[4] declared that interrogation, in the Fifth Amendment *Miranda* context, occurs when an individual "is subjected to either express questioning or its functional equivalent." It further explained that whether a suspect is interrogated is viewed "primarily" from the perspective of the interrogated individual. An officer's subjective awareness of the personal characteristics of the interrogated individual can be relevant to the interrogation inquiry.

On the other hand, the focus of the Sixth Amendment's "deliberate elicitation" inquiry is not upon the suspect but upon the underlying intent of the officer. In the Sixth Amendment context, the central inquiry is whether the government engaged in conduct that was deliberately designed to obtain incriminating remarks. The following two cases, *United States v. Henry*[5] and *Kuhlmann v. Wilson*,[6] will help illustrate this principle.

Henry and *Kuhlmann* involved incriminating statements uttered by an incarcerated individual to a fellow inmate who, unbeknownst to the defendant/speaker, was working for the government as a paid informant. In each instance, adversary proceedings had commenced and the cooperating individual (the fellow inmate) was instructed not to instigate any discussions but to merely listen for any relevant conversations. According to the Court in *Henry*, however, the informant in that case "was not a passive listener," but engaged in conversations with the defendant that ultimately led to his incriminating remarks. The Court found that the statements at issue were deliberately elicited in violation of the Sixth Amendment. In reaching this conclusion, the Court cited three critical factors: the informant's status as a paid cooperative, his covert status, and the fact that he "was not a passive listener," but was actively conversant with an individual who was incarcerated. As stated by the Court:

> [T]he mere fact of custody imposes pressures on the accused; confinement may bring into play subtle influences that will make him particularly susceptible to the ploys of undercover Government agents. The Court of Appeals determined that, on this record, the incriminating conversations between Henry and Nichols were facilitated by Nichols' conduct and apparent status as a person sharing a common plight. . . .
>
> [W]e conclude that the Court of Appeals did not err in holding that Henry's statements to Nichols should not have been admitted at trial. By intentionally creating a situation likely to induce Henry to make incriminating statements without the assistance of counsel, the Government violated Henry's Sixth Amendment right to counsel.

In *Kuhlmann*, however, the Court reached a different conclusion. Finding that the Sixth Amendment had not been violated, the Court held that the informant's conduct was not deliberately designed to procure incriminating statements. It noted that in *Maine v. Moulton*[7] — where a defendant who was not in custody made incriminating remarks to an accomplice who was cooperating with the government and was

---

[3] 475 U.S. 625 (1986).
[4] 446 U.S. 291 (1980).
[5] 447 U.S. 264 (1980).
[6] 477 U.S. 436 (1986).
[7] 474 U.S. 159 (1985).

wearing a wire transmitter—there was a Sixth Amendment violation given that the accomplice's "'active conversation about their upcoming trial was certain to elicit' incriminating statements from the defendant." The *Moulton* Court, citing *Henry*, declared that the government's conduct was the "functional equivalent of interrogation." In contrast to *Henry* and *Moulton*, however, the Court in *Kuhlmann* concluded that there was no Sixth Amendment violation given the comparative inactivity of the accomplice. In *Kuhlmann*, the accomplice did little more than listen to the words uttered in his presence by the defendant. The Court explained that a Sixth Amendment violation is not demonstrated "by showing that an informant, either through prior arrangement or voluntarily, reported his incriminating statements to the police. Rather, the defendant must demonstrate that the police and their informant took some action, beyond merely listening, that was designed deliberately to elicit incriminating remarks."

F A Q

Q: The *Miranda* right to counsel is non-offense-specific. Is the rule the same regarding the Sixth Amendment right to counsel?

A: No. In contrast to the *Miranda* right to counsel under the Fifth Amendment, the Sixth Amendment right to counsel is offense-specific. In other words, the Sixth Amendment affords a defendant protection from police questioning, in the absence of counsel, regarding the offense(s) for which the defendant has been charged. Conversely, protection does not extend to police questioning regarding criminal activity for which the defendant has not been charged. As stated by the Supreme Court in *McNeil v. Wisconsin*,[8] "The Sixth Amendment right . . . is offense-specific. It cannot be invoked once for all future prosecutions, for it does not attach until a prosecution is commenced. . . ." Naturally, this raises the question, what constitutes an "offense" for Sixth Amendment purposes? The Court in *Texas v. Cobb*[9] held that the term refers only to the offense(s) for which a defendant has been actually charged and those offenses for which double jeopardy would attach.[10] Therefore, it does not encompass criminal offenses that are merely factually related to the charged offense. Thus, a defendant who is charged with the murder of a cashier committed during a robbery of a grocery store could, after the commencement of adversary proceedings, be questioned by the police in the absence of counsel about the theft of various items taken from that store at the time of the killing. Given that the criminal offense of theft requires the proof of facts different from the criminal offense of homicide, the Sixth Amendment provides no safeguard in this instance.

---

[8]501 U.S. 171 (1991).

[9]532 U.S. 162 (2001).

[10]As to what constitutes "double jeopardy," the Court in *Cobb* observed that "[i]n *Blockburger* v. *United States*, 284 U.S. 299 (1932), we explained that 'where the same act or transaction constitutes a violation of two distinct statutory provisions, the test to be applied to determine whether there are two offenses or only one, is whether each provision requires proof of a fact which the other does not.' *Id.*, at 304. We have since applied the *Blockburger* test to delineate the scope of the Fifth Amendment's Double Jeopardy Clause, which prevents multiple or successive prosecutions for the 'same offence' (citation omitted). We see no constitutional difference between the meaning of the term 'offense' in the contexts of double jeopardy and of the right to counsel. Accordingly, we hold that when the Sixth Amendment right to counsel attaches, it does encompass offenses that, even if not formally charged, would be considered the same offense under the *Blockburger* test."

C. Waiver

As in the Fifth Amendment *Miranda* context, an individual may waive his Sixth Amendment right to counsel. The means by which a valid waiver is achieved vary somewhat depending upon the factual context.

Generally, the recitation of *Miranda* warnings provides an individual with sufficient information regarding his Sixth Amendment right to counsel. Accordingly, a waiver of an individual's *Miranda* rights is usually sufficient to waive this counsel right. As stated by the Supreme Court in *Montejo v. Louisiana*:[11]

> And when a defendant is read his *Miranda* rights (which include the right to have counsel present during interrogation) and agrees to waive those rights, that typically does the trick, even though the *Miranda* rights purportedly have their source in the *Fifth* Amendment: "As a general matter . . . an accused who is admonished with the warnings prescribed by this Court in *Miranda* . . . has been sufficiently apprised of the nature of his Sixth Amendment rights, and of the consequences of abandoning those rights, so that his waiver on this basis will be considered a knowing and intelligent one." *Patterson* [*v. Illinois*].

Sidebar

WAIVER OF SIXTH AMENDMENT RIGHT TO COUNSEL INAPPLICABLE DURING SURREPTITIOUS INTERROGATIONS

The Supreme Court in *United States v. Henry*[12] declared that "the concept of a knowing and voluntary waiver of Sixth Amendment rights does not apply in the context of communications with an undisclosed undercover informant acting for the Government (citation omitted). In that setting, [the interrogated individual] being unaware that [he was being questioned by] a Government agent expressly commissioned to secure evidence, cannot be held to have waived his right to the assistance of counsel."

[12]447 U.S. 264 (1980).

F A Q

Q: Does the government bear the burden of proving a valid waiver of an individual's Sixth Amendment right to counsel?

A: Yes. If the government seeks to admit statements obtained from an individual after the commencement of adversary proceedings, it must prove that the defendant validly waived his Sixth Amendment right to counsel and that he did so voluntarily, knowingly, and intelligently. A valid waiver can be found irrespective of whether the defendant is already represented.

So under what circumstances will a *Miranda* waiver suffice to waive a right to counsel under the Sixth Amendment? The answer: in virtually every circumstance where an individual has not affirmatively asserted his right to have counsel present under the Sixth Amendment. Thus, in those circumstances where an individual has not made such an affirmative assertion an individual may waive his counsel right under the Sixth Amendment by waiving his *Miranda* rights.

[11]556 U.S. 778 (2009).

To see this, consider the facts in *Montejo*. There, the defendant, who was suspected of murder, was appointed counsel by the court during a preliminary hearing. After the hearing, the defendant was visited by law enforcement personnel while in prison. After being read his *Miranda* warnings, the defendant agreed to accompany the officers on a ride to find the murder weapon. At some point during this trip, the defendant wrote a letter that contained incriminating statements.

In *Montejo*, adversary proceedings had commenced and the police had obtained a waiver of the defendant's *Miranda* rights. At issue was "the scope and continued viability of the rule announced . . . in *Michigan* v. *Jackson*,[13] forbidding the police from initiating interrogation of a criminal defendant once he has requested counsel at an arraignment or similar proceeding." Under *Jackson*, there was a presumption that any waiver obtained by the police after a defendant had requested counsel at an arraignment was invalid. In other words, *Jackson* viewed a request for the appointment of counsel during such proceedings as being the same as an invocation of the Sixth Amendment right.

Jackson involved two cases where the defendants had been arrested, had requested the assistance of counsel during their arraignments, and subsequently made statements to police after having been provided with *Miranda* warnings. In reaching its decision, the Court in *Jackson* drew a distinct line in the sand regarding permissible interrogation practices in the Fifth and Sixth Amendment contexts:

> Indeed, after a formal accusation has been made — and a person who had previously been just a "suspect" has become an "accused" within the meaning of the Sixth Amendment — the constitutional right to the assistance of counsel is of such importance that the police may no longer employ techniques for eliciting information from an uncounseled defendant that might have been entirely proper at an earlier stage of their investigation.

Montejo, however, overturned *Jackson*, thereby removing the *Jackson* presumption of involuntariness that attached to counsel waivers. As a result, the police may now obtain a valid waiver of a defendant's Sixth Amendment counsel right (via the provision of *Miranda* warnings) until such time as the defendant affirmatively communicates or asserts his right to an attorney. The Court explained:

> When a court appoints counsel for an indigent defendant in the absence of any request on his part, there is no basis for a presumption that any subsequent waiver of the right to counsel will be involuntary. There is no "*initial* election" to exercise the right (citation omitted), that must be preserved through a prophylactic rule against later waivers. No reason exists to assume that a defendant like *Montejo*, who has done *nothing at all* to express his intentions with respect to his Sixth Amendment rights, would not be perfectly amenable to speaking with the police without having counsel present. And no reason exists to prohibit the police from inquiring. *Edwards* and *Jackson* are meant to prevent police from badgering defendants into changing their minds about their rights, but a defendant who never asked for counsel has not yet made up his mind in the first instance.

Thus, for example, when an officer approaches a defendant after formal proceedings have commenced and provides him with his *Miranda* warnings, the protections of the Sixth Amendment counsel right will attach only if the defendant affirmatively states his desire to have an attorney present. If, on the other hand, the defendant

---

[13]475 U.S. 625 (1986).

elects to waive his rights, his *Miranda* counsel waiver will serve as a waiver of his Sixth Amendment counsel right. As stated by the Court:

> [A] defendant who does not want to speak to the police without counsel present need only say as much when he is first approached and given the *Miranda* warnings. At that point, not only must the immediate contact end, but "badgering" by later requests is prohibited. If that regime suffices to protect the integrity of "a suspect's voluntary choice not to speak outside his lawyer's presence" before his arraignment (citation omitted), it is hard to see why it would not also suffice to protect that same choice after arraignment, when Sixth Amendment rights have attached

It is important to note that the police may approach a defendant and seek to obtain a waiver irrespective of whether the defendant has hired an attorney or had counsel appointed. Thus, even if a defendant is represented, the police may still obtain a valid waiver. However, once the defendant asserts his right to an attorney, all questioning must cease.

D. The Sixth Amendment Exclusionary Rule

If the Sixth Amendment right to counsel is violated then the substantive use by the state of any resulting statements, as well as any derivative fruits, is prohibited.[14]

However, such evidence can be used as impeachment evidence. This issue was most recently decided by the Supreme Court in *Kansas v. Ventris*.[15] In *Ventris*, the defendant, who was charged with murder, uttered incriminating statements to a government informant while they were in a jail cell. The parties agreed that the government's actions constituted a Sixth Amendment violation, but disagreed as to whether the statements could be used to impeach the defendant. At trial, the defendant took the stand and denied having committed the shooting, but he purportedly made contradictory statements to the government informant.

Addressing "[w]hether otherwise excludable evidence can be admitted for purposes of impeachment," the Court concluded that the Sixth Amendment did not preclude such use.[16] It found that the Sixth Amendment right was a "right to be free of uncounseled interrogation, and is infringed at the time of interrogation," not at the time the statement is introduced at trial. Given such, the Court employed a balancing test, weighing the interests advanced by permitting introduction for impeachment purposes against the deterrence value attendant upon exclusion. The Court determined that the interests in deterring perjury and preserving "the integrity of the trial process" outweighed any deterrent value gained by exclusion. The Court noted, inter alia, that law enforcement agents have a "significant incentive" to comply with the Sixth Amendment given that incriminatory remarks lawfully obtained may be used substantively as well as for impeachment purposes.

---

[14]*United States v. Wade*, 388 U.S. 218 (1967) (finding that a violation of the Sixth Amendment right to counsel may require the suppression of a later courtroom identification at trial). For a more in-depth discussion of *Wade*, see Chapter 20.

[15]556 U.S. 586 (2009).

[16]The Supreme Court reached the same result in *Michigan v. Harvey*, 494 U.S. 344 (1990). Note that the Court's Sixth Amendment review in that case focused upon the since-overruled *Michigan v. Jackson*, 475 U.S. 625 (1986). See discussion of *Montejo v. Louisiana*, 556 U.S. 778 (2009) earlier in this chapter.

Moreover, the Court reasoned that an alternative holding would grant the testifying defendant a "shield against contradiction" by prior inconsistent statements.

SUMMARY

- The Sixth Amendment right to counsel attaches only after the commencement of adversary proceedings (e.g., indictment, preliminary hearing, arraignment).

- Once the adversary process has commenced, the government may not deliberately elicit statements from an individual about the subject for which he has been charged unless counsel is present. This Sixth Amendment right attaches to both overt and covert interrogations.

- Whether a statement is deliberately elicited is viewed from the perspective of the government officer. Thus, to satisfy this requirement, it must be determined that the government engaged in conduct that was deliberately designed to obtain incriminating remarks.

- The Sixth Amendment right to counsel is offense-specific. In other words, the Sixth Amendment affords a defendant protection from police questioning, in the absence of counsel, regarding the offense(s) for which the defendant has been charged.

- An individual may waive his Sixth Amendment right to counsel. A valid waiver must be voluntary, knowing, and intelligent. Moreover, a waiver of an individual's *Miranda* rights is often sufficient to waive his Sixth Amendment right to counsel.

- The exclusionary rule applies to Sixth Amendment violations. Therefore, if statements are obtained in violation of the Sixth Amendment right to counsel, then the government is prohibited from introducing such evidence, as well as any fruits derived therefrom, for substantive purposes. However, such evidence can be introduced for impeachment purposes.

CONNECTIONS

Relationship to Involuntary Confessions and the Due Process Clause Cases (Chapter 17)

The Fifth Amendment *Miranda* rule applies to custodial *interrogations* that occur prior to the commencement of adversarial proceedings. The Sixth Amendment right to counsel applies to statements that are *deliberately elicited* after the commencement of adversarial proceedings. Due process challenges can be brought at any stage of the litigation process. A *Miranda* waiver will often suffice to waive an individual's Sixth Amendment right to counsel. While an individual is entitled to waive his Fifth Amendment *Miranda* rights and his Sixth Amendment right to counsel, an individual cannot waive his Sixth

Amendment right to counsel when being questioned surreptitiously. The *Miranda* right to counsel is non-offense-specific. On the other hand, the Sixth Amendment right to counsel is offense-specific.

Relationship to Fourth Amendment Violations and Their Associated Remedies (Chapter 15)

Evidence (and its fruits, subject to various exceptions) seized in violation of the Fourth Amendment is subject to suppression. Such evidence may be employed to impeach the testimony of the defendant, though not that of defense witnesses. Evidence obtained in violation of the Sixth Amendment right to counsel is also subject to exclusion (as are derivative fruits). However, such evidence may be used for impeachment purposes.

Relationship to the Privilege Against Self-Incrimination — General Principles (Chapter 16) and Involuntary Confessions and the Due Process Clause Cases (Chapter 17)

The exclusionary rule applies to violations of the Fifth and Fourteenth Amendment due process clauses and the Fifth Amendment privilege against self-incrimination. Similarly, evidence obtained in contravention of the Sixth Amendment counsel right is subject to exclusion. Derivative fruit is also excludable in the Sixth Amendment context. The admissibility of such fruit is dependent upon the Fifth Amendment context.

Relationship to Involuntary Confessions and the Due Process Clause Cases (Chapter 17), The *Miranda* Rule (Chapter 18), and Identifications, the Sixth Amendment, and the Due Process Clause (Chapter 20)

The Fifth Amendment *Miranda* right to counsel attaches to custodial interrogations that occur prior to the commencement of adversarial proceedings. The Sixth Amendment right to counsel, on the other hand, attaches after the commencement of adversarial proceedings. Thus, suspect identifications (excluding photographic displays) that occur after the commencement of adversary proceedings implicate this Sixth Amendment right. The Sixth Amendment, therefore, does not attach to identification procedures that occur prior to this time. Fifth Amendment due process challenges to statements made during government interviews or to out-of-court identifications can be made irrespective of whether adversary proceedings have commenced.

Identifications, the Sixth Amendment, and the Due Process Clause

20

At any criminal trial it is essential that the prosecution establish the identity of the individual accused of criminal activity. This is often accom-

OVERVIEW

plished by means of a witness's in-court identification. However, such testimony is often not very compelling given that, outside of the litigants themselves, there are usually few other individuals in the courtroom. Therefore, the government will frequently seek to bolster its case through the admission into evidence of out-of-court identifications.

Identification evidence is all the more essential when the perpetrator's identity is a focal point of a trial. In such instances, identification testimony, particularly if left unchallenged, can be of enormous benefit to the prosecution. What are the different types of identification evidence? What are the constitutional parameters regarding identification evidence? What remedial options are available to defendants who seek to challenge the admissibility of such evidence? These and other questions will be addressed in this chapter.

A. **SUSPECT IDENTIFICATIONS AND THE SIXTH AMENDMENT RIGHT TO COUNSEL**

B. **SUSPECT IDENTIFICATIONS AND THE DUE PROCESS CLAUSE**

1. Suggestive, but Necessary
2. Suggestive and Unnecessary/Unreliable
3. Suggestive, but Reliable

A. Suspect Identifications and the Sixth Amendment Right to Counsel

United States v. Wade[1] and *Gilbert v. California*[2] were decided by the Supreme Court on the same day, and addressed related issues concerning the admissibility of identification testimony. Common to each case was that the out-of-court identifications occurred post-indictment and was made in the absence of appointed counsel. A key fact distinguishing *Wade* from *Gilbert* is that in *Wade* the government admitted only an in-court identification in its case-in-chief, while in *Gilbert* the government admitted both the out-of-court as well as an in-court identification in its direct case. The significance of this distinction will become apparent later in this section.

Wade observed that out-of-court identifications — whether by a lineup (where several individuals are gathered and, in essence, stand together in order to be identified) or by showups (presenting a single individual for identification) — present imposing challenges for defendants as well as dangers that could potentially detract from the fairness of the trial itself. As the Court declared, "[T]he accused's inability effectively to reconstruct at trial any unfairness that occurred at the lineup may deprive him of his only opportunity meaningfully to attack the credibility of the witness' courtroom identification."

Given this problem, the Court concluded that the pretrial lineup was a "critical stage of the prosecution," thus affording a defendant the right to counsel protections of the Sixth Amendment. In fact, the Court deemed the necessity for counsel every bit as essential at this pretrial stage as it is at trial. As stated by the Court:

> Since it appears that there is grave potential for prejudice, intentional or not, in the pretrial lineup, which may not be capable of reconstruction at trial, and since presence of counsel itself can often avert prejudice and assure a meaningful confrontation at trial, there can be little doubt that, for *Wade*, the post-indictment lineup was a critical stage of the prosecution at which he was "as much entitled to such aid [of counsel] . . . as at the trial itself." *Powell v. Alabama* (citation omitted).

F   A   Q

Q: Is defense counsel entitled to influence the ultimate composition of a lineup?

A: Essentially, no. The function of the defense attorney in this context could be described as that of an inactive participant. Though suggestions can certainly be proffered by defense counsel, her advice need neither be considered nor heeded. As with other constitutional contests, identification challenges are presented, and ultimately settled, at the pretrial motions stage. In order for a trial court to adequately assess these arguments, however, the Supreme Court deemed it essential that defense counsel be present at the challenged identification procedure. Without the presence of counsel, the Court in *Wade* believed that a

---

[1]338 U.S. 218 (1967).
[2]338 U.S. 263 (1967).

defense attorney would have a difficult time presenting the factual constructs surrounding the contested identification. As the Court declared: "Insofar as the accused's conviction may rest on a courtroom identification, in fact, the fruit of a suspect pretrial identification which the accused is helpless to subject to effective scrutiny at trial, the accused is deprived of that right of cross-examination which is an essential safeguard to his right to confront the witnesses against him (citation omitted). And even though cross-examination is a precious safeguard to a fair trial, it cannot be viewed as an absolute assurance of accuracy and reliability. Thus, in the present context, where so many variables and pitfalls exist, the first line of defense must be the prevention of unfairness and the lessening of the hazards of eyewitness identification at the lineup itself. The trial which might determine the accused's fate may well not be that in the courtroom but that at the pretrial confrontation, with the State aligned against the accused, the witness the sole jury, and the accused unprotected against the overreaching, intentional or unintentional, and with little or no effective appeal from the judgment there rendered by the witness — 'that's the man.'"

Sequentially, the in-court identification in *Wade* followed an out-of-court identification that was not admitted during the prosecution's direct case and was deemed by the Court to be unconstitutional. Given such, the Court considered whether to adopt a per se rule requiring the exclusion of the in-court identification in this context. Though the Court declined to adopt a per se rule, it did declare that the admissibility of such in-court identifications are subject to a fruit of the poisonous tree analysis. Quoting *Wong Sun v. United States*,[3] the Court stated that the governing test should be "whether granting establishment of the primary illegality, the evidence to which instant objection is made has been come at by exploitation of that illegality or instead by means sufficiently distinguishable to be purged of the primary taint." Unable to make this determination on the record before it, the Court remanded the case to the lower court.

In the end, *Wade* established two critical principles: 1) post-indictment identification procedures where the defendant is presented are critical stages of the prosecution, which trigger the right to counsel protections of the Sixth Amendment; and 2) where this constitutional right has been infringed, testimony regarding the later in-court identification could be suppressed as well, unless the government can demonstrate that the subsequent identification was sufficiently purged from the earlier tainted identification. As alternatively summarized by the Court in *Gilbert*:

> [*Wade*] held that a post-indictment pretrial lineup at which the accused is exhibited to identifying witnesses is a critical stage of the criminal prosecution; that police conduct of such a lineup without notice to, and in the absence of his counsel denies the accused his Sixth Amendment right to counsel and calls in question the admissibility at trial of the in-court identifications of the accused by witnesses who attended the lineup.

As noted, *Gilbert* differed from *Wade* in that the unconstitutional pretrial identification in *Gilbert* was admitted during the prosecution's direct case. Given this fact, *Gilbert* addressed an issue not addressed in *Wade*: namely, whether a violation of a defendant's counsel right at an out-of-court identification procedure mandated the exclusion of such testimony at the subsequent trial. The Court

---

[3]371 U.S. 471 (1963).

answered this question in the affirmative. Accordingly, a violation of a defendant's Sixth Amendment right to counsel at an out-of-court identification procedure results in a "per se exclusionary rule as to such testimony" at a later trial.

A few years after *Wade* and *Gilbert*, the Court decided *Kirby v. Illinois*.[4] Unlike *Wade* and *Gilbert*, *Kirby* involved a one-on-one encounter ("a police station showup") between an eyewitness and the defendant that took place prior to indictment or any formal charge. As in *Gilbert* and *Wade*, counsel was not present at the identification procedure. *Kirby* considered, and rejected, the contention that the Sixth Amendment right to counsel should attach to such early-stage identifications. It noted that it was well-established that the Sixth Amendment right to counsel attaches only after adversary proceedings have commenced. And it concluded that adversary proceedings had not begun in this instance. The pretrial showup at issue in *Kirby* was, in the Court's view, simply part of "a routine police investigation" and not a critical or vital aspect of the prosecution process requiring Sixth Amendment protection. Though Sixth Amendment safeguards may be inapplicable in this context, *Kirby* indicated that abusive identification practices at such early stages were not without remedy. As noted by the Court — and discussed at greater length in the very next section — constitutional challenges to such early-stage identification measures can be pursued pursuant to the Fifth and Fourteenth Amendment due process clauses. Specifically, due process claims can be asserted to challenge any identification procedure, whether pre- or post-indictment, that is needlessly suggestive and presents the risk of an erroneous and irreparable identification.

Sidebar

NO SIXTH AMENDMENT RIGHT TO COUNSEL DURING PHOTOGRAPHIC DISPLAYS

The Supreme Court in *United States v. Ash*[5] held that the Sixth Amendment right to counsel is inapplicable to photographic identifications. Thus, the timing of such identifications — whether the identification occurs pre- or post-indictment — is wholly irrelevant in this context. The Court explained that, in the Sixth Amendment right to counsel context, the central inquiry is whether an attorney's assistance is necessary to aid the accused in meeting his "legal problems" as well as "his adversary." The Court added that "[i]f accurate reconstruction [of the challenged identification procedure] is possible, the risks inherent in any confrontation still remain, but the opportunity to cure defects at trial causes the confrontation to cease to be 'critical.'" The Court concluded that an identification made during a photographic display is not a "critical stage" requiring the assistance of counsel. In contrast to a lineup, the Court noted that a photo display does not require a defendant's physical presence. Given such, there is absolutely no risk, according to the Court, of an accused being manipulated by governmental influences or suggestions. In addition, the Court declared that the events surrounding the photographic identification could be effectively reconstructed at trial. The adversarial trial process "remains as effective for a photographic display as for other parts of pretrial interviews. No greater limitations are placed on defense counsel in constructing displays, seeking witnesses, and conducting photographic identifications than those applicable to the prosecution."

[5]413 U.S. 300 (1973).

[4]406 U.S. 682 (1972).

B. Suspect Identifications and the Due Process Clause

As noted, the Supreme Court in *Kirby* indicated that the due process clauses of the Fifth and Fourteenth Amendments provided another avenue by which pretrial identification procedures could be challenged. What is perhaps most notable about due process claims is their scope, which is broader than Sixth Amendment right to counsel challenges. Specifically, identification procedures of all types, whenever performed, are subject to due process challenges. Thus, identifications made during lineups, showups, and even photographic displays may be subjected to such review. The same is true of identifications made before and after the commencement of adversary proceedings.

Under this formulation, a pretrial identification could be suppressed pursuant to a due process challenge at trial if an out-of-court identification was "unnecessarily suggestive and conducive to irreparable mistaken identification."[6] Thus, three elements must be satisfied in order to successfully prove a due process violation: first, that the identification procedure was suggestive; second, that it was unnecessary for the government to employ this suggestive identification procedure; and third, that the identification was attributable to this suggestive process and not some other reliable factor. It necessarily follows, therefore, that an identification made pursuant to an extremely suggestive and unnecessary procedure may yet be admissible at trial if, when considering the totality of the circumstances, the identification is deemed to be reliable. To see these factors at work, consider the following cases.

(1) Suggestive, but Necessary

Stovall v. Denno involved the government's employment of an identification procedure that was highly suggestive, yet was upheld given that it was deemed by the Court to have been necessary. In that case, the defendant had been arrested on suspicion of murder. After a prompt arraignment, the defendant was presented by law enforcement for identification to an eyewitness to the murder (she was the wife of the victim, had been attacked herself during the confrontation, and was seriously injured during the incident). After "major surgery to save her life," the defendant was taken to her hospital room the following day. He was handcuffed to one of the officers and was the only African-American individual in the room. The defendant was identified during this encounter as the attacker. The Court found that though the identification procedure was suggestive, it was necessary given an array of factors, including the gravity of the eyewitness's health.

The Court declared that whether a particular identification practice offends due process is assessed pursuant to a totality of the circumstances standard. And the Court was satisfied that the totality of the situation in *Stovall* presented an "imperative" circumstance that justified the showing of a single suspect for identification purposes. In support, the Court observed that it was uncertain whether the eyewitness would survive, that given her condition she was unable to depart

---

[6]*Stovall v. Denno*, 388 U.S. 293 (1967).

the hospital and participate in a lineup of suspects, that she was the only individual capable of exonerating the defendant, and that the police, under the circumstances, pursued the only practical pathway to obtain a possible identification of the attacker.

(2) Suggestive and Unnecessary/Unreliable

In *Foster v. California*,[7] the defendant had been arrested for robbery of a business. After his arrest, the defendant was placed in a three-person lineup and was presented before one of the business's managers for identification. The defendant was approximately six inches taller than the other lineup participants. However, the manager was unable to make an identification. Moments thereafter, there was a "one-to-one" meeting between the manager and the defendant, given that the witness "thought" the defendant was the robber, though he remained uncertain. The manager was still unable to make an identification. At a lineup held approximately seven to ten days later, the manager identified the defendant. This lineup consisted of five individuals, of which the defendant was the sole participant from the earlier lineup.

Characterizing this case as a forceful representation of an unfairly suggestive identification process, the Court found that the "pretrial confrontations clearly were so arranged as to make the resulting identifications virtually inevitable." The Court concluded that due process was violated given that the suggestive procedure "undermined the reliability of the eyewitness identification."

(3) Suggestive, but Reliable

Neil v. Biggers[8] involved a rape victim who identified the defendant as her assailant during a one-on-one showup that took place in a police station seven months after the assault. During the preceding months, several other individuals had been shown to the victim (via lineups, showups, and photographs) without an identification being made. The Court addressed whether the defendant's identification violated due process.

The Court held that it did not. It acknowledged that the showup may have been unnecessarily suggestive. However, it declared that more is required before a due process violation can be found. In other words, an identification is not subject to per se exclusion merely because it emanated from an identification procedure that was unnecessarily suggestive. Rather, "[i]t is the likelihood of misidentification which violates a defendant's right to due process." Evaluating the totality of the circumstances, the Court declared that several factors should be considered when ascertaining the reliability of an identification. These factors "include the opportunity of the witness to view the criminal at the time of the crime, the witness' degree of attention, the accuracy of the witness' prior description of the criminal, the level of certainty demonstrated by the witness at the confrontation, and the length of time between the crime and the confrontation."

---

[7]394 U.S. 440 (1969).
[8]409 U.S. 188 (1972).

In the end, the Court found that various factors supported its conclusion that the identification was reliable. It noted, inter alia, that the victim had not made a previous identification during the preceding months, that she expressed that she had "no doubt" that the defendant was her attacker, and that she had spent an extended period of time with her assailant during the commission of the crime and had an adequate opportunity to observe his features.

In *Manson v. Brathwaite*,[9] the Court, again, emphasized the principle that unnecessary suggestiveness alone does not give rise to a due process violation. Rather, the Court held, a successful due process challenge requires a finding that the subject identification was unreliable. *Manson* involved a photographic identification made by an undercover narcotics officer of the defendant from whom the officer had purchased narcotics. The identification was made after the presentation of a single photograph. The parties agreed that the identification procedure at issue was both suggestive and unnecessary. Nevertheless, after consideration of the aforementioned reliability factors delineated in *Biggers*, the Court found that the defendant's due process rights were respected. The Court declared that "[a]lthough identifications arising from single-photograph displays may be viewed in general with suspicion," the identification in this instance was reliable. "Surely," the Court concluded, "we cannot say that under all the circumstances of this case there is 'a very substantial likelihood of irreparable misidentification.'"[10]

SUMMARY

- The Sixth Amendment right to counsel applies to identification procedures (excluding photographic displays) that take place after the commencement of adversary proceedings. Such identification procedures are deemed to be "critical stages" of the criminal trial process.

- A violation of the Sixth Amendment right to counsel requires the exclusion of trial testimony relating to the out-of-court identification. Moreover, it may result in the exclusion of a subsequent in-court identification at trial, unless it is demonstrated that the in-court identification is not a product of the earlier tainted identification.

- The due process clauses of the Fifth and Fourteenth Amendments allow for the exclusion of testimony regarding out-of-court identifications if it can be demonstrated that the subject identification was unnecessarily suggestive and was not reliable.

- This due process right is broader than the Sixth Amendment protection given that it applies to any and all types of identification procedures, irrespective of whether they occurred before or after the commencement of adversary proceedings.

- An identification that is the product of an identification process that is both suggestive and unnecessary may still be admissible at trial if its reliability can be demonstrated.

---

[9]432 U.S. 98 (1977).
[10]*Manson*, 432 U.S. at 116 (citing *Simmons v. United States*, 390 U.S. 377, 384 (1968).

CONNECTIONS

Relationship to Involuntary Confessions and the Due Process Clause Cases (Chapter 17), The Miranda Rule (Chapter 18), and The Sixth Amendment Right to Counsel — General Principles (Chapter 19)

The Fifth Amendment *Miranda* right to counsel attaches to custodial interrogations that occur prior to the commencement of adversarial proceedings. The Sixth Amendment right to counsel, on the other hand, attaches after the commencement of adversarial proceedings. Thus, suspect identifications (excluding photographic displays) that occur after the commencement of adversary proceedings implicate this Sixth Amendment right. The Sixth Amendment, therefore, does not attach to identification procedures that occur prior to this time. Fifth Amendment due process challenges to statements made during government interviews or to out-of-court identifications can be made irrespective of whether adversary proceedings have commenced.

Relationship to Fourth Amendment Violations and Their Associated Remedies (Chapter 15)

Out-of-court identifications made in violation of the Sixth Amendment are subject to automatic exclusion. Subsequent in-court identifications are also subject to exclusion, unless the proponent can demonstrate that the later identification was not tainted by the former violation. Out-of-court identifications that are made pursuant to unnecessarily suggestive procedures are also subject to exclusion. However, such identifications do not violate due process if the identifications are otherwise reliable. By analogy, evidence seized in violation of the Fourth Amendment is subject to exclusion (as are its fruits). However, such evidence may be admissible if, inter alia, there is an independent source for the evidence or if attenuated circumstances exist.

Table of Cases

Index